G. W. Leibniz's
Monadology

G. W. Leibniz's *Monadology*

An Edition for Students

Nicholas Rescher

University of Pittsburgh Press

Published by the University of Pittsburgh Press,
Pittsburgh, Pa. 15260
Copyright © 1991, University of Pittsburgh Press
All rights reserved
Manufactured in the United States of America

Library of Congress Cataloging-in-Publication Data

Leibniz, Gottfried Wilhelm, Freiherr von, 1646–1716.
   [Monadologie. English & French]
   G. W. Leibniz's Monadology : an edition for students / Nicholas Rescher.
     p.   cm.
   Contains original text and English translation of: Monadologie.
   Includes bibliographical references and indexes.
   ISBN 0-8229-3670-4. — ISBN 0-8229-5449-4 (pbk.)
   1. Monadology—Early works to 1800.   I. Rescher, Nicholas. II. Title.
   III. Title: Monadology.
B2580.E5R47   1991
193—dc20   90-24820

 # Contents

❧ Preface

The present work is an act of piety in its attempt to compile on his behalf the book that Leibniz himself never wrote. For there is no representative work of his to which teachers of seventeenth-century thought can send their students as they send them to Descartes' *Meditations* or Spinoza's *Ethics*. The object of the book is to fill this gap.

Taking the *Monadology*—that telegraphic summary of Leibniz's system of philosophy—as its organizing table of contents, the book collects together some of his widely scattered discussions of the philosophical ideas and theses at issue. This procedure achieves a dual result, providing on the one hand a commentary on the *Monadology* by Leibniz himself, and, on the other, an exposition of his philosophy using the *Monadology* as an outline. Such an approach assigns to the *Monadology* what is surely its most useful and appropriate function: that of a gateway into the thought-structure of the Leibnizian philosophy at large.

Several people have rendered invaluable aid in the course of preparing the book: David Carey helped to compile the complex indices; Valentine Butts checked my translations from French; Jan Cover offered constructive suggestions; Linda Butera and Marian Kowatch patiently produced a usable typescript; Irma Garlick edited the copy with care and competence, and those involved in the project at the University of Pittsburgh Press were—as usual—splendidly cooperative. I am deeply grateful to all concerned.

Pittsburgh
June 1990

G. W. Leibniz's
Monadology

◄ 1. Introduction

A. Gottfried Wilhelm Leibniz (1646–1716)

Gottfried Wilhelm von Leibniz was born on July 1, 1646, at Leipzig in Germany, where his father was professor of moral philosophy at the university. Although he attended the finest school in his native city, he loved working on his own and was largely self-taught from the German and Latin books of his father's library. A child prodigy with an insatiable appetite for learning, he launched into an intensive study of logic, scholastic philosophy, and Protestant theology already in his early teens. At 15 he entered the University of Leipzig. During the first preparatory years, one semester of which he spent at the University of Jena, he studied principally philosophy, natural philosophy, and mathematics. His baccalaureate dissertation of 1663 (*De principio individui*) was devoted to the principle of individuation, a topic to which he was to give lifelong attention. The next three years were largely devoted to legal studies, and in 1666, Leibniz applied for the degree of doctor of law at Leipzig. Since he was still only 20 years of age, his application was rejected on the grounds of youth by the university of his native city, but was immediately granted at the University of Altdorf (near Nuremberg), where his highly original dissertation "On Difficult Problems in the Law" (*De casibus perplexis in jure*) secured him the offer of a university post. This he declined, his goal being to enter into public service rather than academic life.

Before reaching age 21, Leibniz had not only earned his doctorate in law, but had published several original studies in logic and legal theory. The presence of such a prodigy in Nuremberg was brought to the attention of Baron Johann Christian von Boineburg (1622–72), a former prime minister to the elector of Mainz, and one of the most prominent political figures in Germany. Through his aid, Leibniz entered the service of the elector of Mainz in 1668, after some months in Frankfurt seeing a legal book through the press. Apart from travels to conduct research, the rest of his life was spent in residence in various courts.

At Mainz, Leibniz was set to working on writings of a political nature. The most important was a memorandum for Louis XIV suggesting that Holland, as a merchant power with extensive trade in the East, might be seriously injured through France's conquest of Egypt—a scheme which would incidentally serve Germany's interests by diverting French expansion from Europe. Nothing came of the project at the time, but the idea somehow stayed alive in French official circles until it came to fruition in the time of Napoleon. In 1672, Leibniz was sent from Mainz to Paris to promote the Egyptian scheme. Although the mission failed to realize its objective, it, and the trip that Leibniz made to London in conjunction with it, proved crucially important to his intellectual development, for he now came into direct contact with the wider world of European learning.

In 1672, when Leibniz was 26, Descartes's followers and disciples were in possession of the philosophical arena, and some who had personally known and corresponded with him were still alive—for example, Thomas Hobbes (1588–1679). Leibniz was able to establish personal contact with such important Cartesian followers as Antoine Arnauld (1612–94), Nicolas Malebranche (1636–1715), and Spinoza (1632–77), whom Leibniz visited in the Netherlands in 1675.

Modern physical science was then in its lusty infancy. Robert Boyle (1627–91) still had many years before him. Isaac Newton (1642–1727), with whom Leibniz was to enter into a fateful correspondence, was only at the beginning of his career. The mathematician-physicist Christian Huygens (1629–95) became Leibniz's mentor and friend in the course of the Paris visit. The scientific firmament was replete with such luminaries as von Guerike, Mariotte, Papin, and Perrault in physics, van Leeuwenhoek in biology, and the Bernouillis, Sturm, Wallis, and Varignon in mathematics. Leibniz entered into contact and correspondence with virtually all of these scholars. (He came to collect correspondents on scientific and scholarly topics as another person might collect rare books.) The doors to this far-flung realm of European learning were first opened to Leibniz in the course of his Parisian mission.

In January 1673, Leibniz traveled to London as attaché on another political mission for the elector of Mainz. There he became acquainted with Henry Oldenburg, secretary of the Royal Society, and other of its members. He exhibited to the Royal Society a calculating machine of his own devising, more versatile than the earlier machine of Pascal. In April 1673, shortly after returning to Paris, Leibniz was elected a fellow of the Royal Society. In Paris he devoted himself intensively to higher mathematics, especially geometry, largely under the tutelage of Huygens, and at this point began a series of original studies that culminated in his invention of the differential and integral calculus.

While still in Paris, Leibniz transferred from the service of the elector of Mainz to that of Duke John Frederick of Brunswick-Lüneburg. In 1676, now aged 30, he settled in Hanover at the duke's request, traveling there via London and Amsterdam, where he held conversations with Spinoza, of whose (then unpublished) *Ethics* he was able to make notes.

For the forty remaining years of his active life, Leibniz continued—under three successive princes—in the service of the Hanoverian Brunswick dukes. He was on excellent terms with the Duke John Frederick (d. 1679) and his son and successor Ernest August (d. 1698), but with the accession of George Louis—later George I of Great Britain—his position was much less favorable, and Leibniz eventually dropped from favor at court, although he always remained on excellent personal terms with the princesses of the house. In his heyday Leibniz was for all practical purposes a minister without portfolio in charge of historico-legal, cultural, and scientific affairs. He managed the royal libraries and archives, conducted legal and historical researches, composed polemical tracts to justify various rights and claims of the dukes of Hanover, and he planned a reformation of the coinage and tried to reorganize the mines. Though Leibniz lived in the atmosphere of petty politics in a small German principality, his interests and outlook were always wide-ranging and international.

Leibniz's dedicated service to the court of Hanover was matched with an intense commitment to the furtherance of learning, scholarship, and science. Regularly laboring in his workroom late into the night hours, Leibniz produced an astounding variety of original ideas in logic, mathematics, physics, natural science, historical studies, and philosophy. He published only a fraction of his work, with most of it set aside to await the attention of later generations of scholars. In particular, the philosophical system sketched in the *Monadology*, though almost fully developed during the 1684–86 period, was never systematically set down on paper. (The *Monadology*, itself, written when Leibniz was almost 70, was, as it were, a last-minute attempt to provide a systematic sketch of his overall system.)

From 1687 to 1690, Leibniz traveled extensively through Germany, Austria and Italy searching public records and archives to gather information for an official history of the house of Brunswick, and gathering materials for his extensive collections on European diplomatic and political history. After returning from Italy in 1690, he also became librarian of the important library at Wolfenbüttel established by Duke Anton of Brunswick-Wolfenbüttel. He now organized material collected in his travels for a code of international law into two great books.

The electress Sophia, wife of Ernest August and heir apparent to the British throne, as well as her daughter, Sophie Charlotte, who became queen of Prussia, were particular friends of Leibniz. Some of his philosophical writings, including the *Théodicée*, grew out of his discussions with these influential princesses. When Sophie Charlotte reigned in

Berlin, Leibniz frequently visited there, but after her death in 1705 his visits to Berlin became less frequent.

After the accession of George Louis in 1698, Leibniz was pressed to concentrate his official efforts on his history of the house of Brunswick (which at his death had gone no further than the period 768–1005). As the seventeenth century drew toward it close, he began to feel increasingly constricted. To one correspondent he wrote: "But here [in Hanover] one hardly finds anyone to talk to, or rather one does not count as a good courtier in this country if one speaks of scientific matters. Without the Electress [Sophia] one would speak of them even less" (G III, 175).

Leibniz now looked increasingly in other directions. He used his influence at the court of Berlin to promote the establishment there in 1700 of the royal academy (*Akademie der Wissenschaften*), of which he was elected president for life. Founding academies modeled on those of Paris and London was a favorite project with Leibniz. He urged upon Peter the Great the plan for an academy at St. Petersburg which was not carried out until after the czar's death. In the course of an official visit to Vienna from 1712 to 1714 he promoted (unsuccessfully) a plan for establishing an academy there. This Viennese visit did give Leibniz some satisfaction, however, for he received the honor of an imperial privy councillorship and ennoblement. However, these démarches in other directions caused annoyance at the Hanoverian court, where Leibniz came into increasing disfavor and his long absence in Vienna was much resented.

Upon the death of Queen Anne in August 1714, Leibniz's master, the elector George Louis of Hanover, succeeded to the throne of England as King George I. Leibniz returned to Hanover in mid-September, but his master had already departed for England. Leibniz was eager to follow him to London and play a greater role on a larger stage, but he was by now *persona non grata* with the king. He was instructed to remain at Hanover and finish his history of the house of Brunswick, working in the vacuum left by the general exodus of important courtiers. He died on November 14, 1716 aged 70, his last years made difficult by neglect, illness, and the distrust of the local public. (Some Hanover clergymen called him "Lövenix"—believer in nothing—and the reputation of an unbeliever made him locally unpopular.) Despite this, he retained to the end his capacity for hard work in the pursuit of active researches in many fields of learning.

Leibniz possessed an astounding range of interests and capacities. Mathematics, physics, geology, philosophy, logic, philology, theology, history, jurisprudence, politics, and economics are all subjects to which he made original contributions of the first rank. The universality of the range of his abilities and achievements is without rival in modern times. And his work in philosophy (including logic) is of a caliber to put him on a par with the very greatest: Plato, Aristotle, Aquinas, and Descartes.

By prodigious energy, ability, and effort, Leibniz managed to be three persons in one—a scholar, a public servant and man of affairs, and a courtier—without letting any one suffer at the expense of the others. He possessed amazing powers for swift and sustained work, sometimes taking meals at his desk and spending days on end there, except for a few occasional hours of sleep. He was fond of travel, and even while traveling in the rough conveyances of the day he worked at mathematical problems. The interpersonal interaction which another might have found in family life, Leibniz derived from his vast correspondence.

Leibniz was a man of middling height, pale complexion, and rather slender build, his bald pate always covered by a huge wig of the type popular in the Paris of his youth. Though he lived a sedentary life, he was generally in good health—a sound sleeper with a good digestion and an even temper. He was a night-worker who did not like to rise early, generally having worked late into the morning hours. While reading was a favored activity, he also loved to mingle with people in society and hoped to learn something from everyone. He was somewhat irascible and did not suffer fools gladly. Contemporary accounts describe Leibniz as being of moderate habits, quick in temper but easily appeased, very self-assured, and impatient of contradiction, his irascibility no doubt the result of chronic overwork. Although somewhat impractical in the management of his own affairs, he nevertheless was, by all evidence, a person of wise understanding in human affairs, wide-ranging in interests, charitable in judgment of others, and tolerant of differences in customs and opinions. His secretary said that he spoke well of everybody and made the best of everything. He is said to have been money-conscious and somewhat tightfisted. He was perhaps over-anxious to secure the recognition he believed to be his due for his work and services. But behind this lay an inseparable mixture of personal ambition and public-spirited desire to be in a position to advance the general good, which could, then as now, only be done from a position of influence.

Leibniz's interests imbued him with a thoroughly cosmopolitan point of view. In discussing resumption of the work of the French Academy after the Peace of Ryswick (1697), he wrote: "Provided that something of consequence is achieved, I am indifferent whether this is done in Germany or in France, for I seek the good of mankind. I am neither a *phil-Hellene* nor a *philo-Roman*, but a *phil-anthropos*" (G VII, 456). Leibniz's services to the advancement of learning were indefatigable and incredibly many-sided. In learned controversy and correspondence he was immensely patient and good tempered. He had a voracious appetite for knowledge of all sorts, and his interests were literally bound-less. (In this regard, as in some others, he was quite like his interesting contemporary, Samuel Pepys.)

A word about Leibniz's philosophical development is in order. Until the age of around 16, he was under the influence of the Scholastics whose works he read in his father's library. Thereafter, in the course of his studies of the sciences at the university, he inclined to a material-istic atomism (of the sort to be found in Gassendi and Bacon), a position from which he was weaned in the early 1670s by a complex combina-tion of antimaterialistic influences. (Leibniz's thought was molded by a diversified multitude of thinkers whose influence will perhaps never be unraveled: among the ancients are the Platonic tradition and Plato himself; among the medievals, the Scholastics as well as the "new" Aristotle; in the Renaissance, Nicholas of Cusa and the entire Platonic movement of the late Renaissance; and thereafter Suarez and Des-cartes.) The rudiments of his monadism were conceived by 1675, but for the long interval 1675–84 Leibniz devoted his intellectual energies mainly to mathematics, logic, and physics. However, during the period 1684–86 he resumed intensive work in philosophy and tied up various loose ends in his philosophical system, of which he now proceeded to write various sketches (preeminently including the *Discourse on Meta-physics*). As of 1686, Leibniz's philosophy had pretty much reached its mature completion, and his subsequent writing on the subject was in large measure an exposing to public view of the further details of an existing structure to which only a few substantial additions were needed.

The story of Leibniz's philosophical writings is complex. During his whole life he published only one single philosophical book, the *Essais de Théodicée* (1710), although he had written another, the *Nouveaus Essais sur l'Entendement Humain*, a critique of John Locke's *Essay Concerning Human Understanding*, which he left unpublished upon Locke's death in 1704. The essence of Leibniz's mature philosophy was contained in a series of occasional articles he published between 1686 and 1706 in such journals as the *Acta Eruditorum* of Leipzig and the *Journal des savants* of Paris. But behind these generally sketchy articles lay a vast series of essays and memoranda prepared for personal use and never put into form for publication, as well as a great multitude of ex-planatory letters. For the format Leibniz selected for propagation of his ideas was letters to select correspondents. (It would seem that he was less concerned about publishing his system for the world than securing the adherence, or at any rate understanding, of a score or two of leading intellects.) It is from the personal memoranda and his vast correspon-dence that one is able to obtain a firm and balanced grasp upon his philosophical system: the published works are but a window through which one can glance into the various parts of a larger structure. "One who knows me only by the published works does not know me at all" (*Qui me non nisi editis novit, non novit*), Leibniz very properly wrote on one occasion.[1]

B. The Monadology

In the summer of 1714, Leibniz, then aged 68, was in Vienna, fostering his contacts with the imperial court, much to the chagrin of his Hanoverian employers. There, in June and July of that year, he wrote in French two very short overviews of some of the leading ideas of his philosophical system. The first, entitled *Principes de la nature et de la grâce fondés en raison*, ("Principles of Nature and of Grace Founded on Reason"), a rather less comprehensive and more popular account, was elegantly bound with a number of other philosophical essays and presented to Prince Eugene of Savoy, the famous imperial field marshal and co-victor with the Duke of Marlborough in the great allied victory over France at Blenheim. The second, prepared at the behest of Nicolas Remond, counselor to the Duke of Orleans, was also begun that summer, though probably not completed until later in the year. For in July, Leibniz wrote from Vienna to Remond (G III, 618, 624) that this overview of the monadic theory—described as an *Éclaircissement sur les monades*—was growing to larger proportions than he had anticipated and was being delayed by various interruptions, and eventually he sent Remond a copy of the aforementioned *Principes* instead (on August 26, 1714). Leibniz himself gave no further title to his *Éclaircissement*, but the copy in the Vienna State Library (Nationalbibliothek) bears the title *Les Principes de la Philosophie, par Monsieur Leibniz*, and it is plausible that Leibniz himself would have thought of this opuscule as the *Principles of (My) Philosophy*. However, Heinrich Koehler, who first published this work in 1720 in German translation, gave it the label *Monadology*, and this eminently apt title has stuck. It is clear that Leibniz considered the *Monadology* a sound and satisfactory overview of his philosophical position, for he took the trouble to work through it himself to provide cross-references to the relevant passages of the *Theodicy*, his only philosophical book available to contemporary readers. (Leibniz's original manuscript is still in the possession of the Nether-Saxon State Library, the Niedersächsiche Landesbibliothek, in Hanover.)

The *Monadology* was Leibniz's substitute for a book he never wrote.

1. This account of Leibniz's life and work is largely drawn from the editor's *Leibniz: An Introduction to His Philosophy* (Oxford: Blackwell, 1979), which provides a compact overview of Leibniz's philosophical views.

For although he devised one of the most complex and many-sided philosophical systems ever contrived by the mind of man, he never wrote a book to present it in a systematic way. Instead Leibniz wrote numerous small essays and sketches—and innumerable letters to a vast array of correspondents. The only philosophical book that he published in his lifetime (at age 60), was the *Theodicy*, a study of major issues in philosophical theology published in 1706. Though this book dealt primarily with "the problem of evil"—the issue of how the perfection of a creator God can be reconciled with the imperfection of his creation—it gave many incidental indications regarding Leibniz's philosophical doctrines. This led to various requests for a systematic exposition of his position, which Leibniz was unable to meet because of the pressure of other commitments. However, the comparative leisure of a long visit at the court of Vienna enabled him to write a brief overview. He initially projected a diminutive sketch of some half-dozen (printed) pages, but the project "grew between his hands" to roughly twice its initially envisioned scale. The ultimate product, the *Monadology*, was a sketchy outline of his thought in ninety brief sections, most of them only two or three sentences long. In writing the *Monadology*, the now almost seventy-year-old Leibniz seized virtually the last available moment to set out for posterity just exactly how he conceived of the "system" of philosophy that had existed in his mind so clearly for almost a generation. Its concise indications clarify how Leibniz conceived of the "system" of philosophy he had been expounding piecemeal for many years—and enable us to appreciate just how systematic a thinker he really was. It is a masterpiece of concise exposition—perhaps too much so to serve really well its intended purpose of providing an adequate introduction to his philosophy.

Within the limitations of its size, however, the *Monadology* is as helpful as the nature of the project permits. Leibniz's philosophy is a complex, many-sided system worked out in great detail across a vast range of themes and issues. The dramaturgy of the text moves smoothly and swiftly along its ontological ascent from individual substances to organic nature to God as the ultimate author and monarch of all. To give a good synoptic overview of it in a few pages is an impressive *tour de force*. And yet it remains unsatisfying—as Leibniz himself fully realized. For to present a complex position in this telegraphic way is also to make a caricature of it.

In the end, Leibniz took one further step to compensate for this unsatisfactory compression. For after completing his opuscule, he worked his way through the text adding references to those passages of the *Theodicy* where the particular ideas at issue are further explained and developed. In this way, he believed, the interested reader could obtain a somewhat fuller picture of his thought.

Our presentation of the *Monadology* follows Leibniz's lead by reaching beyond the text itself to present throughout also those discussions from the *Theodicy* to which he made reference. And it moves even further in this direction, generally adding also some other passages where Leibniz further develops the ideas at issue. (In particular, it subsumes the entire text of the *Principles of Nature and of Grace* into this framework.) The sort of compilation provided here would very likely meet with approval by Leibniz himself. In July 1714 he wrote to Nicolas Remond: "It is true that my *Theodicy* does not suffice to present my system as a whole. But if it is joined with what I have published in various journals, those of Leipzig, Paris, and those of Mr. Bayle and Mr. Basnage, it does not fall short of doing so, at least as regards the principles" (G III, 618). The result is, in effect, one that proceeds in the belief that Leibniz himself is his own best commentator by letting his own discussions explain the ideas treated in the *Monadology*, drawing on other parts of his enormously diversified corpus for this purpose.[2] On this basis, the present edition principally lets Leibniz speak for himself, with only a very brief commentary to help the reader keep the principal ideas in clearer focus. Such a provision of context relieves the *Monadology* of the aura of strangeness with which its bare-bones statements of doctrines otherwise impress the reader. As one profound student of Leibniz was to remark: "I felt—as many others have felt—that the *Monadology* was a kind of fantastic fairy tale, coherent perhaps, but wholly arbitrary."[3] Only by reading a good many peripheral writings can this strangeness be removed.

Though the *Monadology* is, in its telegraphic way, the fullest exposition of Leibniz's philosophy that we have from his own pen, it is nevertheless far from complete. It leaves out of view his natural philosophy (theory of space and time, of force, the nature of matter, the critique of the vacuum), it does not report his theory of the will (free will, inclining reasons), it omits major pieces of his theory of knowledge (the analysis of ideas into simples, the theory of innate ideas and truths), and his social philosophy (theory of justice, theory of the state) goes unmentioned save in the context of God's relationship to man. Even in metaphysics, the theory of individuation and the conception of well-founded phenomena are passed over in silence.[4] Although the *Monadology* covers an immense range for a brief a text, it has shortcomings

2. The ablest Leibniz scholars have always appreciated this fact. For example, André Robinet's edition of the *Monadology* appends a chart giving cross-references to a half-dozen Leibnizian texts.

3. Bertrand Russell, *A Critical Exposition of the Philosophy of Leibniz*, 2d ed. (London: Allen & Unwin, 1937), p. xiii.

4. The very words *phenomenon (phénomène), matter (matière), space (l'espace), time (temps),* and *free will (volonté, libre, libre arbitre)* do not occur in the *Monadology*.

even as a table of contents in relation to the vast complexity of Leibniz's philosophical system. While Leibniz may have felt that he had done justice to these omitted topics in his various publications, their setting within his overall system ought surely to have been indicated. But in any case, the *Monadology* does give a faithful sketch of the metaphysical theory of substances which had stood pretty much complete in his mind ever since the *Discourse on Metaphysics* of 1686 and the subsequent correspondence with Arnauld. This was a theory of aggregated physical quasi-substances unified by the unextended substantial entelechies on substantial forms characterized as monads in his later writings—those "true atoms of nature," lacking the extendedness of classical atoms, but each endowed with its own characteristic "point of view." Leibniz was the first metaphysician of the Western tradition, who sought to construct reality out of units possessing a property structure wholly beyond the reach of our everyday experiences. Anticipating twentieth-century physics in this respect, Leibniz dared for the first time to envision a reality that emerged from the operation of a reality that lies totally beyond the reach of human observation. His theory of substance is a leap into an order of reality which, for the sake of being intelligible, leaves the sensible domain almost totally behind, a position which the more conservative Kant was to regard as a decisive defect.

In this regard, it is necessary to give a word of warning to those taking the *Monadology* in hand for the first time. Leibniz's opuscule is the work of an era far removed from our own. In our day, specialization and division of labor have created an intellectual situation radically different from that of the seventeenth century, when science ("natural philosophy") and philosophy proper ("theoretical philosophy") were parts of one unified whole that also included not only ethics ("practical philosophy") and theology ("religious philosophy") but much else besides. Any sympathetic reader of the *Monadology* has to accept from the outset that its point of view is altogether olympian. Its purview is not confined to issues of technical philosophy; it seeks to provide a view of the entire range of man's attempts to grasp the world we live in from a unified theoretical perspective, encompassing science, metaphysics, theology, and scholarship in a seamlessly integrated whole. It is this drive to system that makes Leibniz's project both fascinating and admirable and yet rather strange in our eyes. Be it in politics, scholarship, or science, Leibniz insisted on a synoptic perspective from which boundaries are a regrettable, fundamentally irrelevant concession to human frailties.

What Leibniz endeavored to do in his philosophizing was to integrate the available knowledge of the world in all of its diversified complexity into a unified whole that exhibits the operation of certain pervasive principles. These principles are primarily those reflected in the concepts of: rationality (sufficient reason), continuity, harmony, fertility, organic unity, and plenitude. Be it in cosmology or biology, in psychology or in statecraft, Leibniz sees these principles as based in metaphysical and theological considerations and yet as operative throughout nature and thus illustrated and instantiated throughout the whole range of natural science. For Leibniz, science is philosophy teaching by examples, and there is no effective line of separation between these modes of intellectual endeavor.

C. Sources and Resources

The *Monadology* was first published by Heinrich Koehler in a German translation (*Leibnizens Lehr-Sätze über die Monadologie, etc.* [Frankfurt and Leipzig, 1720]). In his subsequent edition of Leibniz's works (*Opera Omnia* [Geneva, 1768]), Ludovico Dutens included a Latin translation based on this German version of Koehler's. A version of the original French text was first published in J. E. Erdmann's edition of Leibniz's philosophical works (*Opera Omnia* [Berlin, 1840]).

The French text of the *Monadology* that is given here is based on the magisterial edition of André Robinet, *G. W. Leibniz: Principes de la Nature et de la grâce fondés en raison et Principes de la philosophie ou Mondalogie* (Paris: Presses Universitaires de France, 1954). For other Leibniz texts, I rely on C. I. Gerhardt, *Die philosophischen Schriften von Gottfried Wilhelm Leibniz*, 7 vols. (Berlin: Weidmann, 1875–90). This work I cite simply as G, with the *Monadology* given in G VI, 607–23.

From the textual point of view, the manuscript basis of the *Monadology* affords an embarrassment of riches. The Nether-Saxon State Library (Niedersächsische Landesbibliothek) preserves Leibniz's initial manuscript draft and also two secretarial copies, designated by Robinet as A and B, respectively, each of them furnished with Leibniz's corrections and additions. Robinet's edition presents all this material in an accurate, usefully organized way. He himself takes as the definitive text that of copy B in its final version. And in presenting the text here I have followed this precedent, though occasionally drawing on A, sometimes for the sake of linguistic uniformity (especially with regard to punctuation), and sometimes for greater informativeness. Leibniz' own usage is followed in all matters of grammar, spelling, and (especially) accentuation; there is no attempt to modernize his seventeenth century practices.

The translation of the *Monadology* is my own. As regards the *Theodicy*, the translation given is that of E. M. Huggard, *G. W. Leibniz: Theodicy* (New Haven: Yale University Press, 1952). Extracts from

Leibniz's *New Essays on Human Understanding* are presented in the translation of J. Bennett and P. Remnant (Cambridge: Cambridge University Press, 1981). The *Discourse on Metaphysics* and the correspondence with Antoine Arnauld have been cited from *Leibniz: Discourse on Metaphysics etc.*, trans. George R. Montgomery (La Salle: Open Court, 1902). For other Leibnizian texts, the translation given here is generally that of L. E. Loemker, *Leibniz: Philosophical Papers and Letters*, 2d ed. (Dordrecht: D. Reidel, 1969). (I have, however, on occasion emended these translations in the interest of philosophical accuracy.) A useful collection of translated Leibniz materials more recent, albeit less comprehensive than that of Loemker, is Roger Ariew and Daniel Garber (eds. & trs.), *G. W. Leibniz: Philosophical Essays* (Indianapolis: Hackett, 1989).

Readers who want to follow particular words and concepts into their wider Leibnizian context will find indispensable the *Leibniz Lexicon* edited by Reinhard Finster et al. (Hildesheim: G. Olms, 1988), a work whose translation into English would render a real service to anglophone students of Leibniz.

D. Notation

The following notational conventions are adopted with respect to the text of the *Monadology*:

• parentheses ( ) indicate words or expressions used by Leibniz himself.
• single brackets [ ] indicate materials that originally formed part of Leibniz's text that were subsequently deleted by him.
• braces ⟨ ⟩ indicate additions or interpolations supplied by myself.

E. Oft-Cited Leibnizian Writings

DM: "Discourse on Metaphysics." [1686]. G IV, 427–65. Trans. Loemker, pp. 303–328; Ariew & Garber, pp. 35–68. See also the next entry.
To Arnauld: "Correspondence With Antoine Arnauld" [1686–90]. G II, 1–138, Loemker, pp. 331–348 (selections); Ariew & Garber, pp. 69–90 (selections); George R. Montgomery, trans., Leibniz: *Discourse in Metaphysics; Correspondence with Arnauld, and Monadology* (La Salle: Open Court, 1902), pp. 65–248 (complete through January 1688).
NS: "New System of the Nature and Communication of Substances." [1695]. G IV, 471–87. Trans. Loemker, pp. 453–59; Ariew & Garber, pp. 138–45.
NE: *New Essays on Human Understanding.* [1705]. G V, 39–509. Trans. Peter Remnant and Jonathan Bennett (Cambridge: Cambridge University Press, 1981).
Theodicy: Essays on the Goodness of God, the Freedom of Man, and the Origin

of Evil [1710]. G VI, 21–436. Trans. E. M. Huggard (New Haven: Yale University Press, 1952).

PNG: "Principles of Nature and of Grace, Based on Reason." [1714]. G VI, 598–606. Trans. Loemker, pp. 636–41; Ariew & Garber, pp. 206–13.

To Clarke: "Correspondence with Samuel Clarke" [1715–16]. G VII, 352–440. Trans. Loemker, pp. 675–717 (Leibniz's half of the correspondence only); Ariew & Garber, pp. 320–46 (excerpts).

F. Abbreviations of Editions of Leibniz's Works

G: C. I. Gerhardt, *Die philosophischen Schriften von G. W. Leibniz*, 7 vols. (Berlin: Weidmann, 1875–90).

G. Math.: C. I. Gerhardt, *Leibnizen's Mathematische Schriften*, 7 vols. (Berlin and Halle: Weidmann, 1850–63).

Cassirer/Buchenau: Ernst Cassirer, ed., and A. Buchenau, trans., *G. W. Leibniz, Hauptschriften*, 2 vols. (Leipzig: F. Meiner, 1904).

Couturat: Louis Couturat, *Opuscules et fragments inédits de Leibniz* (Paris: Felix Alcan, 1903).

Couturat: Louis Couturat, *La Logique de Leibniz* (Paris: Felix Alcan, 1901).

Foucher de Careil: *Oeuvres de Leibniz*, 7 vols. (Paris: Firmin-Didot, 1859–75).

Grua: Gaston Grua, *G. W. Leibniz: Textes inédits*, 2 vols. (Paris: Presses Universitaires de France, 1948).

Loemker: Leroy E. Loemker, *Leibniz, Philosophical Papers and Letters* (Amsterdam: Reidel, 1970).

Riley: Patrick Riley, *The Political Writings of Leibniz* (Cambridge: Cambridge University Press, 1972).

G. Commentaries on the Monadology

Earlier commentaries on (or extensive annotations of) the *Monadology* include:

Emile Boutroux, *Leibniz: La Monadologie* (Paris: Delagrave, 1887)

Robert Latta, *Leibniz: The Monadology and Other Philosophical Writings* (Oxford: Oxford University Press, 1898).

Henri Lachelier, *Leibniz: La Monadologie* (Paris: Hachette, 1881).

Herbert Wildon Carr, *The Monadology of Leibniz* (London: Favil Press, 1930).

Hermann Glockner, *Gottfried Wilhelm Leibniz: Monadologie* (Stuttgart: Reclam, 1954).

I have found Latta's and Lachelier's annotations particularly useful.

H. Leibniz's Life

For information about Leibniz's life, his personality, and his activities, the reader is referred to:

G. E. Guhrauer, *Gottfried Wilhelm Freiherr von Leibniz: Eine Biographie*, 2 vols. (Breslau, 1842; photoreprinted, Hildesheim: G. Olms, 1966).

Kurt Müller and Gisela Krönert, *Leben und Werk von Gottfried Wilhelm Leib-niz* (Frankfurt am Main: Vittorio Klosterman, 1969).

E. J. Aiton, *Leibniz: A Biography* (Bristol: Adam Hilger, 1985).

Guhrauer's book, though dated in its sources of information, is still the fullest account. The Müller-Krönert volume transcends being a mere chronology by giving many quotations from contemporary correspondence. Aiton's biography, though sparing in detail, is particularly informative in presenting Leibniz's mathematical contributions.

❧ 2. Translation of the *Monadology* of Gottfried Wilhelm von Leibniz

1. *The monad* which we shall discuss here is nothing other than a simple substance that enters into composites. Simple means without parts. (See *Theodicy*, sec. 10.)

2. And there must be simple substances, since there are composites; for the composite is nothing but an accumulation or *aggregate* of simples.

3. However, where there are no parts at all, no extension or figure or divisibility is possible. And these monads are the true atoms of nature, and, in a word, the elements of things.

4. There is also no dissolution to fear in them and there is no way conceivable in which a simple substance can perish naturally. (See *Theodicy*, sec. 89.)

5. For the same reason, there is no way in which a simple substance could begin naturally, since it cannot be formed by composition.

6. So one can say that monads can neither come into being nor end save all at once; that is, they can begin only by creation and end only by annihilation. By contrast, that which is composite begins and ends part by part.

7. There is, furthermore, no way to explain how a monad could be altered or changed in its inner make-up by some other created being. For one can transpose nothing in it, nor conceive in it any internal motion that could be excited, directed, increased, or diminished within it, as can happen in composites, where there is change among the parts. Monads just have no windows through which something can enter into or depart from them. Accidents cannot be detached, nor wander about outside of substances, as the sensible species of the Scholastics formerly did. And so, neither substance nor accident can enter a monad from without.

8. However, monads must have some qualities, otherwise they would not even be beings. And if simple substances did not differ by their qualities at all, there would be no way at all of perceiving any change in things, since that which is present in the composite can only

come from its simple constituents. And then monads, being without qualities, would be indistinguishable from one another, since they do not differ quantitatively at all. In consequence, a plenum being supposed, each place would always receive in any motion only the equivalent of what it already had, and one state of things would be indistinguishable from another. (See *Theodicy*, Preface.)

9. It is even necessary that every monad be different from every other. For there are never in nature two beings that are perfectly alike and in which it would not be possible to find a difference that is internal or founded on an intrinsic denomination.

10. I also take it for granted that every created being is subject to change, and in consequence the created monad also, and even that this change is continuous in each one.

11. It follows from what has just been said that the natural changes of the monads proceed from an *internal principle*. For an external cause cannot influence their inner make-up. (See *Theodicy*, secs. 396, 400.)

12. But beyond the principle of change, there must also be an *internal complexity (détail) of that which changes*, which would produce, so to speak, the specification and the variety of simple substances.

13. This internal complexity (*détail*) must enfold a multiplicity in unity or in the simple. For as every natural change happens by degrees, something always changes and something remains. Consequently, there must be a plurality of properties and relations within a simple substance, even though it has none of parts.

14. The transitory state which enfolds and represents a multiplicity in a unity, or in the simple substance, is exactly what one calls *perception*. One must distinguish this from *apperception* and from *consciousness*, as will become clear below. This is where the Cartesians went badly wrong in taking no account of perceptions that are not apperceived. This led them to think that "spirits" alone are monads, and that there are no souls of beasts nor other entelechies. And it led them to confuse, as ordinary people do, a prolonged stupor with death in the strict sense, which again misled them into the Scholastic prejudice that there are wholly separated souls and even confirmed misguided minds in a belief in the mortality of souls.

15. The action of the internal principle which brings about the change or the passage from one perception to another may be called *appetition*. It is true that appetite cannot always attain altogether the whole perception to which it tends, but it always obtains some part of it, and so attains new perceptions.

16. We ourselves experience multiplicity in a simple substance when we find that the slightest thought of which we are conscious in ourselves enfolds a variety in its object. Accordingly, all who recognize that the soul is a simple substance must also recognize this multiplicity

within the monad, and Monsieur Bayle ought nowise to have found difficulty in this, as he did in his *Dictionary* article "Rorarius."

17. Furthermore, one is obliged to admit that *perception* and what depends upon it is *inexplicable on mechanical principles*, that is, by figures and motions. In imagining that there is a machine whose construction would enable it to think, to sense, and to have perception, one could conceive it enlarged while retaining the same proportions, so that one could enter into it, just like into a windmill. Supposing this, one should, when visiting within it, find only parts pushing one another, and never anything by which to explain a perception. Thus it is in the simple substance, and not in the composite or in the machine, that one must look for perception. Moreover, there is nothing besides this—besides perceptions and their changes—that one could possibly find in a simple substance. It is also in this alone that all the *internal actions* of simple substances can consist.

18. One could give the name *entelechies* to all simple substances or created monads. For they all have in them a certain perfection (*echousi to enteles*); there is a certain self-sufficiency (*autarkeia*) that makes them sources of their own internal actions and, so to speak, incorporeal automata. (See *Theodicy*, sec. 87.)

19. If we are willing to call *soul* anything that has *perceptions* and *appetites* in the general sense I have just explained, then all simple substances or created monads could be called souls. But as sentience is something more than a mere perception, I hold that the generic name of *monads* or *entelechies* suffices for simple substances which have nothing but this, and that one should call *souls* only those whose perception is more distinct and accompanied by memory.

20. For we experience in ourselves a state where we remember nothing and have no distinct perception, as when we fall into a swoon or when we are overcome by a deep and altogether dreamless sleep. In this state the soul does not differ noticeably from a simple monad. But as this state is not at all durable, and the soul emerges from it, the soul is something more. (See *Theodicy*, sec. 64.)

21. But it by no means follows from this that a simple substance is now wholly without perception. This is even impossible for the aforementioned reasons. For a substance cannot perish, nor can it subsist without some affection, which is nothing other than its perception. But when there is a large multiplicity of minute perceptions where there is nothing distinct, one is stupefied, as when we turn continually in the same direction several times in succession, whence arises a dizziness which can make us faint and which lets us distinguish nothing. Death can give this state for a time to animals.

22. And as every present state of a simple substance is a natural con-

sequence of its preceding state, so is its present pregnant with the future. (See *Theodicy*, sec. 360.)

23. Therefore, since when reawakened from unconsciousness one *apperceives* one's perceptions, it must be that one had some of them immediately before, although one was not at all aware of them. For a perception can come naturally only from another perception, just as one motion can come naturally only from another motion. (See *Theodicy*, secs. 401, 403.)

24. One sees from this that if we had in our perceptions nothing distinct and, so to speak, heightened and of an enhanced flavor, we should always remain in unconsciousness. And this is the state of the totally bare monads.

25. We see too that nature has given heightened perceptions to animals by the care she has taken to furnish them with organs which collect many rays of light or many vibrations of air to make them more effective through their unification. There is something similar in smell, taste, and touch, and perhaps in many other senses that are unknown to us. And I shall explain presently how what happens in the soul represents what happens in the organs.

26. Memory provides a kind of *connectedness* (*consécution*) to souls which resembles reason but must be distinguished from it. For we see that animals which have a perception of something that strikes them and of which they have previously had a similar perception expect, from the representation in their memory, that which has been conjoined in that previous perception, and are thus led to sensations similar to those they have had before. For example, when one shows a stick to dogs, they recall the pain that it has caused them and whine and run off. (See *Theodicy*, Preliminary Discourse, sec. 65.)

27. The potent imaging that strikes and moves them comes either from the size or from the number of the preceding perceptions. For often a strong impression has at one blow the effect of a long-formed *habit*, or that of a great many repeated perceptions of modest size.

28. Men function like beasts insofar as the connections among their perceptions come about only through the agency of memory, resembling empirical physicians who have mere practice without theory. We are all mere empirics in three-quarters of our actions. For example, when one expects a sunrise tomorrow, one acts as an empiric, seeing that this has always been so heretofore. Only the astronomer judges this by reason. (See *Theodicy*, Preliminary Discourse, sec. 65.)

29. But the knowledge of necessary and eternal truths is what distinguishes us from mere animals and provides us with *reason* and the sciences, elevating us to a knowledge of ourselves and of God. And it is this within us that is called the rational soul or *spirit*.

30. It is also through the knowledge of necessary truths and through

their abstraction that we are raised to *Reflexive Acts*, which enable us to think of what is called I and to consider that this or that lies within *ourselves*. And, it is thus that in thinking of ourselves we think of being, of substance, of the simple and compound, of the immaterial, and of God himself, by conceiving that what is limited in us is unlimited in him. And these reflexive acts furnish the principal objects of our reasonings. (See *Theodicy*, Preface.)

31. Our reasonings are founded on *two great principles: that of Contradiction*, in virtue of which we judge to be false that which contains contradiction, and to be *true* that which is opposed or contradictory to the false. (See *Theodicy*, secs. 44, 169.)

32. And that of *Sufficient Reason*, in virtue of which we consider that no fact can be real or actual, and no proposition true, without there being a sufficient reason for its being so and not otherwise, although most often these reasons just cannot be known by us. (See *Theodicy*, secs. 44, 196.)

33. There are two kinds of truths, those of *reasoning* and those of *fact*. Truths of reasoning are necessary and their opposite is impossible, while those of fact are contingent and their opposite is possible. When a truth is necessary one can find its reason through analysis, resolving it into ever more simple ideas and truths until one reaches primitives. (See *Theodicy*, secs. 170, 174, 189, 280–82, 367; Abridgment, obj. 3.)

34. This is how, among mathematicians, theoretical *theorems* and practical *rules* are reduced by analysis to definitions, axioms, and postulates.

35. There are, ultimately, simple ideas of which no definition can be given. And there are also axioms and postulates, or, in a word *primitive principles*, which cannot be proved and have no need of it, either. And these are the *identical propositions*, whose opposite contains an explicit contradiction.

36. But a *sufficient reason* must also be present in *contingent truths* or *truths of fact*, that is to say, in the sequence of things dispersed through the universe of created beings. Here the resolution into particular reasons can go on into endless detail, because of the immense variety of things in nature and the *ad infinitum* division of bodies. There is an infinity of shapes and motions, present and past, that enter into the efficient cause of my present writing, and there is an infinity of minute inclinations and dispositions of my soul, present and past, that enter into its final cause. (See *Theodicy*, secs. 36, 37, 44, 45, 49, 52, 121, 122, 337, 340, 344.)

37. And as all this *detail* only contains other prior, or yet more detailed contingents each of which also requires a similar analysis to provide its reason, one is no further ahead. The sufficient or final reason

must lie outside of the sequence or *series* of this detail of contingencies, however infinite it may be.

38. And so the ultimate reason of things must be in a necessary substance in which the detail of the changes is present only eminently, as in its source. It is this that we call *God*. (See *Theodicy*, sec. 7.)

39. Now as this substance is a sufficient reason of all this detail, which is also interconnected throughout, *there is only one God and this God is all-sufficient.*

40. One can also conclude that this Supreme Substance, which is unique, universal, and necessary—having nothing outside it that is independent of it, and being a direct consequence of merely being possible—must be incapable of limits and must contain as much reality as is possible.

41. From this it follows that God is absolutely perfect, *perfection* being nothing but the amount of positive reality taken separately, putting aside the limits or bounds in the things that have them. And where there are no bounds at all, namely in God, perfection is absolutely infinite. (See *Theodicy*, Preface, sec. 22.)

42. It follows also that created beings owe their perfections to the influence of God, but owe their imperfections to their own nature, which is incapable of being without limits. For it is in this that they differ from God. (See *Theodicy*, secs. 20, 27–31, 153, 167, 377–78, 380; Abridgment, obj. 5.)

43. It is true also that in God lies not only the source of existences, but also that of essences, insofar as they are real.

44. For it must be that, if there is a reality in essences or possibilities, or indeed in eternal truths, this reality be founded in something existent and actual, and consequently in the existence of the Necessary Being, in whom essence includes existence, or in whom being possible suffices for being actual. (See *Theodicy*, secs. 184, 189, 335.)

45. Thus only God, or the Necessary Being, has this privilege, that he must exist if he is possible. And since nothing can prevent the possibility of that which contains no limits and no negation, and consequently no contradiction, this by itself suffices to establish the existence of God *a priori*. And we have also proved this through the reality of the eternal truths.

46. However, we must not imagine, as some do, that the eternal truths, being dependent on God, are arbitrary and depend upon his will, as Descartes seems to have held, and Monsieur Poiret after him. That is true only of contingent truths, whose principle is *fitness* or the choice of *the best*. Instead, the necessary truths depend solely on God's understanding, and are its internal object. (See *Theodicy*, secs. 180–84, 185, 335, 351, 380.)

47. Accordingly, God alone is the primary unity or the original sim-

ple substance, of which all the created or derivative monads are products. They originate, so to speak, through continual fulgurations of the divinity from moment to moment, limited by the receptivity of the created being, to which it is essential to be limited. (See *Theodicy*, secs. 382–91, 395, 398.)

48. There is in God *Power*, which is the source of all, and also *Knowledge*, which contains the detail (*détail*) of the ideas of things, and finally *Will*, which effects changes or products according to the *principle of the best*. (See *Theodicy*, secs. 7, 48, 149, 150.)

This triad corresponds in created monads to the subject or basis, the perceptive faculty, and the appetitive faculty. But in God these attributes are absolutely infinite or perfect, while in the created monads or entelechies (or *perfectihabies*, "perfection-havers," as Hermolaus Barbarus rendered this word) they are mere imitations, authentic only to the extent that there is perfection. (See *Theodicy*, secs. 48, 87.)

49. A created being is said *to act* externally insofar as it has perfection, and *to react* to another insofar as it is imperfect. Thus *action* is attributed to the monad insofar as it has distinct perceptions and *reaction* (*passion*) insofar as it has confused ones. (See *Theodicy*, secs. 32, 66, 386.)

50. And one created being is more perfect than another insofar as one finds within it that which provides an *a priori* reason for what happens in the other. And it is because of this that one says that it *acts* upon the other.

51. But in simple substances there is only an ideal influence of one monad on another, which can have its effect only through the intervention of God, insofar in the ideas of God one monad demands with good reason that God should have regard for it in regulating the others from the very beginning of things. For, since one created monad cannot have any physical influence on the inner make-up of another, it is in this way alone that the one can be dependent on the other. (See *Theodicy* secs. 9, 54, 65, 66, 2ol; Abridgment, obj. 3.)

52. And it is in this way that among created beings actions and reactions are reciprocal. For God, comparing two simple substances, finds in each reasons which oblige him to accommodate the other to it, and consequently that which is in certain regards active is passive from another point of consideration. It is *active* insofar as what is distinctly known in it provides the reason for what happens in another, and *reactive* (*passive*) insofar as the reason for what happens in it is found in what is distinctly known in another. (See *Theodicy*, sec. 66.)

53. Now, as there is an infinity of possible universes in the ideas of God, and as only one of them can exist, there must be a sufficient reason for God's choice, which determines him to one rather than another. (See *Theodicy*, secs. 8, 10, 44, 173, 196–99, 225, 414–16.)

54. And this reason can only be found in *fitness* or in the degrees of perfection that these worlds contain, each possible world having the right to lay claim to existence to the extent of the perfection it enfolds. (See *Theodicy*, secs. 74, 130, 167, 201, 345–47, 350, 352, 354.)

55. And this is the cause of the existence of the best: that his wisdom makes it known to God, his goodness makes him chose it, and his power makes him produce it. (See *Theodicy*, secs. 8, 78, 80, 84, 119, 204, 206, 208, and Abridgment, objs. 1, 8.)

56. Now this interlinkage or accommodation of all created things to each other, and of each to all the others, brings it about that each simple substance has relations that express all the others, and is in consequence a perpetual living mirror of the universe. (See *Theodicy*, secs. 130, 360.)

57. And as one and the same town viewed from different sides looks altogether different, and is, as it were, *perspectively* multiplied, it similarly happens that, through the infinite multitude of simple substances, there are, as it were, just as many different universes, which however are only the perspectives of a single one according to the different *points of view* of each monad. (See *Theodicy*, sec. 147.)

58. And this is the way to obtain as much variety as possible, but combined with the greatest possible order, that is to say, it is the way to obtain as much perfection as can be. (See *Theodicy*, secs. 120, 124, 214, 241–43, 275.)

59. Further, no hypothesis but this (which I venture to call established) fittingly exalts the greatness of God. Monsieur Bayle recognized this when in his *Dictionary* (article "Rorarius") he made some objections in which he was even inclined to believe that I ascribed too much to God—more than is possible. But he could give no reason why this universal harmony, which makes every substance express exactly all the others through the relations it has to them, should be impossible.

60. Moreover, one sees in what I have just discussed the *a priori* reasons why things cannot be otherwise than they are. For in regulating the whole, God has had regard for each part, and in particular for each monad, which, its very nature being representative, is such that nothing can restrict it to representing only one part of things. To be sure, this representation is only confused regarding the detail of the whole universe. It can only be distinct in regard to a small part of things, namely those that are nearest or most extensively related to each monad. Otherwise each monad would be a deity. It is not in their object but in the particular mode of knowledge of this object that the monads are restricted. They all reach confusedly to the infinite, to the whole; but they are limited and differentiated by the degrees of their distinct perceptions.

61. And composites accord with simples in this regard. For as all is

a plenum, which renders all matter interconnected, and as in a plenum any motion has some effect on distant bodies in proportion to their distance—so that each body is affected not only by those that touch it, in some way feeling the effects of all that happens to them, but also through their mediation feeling affected by those in contact with the former by which it is directly touched—it follows that this inter-communication extends to any distance, however great. And in consequence, all bodies feel the effects of everything that happens in the universe. Accordingly, someone who sees all could read in each all that happens throughout, and even what has happened or will happen, observing in the present that which is remote, be it in time or in place. *Sympnoia panta* ("all things conspire"), as Hippocrates said. But a soul can read in itself only that which is represented distinctly there; it cannot unfold all-at-once all of its complications, because they extend to infinity.

62. Thus, although every created monad represents the entire universe, it represents more distinctly the body which is especially bound to it and of which it is the entelechy [and which is always organic so that there should be an order in the body]. And even as this body expresses the whole universe through the connection of all matter in the plenum, so the soul also represents the entire universe in representing this body, which belongs to it in a special way. (See *Theodicy*, sec. 400.)

63. The body belonging to the monad that is its entelechy or soul constitutes with this entelechy what may be called an *organism*, and with a soul what is called an *animal*. Now the body of an organism or an animal is always organic; for, since every monad is a mirror of the universe in its own way, and the universe is regulated in a perfect order, there must also be an order in the representer—that is, in the perceptions of the soul, and consequently in the body—through which the universe is represented there. (See *Theodicy*, sec. 403.)

64. Thus each organic body of a living being is a kind of divine machine or natural automaton which infinitely surpasses all artificial automata. For a machine made by human artifice is not a machine in each of its parts. For example, the tooth of a brass wheel has parts or pieces which to us are no longer artificial things, and no longer have something recognizably machine-like about them, reflecting the use for which the wheel is intended. But the machines of nature, namely living organisms, are still machines even in their smallest parts, *ad infinitum*. It is this that constitutes the difference between nature and artifice, that is, between divine artifice and ours. (See *Theodicy*, secs. 134, 146, 194, 403.)

65. And the Author of Nature has been able to practice this divine and infinitely wonderful artifice because each bit of matter is not merely infinitely divisible, as the ancients already realized, but is even

actually endlessly subdivided, every piece into further pieces, each of which has some motion of its own. Otherwise it would be impossible that each bit of matter could express the whole universe. (See *Theodicy*, Preliminary Discourse, sec. 70; sec. 195.)

66. From this one sees that there is a whole world of creatures—of organisms, animals, entelechies, and souls—even in the least piece of matter.

67. Every bit of matter can be conceived as a garden full of plants or a pond full of fish. But each branch of the plant, each member of the animal, each drop of its bodily fluids, is also such a garden or such a pond.

68. And though the earth and the air emplaced between the plants of the garden or the water emplaced between the fish of the pond are certainly neither plant nor fish, they contain yet more of them, though mostly of a minuteness imperceptible to us.

69. Thus nothing is fallow, sterile, or dead in the universe; there is no chaos, no disorder save in appearance. It is somewhat like what appears in a distant pond, in which one might see the confused and, so to speak, teeming motion of the pond's fish, without distinguishing the fish themselves. (See *Theodicy*, Preface.)

70. One sees from this that every living body has a dominant entelechy, which in an animal is the soul. But the members of this living body are themselves full of other organisms—plants or animals—each of which also has its own entelechy or dominant soul.

71. But it must not be imagined, as some have done who misunderstood my thought, that every soul has a bulk or bit of matter of its own that is attached to it forever, and that it consequently possesses other inferior organisms destined always to be at its service. For all bodies are in a perpetual flux, like rivers, and some parts enter into them and some pass out continually.

72. Thus the soul changes its body only slowly and by degrees, so that it is never laid bare of all its organs all at once. There is often a metamorphosis in animals, but never metempsychosis or transmigration of souls. Nor are there *souls* altogether *separated* or disembodied spirits. God alone is wholly detached from any body. (See *Theodicy*, secs. 90, 124.)

73. This also brings it about that there is never either complete birth or complete death, in the strict sense of a separation of the soul. What we call *births* are unfoldings and growths; even as what we call *deaths* are enfoldings and diminutions.

74. Philosophers have been much perplexed about the origin of forms, entelechies, or souls. But today, when we have learned from scientific studies of plants, insects, and animals, that the organic bodies of nature are never products of a chaos or decay, but always grow from

seeds in which there was undoubtedly some *pre-formation*, it has been concluded that not only was the organic body already present before conception, but also the soul in this body and, in short, the animal itself, and that through its conception this animal has only been positioned for a great transformation so as to become an animal of a different kind. One even sees something like this apart from birth, as when larvae become flies and caterpillars become butterflies. (See *Theodicy*, Preface; secs. 86, 89, 90, 187, 188, 397, 403.)

75. The *animals*, some of which are raised through conception to the level of the highest animals, may be called *spermatics*. But those among them which are more typical, that is, the majority, are born, multiply, and are destroyed just like the higher animals, and it is only a few specially chosen ones (the "elect") that achieve a larger role.

76. Yet this is only half of the truth. I have therefore concluded that if an animal never begins by natural means, it does not end by natural means either. Not only will there be no real birth, but also no total destruction, nor death in the strict sense. And these reasonings, made *a posteriori* and drawn from experience, agree perfectly with principles deduced *a priori*, as above. (See *Theodicy*, sec. 90.)

77. Thus we can say that not only the soul, that mirror of an indestructible universe, is indestructible, but also the animal itself, although its bodily mechanism may often perish in part, and leave off or take on organic coverings.

78. These principles have given me a way to explain naturally the union, or rather the conformity of the soul and the organic body. The soul follows its own laws and the body likewise follows its own; and they agree by virtue of the *pre-established harmony* among all substances, because they are all representations of one selfsame universe. (See *Theodicy*, Preface; secs. 340, 352, 353, 358.)

79. Souls act according to the laws of final causes through appetition, ends, and means. Bodies act according to the laws of efficient causes or of motions. And the two realms, that of efficient causes and that of final causes, are harmonious with one another.

80. Descartes recognized that souls are wholly unable to impart force to bodies because there is always the same quantity of force in matter. However, he believed that the soul could change the direction of bodies. But this was because people did not know in his time the law of nature which also maintains the conservation of the same total of directed force in matter. If he had recognized this, he would have hit upon my system of pre-established harmony. (See *Theodicy*, Preface; secs. 22, 59–61, 63, 66, 345–48, 354, 355).

81. This system has it that bodies act as though (to suppose the impossible) there were no souls at all, and souls act as though there were no bodies at all, and both act as though each influenced the other.

82. As regards *spirits* or rational souls, while I find that at bottom the same situation prevails in all organisms and animals, as just said (namely that the animal and the soul begin only with the world and end only with the world), there is nevertheless this peculiarity in rational animals, that their minute spermatic animacules, as long as they are only this, have merely ordinary or sensitive souls. But as soon as those who are, so to speak, elect arrive through an actual conception at human nature, their sensitive souls are elevated to the rank of reason and to the prerogative of spirits. (See *Theodicy*, secs. 91, 397.)

83. Among other differences between ordinary souls and spirits, a part of which I have already noted, there is also this, that souls in general are living mirrors or images of the universe of created beings. But the spirits are also images of divinity itself—of the very Author of nature. They are capable of knowing the system of the universe, and of imitating it to some extent through constructive samples, each spirit being like a minute divinity within its own sphere. (See *Theodicy*, sec. 147.)

84. This brings it about that spirits are capable of entering into a kind of community with God, and that he is in regard to them not only what an inventor is to his machine (as God is in relation to other created beings), but also what a prince is to his subjects, and even a father to his children.

85. From this it is readily concluded that the assemblage of all spirits must compose the City of God, that is, the most perfect state possible, under the most perfect of monarchs. (See *Theodicy*, sec. 146; Abridgment, obj. 2.)

86. This City of God, this truly universal monarchy, is a moral world within the natural world, and is the most exalted and the most divine of the works of God. And it is in it that the glory of God truly consists, for there would be none at all if his grandeur and goodness were not known and admired by the spirits. It is also in relation to this divine city that he particularly has goodness, whereas his wisdom and power are manifested everywhere.

87. As we have already established a perfect harmony between two natural realms, the one of efficient and the other of final causes, we must here also recognize a further harmony between the physical realm of nature and the moral realm of grace, that is, between God considered as architect of the mechanism of the universe, and God considered as monarch of the divine city of spirits. (See *Theodicy*, secs. 62, 74, 112, 118, 130, 247, 248.)

88. This harmony brings it about that all things lead to grace by the ways of nature themselves, so that this globe, for example, must be destroyed and renewed in natural ways at those moments that the gov-

ernment of the spirits requires for the punishment of some and the reward of others. (See *Theodicy*, secs. 18–20, 110, 244, 245, 340.)

89. It can also be said that God as architect fully satisfies God as lawgiver. Thus sins must carry their penalty with them through the order of nature, and even in virtue of the mechanical make-up of things. And similarly, good deeds will obtain their rewards in ways that are mechanical as regards bodies, even though this cannot and need not always happen immediately.

90. Finally, under this perfect government no good deed whatever will be unrewarded and no wicked one unpunished. And all must result for the benefit of the good, that is, of those who are nowise malcontents in this great state, who trust in providence after having done their duty, and who love and imitate, as is proper, the author of all good, taking pleasure in the consideration of his perfections according to the nature of a genuine *pure love*, which makes one take pleasure in the felicity of the beloved. It is this that makes wise and virtuous people work for everything that seems in conformity with the presumptive or antecedent divine will, and nevertheless content themselves with what God actually brings to pass by his secret, consequent or decisive will. They recognize that, if only we could sufficiently understand the order of the universe, we should find that it surpasses all the desires of the wisest, and that it is impossible to make it any better than it is, not only for the whole generally, but also for ourselves in particular, if we are properly attached to the author of all, not only as the architect and efficient cause of our being, but also as our master and as the final cause, who ought to be the whole aim of our will and who alone can bring us happiness. (See *Theodicy*, Preface; secs. 134 *ad fin.*, 278.)

✤ 3. The Thematic Structure of the *Monadology*

Note: References in parentheses indicate section numbers

A. Monads

I. Simple substances or *monads* are the ultimate units of existence in nature. They
- have no parts (1);
- must exist (2);
- lack extension, figure, divisibility (3);
- are "true atoms of nature" (3).

II. Monads are causally impervious and thus
- cannot begin or end in time (4, 5);
- are subject only to creation and annihilation, not to growth or decay (6)
- cannot be causally affected by other things (7).

III. Monads are quantitatively simple but qualitatively complex existents. Specifically, they
- have qualities (8);
- change qualities over time (8);
- differ in their qualities (*identity of indiscernibles*) (9).

B. Monadic Perception

IV. Monadic change is change in the qualities of substances that
- is ever-present (10);
- comes from within through the unfolding of an inner law of development (11);
- roots in the inner complexity (*detail*) of substances (12);
- obeys a *law of continuity* (13).

V. The ever-changing, internally complex make-up (*detail*) of a monad's qualitative state
- can be called *perception* (which need not be conscious, that is, *apperceptive*) (14);

- is subject to an inner drive of developmental change called *appetition* (15);
- reflects a comprehension of multiplicity in unity that we ourselves can and do experience within ourselves (16);
- is inexplicable by mechanical reasons (17);
- proceeds entirely from the monad's own internal make-up through an inherent "programming" that makes each substance into a (fully independent) source of its own actions (18);
- is subject to an inherent orderliness that means that what comes later emerges through a natural explanation from what has gone before (22).

C. Souls and Spirits

VI. All monads have *perception* and *appetition* and the *self-sufficiency* of inherent development. But
- some monads—to be called *souls*—also have consciousness and memory (19, 20, 24);
- these monads enjoy a more heightened and developed mode of (conscious) perception (21);
- this sort of perceptual experience is orderly and coherently interconnected (23).

VII. The more sophisticated perceptual experience of the *conscious* sort that is found only in the more developed *soul*-endowed organisms
- reflects the physiological make-up of the animals that manifest it (25);
- is accompanied by memory in a way that brings a *law of association* into operation (26);
- is also accompanied by a capacity for imagination (27).

VIII. The monads of the highest sort—typified by persons—are called *spirits:*
- they are distinguished by also possessing the capacity for *reasoning* from general truths (28–29);
- this capacity furnished us with access to the necessary and "eternal" truths of mathematics, metaphysics, and theology (29–30).

D. Principles of Truth

IX. The key metaphysical principles which undergird the present deliberations themselves are:
- the *principle of sufficient reason*, which stipulates that for

every truth whatever, there is a sufficient reason for its being
so rather than otherwise (32);
- the *principle of contradiction*, which furnishes (via the insistence or noncontradiction) the sufficient reason for the necessary and eternal truths (31); and
- the *principle of perfection* (or *principle of the best*), which provides the sufficient reason for the contingent truths (36,
  53–55).
- There are accordingly two fundamentally different kinds of
  truth, the truths of reason (necessary truths) and the truths of
  fact (contingent truths) (33).

X. As regards the sufficient reason for truths:
- The sufficient reason for any truth can be found by a process
  of analysis. This analysis is finite in the case of necessary
  truths, where it ultimately terminates in self-evident propositions (33–35);
- the analysis involved in providing a sufficient reason for truths
  of fact is of unending complexity and infinite detail (36–37).

E. God

XI. The sufficient reason of truths of fact extends into something beyond the entire series of contingent existence in its endless detail.
This "ultimate reason of things" is God himself (38). And this
God must, of metaphysical necessity, be conceived of
- as unique and uniquely sufficient (39);
- as necessary and unlimited in existence (40);
- as perfect and infinite (41);
- as the creator and sustainer of everything that is good in existing things (42).

XII. But while God is perfect, creatures are not.
- For imperfections lie in their own nature, over which God has
  no control (42).
- God finds these creatures as abstract possibilities in his intellect; his will has no part in making them what they are (43).
- The intellect of God is thus the region of possibilities: if (*per
  impossible*) God did not exist, not only would nothing else
  exist, but nothing would even be possible (44).

XIII. Accordingly the existence of God is necessary (45). And moreover,
- the necessary truths hinge upon his intellect, unlike the contingent truths which depend on his will as well (46);
- God is thus the self-necessitated source of all else that exists,
  and everything else depends contingently upon him (47);

- God is accordingly the perfect being, at once all-powerful, all-being, and all-good (48).

XIV. God alone is a genuine agent. The agency of created substances is an agency in name only.
- The created monads are *active* insofar as their nature involves perfections and *inactive* insofar as their nature involves imperfections (49).
- They are perfect, and thus active, exactly insofar as God finds in the nature of the one that which provides a reason for selecting another that is coordinated with it (50).
- The agency of one substance on another is ideal only; one substance can have no actual influence on one another (51).
- God's creation choice is the only real action that there is. His selection among alternatives adjusts monads to one another. The superior, to whose interests others are accounted are thereby "active"; the inferior, who give way to others in the accommodation process are thereby passive (52).

F. God's Choice Among Possible Worlds

XV. God's mind is the domain of possibilities.
- God chooses one alternative over others for actualization (53).
- In so doing he is guided by the inherent perfection that the concept of these possibilities enfolds (54).
- The existence of the best accordingly roots in the free will of God (55).

XVI. God's commitment to the realization of perfection in the real world
- involves a coordination among all existing situations which attunes all things to one another in smoothly coordinated interrelations (56);
- means that each substance represents a particular point of view regarding one single unified whole (57);
- maximizes realizable perfection by way of an optimal combination of variety and orderliness (58).

XVII. God's maximization of the world's *realizable* perfection
- is the theologically most appropriate hypothesis for explaining the real (59);
- renders the world's content of some imperfections understandable, on the ground of their being unavoidable (60).

G. A Pan-Organic Conception of Nature

XVIII. God's concern for the world's orderliness and harmony makes it possible to

- account for the coordination and interconnectedness of all things throughout nature (61);
- explain the consonance between individual substances and their environing nature that coordinates microcosm (monad) and macrocosm (universe) (62);
- understand how its immediate environing substances are organically interrelated with a particular (dominant) monad (63);
- see that nature is an integrated whole that is everywhere living and is organized into an orderly cosmos on the basis of organic principles (64–69).

XIX. Nature is organized throughout into living organisms which
- though constituted of pluralities, are bonded together into units through the operation of a dominant monad, be it entelechy, soul, or spirit (70);
- constantly change as regards the population of individual substances that compose them (71);
- never fall into such utter disarray that higher-level substances (souls or spirits) lose all prospect of recovery (72–73);

XX. This view of the pervasively organic structure of nature
- is substantiated in recent advances in biology made possible by microscopy (74)
- reflects the fact that life comes from life and also, never actually loses its organic character (75–77).

H. Mind-Body Coordination

XXI. The "organic" coordination of the states of all substances with one another
- explains the conformity of soul and body (78);
- coordinates the "mechanical" efficient causation of bodies and the "teleological" final causation of souls (79);
- explains how mind-body coordination is possible without any actual interaction (80–81).

XXII. The *spirits* or monads of the highest order
- can attain the level of rational beings (82);
- resemble God in their capacity to know, to evaluate, and to act in pursuit of the good (83);
- can enter into a special relationship with God (84).

I. The City of God

XXIII. Because of their special status, the spirits
- constitute a special community, the City of God (85);
- are, as it were, the pride and glory of God's creation (86).

XXIV. The overall harmony of all creation and particularly of the
      spirits within it
  • coordinates the order of nature with the order of God's grace
    (87–88);
  • indicates that what happens in the world is all part of God's
    plan, in which the welfare of spirits has a prime place (89);
  • means that we humans should be content with our place in
    the world's natural order (90).

🎄 4. Leibniz's Use of Analogies and Principles

In the *Monadology* (as elsewhere), Leibniz often expounds his ideas by means of analogies involving a proportion of the form: X is to X' even as Y is to Y'. In fact, virtually the whole of Leibniz's discussion here is a complex fabric of such analogies or proportions—as is made transparently clear by the inventory given below. (Observe that it is only in the basic expository discussion that describes the *modus operandi* of monads [secs. 1–13] that Leibniz relies more heavily on direct description than on explanatory comparisons.)

Regarding the use of analogies in science, Leibniz himself comments as follows:

> The hypothetical method a posteriori [i.e., the inductive method of science] which proceeds from experiments, rests for the most part upon analogies. For instance, seeing that many terrestrial phenomena agree with magnetic phenomena, some men teach that the earth is a great magnet, that the structure of the earth corresponds to this, and that heavy bodies are drawn to earth as a magnet draws to iron. Others explain everything by fermentation, even the ebb and flow of the tides. Still others, seeing that lye fights against acids, reduce all corporeal conflicts to those of acid and alkali. While we must guard against the abuse of analogies, yet they can be of exceedingly great use in making inductions and in setting up aphorisms from inductions by means of which we can also make predictions about matters of which we as yet have little experience. This too is useful in investigating the true causes of things, for it is always easier to discover the cause of a phenomenon which several things have in common. So it is also easier to solve cryptographs when we have found a number of letters in the concealed meaning which are written according to the same key. Then, too, the cause of the same phenomenon can be investigated more easily in one subject than in another, as anatomists who dissect different animals well know. (Loemker, p. 284)

For other statements of Leibniz regarding analogy, see R. Finster et al., eds., *Leibniz Lexicon*, pp. 15–16, s.v. *analogia*, noting in particular his dictum: *omnia in natura sunt analogica*.

This analogy-intensive mode of treatment reflects Leibniz's methodology of thought—in philosophy as well as in science and mathematics. He is *par excellence* the philosopher of cosmic harmony, and since the days of the Pythagoreans of classical antiquity, proportion has been viewed as a prime vehicle of harmony. It is thus interesting—and deeply fitting—that Leibniz's substantive philosophy of harmony should find its expression in a mode of exposition that uses proportion as its preeminent instrumentality.

To be sure, Leibniz does not deploy such analogies as substantiating *arguments* for his position: their use is merely expository and explanatory. Nevertheless, he doubtless regards the circumstance that his philosophy lends itself so smoothly to a formulation in terms of proportions as constituting a substantiating consideration in its behalf. Leibniz's talent as a philosopher lies—*inter alia*—in his capacity to flesh out these picturesque analogies with a mass of theoretical detail that transforms them into a comprehensive and detailed explanatory system.

Inventory of Analogies in the *Monadology*
(Numbers indicate sections.)

2. Even as the traditional atoms are the ultimate physical building blocks of material objects, so the monads are the ultimate metaphysical building blocks of substances.

7. Even as material simples (atoms) cannot be changed by external physical influences (or causes), so metaphysical simples (monads) cannot be changed by external metaphysical influences (or causes).

7. Even as external images cannot enter a windowless house so external influences cannot enter a monad.

8. Even as perceptible objects can only be distinguished through their perceptible qualities, so metaphysical objects (monads) can only be distinguished through their metaphysical qualities.

14. Basic (monadic) "perception" is to full-fledged *perception* as unconscious awareness is to conscious awareness.

15. Monadic appetition is to (conscious) appetite as monadic (basic) perception is to conscious awareness.

16. The unity of a (conscious) thinker is to the diversity of a thought-content as the unity of an (unconscious) perceiver is to the diversity of a perceptual content.

17. A strictly mechanical "mind" would be to perception as a mechanism would be to conscious thought. (Hence perception—and mental process generally—cannot be explained in mechanical principles.)

18. Even as an Aristotelian entelechy is an organically self-developing organism, so a monad is a metaphysically self-developing mechanism (an "incorporeal automaton").

19. Even as souls have conscious perception and appetites, so simple monads have unconscious perception and appetition.

20. Even as in sleep and fainting human minds fall into occasional unconsciousness, so bare monads standardly function in unconsciousness.

21. Unconscious is to conscious perception as death and fainting are to the waking experience of souls.

22. As an embryonic state of an organism is to its later more developed later stages, so is the present state of a substance to its later more developed stages.

23. Even as in mechanics the later physical stages of a system are lawful consequences of its earlier stages, so in metaphysics are the later perceptual states of a substance the lawful consequences of its earlier states.

24. Conscious perception is to minds (spirits) as unconscious perception is to bare monads.

25. Even as complex sense-organs enable humans to organize sensory inputs into self-conscious experience, so do more rudimentary organic structures enable higher animals to have conscious experience.

26. Even as reasoning connects beliefs by logical relationships, so memory connects experiences by association.

27. Even as many small weights amount to one large one, so a strong impression is like a long-formed habit built up by many small impressions (in that both make a comparably sizeable cognitive impact).

28. Habit based on experience is for the ordinary person what reason is to the scientist. Ordinary men are to scientists as empirical physicians are to scientifically trained physicians: the former both proceed without a theory that enables them to understand and explain the connections among experiences.

30. Human knowledge is to God's knowledge as the finite is to the infinite.

33. Truths of reason are to truths of fact as the (finitely) analytical is to the (infinitely) unanalyzable.

35. Simple (unanalyzable) ideas are to complex (definable) ideas as unprovable propositions (axioms and postulates) are to provable propositions (theorems).

35. Identical propositions are to necessary truths what axioms and postulates are to mathematical truths.

36. The infinite analysis of substantiating detail is to contingent truths what demonstration (i.e., finite analysis) is to necessary truths.

37. We humans stand to facts about our actions as God stands to facts about the world.

41. In point of perfection (including knowledge, goodness, power, reality, etc.) humans are to God as the finite is to the infinite.

42. Confusedness is to the perception of creatures as inertia is to the bodies of creatures. (Both betoken the same sort of limitedness and imperfection.)

43–44. Even as our minds sustain our ideas, so God's mind sustains God's ideas (and is accordingly the region where necessary truths exist).

45. Even as a particular contingent being must have some ground or basis outside itself (in an external cause) so the realm of integral fact at large must have some ground outside itself (and so in something which, being extra-contingent must be necessary.

45. In general we have the proportion:

possibly : actuality :: actuality : necessity (and thus $P/A = A/N$). But in God (and in God alone) we have $P = A$. Hence for God (and for God alone) we have $P = A = N$.

47. Even as the sun's physical fulgurations provide the light that renders material things visible, so the fulgurations of God's will render created substances existent. (Here Leibniz the neo-Platonist comes to the fore.)

47–48. As in God there is unlimited scope for power, knowledge, and will, so in the created mind there is primitive force, perception, and appetition. Its perfections are to the nature of a finite being what God's perfections are to the divine nature—namely: the former are inherently limited, the latter inherently unlimited.

49. Action is to passion as distinct perception is to confused perception.

50. Cause is to effect as explaining reason is to explained fact.

51. The influence of one monad upon another is like the influence of one statement upon another in a book: God adjusts monads to one another even as the author adjusts statements to one another with a view to their compatibility in logical or material regards.

52. Action is to passion as ground is to consequence: that substance is the agent whose nature provides the reason for the accommodation of another.

53. Even as among mutually incompatible statements only one can be true, so among mutually incompossible worlds only one can be existent.

54–55. Even as in deliberations among alternative choices the chooser will prefer the most appealing (i.e. the seemingly best), so in his choice among possible worlds will God prefer the *fittest* (i.e., the actually best or most perfect).

56. Every substance contains a representation of every other even as every object facing a mirror is represented by an image upon it.

57. The different perceptions of a common world from the varying perspectives of different monads are as the different appearances of a

common object (city) from the different points of view of different observers.

60. Even as God knows clearly everything that happens in the possible worlds, so each monad perceives infinitely everything that happens in the actual world.

61. Even as a motion anywhere makes itself felt everywhere in a body of water (though with lessened impact at greater distances), so in the world at large any change anywhere has repercussions everywhere (though again with lessened force at greater distances). (Thus a monad perceives everything—albeit in general confusedly.)

62. Even as each body is bound up with the changes of all others through physical laws (e.g., universal gravitation), so each monad is bound up with all others through metaphysical principles of universal order.

63. Even as a body mirrors its environing universe, so a soul mirrors its environing body (and consequently the entire universe).

64. An organism is to a machine as the infinitely complex is to the finity complex (the latter is a work of finite and imperfect artifice, the former a work of infinite and perfect artifice). Thus art is to nature as man is to God.

65–67. Every bit of matter is like "a garden full of plants or a pond full of fish." Nature is like a "Chinese box": a manifold of organisms containing ever-smaller organisms. (The organisms in our blood and cellular make-up at the microscopic level themselves contain smaller organisms that play a similar role. And so on *ad indefinitum*.)

69. The things of this world are like a teeming pond seen from the distance as a single whole: on closer inspection there are masses of organisms everywhere.

70. The dominant entelechy is the "soul" of an organism even as the soul of a person is what effects the unity of a single being.

71. "All bodies are in a perpetual flux, like rivers, and parts are passing into and out of them continually."

74. Even as plants grow from seeds and insects from larvae, so all compound organisms emerge from preexisting organisms.

75. The lower, spermatic organisms are just like the higher animals: they too "are born, reproduce, and die," generation on generation.

73–76. What we call "birth" is a growth, what we call "death" is a diminuition. (In nature there are no absolute beginnings and ends.)

77. Much as any monad (weakly) reflects its environing universe, so the dominant monad of an organism (strongly) reflects its environing body.

78. The perception of monads follows metaphysical laws of order even as the actions of bodies follow physical laws of order (and both sorts of laws reflect the inherent order of the universe).

79. Even as bodies act according to the efficient causation of the laws of motion, so souls act according to the final causation of the laws of appetition.

81. Even as bodies act according to the laws of bodies (as though there were no souls), so souls act according to the laws of souls (as though there were no bodies). (But the orders of action are entirely consonant.)

82. Souls are to lower animals as spirits are to humans (that is, in both cases we have unification through the dominant monads of aggregates).

82. Souls are to spirits as common folk are to the nobility (the "elect" who are raised to a higher rank and accorded its priorities).

83. Souls are (confused, yet living) reflectors of their environing world even as mirrors are (partial and inert) reflectors of their environment. And even as God is to the world (namely its creator), so is the spirit to the micro-world represented by the efficacy-range of a human being's agency.

83. As souls are to the universe so spirits are to God himself (viz., both reflect—albeit imperfectly—the larger law-structure of their coordinate).

84–85. God is to the world that is his creation as an inventor is to his machine. But more yet: God's relations to the spirits are as a prince's relations to his subjects (or a father's to his children)—viz., in each case there is not only creative agency but moral responsibility as well.

86. Even as the grandeur of his principality manifests the glory and power of a prince, so the principality of God ("City of God") constituted by the spirits manifests the glory and power of God.

87. Even as the coordination of efficient and final causation within nature manifests a preestablished perfect harmony, so the coordination between the entire realm of nature and the moral kingdom of grace manifests a preestablished perfect harmony.

87–89. God's perfect creativity as architect of the machinery of nature parallels God's perfect statecraft as legislator of the "divine city of spirits."

88–89. The order of the realm of grace parallels the order of the realm of nature in that each provides for a perfect moral balance of desert and reward.

90. Even as God is the ultimate efficient cause (or architect) of the world's existence, so God is also the ultimate final cause (or master) of the world's existence: reality's final purpose-endower.

A stylistic feature of the *Monadology* that is particularly striking is that Leibniz clothes the whole tract in the garment of mathematical exposition. Even in this metaphysical discourse we see Leibniz the logician at work, constantly employing the language of formal reasoning. One of his favored expressions is "thus" (*ainsi*), as per secs. 6, 34, 45, 47, 62, 64, 69, 72, and 77. Then too there is "one sees from this" (*on voit para là*, sec's 24, 60, 66, 70) and "whence it follows" (*d'où il s'en-suit*, secs. 11, 21, 41, 61). And note also *célà posé* (17), *il se prend pour accordé* (10), *c'est par là* (52), and *comme nous avons établi ci-dessus* (87). Leibniz clearly views his discussions not as a matter of description but of rational exfoliation, and it is indicative of his approach that he refers to his exposition as *nos raisonnements* (31). Leibniz's devotion to the geometric mode (to thinking things out *more geometrico*) is less explicit but no less emphatic than that of Spinoza.

Leibniz's way of visualizing a fabric of analogies as a systemic structure imbued with mathematical rigor affords a striking illustration of the Baroque era's penchant for unity amidst diversity and coherence amidst complexity (as illustrated in the music, architecture, and painting of the day).

And so, notwithstanding its extensive use of explanatory analogies, Leibniz's system consists in a *system of principles*, a collection of far-reaching generalizations on whose basis substantial parts of the detail of our understanding of the world can be accounted for. Some salient examples of such principles at work in the *Monadology* are as follows:

Principles of Existence

• *Substantiality:* Whatever really exists is either itself a thing (substance) or a collection or a feature of things. Individual substances have no physical parts (secs. 1–3).

• *Change:* Everything constantly changes. All metaphysical (substantival) change is a matter of property-alteration. All physical (natural) change is a matter of rearrangement (transposition) (secs. 4–8, 10).

• *Individuality:* Substances are *identified* through their properties (attributes, accidents). Hence there cannot be two distant substances with the same attributes. ("Identity of Indiscernibles") (sec. 9).

Principles of Intelligibility

• *Sufficient Reason: Nihil est sine ratione,* for every fact there is a sufficient reason for its being so rather than otherwise (sec. 32).

• *Contradiction:* Every necessary truth finds its sufficient reason in the self-contradictioness of its denial (sec. 31).

• *Perfection:* Every contingent truth finds its sufficient reason in its being better that matters stand thus rather than otherwise (secs. 36, 53–54).

Principles of Logic

• *Ideation:* Every feature of the possible can be represented by an *idea.* Such ideas are either simple (undefinable) or complex (definable through the conjoining of simple ideas) (sec. 35).

• *Proposition:* Every state of the possible can be represented by a proposition. Such propositions are either primitive (primary, underivable) or derivative (derivable from primary propositions). The primitive truths are necessary "identities," that is, propositions whose denial involves contradiction (cf. the above-mentioned Principle of Contradiction) (sec. 35).

Principles of Metaphysics

• *Reflection:* Everything that exists reflects everything else: each existent is coordinated with all the rest (secs. 13–14, 62).

• *Agency:* Everything that exists acts. Its "acting" consists in its involvement in changes the reason for which lie in its own nature (secs. 9–13, 15–17).

• *Organicism:* Everything that exists has life: all existence is organic (secs. 66–70).

• *Harmony:* Every occurrence and every arrangement of things in the world's stage is preprogrammed into coordination and alignment with everything else. In nature nothing is haphazard or fortuitious. Whatever occurs, occurs in line with an all-encompassing order (secs. 79, 81, 87, 88).

• *Community:* The intelligent beings that exist in the world form part of one grand, overarching community, united by their (potential) understanding of cosmic and moral order, and (as it were) forming a monarchial state whose presiding ruler is God himself (secs. 86, 89–90).

These principles are only some salient illustrations. Leibniz's entire "system," in fact, involves an orchestration of mutually coordinated principles, which is exactly why he designated the so-called *Monadology* as "The Principles of (My) Philosophy" (*Principes de la Philosophie*), as well as entitling its cognate sketch "The Principles of Nature and Grace." Philosophy, for Leibniz, is a complex structure of duly constructed explanatory principles, even as the world is a complex structure of coordinated units of existence. Leibniz's commitment to harmony is once again illustrated in the fact that, for him, the rational structure of philosophy itself reflects the intelligible structure of the world it seeks to explain.

☙ 5. Text and Commentary

SECTION 1

1. ***The monad*** **which we shall discuss here is nothing other than a simple substance that enters into composites.** ***Simple*** **means without parts. (See *Theodicy*, sec. 10.)**

1. La Monade *dont nous parlerons ici, n'est autre chose, qu'une substance simple, qui entre dans les composés;* simple, *c'est à dire, sans parties. (*Théodicée, *sec. 10.)*

(*Theodicy*, sec. 10.) There are of necessity substances which are simple and without extension, scattered throughout all Nature, and these substances must subsist independently of every other except God.

(PNG, sec. 1) *Substance* is a being capable of action. It is simple or compound. *Simple substance* is that which has no parts. *Compound substance* is a collection (*assemblage*) of simple substances, or *monads*. *Monas* is a Greek word signifying unity or that which is one.

(G VI, 585–86; Loemker, p. 622; Ariew & Garber, p. 262; "Conversation of Philarète and Ariste" [1712].) There is nothing but monads, that is, simple or indivisible substances, which are truly independent of every other concrete created thing.

COMMENTARY

Leibniz espoused a philosophy predicated on a concept of substance, exactly as did his predecessors Descartes and Spinoza. And he, like them, conforms his conception of substance to the traditional idea of a substance as an independent unit of existence, a *being* (*ens, un être*). As Spinoza put it in book I of the *Ethics* (definition 3), a substance is "something which exists in itself and can be conceived through itself" (*quod in se est et per se concipitur*). (This insistence on the indivisibility of substance goes back at least to Parmenides.) Substances are "true unities" and any genuine unit of existence must be substantial. But for Leibniz this means that a substance can have no parts; for if it did, then its own existence would depend on that of its parts. It has no material or physical components at all. However a substance must have features of some sort—properties (or "accidents")—for otherwise it would be nothing. Its *descriptive* make-up must accordingly be complex.

The "simplicity" of simple substances accordingly has to be construed as strictly *spatial* simplicity, that is, partlessness. (The simplicity at issue is thus emphatically *not* a qualitative one.) Being without parts, substances must be immaterial. What we perceive in the world about us is the *result* of the conjoint operation of monads. But they themselves are altogether immaterial. They are "metaphysical points" which in themselves have no size at all, although they "enter into" and indeed somehow go to make up sizeable objects.

According to Leibniz, the monads do not just "enter into" the composite things of this world, but actually *constitute* them. Exactly how they do so is one of the deep problems of the Leibnizian philosophy, which, strictly speaking, countenances only individual substances and treats composites or aggregates as mere illusions. (Note that Leibniz standardly speaks of composites or aggregates and not of composite or aggregate *substances*.) But he felt somewhat uneasy about the matter. The manuscript shows that he first added "which enter into composites" (*qui entre dans les composés*) as a marginal addendum, then crossed it out, and then finally reinserted it. Only in sections 61–64 do we get a clearer picture of the matter: composites or aggregates are substances by courtesy only, mere collectives of totally separate units integrated and coordinated by the dominance of a linking substance (entelechy) that links them all together through its perceptions. This unity is thus a matter of the same sort of organic coordination of interrelating operation that makes my finger a part of my body rather than of yours.

The monadic substances are not, of course, accessible to empirical experience but only to theoretical projection. Monads are not an observable part of physical reality. They are "hypothetical entities" postulated by Leibniz with a view to providing an effective explanatory instrumentality for a whole range of scientific, philosophical, and theological facts.

Leibniz began to use the term *monad* only in 1690 (in a letter to Fardella); until then he spoke of his unextended and immaterial unit of existence as a *simple substance* or also as an *entelechy*, another borrowing from Greek philosophy. The word *monad* had been used earlier by Giordano Bruno (1591), and more recently by Henry More (1671) and F. M. von Helmont (1685), from whom Leibniz probably borrowed the term. The Greek word *monas* ("unit") had been used by Euclid in book VII of the *Elements* and was employed by Aristotle (*Meteorology*, 1016b25e30, 1089b35, etc.) to designate something that is "indivisible in every direction." For ancient Pythagoreans, *monas* ("the unit") was the generating principle (*archê*) of numbers. For Giordano Bruno, like Leibniz, monads were the ultimate constituents (elemental *minima*) of all things, and contained both a physical and a psychic aspect (*De monade, numero et figura,* 1591).

KEY WORDS:

monad/*monade*
simple substance/*substance simple*
simple/*simple*
partless/*sans parties*
composite/*composé*

SECTION 2

2. And there must be simple substances, since there are composites; for the composite is nothing but a [collection or] accumulation or *aggregate* of simples.

2. Et il faut qu'il y ait des substances simples, puisqu'il y a des composés; car le composé n'est autre chose, qu'un [recueil ou] amas ou aggregatum des simples.

(PNG, sec. 1.) Compounds, or bodies, are pluralities; and simple substances—organisms, souls, and spirits—are unities. And there must certainly be simple substances everywhere, for without simples there would be no compounds.

(NS, sec. 11.) Furthermore, by means of the soul or form there is a true unity corresponding to what is called "I" in us. Such a unity could not occur in artificial machines or in a simple mass of matter, however organized it may be. For such a mass can be compared only to an army or a herd, or to a pond full of fish, or a watch made of springs and wheels. If there were no true substantial unities, however, there would be nothing substantial or real in the collection.

(G II, 76; Ariew & Garber, p. 79; to Arnauld [1686].) I think that a block of marble is, perhaps, only a mass of stones and thus cannot be taken as a single substance but as an assembly of many. For, supposing there are two stones, (for example, the diamond of the Grand Duke and that of the Great Mogul), the same collective name could be put for both of them, and we could say that it is a pair of diamonds, although they are very far apart; but, we should not say that these two diamonds compose one substance. Matters of greater or less in this case would make no difference. They might be brought nearer together, even to touching. Yet they would not be substantially one, and if, after they had touched they were joined together by some other body, constructed to prevent their separation—for instance, if they were set in the same ring—all this would make only what is called a unity by accident, for it is as by accident that they are subjected to the same motion. I hold, therefore, that a block of marble is no more a thoroughly single substance than would be the water in a pond with all the fish included, even when all the water and all the fish were frozen; or any more than a flock of sheep, even when the sheep were tied together so that they could only walk in step and so that one could not be touched without producing a cry from all. There is as much difference between a substance and such a being, as there is between a man and a community—say a people, an army, a society or committee, which are moral beings, yet they have an imaginary something and depend upon the fiction of our minds. Substantial unity calls for a thoroughly indivisible being, naturally indestructible since its concept involves all that must happen to it. This characteristic cannot be found either in forms or in motions, both of which involve something imaginary as I could demonstrate. It can be found, however, in a soul or a substantial form, such as is the one called the me. These latter are the only thoroughly real beings as the ancients recognized and, above all, Plato, who showed very clearly that matter alone does not suffice for forming a substance. Now, the me mentioned above or whatever corresponds to it, in each individual substance can neither be made nor destroyed by the bringing together or the separation of the parts. Such juxtapositions are wholly apart from the constitution of a substance.

(G II, 77; Ariew & Garber, p. 80; to Arnauld [1686].) If I am asked in particular what I say about the sun, the earthly globe, the moon, trees, and other similar bodies, and even about beasts, I cannot be absolutely certain whether they have souls, or even whether they are substances, or, indeed, whether they are simply machines or aggregates of several substances. But at least I can say that if there are no corporeal substances such as I claim, it follows that bodies would only be true phenomena, like the rainbow. For the continuum is not merely divisible to infinity, but every part of matter is actually divided into other parts as different among themselves as the two aforementioned diamonds. And since we can always go on in this way, we would never reach anything about which we could say, here is truly a being, unless we found besouled machines whose soul or substantial form produced a substantial unity independent of the external union arising from contact. And if there were none, it then follows that, with the exception of man, there is nothing substantial in the visible world.

(G II, 96–97; Ariew & Garber, p. 85; to Arnauld [1687].) If my opinion, that substances require a true unity, is founded only upon a definition which I have made up contrary to the common usage, this would be a mere question of words; but besides the fact that most philosophers have understood this term in nearly the same way, namely, that a distinction should be made between unity itself and unity through accident, between substantial form and accidental form, between an imperfect and a perfect compound, between natural and artificial. I take still higher ground and, leaving the question of terminology, I believe that where there are only beings by aggregation, there are not even real beings, because every being by aggregation pre-supposes beings endowed with true unity, because it obtains its reality only from the reality of those of which it is composed, so that it will have no reality at all if every being of which it is composed is again a being by aggregation; or else we must seek some other foundation for its reality, seeing that by this method it can never be reached, even by searching forever. I grant. . . . that in all corporeal nature there exist only machines (some of which are alive), but I do not grant that there exist only aggregations of substances, and if there do exist aggregations of substances it must be that there are also real substances of which all these aggregations are the product. . . .

It seems also that what constitutes the essence of a being by aggregation consists solely in the mode of the being of its component elements. For example, what constitutes the essence of an army? It is simply the mode of being of the men who compose it. This mode of being presupposes, accordingly a substance of which the essence is not a mode of being of a substance. Every machine therefore presupposes some substance in the parts out of which it is made, and there is no plurality without true unities; in short, I consider as an axiom this identical proposition, which receives two meanings only through a change in accent; namely, that what is not truly *a* being is not truly a *being*. It has always been thought that one and being are reciprocal terms. Being is very different from beings, but the plural presupposes the singular; and where there is no being, there are still less several beings. What can be clearer? I thought, therefore, that I should be permitted to distinguish beings by aggregation from substances, since these beings have their unity only in our minds, and our minds repose only upon the relations or the modes of real substances. If a machine is a substance, a circle of men who are holding hands would be one also, so an army, and in fact, any gathering together of substances. I do not say that there is nothing substantial or nothing but appearance in things which have not a true unity, for I acknowledge that they have as much of reality or substantiality as there is of true unity in that which enters into their composition.

(G II, 100–101; Ariew & Garber, pp. 88–89; to Arnauld [1687].) I agree that there are degrees of accidental unity, that a regulated society has more unity than a confused mob and that an organized body or indeed a machine has more unity than a society. That is, it is more appropriate to conceive of them as a single thing because there is more relation between the component elements. All these unities, however, receive their name only through thoughts and through appearances like colors and other phenomena that are, nevertheless, called real. The fact that a pile of stones or a block of marble can be touched does not prove its substantial reality any more successfully than the visibility of a rainbow proves its reality; and as nothing is so solid that it has not a certain degree of fluidity, perhaps the block of marble itself is only a mass of an infinite number of living bodies like a lake full of fish, although such animals in a body can be ordinarily distinguished by the eye only when the body is partially decayed. . . . Our mind sees or conceives of certain true substances which have certain modes. These modes involve relations to other substances whenever the mind finds occasion to join them in thought and to make one name stand for the whole assembly of these things, which name shall serve as a means of reasoning; but we must not make the mistake of thinking that they are substances or veritably real beings. This position can be held only by those who go no farther than appearances, or else by those who consider as realities all the abstractions of the mind and who conceive number, time, place, motion, form and sensible quality as so many beings by themselves. I, on the contrary, hold that philosophy cannot be restored in a better way nor better reduced to precision than by recognizing substances or complete beings endowed with a true unity in which different states succeed. All the rest are to be considered only as phenomena, abstractions or relations. Nothing will ever be found fitted to constitute a true substance out of several beings by means of aggregation; for example, if the parts which fit together for a common design are more appropriate to constitute a true substance than those which are in contact, all the officials of the India Company in Holland would constitute a real substance better than would a pile of stones. But such a common design—what is it but a resemblance, or rather an arrangement of actions and passions? If this unity by contact should be preferred as the most reasonable hypothesis, other difficulties would be found: the parts of solid bodies are perhaps united only by the pressure of surrounding bodies and by their own pressure, and in their substance they may have no more unity than a pile of sand.

(G II, 118; to Arnauld [1687].) There are not several beings where there is not even one which may be truly a being, and I hold that every multitude presupposes a unit.

(G II, 135; to Arnauld [1690].) Body is an aggregate of substances, and is not a substance properly speaking. It is consequently necessary that everywhere in body there should be indivisible substances, ingenerable and incorruptible, having something corresponding to souls.

(G II, 193; to de Volder [1699].) Since every extended body, as it is really found in the world, is in fact like an army of creatures, or a herd, or a place of confluence, like a cheese filled with worms, a connection between the parts of a body is no more necessary than is a connection between the parts of an army. And just as some soldiers can be replaced by others in an army, so some parts can be replaced by others in every extended body. Thus no part has a necessary connection with any other part, even though it is true of matter in general that when any part is removed, it must necessarily be replaced by some other part, just as it is necessary, when soldiers are confined in a small enclosure or one which will not hold many, for another to take the place of anyone who goes out. I have already made enough suggestions about this in my previous letter, and I do not see any point that can be made about any body whatsoever, apart from the soul, which would not be equally valid for an army or a machine. Therefore I understand a true unit (and not merely a sensible one), or a *monad*, to exist only where there is something which does not contain many substances.

(G II, 267; to de Volder [1704].) A thing which can be divided into several (already actually existing) is an aggregate of several, and . . . is not one except mentally, and has no reality but what is borrowed from its constituents. Hence I inferred that there must be in things indivisible unities, because otherwise there will be in things no true unity, and no reality not borrowed. Which is absurd. For where there is not true unity, there is not true multiplicity. And where there is no reality not borrowed, there will never be any reality, since this must in the end belong to some subject. . . . But you [de Volder] . . . hold that the right conclusion from this is that in the mass of bodies no indivisible unities can be assigned. I, however, think that the contrary is to be concluded, namely that we must recur, in bodily mass, or in constituting corporeal things, to indivisible unities as prime constituents. Unless indeed you hold the right conclusion to be, that bodily masses are not themselves indivisible unities, which I say, but this is not the question. For bodies are always divisible, and even actually subdivided, but not so their constituents. . . .

(G IV, 491–92; "Objections to Foucher" [1695].) In actual substantial things the whole is a sum or aggregate of simple substances or rather of a multitude of real units (*unités*). . . . But in realities, in which there are only divisions actually made, the whole is merely a sum or aggregate, as in the case of a flock of sheep. It is true that the number of simple substances which enter into a mass, however small it be, is infinite, since in addition to the soul which constitutes the real unit of the animal, the body of the sheep (for instance) is actually subdivided, that is to say it is also an aggregate of invisible animals or plants (which are likewise compound) besides that which constitutes also their real unity; and although this proceeds *ad infinitum*, it is manifest that ultimately all is reducible to these unities, the remainder or the aggregates being merely well-founded phenomena.

(Loemker, p. 278; "Elements of Natural Science" [ca. 1684].) Without soul or form of some kind, body would have no being, because no part of it can be designated which does not in turn consist of more parts. Thus nothing could be designated in a body which could be called "this thing," or a unity.

COMMENTARY

Although there is only one type of genuine substance for Leibniz, namely monads, there are infinitely many instances of this type. In fact, every monad is, in a way, its own species; the only exemplar of its complete individual concept. Leibniz's commitment to a plurality—indeed an infinite plurality—of individual substances contradistinguishes him from one-substance ("monistic") philosophers such as Parmenides or Spinoza.

Like the Greek atomists, Leibniz thinks of nature as having two levels, a basic metaphysical micro-level of individual substances (monads), and a derivative macro-level of compounds—organized collectivities of substance—that are the very fabric of nature as we experience it. But substances are fundamental; whatever else there is over and above individual substances and their features and operations is somehow a product that results from their compounding and combination. Natural process came about through changes among the basic units (the atoms, the monads)—through their mutual realignments, as it were. Leibniz's theory of monads is, in effect, an atomism of sorts.

Leibniz holds that only a unit can unify—only what has unity can engender unity. The unity of any large-scale unit that underlies a plurality of substances must therefore itself be encapsulated in a single substance that serves as the unifier of that whole by suitably representing all of its parts through linkages of qualitative kinship—somewhat as a monarch unifies his people by a system of allegiances. It is because he regards such representative unification as the only possible road to unity that Leibniz stands committed to the view that if there were no simple substances to do this unifying, then there would be no way to unify pluralities into composite wholes. The idea of this section is accordingly *not* just the trivial point that composites require units because composites are pluralities, but rather the more interesting idea that composites which are themselves unified require true units to serve as unifiers.

KEY WORDS:

simple substance/*substance simple*
composite/*composé*
aggregate/*aggregatum* (Lat.)

SECTION 3

3. However, where there are no parts at all, no extension or figure or divisibility is possible. And these monads are the true atoms of nature, and, in a word, the elements of things.

3. Or là, où il n'y a point de parties, il n'y a ni étendue, ni figure, ni divisibilité possible. Et ces Monades sont les véritables Atomes de la Nature et en un mot les Elemens des choses.

(PNG, sec. 2.) They <i.e., the monads> cannot have shapes, for then they would have parts. In consequence, one monad by itself and at a single moment cannot be distinguished from another except by its internal qualities and actions and these can only be its *perceptions*, that is to say, the representations of the compound, or of that which is without, in the simple—and its appetitions—that is to say, its tendencies from one perception to another—which are the principles of change.

(NE, p. 317.) It seems that substantial forms have recently acquired a bad name in certain quarters in which people are ashamed to speak of them. However, this is perhaps more a matter of fashion than of reason. When particular phenomena were to be explained, the Scholastics inappropriately used this general notion, but such misuse does not destroy the thing itself. The human soul somewhat shakes the confidence of some of our modern thinkers. Some of them acknowledge that it is the substantial form of the man, but add that it is the only substantial form in the known part of nature. M. Descartes speaks of it in this way; and he reproved M. Regius for challenging the soul's quality of being a substantial form and for denying that man is *unum per se*, a being endowed with a genuine unity. Some believe that this distinguished man did so out of prudence. I rather doubt that, since I think that he was right about it. But the privilege should not be restricted to man alone, as though the rest of nature were put together higgledy-piggledy. There is reason to think that there is an infinity of souls, or rather, more generally, of primary entelechies, possessing something analogous to perception and appetite, and that all of them are and forever remain substantial forms of bodies.

(NS, sec. 3.) At first, after freeing myself from bondage to Aristotle, I accepted the void and the atoms, for it is these that best satisfy the imagination. But in turning back to them after much thought, I perceived that it is impossible to find *the principles of a true unity* in matter alone or in what is merely passive, since everything in it is but a collection or aggregation of parts to infinity. Now a multitude can derive its reality only from the *true unities*, which have some other origin and are entirely different from points, for it is certain that the continuum cannot be compounded of points. To find these *real unities*, therefore, I was forced to have recourse to a formal atom, since a material being cannot be at the same time material and perfectly indivisible, or endowed with true unity. It was thus necessary to restore and as it were, to rehabilitate the *substantial forms* which are in such disrepute today, but in a way which makes them intelligible and separates their proper use from their previous abuse. I found then that their nature consists of force and that there follows from this something analogous to sense and appetite, so that we must think of them in terms similar to the concept which we have of *souls*. But just as the soul ought not to be used to explain the details of the economy of the animal's body, so I concluded that one ought not to use these forms to explain the particular problems of nature, though they are necessary to establish its true general principles. Aristotle calls them *first entelechies*. I call them, more intelligibly perhaps, *primitive forces*.

(NS, sec. 11.) But *material atoms* are contrary to reason, besides being still further composed of parts, since an invincible attachment of one part to another (if we could reasonably conceive or assume this) would not at all destroy the diversity of these parts. It is only *atoms of substance*, that is to say, real unities that are absolutely destitute of parts, which are the sources of action and the absolute first principles out of which things are compounded, and as it were, the ultimate elements in the analysis of substance. One could call them *metaphysical points*. They have something vital, and a kind of *perception*, and *mathematical points* are the *points of view* from which they express the universe. But when a corporeal substance is contracted, all its organs together make only one *physical point* with respect to us. Physical points are thus indivisible in appearance only, while mathematical points are exact but are nothing but modalities.

(DM, sec. 8.) The nature of an individual substance or of a complete being is such as to afford a conception so complete that the concept shall be sufficient for the understanding of it and for the deduction of all the predicates of which the substance is or may become the subject. Thus the quality of king, which belonged to Alexander the Great, an abstraction from the subject, is not sufficiently determined to constitute an individual, and does not contain the other qualities of the same subject, nor everything which the idea of this prince includes. God, however, seeing the individual concept, or haecceity, of Alexander, sees there at the same time the basis and the reason of all the predicates which can be truly uttered regarding him; for instance that he will conquer Darius and Porus, even to the point of knowing *a priori* (and not by experience) whether he died a natural death or by poison—facts which we can learn only through history. When we carefully consider the connection of things we see also the possibility of saying that there were always in the soul of Alexander marks of all that had happened to him and evidences of all that would happen to him and traces even of everything which occurs in the universe, although God alone could recognize them all.

(DM, sec. 9.) There follow from these considerations several noticeable paradoxes; among others that it is not true that two substances may be exactly alike and differ only numerically, *solo numero*, and that what St. Thomas says on this point regarding angels and intelligences (*quod ibi omne individuum sit species infima*) is true of all substances.

(DM, sec. 12.) The whole nature of bodies is not exhausted in their extension, that is to say, in their size, figure and motion, but we must recognize something which corresponds to soul, something which is commonly called substantial form, although these forms effect no change in the phenomena, any more than do the souls of beasts, that is if they have souls. It is even possible to demonstrate that the ideas of size, figure and motion are not so distinctive as is imagined, and that they stand for something imaginary relative to our perceptions as do, although to a greater extent, the ideas of color, heat, and the other similar qualities in regard to which we may doubt whether they are actually to be found in the nature of things outside of us. This is why these latter qualities are unable to constitute "substance" and if there is no other principle of identity in bodies than that which has just be referred to a body would not subsist more than for a moment.

(G III, 606; Loemker, p. 657; to Remond [1714].) When I looked for the ultimate reasons for mechanisms, and even for the laws of motion, I was greatly surprised to see that they could not be found in mathematics but that I should have to return to metaphysics. This led me back to entelechies, and from the material to the formal, and at last brought me to understand, after many corrections and forward steps in my thinking, that monads or simple substances are the only true substances and that material things are only phenomena, though well founded and well connected.

(Couturat, *Opuscules*, p. 521; Loemker, pp. 269–70; Ariew & Garber, p. 33; "First Truths" [ca. 1685].) *There is no corporeal substance in which there is nothing but extension, or magnitude, figure, and their variations.* For otherwise there could exist two corporeal substances perfectly similar to each other, which is absurd. Hence it follows that there is something in corporeal substances analogous to the soul, which is commonly called form. *There is no vacuum.* For the different parts of empty space would be perfectly similar and congruent with each other and could not by themselves be distinguished. So they would differ in number alone, which is absurd. Time too may be proved not to be a thing, in the same way as space. *There are no atoms;* indeed, there is no body so small that it is not actually subdivided. By this very fact, since it is affected by all other things in the entire world and receives some effect from all, which must cause a change in the body, it has even preserved all past impressions and anticipates the future ones. If anyone says that this effect is contained in the motions impressed on the atom, which receives the effect *in toto* without any division in it, it can be replied that not only must an effect in the atom result from all the impressions of the universe but conversely, the entire state of the universe must be gathered from the atom. Thus the cause can be inferred from the effect. But from the figure and motion of the atom alone, we cannot by regression infer what impressions have produced the given effect on it, since the same motion can be caused by different impressions, not to mention the fact that we cannot explain why bodies of a definite smallness should not be further divisible. . . . Extension, motion, and bodies themselves, insofar as they consist in extension and motion alone, are not substances but true phenomena, like rainbows and parhelia. For figures do not exist in reality and if only their extension is considered, bodies are not one substance but many.

COMMENTARY

Even as geometric figures (lines, triangles, spheres) somehow contain points without being composed of them by mere aggregation through the successive addition of more individual units, so the things of this world are, as Leibniz sees it, made up of monadic punctiform substances. (By "no parts," Leibniz means "no *spatial* parts"; monads can certainly have *qualitative* components, as pieces of music do.)

Leibniz is thus a neo-atomist. But his monads, unlike the classical atoms, have no size at all, and hence lack the spatial features (extension and figure) possessed by the classical atoms. (They are "*true* atoms" because they cannot be spatially subdivided—neither physically nor even in thought. Yet even as the atoms of the ancient atomists were only distinguishable by intrinsic properties (namely their extension and figure), so Leibniz's monads are distinguishable from one another only by intrinsic features, namely their modes of action. Since monads are physically without parts and thus point-like, there is no other basis for effecting their differentiation apart from their *modus operandi*.

KEY WORDS:

atoms of nature/*atomes de la nature*
elements/*éléments*

extension/*l'étendue*
partless/*point de parties*

SECTION 4

4. There is also no dissolution to fear <in the monads>, and there is no way conceivable [by us] in which a simple substance can perish [or change] naturally. (See *Theodicy*, sec. 89.)

*4. Il n'y a aussi point de dissolution à craindre, et il n'y a aucune manière [qui nous soit] concevable, par laquelle une substance simple puisse perir [ni changer] naturellement. (*Théodicée, *sec. 89.)*

(*Theodicy*, sec. 89.) <Accidents> are only modifications of the substance, and their origin may be explained by eduction, that is, by variation of limitations, in the same way as the origin of shapes. But it is quite another matter when we are concerned with the origin of a substance as such, whose beginning and destruction are equally difficult to explain.

(*Theodicy*, sec. 396.) As for the souls or substantial forms, M. Bayle is right in adding: "that there is nothing more inconvenient for those who admit substantial forms than the objection which is made that they could not be produced save by an actual creation. . . ." But there is nothing more convenient for me and for my system than this same objection. For I maintain that all the Souls, Entelechies or primitive forces, substantial forms, simple substances, or Monads, whatever name one may apply to them, can neither spring up naturally nor perish. And the qualities or derivative forces, or what are called accidental forms, I take to be modifications of the primitive Entelechy, even as shapes are modifications of matter. That is why these modifications are perpetually changing, while the simple substance remains.

(PNG, sec. 2.) Monads, having no parts, can neither be formed nor unmade. They can neither begin nor end naturally.

(DM, sec. 9.) A substance will be able to commence only through creation and perish only through annihilation; a substance cannot be divided into two nor can one be made out of two, and thus the number of substances neither augments nor diminishes through natural means, although they are frequently transformed.

(DM, sec. 34.) Supposing that the bodies which constitute a *unum per se*, as human bodies, are substances, and have substantial forms, and supposing that animals have souls, we are obliged to grant that these souls and these substantial forms cannot entirely perish, any more than can the atoms or the ultimate elements of matter, according to the position of other philosophers; for no substance perishes, although it may become very different. . . . Also the immortality which is required in morals and in religion does not consist merely in this perpetual existence, which pertains to all substances, for if in addition there were no remembrance of what one had been, immortality would not be at all desirable. Suppose that some individual could suddenly become King of China on condition, however, of forgetting what he had been, as though being born again, would it not amount to the same practically, or as far as the effects could be perceived, as if the individual were annihilated, and a king of China were the same instant created in his place? The individual would have no reason to desire this.

(G II, 76; to Arnauld [1686].) The unity of a substance demands a complete, indivisible, and naturally indestructible being, since its notion involves all that is ever to happen to it.

(Loemker, p. 270; Ariew & Garber, p. 34; "First Truths" [ca. 1685].) *Corporeal substance can neither come into being nor perish except through creation or annihilation.* For, once it does last, it will last always, for there is no reason for a change. Nor does the dissolution of a body have anything in common with its destruction. *Therefore ensouled beings neither begin nor perish; they are only transformed.*

COMMENTARY

Leibniz thinks of natural death as a matter of dissolution or decomposition, which must be a disassembling of some sort. Since the monads have no parts, they are not subject to such a physical process. By a "natural process" Leibniz means a physical process of the sort that can in principle be examined and explained through the instrumentalities of natural science. (Compare sec. 17.) For Leibniz, the operation of substances must be understood *metaphysically* with reference to God, rather than *naturally* with reference to nature's processes alone, seeing that it is in the metaphysical, monadic order that the explanation of nature's processes themselves must be sought.

KEY WORDS:
simple substance/*substance simple*
dissolution/*dissolution*
to perish naturally/*périr naturellement*

SECTION 5

5. For the same reason, there is no way in which a simple substance could begin naturally, since it cannot be formed by composition.

5. Par la même raison il n'y en a aucune <manière> par laquelle une substance simple puisse commencer naturellement, puisqu'elle ne sçauroit être formée par composition.

(PNG, sec. 2.) *Monads,* having no parts, can neither be formed nor unmade. They can neither begin nor end naturally.

(NS, sec. 5.) As all simple substances which have a genuine unity can have a beginning and an end only by miracle, it follows that they can come into being only by creation and come to an end only by annihilation. Thus I was obliged to recognize that (with the exception of the souls which God still intends specially to create) the constitutive forms of substances must have been created with the world and subsist always.

COMMENTARY

For Leibniz, all *natural* processes are a matter of the reassembly or transformation of preexisting items. To come into being naturally is to develop from a preexisting something else. But there is no preexisting something else that can turn into a monad. And things which have no parts—that is, individual substances—cannot come into being by a recombination of preexisting parts. Simple substances can only arise through actual creation—origination *ex nihilo*—which is something inherently supra- or extra-natural. Since monads cannot come about through division and recombination, they cannot be created "naturally"—and they cannot be destroyed naturally through physical dissolution either. Their origination (or destruction) is possible only by a supra-natural creation from nothing or vanishing into nothingness.

This situation that substances can neither be created nor destroyed accords perfectly with the world-picture of classical physics that was being forged in Leibniz's day, in which no place can be found for the origination or annihilation of matter.

KEY WORDS:

simple substance/*substance simple*
to begin naturally/*commencer naturellement*
composition/*composition*

SECTION 6

6. So one can say that monads can neither come into being nor end save all at once; that is, they can begin only by creation and end only by annihilation. By contrast, that which is composite begins and ends part by part.

6. Ainsi on peut dire que les Monades ne sçauroient commencer, ni finir, que tout d'un coup, c'est à dire, elles ne sçauroient commencer que par creation et finir que par annihilation; au lieu que ce qui est composé, commence ou finit par parties.

(PNG, sec. 2.) Monads, having no parts, can neither be formed nor unmade. They can neither begin nor end naturally, and therefore they last as long as the universe, which will change but will not be destroyed.

(NS, sec. 4.) I saw that these forms and these souls must be indivisible, just as is our mind; in fact, I remembered that this was the opinion of St. Thomas with regard to the souls of beasts. But this truth revived the great difficulties about the origin and duration of souls and forms. For since every substance which has a true unity can begin and end only by a miracle, it follows that souls can begin only by creation and end only by annihilation.

COMMENTARY

Leibniz thinks of his simple substances as existing continually in the world throughout the whole expanse of time. They come into being all at once, with the creation of the universe as a whole, and can cease to exist only all at once with the ending of physical existence as such. All the monads are thus contemporaries with one another and with the entire universe. Like the atoms of the ancients, their history is co-extensive with that of the whole world; they are co-eternal with the entirety of nature. Birth and death play no part in their career.

KEY WORDS:

monad/*monade*
creation/*création*
annihilation/*annihilation*
composite/*composé*

SECTION 7

7. There is, furthermore, no way to explain how a monad could be altered or changed in its inner make-up by some other created being. For one can transpose nothing in it, nor conceive in it any internal motion that could be excited, directed, increased, or diminished within it, as can happen in composites, where there is change among the parts. Monads just have no windows through which something can enter into or depart from them. Accidents cannot be detached, nor wander about outside of substances, as the sensible species <*species sensibiles*> of the Scholastics formerly did. And so, neither substance nor accident can enter a monad from without.

7. *Il n'y a pas moyen aussi d'expliquer, comment une Monade puisse être altérée ou changée dans son intérieur par quelque autre creature; puisqu'on n'y sçauroit rien transposer, ni concevoir en elle aucun mouvement interne qui puisse être excité, dirigé, augmenté ou diminué là dedans; comme cela se peut dans les composés, où il y a du changement entre les parties. Les Monades n'ont point de fenêtres, par lesquelles quelque chose y puisse entrer ou sortir. Les accidens ne sçauroient se détacher, ni se promener hors des substances, comme faisoient autrefois les especes sensibles des scholastiques. Ainsi, ni substance, ni accident peut entrer de dehors dans une Monade.*

(NE, p. 110.) Does the soul have windows? Is it similar to writing-tablets, or like wax? Clearly, those who take this view of the soul are treating it as fundamentally corporeal. Someone will confront me with this accepted philosophical axiom, that there is nothing in the soul which does not come from the senses. But an exception must be made of the soul itself and its states. "Nothing is in the intellect that has not been in a sense organ, except for one thing, the intellect itself" (*Nihil est in intellectu quod non fuerit in sensu, excipe: nisi ipse intellectus*).

(NS, sec. 14.) Being constrained, then, to admit that it is impossible for the soul or any other true substance to receive something from without, except by the divine omnipotence, I was led insensibly to an opinion which surprised me, but which seems inevitable, and which has in fact very great advantages and very significant beauties. This is that we must say that God has originally created the soul, and every other real unity, in such a way that everything in it must arise from its own nature by a perfect *spontaneity* with regard to itself, yet by a perfect *conformity* to things without.

(DM, sec. 13.) The concept of an individual substance includes once for all everything which can ever happen to it and in considering this concept one will be able to see everything which can truly be said concerning that individual, just as we are able to see in the nature of a circle all the properties which can be derived from it. . . . Let us give an example. Since Julius Caesar will become perpetual Dictator and master of the Republic and will overthrow the liberty of Rome, this action is contained in his concept. . . .

(G II, 76; to Arnauld [1686].) The unity of a substance demands a completely, indivisible and naturally indestructible being, since its notion embraces all that is ever to happen to it.

COMMENTARY

Species (Fr. *espèce*) is not a *kind* but the characteristic *property* or qualitative feature that distinguishes one kind of thing from another. The "sensible species" of the Scholastic philosophers are images or immaterial representations of material qualities that could leave their possessors behind to enter into the sensorium in acts of observation. Leibniz rejects any such transactional theory of perception. Since monads are not material things, nothing can make a physical impact upon them. They are altogether *impervious*; they admit of no *causal* impact through the agency of others.

Moreover any idea of an ideational, nonphysical external impact or impetus would also be unintelligible. Nothing can affect monads from without: they are "windowless." Their inner nature (their defining *notion* or *complete individual concept*) fixes everything about them. Their changes are the result of inner programming and not of any external causal impetus. (As sec. 11 will insist, all monadic changes are generated internally, "from within," through the chronological exfoliation of the exigencies of their own inner natures.) Any theory that would put substances at the mercy of the causal operation of others would, as Leibniz sees it, be at odds with the self-sufficiency of substances.

However, while monads cannot act on one another by way of causality, their inner states can be aligned by way of coordination or synchronization which effects a mutual adjustment that is not causal but *ideal*. (See secs. 51, 81.) Monads are *causally* independent, but not *totally* independent because of such a reciprocal coordination through alignment rather than influence.

Note that Leibniz here reasons: "There is no way to explain how X can be so; therefore X cannot actually be so." It is this commitment to the idea that "the real must be rational" (to the "principle of sufficient reason") that marks Leibniz as a *"rationalist"* philosopher.

KEY WORDS:

change/*changement*
composite/*composé*
windowless/*point de fenêtres*
substance/*substance*
internal constitution/*intérieur*
accident (or attribute)/*accident*
mathematical points/*points mathématiques*
monad/*monade*

SECTION 8

8. However, monads must have some qualities [and some changes], otherwise they would not even be beings [and if simple substances were nonentities, compounds would also be reduced to nothing]. [Monads are not mathematical points, for such points are only extremities, and a line cannot be made up of points.] And if simple substances did not differ by their qualities at all, there would be no way at all of perceiving any change in things, since that which is present in the composite can only come from its simple constituents. And then monads, being without qualities, would be indistinguishable from one another, since they do not differ quantitatively at all. In consequence, a plenum being supposed, each place would always receive in any motion only the equivalent of what it already had, and one state of things would be indistinguishable from another. (See *Theodicy*, Preface.)

8. *Cependant il faut que les Monades ayent quelques qualités [et quelques changemens], autrement ce ne seroient pas même des Etres [et si les substances simples étoient des riens, les composés aussi seroient reduits à rien]. [Les monades ne sont pas des points mathematiques. Car ces points ne sont que des extremités et la ligne ne sçauroit être composée de points.] Et si les substances simples ne differoient point par leurs qualités, il n'y auroit pas moyen de s'appercevoir d'aucun changement dans les choses; puisque ce qui est dans le composé ne peut venir que des ingrediens simples; et les Monades étant sans qualités, seroient indistinguables l'une de l'autre, puisqu'aussi bien elles ne diffèrent point en quantité: et par consequent, le plein étant supposé, chaque lieu ne recevroit toûjours dans le mouvement, que l'Equivalent de ce qu'il avoit eu, et un état des choses seroit indistinguable* de l'autre. (Théodicée, Préface,***2b.)*
<*Leibniz initially wrote *indiscernable*.>

(*Theodicy*, Preface [G VI, 45].) One may say also in a metaphysical sense that the soul acts upon the body and the body upon the soul. Moreover, it is true that the soul is the Entelechy or the active principle, whereas the corporeal alone or the mere material contains only the passive. Consequently the principle of action is in the soul . . . and . . . I have even demonstrated that, if bodies contained only the passive, their different conditions would be indistinguishable.

(PNG, Sec. 2.) It follows that one monad by itself and at a single moment cannot be distinguished from another except by its internal qualities and actions, and these can only be its perce'ptions—that is to say, the representations of the compound, or of that which is without, in the simple—and its appetitions—that is to say, its tendencies from one perception to another—which are the principles of change. For the simplicity of a substance does not prevent the plurality of modifications which must necessarily be found together in the same simple substance; and these modifications must consist of the variety of relations of correspondence which the substance has with things outside. In the same way there may be found, in one center or point, though it is perfectly simple, an infinity of angles formed by the lines which meet in it.

(G II, 252; Loemker, p. 531; Ariew & Garber, p. 177; to de Volder [1703].) Since only simples are truly things, what remain are only entities by aggregation; to that extent they are phenomena, and, as Democritus put it, exist by convention and not by nature. So it is obvious that unless there were change in simple things, there would be no change in things at all. Indeed, not even change can come from without, since, on the contrary, an internal tendency to change is essential to finite substance, and change could not arise naturally in monads in any other way. But in phenomena or aggregates, all new change derives from the collision of bodies in accordance with laws. . . .

(G II, 295; to des Bosses [1706].) If we were to admit, as the Cartesians desire, the *plenum* and the uniformity of matter, adding to these motion alone, it would follow that nothing would ever take place among things but a substitution of equivalents, as if the whole universe were reduced to the motion of a perfectly uniform wheel about its axis or, again, to the revolutions of concentric circles each made of exactly the same materials. The result of this would be that it would not be possible, even for an angel, to distinguish the state of things at one moment from their state at another. For there could be no variety in the phenomena. Accordingly, in addition to figure, size, and motion, we must allow certain Forms, whence there arises a distinction among the phenomena of matter; and I do not see whence these Forms are to be taken, if they are to be intelligible, unless it be from Entelechies.

COMMENTARY

Despite their *quantitative* (arithmetico-geometric) simplicity, monads are *qualitatively* complex; each has a plurality of properties (qualities). Substances require qualities to endow them with a character that provides for the distinction of each from the rest. These qualities represent the inner reflections of outer conditions unfolding over time. The force or activity of *action*—of qualitative change—is of the very essence of monads.

For Leibniz, the world's dynamical character as theater of operation for the unfolding of processes, is its most important ontological feature, and a metaphysical position which—like the theories of his predecessors Descartes and Spinoza—does not provide an adequate way of coming to terms with change is thereby foredoomed to failure. As Leibniz sees it, the ever-changing quality-structure of each monad determines its particular position in the overall scheme of things. For each monad must have its individually characteristic quality-structure because if two are exactly alike in point of their qualities they could not be differential at all; they would simply be one and the same. (This is Leibniz's "principle of the identity of indiscernibles," which is also treated in sec. 9.)

Note also that we are now informed that the universe as a whole is an integrally connected system of coordinated monads, a plenum. In fact, the qualitative complexity of monads lies in the circumstance that each of them provides a representation of the entire universe (sec. 62)—albeit in different ways (from different "points of view," and with variable degrees of clarity).

Leibniz's supposition of a plenum does not mean that he thinks of space as an empty preexisting Newtonian container that is filled up with monads. In fact, he rejects that view altogether, and considers space as being derivative from the organization of the punctiform monads in their qualitative interrelations. The world's being a plenum simply means its being and that no point of view is unoccupied by an existing substance. (If the world's substances were annihilated, then its "space" would vanish as well; it is "merely phenomenal.")

Originally Leibniz wrote after the first sentence "and if simple substances were nonentities, compounds would also be reduced to nothing." In the end, however, he set this question-begging ontological formulation aside in favor of the subtler epistemic approach of the second sentence. (In any case, the idea had already been covered in sec. 2.)

KEY WORDS:

monad/*monade*
simple substances/*substances simples*
composites/*composés*
quality/*qualité*
change/*changement*
indistinguishable/*indistinguable*
motion/*mouvement*
plenum/*le plein*

SECTION 9

9. It is even necessary that every monad be different from every other. For there are never in nature two beings that are perfectly alike and in which it would not be possible to find a difference that is internal or founded on an intrinsic denomination.

9. Il faut même que chaque Monade soit differente de chaque autre. Car il n'y a jamais dans la nature deux Etres, qui soient parfaitement l'un comme l'autre, et où il ne soit possible de trouver une difference interne, ou fondée sur une denomination intrinseque.

(PNG, sec. 2.) For the simplicity of a substance does not prevent the plurality of modifications which must necessarily be found together in the same simple substance; and these modifications must consist of the variety of relations of correspondence which the substance has with things outside. In the same way there may be found, in one *center* or point, though it is perfectly simple, an infinity of angles formed by the lines which meet in it.

(NE, p. 57.) I have also pointed out that in consequence of imperceptible variations no two individual things could be perfectly alike, and that they must always differ more than numerically. This puts an end to the blank tablets of the soul, a soul without thought, a substance without action, empty space, atoms, and even to portions of matter which are not actually divided, and also to absolute rest, completely uniform parts of time or place or matter, perfect spheres of the second element which take their origin from perfect cubes, and hundreds of other fictions which have arisen from the incompleteness of philosophers' notions. They are something which the nature of things does not allow of. They escape challenge because of our ignorance and our neglect of the insensible; but nothing could make them acceptable, short of their being confined to abstractions of the mind, with a formal declaration that the mind is not denying what it sets aside as irrelevant to some present concern. On the other hand if we meant literally that things of which we are unaware exist neither in the soul nor in the body, then we would fail in philosophy as in politics, because we would be neglecting *to mikron*, imperceptible changes. Whereas abstraction is not an error as long as one knows that what one is pretending not to notice, is *there*. This is what mathematicians are doing when they ask us to consider perfect lines and uniform motions and other regular effects, although matter (i.e. the jumble of effects of the surrounding infinity) always provides some exception. This is done so as to separate one circumstance from another and, as far as we can, to trace effects back to their causes and to foresee some of their results; the more care we take not to overlook any circumstance that we can control, the more closely practice corresponds to theory. But only the supreme Reason, which overlooks nothing, can distinctly grasp the entire infinite and see all the causes and all the results. All we can do with infinities is to know them confusedly and at least to know distinctly that they are there. Otherwise we shall not only judge quite wrongly as to the beauty and grandeur of the universe, but will be unable to have a sound natural science which explains the nature of things in general.

(NE, p. 110.) And I think I can demonstrate that every substantial thing, be it soul or body, has a unique relationship to each other thing; and that each must always differ from every other in respect of *intrinsic denominations*. Not to mention the fact that those who hold forth about the "blank page" cannot say what is left of it once the ideas have been taken away—like the Scholastics who leave nothing in their prime matter. It may be said that this "blank page" of the philosophers means that all the soul possesses, naturally and inherently, are bare faculties. But inactive faculties—in short, the pure powers of the Schoolmen—are also mere fictions, unknown to nature and obtainable only by abstraction. For where will one ever find in the world a faculty consisting in sheer power without performing any act? There is always a particular disposition to action, and towards one action rather than another.

(NE, p. 230.) In addition to the difference of time or of place there must always be an internal *principle of distinction*: although there can be many things of the same kind, it is still the case that none of them are ever exactly alike. Thus, although time and place (i.e. the relations to what lies outside) do distinguish for us things which we could not easily tell apart by reference to themselves alone, things are nevertheless distinguishable in themselves, Thus, although diversity in things is accompanied by diversity of time or place, time and place do not constitute the core of identity and diversity by impressing different states upon the thing.

(NE, p. 231.) If there were atoms, i.e. perfectly hard and perfectly unalterable bodies which were incapable of internal change and could differ from one another only in size and in shape, it is obvious that since they could have the same size and shape they would then be indistinguishable in themselves and discernible only by means of external denominations with no internal foundation; which is contrary to the greatest principles of reason. In fact, however, every body is changeable and indeed is actually changing all the time, so that it differs in itself from every other. I remember a great princess <the electress Sophia>, of lofty intelligence, saying one day while walking in her garden that she did not believe there were two leaves perfectly alike. A clever gentleman who was walking with her believed that it would be easy to find some, but search as he might he became convinced by his own eyes that a difference could always be found.

(DM, sec. 8.) The nature of an individual substance or of a complete being is such as to afford a conception so complete that the concept shall be sufficient for the understanding of it and for the deduction of all the predicates of which the substance is or may become the subject. Thus the quality of king, which belonged to Alexander the Great, an abstraction from the subject, is not sufficiently determined to constitute an individual, and does not contain the other qualities of the same subject, nor everything which the idea of this prince includes. God, however, seeing the individual concept, or haecceity, of Alexander, sees there at the same time the basis and the reason of all the predicates which can be truly uttered regarding him; for instance that he will conquer Darius and Porus, even to the point of knowing *a priori* (and not by experience) whether he died a natural death or by poison—facts which we can learn only through history. When we carefully consider the connection of things we see also the possibility of saying that there were always in the soul of Alexander marks of all that had happened to him and evidences of all that would happen to him and traces even of everything which occurs in the universe, although God alone could recognize them all.

(DM, sec. 9.) There follow from these considerations several noticeable paradoxes; among others that it is not true that two substances may be exactly alike and differ only numerically, *solo numero*, and that what St. Thomas says on this point regarding angels and intelligences (*quod ibi omne individuum sit species infima*) is true of all substances, provided that the specific difference is understood as Geometers understand it in the case of figures.

(G VII, 371–72; to Clarke IV.1–2 [1716].) In things absolutely indifferent there is no (foundation for) choice, and consequently no election or will, since choice must be founded on some reason or principle. A mere will without any motive is a fiction, not only contrary to God's perfection but also chimerical and contradictory, inconsistent with the nature of the will.

(G VII, 393; to Clarke V.21 [1716].) It must be confessed that though this great principle ⟨of sufficient reason⟩ has been acknowledged, yet it has not been sufficiently made use of. Which is in great measure the reason why the *prima philosophia* has not been hitherto so fruitful and demonstrative as it should have been. I infer from that principle, among other consequences, that there are not in nature two real, absolute beings, indiscernible from each other, because, if there were, God and nature would act without reason in ordering the one otherwise than the other; and that therefore God does not produce two pieces of matter perfectly equal and alike. The author answers this conclusion without confuting the reason of it, and he answers with a very weak objection. "That argument," says he, "if it was good, would prove that it would be impossible for God to create any matter at all. For the perfectly solid parts of matter, if we take them of equal figure and dimensions (which is always possible in supposition), would be exactly alike." But 'tis a manifest *petitio principii* to suppose that perfect likeness, which, according to me, cannot be admitted. This supposition of two indiscernibles, such as two pieces of matter perfectly alike, seems indeed to be possible in abstract terms, but it is not consistent with the order of things, nor with the divine wisdom by which nothing is admitted without reason. The vulgar fancy such things because they content themselves with incomplete notions. And this is one of the faults of the atomists.

(G II, 250; Loemker, p. 529; Ariew & Garber, p. 175; to de Volder [1703].) It cannot happen in nature that two bodies are at once perfectly similar and equal. Also, things which differ in position must express their position, that is, their surroundings, and are hence not to be distinguished merely by their location or by a solely extrinsic denomination, as such things are commonly understood. Hence there can be no bodies in nature as they are commonly conceived, like the atoms of the Democriteans and the perfect globules of the Cartesians, and these are nothing but the incomplete cogitations of philosophers who have not thoroughly investigated the natures of things. . . . I have used another unassailable argument besides to demonstrate that, given a plenum, it is impossible for matter as it is commonly thought of as formed solely out of the modifications of extension, or if you prefer, out of passive mass, to suffice for filling the universe, but that it is obviously necessary to assume something else in matter from which we may get a principle of change and one by which to distinguish among phenomena; and hence we need some alteration and therefore some heterogeneity, in matter in addition to increase, diminution, and motion. But I do not admit any generation or corruption in substance itself.

(Couturat, *Opuscules*, pp. 519–20; Loemker, p. 268; Ariew & Garber, p. 32, "First Truths" [ca. 1685].) It follows also that *there cannot be two individual things in nature which differ only numerically*. For surely it must be possible to give a reason why they are different, and this must be sought in some differences within themselves. Thus the observation of Thomas Aquinas about separate intelligences, which he declared never differ in number alone, must be applied to other things also. Never are two eggs, two leaves, or two blades of grass in a garden to be found exactly similar to each other. So perfect similarity occurs only in incomplete and abstract concepts, where matters are conceived, not in their totality but according to a certain single viewpoint, as when we consider only figures and neglect the figured matter. So geometry is right in studying similar triangles, even though two perfectly similar material triangles are never found. And although gold or some other metal, or salt, and many liquids, may be taken for homogeneous bodies, this can be admitted only as concerns the senses and not as if it were true in an exact sense.

COMMENTARY

A thing's "intrinsic denominations" or inner determinations are those of its features that inhere in its descriptive make-up, encompassing all the features that indicate its qualitative properties as contrasted with its relationships to other things. (The term is taken from the *Port Royal Logic* (pt. I, chap. 2) of 1662 by Leibniz's correspondent Antoine Arnauld, one of the major theorists of the Cartesian school.)

From his earliest years, Leibniz was intrigued by the question of a "principle of individuation" to address the problem of what determines a substance as the individual item it is, in its distinction from all others. We are here told that the crux lies in its *qualitative makeup*: no two things are qualitatively entirely alike (though they can, of course, be qualitatively similar in many respects). This "principle of the identity of indiscernibles" has also been characterized as a "principle of the dissimilarity of the diverse." If distinct things could be wholly alike in their internal constitution, then there would be no assignable reason why one of those should bear the particular (and differentiating) relationships it bears to others, thus violating Leibniz's fundamental "principle of sufficient reason." (See sec. 32 below.)

Leibniz is indebted for his Principle of the Identity of Indiscernibles to Nicholas of Cusa (1401–64), who asserted that "there cannot be several things exactly the same (*aequalia*), for in that case there would not be several things, but the same thing itself. Therefore all things both agree with and differ from one another" (*De Venatione Sapientiae*, 23). Compare *De docta ignorantia*, iii, I: "All things must of necessity differ from one another. Among several individuals of the same species there is necessarily a diversity of degrees of perfection. There is nothing in the universe which does not enjoy a certain *singularity*, which is to be found in no other thing." The principle also plays a role in Spinoza's *Ethics*, where he maintains that "In the natural realm two or more things cannot be of the same nature or attribute" (I, prop. 5).

KEY WORDS:

monad/*monade*
difference/*différence interne*
internal intrinsic denomination/*dénomination intrinsèque*

SECTION 10

10. I also take it for granted that every created being is subject to change, and in consequence the created monad also, and even that this change is continuous in each one.

10. Je prends aussi pour accordé, que tout être créé est sujet au changement, et par consequent la Monade créée aussi, et même que ce changement est continuel dans chacune.

(PNG, sec. 2.) One monad by itself and at a single moment cannot be distinguished from another except by its internal qualities and actions, and these can only be its *perceptions*—that is to say, the representations of the compound, or of that which is without, in the simple—and its *appetitions*—that is to say, its tendencies from one perception to another—which are the principles of change.

(NE, p. 56.) Nothing takes place suddenly, and it is one of my great and best confirmed maxims that *nature never makes leaps.* I called this the Law of Continuity. . . . I have also pointed out that in consequence of imperceptible variations no two individual things could be perfectly alike, and that they must always differ more than numerically.

(NE, p. 473.) In nature everything happens by degrees, and nothing by jumps; and this rule about change is one part of my law of continuity. But the beauty of nature, which insists upon perceptions which stand out from one another, asks for the appearance of jumps.

(G II, 168; Loemker, p. 515; Ariew & Garber, p. 516; to de Volder [1699].) No transition happens by a leap. . . . This holds, I think, not only of transitions from place to place, but also of those from form to form, or from state to state. For not only does experience confute all sudden changes, but also I do not think any *a priori* reason can be given against a leap from place to place, which would not militate also against a leap from state to state.

(G III, 52; Loemker, p. 351; "Reply to Malebranche" [1687].) A principle of general order which I have noticed . . . is of great utility in reasoning. . . . It takes its origin from the infinite, it is absolutely necessary in Geometry, but it succeeds also in Physics, because the sovereign wisdom, which is the source of all things, acts as a perfect geometer, following a harmony to which nothing can be added. . . . It may be enunciated thus: "When the difference of two cases can be diminished below every given magnitude in the data or in what is posited, it must also be possible to diminish it below every given magnitude in what is sought or in what results," or, to speak more familiarly, "When the cases (or what is given) continually approach and are finally merged in each other, the consequences or events (or what is sought) must do so too." Which depends again on a still more general principle, namely: "When the data form a series, so do the consequences" (*datis ordinatis etiam quaesita sunt ordinata*).

COMMENTARY

Change—and the activity that produces it—is the most fundamental feature of a monad. Its characteristic mode of operation is, after all, what defines it as the thing that it is. The internal principle which regulates a monad's changes is called *appetition* by Leibniz. (See sec. 15.)

Life is change. If monads did not constantly change, they would be to this extent inert and so fail to be living beings. And this would run counter to Leibniz's fundamentally organic view of nature. Only God, who is altogether extratemporal, is an exception here. To be sure, change is sometimes so slow as to be unobservable. His theory of "minute perceptions" lying beneath the threshold of conscious recognition serves Leibniz at this point also.

His speaking of "the created monad" here suggests that Leibniz is quite prepared to characterize God, the *necessary* being or substance as a monad, as well. (Compare secs 18 and 47.) But God is, of course, unchanging, whereas all created monads are changeable, and indeed ever-changing. They are accordingly en-

dowed with an inexorably *temporal and historical* dimension, as, consequently, are the macro-entities which they compose. Moreover these changes
proceed under the aegis of natural laws that are mathematically tractable in
being *continuous*. (The curves defined by the equations of physics are continuous, smooth, everywhere differentiable.) There are no gaps, leaps, or discon-
tinuities in nature, but everything happens by degrees. Leibniz accordingly
insists on a "Law of Continuity" (*lex continuitatis*) in nature, and sees its continuities as a part of what binds the universe together into a unified whole.
(Compare sec. 13.)

KEY WORDS:

created being/*être créé*
monad/*monade*
continuous change/*changement continuel*

SECTION 11

11. It follows from what has just been said that the natural changes of the
monads proceed from an *internal principle* [that one can call an active force].
For an external cause cannot influence their inner make-up. [And one can say,
generally, that Force is nothing but the principle of change.] (See *Theodicy*, secs.
396, 400.)

11. *Il s'ensuit de ce que nous venons de dire, que les changemens naturels
des Monades viennent d'un* principe interne *[qu'on peut appeler force active],
puisqu'une cause externe ne sçauroit influer dans son interieur. [Et generale-
ment on peut dire que la Force n'est autre chose que le principe du changement.]* (Théodicée, *secs. 396, 400.*)

(*Theodicy*, sec. 369.) Adam sinned freely and. . . . God saw him sinning already in conceiving the very possibility of Adam which became actual in accordance with the decree of the divine permission. It is true that Adam was
determined to sin in consequence of certain prevailing inclinations ⟨of his
inner nature⟩: but this inner determination destroys neither contingency nor
freedom.

(*Theodicy*, sec. 396.) And the qualities. . . . or what I call the accidental forms
⟨of a substance⟩ I take to be modifications of this primitive entelechy, much as
shapes are modifications of matter. That is why these modifications are perpetually changing, while the simple substance remains.

(*Theodicy*, sec. 400.) The force of these proofs, which he praises, must not
be so great as he thinks, for if it were they would prove too much. They would
make God the author of sin. I admit that the soul cannot stir the organs by a
physical influence; for I think that the body must have been so formed beforehand that it would do in time and place that which responds to the volitions
of the soul, although it be true nevertheless that the soul is the principle of the
operation. But if it be said that the soul does not produce its thoughts, its sensations, its feelings of pain and pleasure, that is something for which I see no

reason. In my system every simple substance (that is, every true substance) must be the true immediate cause of all its actions and inward passions; and, speaking strictly in a metaphysical sense, it has none other than those which it produces. Those who hold a different opinion, and who make God the sole agent, are needlessly becoming involved in expressions whence they will only with difficulty extricate themselves without offence against religion; moreover, they unquestionably offend against reason.

(PNG, sec. 2.) One monad by itself and at a single moment cannot be distinguished from another except by its internal qualities and actions, and these can only be its *perceptions*—that is to say, the representations of the compound, or of that which is without, in the simple—and its *appetitions*—that is to say, its tendencies from one perception to another—which are the principles of change. For the simplicity of a substance does not prevent the plurality of modifications which must necessarily be found together in the same simple substance.

(NS, sec. 14.) And thus, since our internal sensations ... are merely phenomena which follow upon external events or better, are really appearances or like well-ordered dreams, it follows that these perceptions internal to the soul itself come to it through its own original constitution, that is to say, through its representative nature, which is capable of expressing entities outside of itself in agreement with its organs—this nature having been given it from its creation and constituting its individual character. It is this that makes each substance represent the entire universe accurately in its own way and according to a definite point of view.

(DM, sec. 8.) Now it is evident that every true prediction has some basis in the nature of things, and even when a proposition is not identical, that is, when the predicate is not expressly contained in the subject, it is still necessary that it be virtually contained in it, and this is what the philosophers call *in-esse*, saying thereby that the predicate is in the subject. Thus the content of the subject must always include that of the predicate in such a way that if one understands perfectly the concept of the subject, he will know that the predicate appertains to it also. This being so, we are able to say that this is the nature of an individual substance or of a complete being, namely, to afford a conception so complete that the concept shall be sufficient for the understanding of it and for the deduction of all the predicates of which the substance is or may become the subject. Thus the quality of king, which belonged to Alexander the Great, an abstraction from the subject, is not sufficiently determined to constitute an individual, and does not contain the other qualities of the same subject, nor everything which the idea of this prince includes. God, however, seeing the individual concept, or haecceity, of Alexander, sees there at the same time the basis and the reason of all the predicates which can be truly uttered regarding him; for instance that he will conquer Darius and Porus, even to the point of knowing *a priori* (and not by experience) whether he died a natural death or by poison,—facts which we can learn only through history. When we carefully consider the connection of things we see also the possibility of saying that there were always in the soul of Alexander marks of all that had happened to him and evidences of all that would happen to him and traces even of everything which occurs in the universe, although God alone could recognize them all.

(NE, pp. 65–66.) It must be borne in mind above all that the modifications which can occur to a single subject naturally and without miracles must arise from limitations and variations of a real genius, i.e. of a constant and absolute inherent nature. . . . Whenever we find some quality in a subject, we ought to believe that if we understood the nature of both the subject and the quality we would conceive how the quality could arise from it. So within the order of nature (miracles apart) it is not at God's arbitrary discretion to attach this or that quality haphazardly to substances. He will never give them any which are not natural to them, that is, which cannot arise from their nature as explicable modifications.

(Couturat, *Opuscules*, pp. 520–21; Loemker, pp. 268–69; Ariew & Garber, p. 32; "First Truths" [ca. 1685].) *The complete or perfect concept of an individual substance involves all its predicates, past, present, and future.* For certainly it is already true now that a future predicate will be a predicate in the future, and so it is contained in the concept of the thing. Therefore there is contained in the perfect individual concepts of Peter or Judas, considered as merely possible concepts and setting aside the divine decree to create them, everything that will happen to them, whether necessarily or freely. And all this is known by God. Thus it is obvious that God elects from an infinity of possible individuals those whom he judges best suited to the supreme and secret ends of his wisdom. In an exact sense, he does not decree that Peter should sin or Judas be damned but only that, in preference to other possible individuals, Peter, who will sin—certainly, indeed, yet not necessarily but freely—and Judas, who will suffer damnation—under the same condition—shall come into existence, or that the possible concept shall become actual. And although the future salvation of Peter is contained in his eternal possible notion, yet this is not without the help of grace, for in the same perfect notion of this possible Peter, there are contained as possibilities the helps of the divine grace to be granted to him. *Every individual substance involves the whole universe in its perfect concept,* and all that exists in the universe has existed or will exist. For there is no thing upon which some true denomination, at least of comparison or relation, cannot be imposed from another thing. Yet there is no purely extrinsic denomination. I have shown the same thing in many other ways which are in harmony with each other.

(G VI, 589; Loemker, p. 625; Ariew & Garber, p. 265; "Conversation of Philarète and Ariste" [1712].) But the viewpoint which ascribes all external actions to God alone has recourse to miracles, and even to unreasonable miracles hardly worthy of the divine wisdom. By the same right by which we set up such fictions which only a miraculous omnipotence of God could make possible, it would be permissible to maintain that I am alone in the world and that God produces all the phenomena in my soul as if there were other things outside of me, without there actually being any.

COMMENTARY

Section 15 will inform us that the action of the "internal principle of change"—this inner "active force" of monadic development over time—is to be characterized as *appetition.* This mode of force is operative within all created monads, providing them with a "program," as it were, specifying once and for all how their entire history unfolds in a predetermined fashion. Leibniz entertained the radical idea—not projected in modern science until the double helix of contemporary genetics—that information could be encoded in the internal make-up of a substance in such a way as to pre-program in its natural make-up the entire course of its subsequent development. Such a pre-ordained process of change determines a substance's orderly unfolding over time in much the way in which an acorn embodies the developmental instructions that lead it to grow into an oak tree rather than a maple. Leibniz considers the internal principles as akin to the algebraic rule for generating a numerical series or (better yet) as the generating equation for a continuous curve. This systemic unfolding of its own successive states—the whole history of its particular actions, so to speak—serves to endow each substance with its own particular individuality.

The fact that monadic change proceeds from within marks substances as units of activity—as *agents*—and thus is the definitively important aspect of their nature. This doctrine marks Leibniz as a philosopher of process, and sets him apart from the succession of theorists (reaching from Parmenides to Spinoza to Bradley) who see time and change as insignificant and somehow illusory features of a fundamentally timeless and unchanging universe.

KEY WORDS:

monad/*monade*
natural changes/*changements naturels*
internal constitution/*intérieur*
(internal) principle of change/*principe (interne) du changement*
external cause/*cause externe*

SECTION 12

12. But beyond the principle of change, there must also be an *internal complexity (détail) of that which changes*, which would produce, so to speak, the specification and the variety of simple substances.

12. Mais il faut aussi qu'outre le principe du changement, il y ait un detail *de ce qui change, qui fasse pour ainsi dire la specification et la varieté des substances simples.*

(PNG, sec. 3.) Everywhere there are simple substances actually differentiated from each other by their actions, which continually change their relations.

(DM, sec. 8.) It is true, indeed, that when several predicates can be attributed to same subject, and this subject can no longer be attributed to any other, we call it an individual substance; but that is not enough, and such an explanation is only nominal. We must therefore consider what it is to be truly attributed to a certain subject. Now it is evident that every true prediction has some basis in the nature of things, and even when a proposition is not idential, that is, when the predicate is not expressly contained in the subject, it is still necessary that it be virtually contained in it, and this is what the philosophers call *in-esse*, saying thereby that the predicate is in the subject.

COMMENTARY

In speaking of specification (*specificatio*), the Scholastics had in view those properties of a thing whose possession marks it as a member of the kind (or *species*) to which it belongs—the features that identify it as the sort of thing it is.

All monads have a complex inner structure, an internal complexity of differentiated *détail* that runs on into endless variation, somewhat like the infinite decimal expansion of a unit like pi or the square root of two. (On *détail*, see also sec 37.) This complexity serves both to differentiate substances from one another, and to differentiate every state of the substance from every other over time. In fact substantial change simply consists in this alteration of detail. For Leibniz, it is the totality of its properties (i.e., its "complete individual concept") that establish its characteristic identity. On this basis each individual substance is, as it were, a species unto itself.

This qualitative complexity of monads stands in stark contrast to their quantitative simplicity. This may explain why Leibniz eventually came to prefer terms of art like *monad* or *entelechy* when referring to "simple substances."

KEY WORDS:

simple substance/*substance simple*
(inner) principle of change/*principe (interne) du changement*
internal complexity/*détail*
specification/*spécification*
variety/*variété*

SECTION 13

13. This internal complexity (*détail*) must enfold a multiplicity in unity or in the simple. For as every natural change happens by degrees, something always changes and something remains. Consequently, there must be a plurality of properties (*affections*) and relations within a simple substance, even though it has none <i.e., no plurality> of parts.

13. Ce detail doit envelopper une multitude dans l'unité ou dans le simple. Car tout changement naturel se faisant par degrés, quelque chose change, et quelque chose reste; et par consequent il faut que dans la substance simple il y ait une pluralité d'affections et de rapports, quoiqu'il n'y en ait de parties.

(PNG, sec. 2.) *Monads* cannot have shapes, for then they would have parts. It follows that one monad by itself and at a single moment cannot be distinguished from another except by its internal qualities and actions, and these can only be its *perceptions*—that is to say, the representations of the compound, or of that which is without, in the simple—and its *appetitions*—that is to say, its tendencies from one perception to another—which are the principles of change. For the simplicity of a substance does not prevent the plurality of modifications which must necessarily be found together in the same simple substance; and these modifications must consist of the variety of relations of correspondence which the substance has with things outside. In the same way there may be found, in one *center or point, though it is perfectly simple, an infinity of angles formed by the lines which meet in it.*

(PNG, sec. 3.) Everywhere there are simple substances actually separated from each other by their own actions, which continually change their relations.

(NE, p. 56.) Nothing takes place suddenly, and it is one of my great and best confirmed maxims that *nature never makes leaps.* I called this the Law of Continuity when I discussed it formerly. . . . There is much work for this law to do in natural science. It implies that any change from small to large, or vice versa, passes through something which is, in respect of degrees as well as of parts, in between; and that no motion ever springs immediately from a state of rest, or passes into one except through a lesser motion; just as one could never traverse a certain line or distance without first traversing a shorter one. Despite which, until now those who have propounded the laws of motion have not complied with this law, since they have believed that a body can instantaneously receive a motion contrary to its preceding one. All of which supports the judgment that noticeable perceptions arise by degrees from ones which are too minute to be noticed.

(G II, 168–69; Loemker, pp. 515–16; to de Volder [1699].) This is the axiom that I use—*no transition is made through a leap.* I hold that this follows from the law of order and rests upon the same reason by which everyone knows that motion does not occur in a leap; that is, that a body can move from one place to another only through intervening positions. I admit that once we have assumed that the Author of things has willed continuity of motion, this itself will exclude the possibility of leaps. But how can we prove that he has willed this, except through experience or by reason of order? For since all things happen by the perpetual production of God, or, as they say, by continuous creation, why could he not have transcreated a body, so to speak, from one place to another distant place, leaving behind a gap either in time or in space; producing a body at *A,* for example, and then forthwith at *B,* etc.? Experience teaches us that this does not happen, but the principle of order proves it too, according to which, *the more we analyze things, the more they satisfy our intellect.* This is not true of leaps, for here analysis leads us to mysteries.

(G IV, 364; "Against the Principle of the Cartesians" [1697].) I know not whether the definition of substance as that which needs the concurrence of God only for its existence, is appropriate to any created substance known to us, unless interpreted in a somewhat unusual sense. For we need not only other substances, but also, much more, other accidents. Since there will be need of other criteria for distinguishing substance from accident, among which this may be one, that a substance, though it does need some accident, yet often has no need of one determinate accident, but when this is taken away, is content with the substitution of another; whereas an accident does not need merely some substance in general, but also that one of its own in which it once inheres, so as not to change it.

(G IV, 562; Loemker, p. 579; "Reply to Bayle" [1702].) The soul, on the other hand, though entirely indivisible, involves a composite tendency, that is to say, a multitude of present thoughts, each of which tends to a particular change according to what it involves and what is found in it at the time by virtue of its essential relationship to all the other things in the world. Among other things, it is also their lack of this relationship which bans the atoms of Epicurus from nature. For each thing or part of the universe must point to all the rest, in such a way that the soul, as concerns the variety of its modifications, must be compared, not with a material atom, but with the universe which it represents according to its point of view—and in some ways even with God himself, whose infinity it represents finitely because of its confused and imperfect perception of the infinite. The thought of pleasure seems to be simple, but it is not, and anyone who studies its anatomy will find that it involves everything that surrounds us and therefore everything which surrounds our environment. And the reason for the change of thoughts in the soul is the same as that of the change of things in the universe which it represents. The mechanical reasons which are developed in the bodies are united and concentrated, so to speak, in the souls or entelechies; indeed, they have their source there. It is true that not all the entelechies are, like our soul, images of God, for they are not all made to be members of a society or of a state of which he is the head. But they are always images of the universe. They are after their manner worlds in abridged form, fruitful simplicities, substantial unities, but virtually infinite by the multitude of their modifications, centers which express an infinite circumference.

COMMENTARY

Their complex and dynamic inner property structure is a crucial aspect of simple substances. Such a substance is "simple" only *physically* (in having no parts); it is certainly not "simple" in a *descriptive* sense. For it has both (1) a complex descriptive state at any given time (its *détail*), and (2) an internalized "program" for changing this constantly over time. Note that Leibniz does not deny the relationship (*rapport*) of substances to one another. On the contrary, he insists upon such interrelatedness, but holds that interrelationships are always *internalized* through mutual attunenement. (Compare sec. 51.) It is this latter circumstance of ongoing readjustments that is the basis of agency, which is always naturally produced from internally pre-programmed changes, and never caused from without, seeing that the monads are "windowless."

On the present section's insistence that all *natural* change happens by degrees, compare also section 6's contention that all changes in compounds occur by parts. As Leibniz sees it, the quantitative changes of the material realm are thus related to—and indeed ultimately rooted in—the qualitative changes of the metaphysical, monadic realm.

The circumstance that "natural change always happens by degrees" is significant for Leibniz. He characterized the fact that physical nature everywhere exhibits such continuities in its laws of operation as the Law of Continuity (*lex continuitatis*). (Compare sec. 10.) Throughout its various presentations, this Law of Continuity was presented by Leibniz as a consequence of the Principle of Perfection. As usual when he is in possession of a useful mathematical or physical principle, Leibniz applies it in philosophy, where it is given the formulation: "Jumps are forbidden not only in motions, but also in every order of things and of truths" (G III, 635).

KEY WORDS:

simple substance/*substance simple*
internal complexity/*détail*
natural change/*changement naturel*
by degrees/*par degrés*
plurality (of properties and relations)/*pluralité d'affections et de rapports*
multiplicity in unity/*multitude dans l'unité*
affections (i.e., properties)/*affections*
relations/*rapports*

SECTION 14

14. The transitory state which enfolds and represents a multiplicity in a unity, or in the simple substance, is exactly what one calls *perception*. One must distinguish this from *apperception* and from *consciousness*, as will become clear below. <See secs. 19, 23–24.> This is where the Cartesians went badly wrong in taking no account of perceptions that are not apperceived. This led them to think that "spirits" alone are monads, and that there are no souls of beasts nor other entelechies. And it led them to confuse, as ordinary people do, a prolonged stupor with death in the strict sense, which again misled them into the Scholastic prejudice that there are wholly separated souls and even confirmed misguided minds in a belief in the mortality of souls.

14. L'état passager qui enveloppe et represente une multitude dans l'unité, ou dans la substance simple, n'est autre chose que ce qu'on appelle la Perception, *qu'on doit distinguer de l'apperception et de la conscience, comme il paroîtra dans la suite. Et c'est en quoi les Cartesiens ont fort manqué, ayant compté pour rien les perceptions dont on ne s'apperçoit pas. C'est aussi ce qui les a fait croire, que les seuls Esprits étoient des Monades, et qu'il n'y avoit point d'Ames des Bêtes ni d'autres Entelechies, et qu'ils ont confondu avec le vulgaire un long étourdissement avec une mort à la rigueur, ce qui les a fait encore donner dans le prejugé scholastique des Ames entièrement separées et a même confirmé les esprits mal tournés dans l'opinion de la mortalité des Ames.*

(PNG, sec. 4.) So it is well to make a distinction between *perception*, which is the inner state of the monad representing external things, and *apperception*, which is consciousness or the reflective knowledge of this inner state itself and which is not given to all souls or to any soul all the time. It is for lack of this distinction that the Cartesians have made the mistake of disregarding perceptions which are not themselves perceived, just as people commonly disregard imperceptible bodies. It is this too which has made these same Cartesians think that only spirits are monads and that there is no soul in beasts, still less other *principles of life*. And after having defied the everyday opinion of men too much in denying that beasts have feeling, they adjusted their views too far to popular prejudices, on the other hand, when they confused a *long stupor* coming from a great confusion of perceptions with *death* in the rigorous sense, in which all perception would cease. This has confirmed the poorly grounded opinion that certain souls are destroyed and has supported the pernicious view of certain so-called free-thinkers who have denied the immortality of our souls.

(NE, p. 54.) Memory is needed for attention: when we are not alerted, so to speak, to pay heed to certain of our own present perceptions, we allow them to slip by unconsidered and even unnoticed. But if someone alerts us to them straight away, and makes us take note, for instance, of some noise which we have just heard, then we remember it and are aware of just having had some sense of it. Thus, we were not straight away aware of these perceptions, and we became aware of them only because we were alerted to them after an interval, however brief. To give a clearer idea of these minute perceptions which we are unable to pick out from a crowd, I like to use the example of the roaring noise of the sea which impresses itself on us when we are standing on the shore. To hear this noise as we do, we must hear the parts which make up this whole, that is the noise of each wave, although each of these little noises makes itself known only when combined confusedly with all the others, and would not be noticed if the wave which made it were by itself. We must be affected slightly by the motion of this wave, and have some perception of each of these noises, however faint they may be; otherwise there would be no perception of a hundred thousand waves, since a hundred thousand nothings cannot make something. Moreover, we never sleep so soundly that we do not have some feeble and confused sensation; and the loudest noise in the world would never waken us if we did not have some perception of its start, which is small, just as the strongest force in the world would never break a rope unless the least force strained it and stretched it slightly, even though that little lengthening which is produced is imperceptible.

(NE, pp. 115–16.) Every impression has an effect, but the effects are not always noticeable. When I turn one way rather than another, it is often because of a series of tiny impressions of which I am not aware but which make one movement slightly harder than the other. All our undeliberated actions result from a conjunction of minute perceptions; and even our customs and passions, which have so much influence when we do deliberate, come from the same source; for these tendencies come into being gradually, and so without the minute perceptions we would not have acquired these noticeable dispositions.

(NS, sec. 14.) God has originally created the soul, and every other real unity, in such a way that everything in it must arise from its own nature by a perfect *spontaneity* with regard to itself, yet by a perfect *conformity* to things without. And thus, since our internal sensations, that is, those which are in the soul itself and not in the brain or in the subtle parts of the body, are merely phenomena which follow upon external events or better, are really appearances or like well-ordered dreams, it follows that these perceptions internal to the soul itself come to it through its own original constitution, that is to say, through its representative nature, which is capable of expressing entities outside of itself in agreement with its organs—this nature having been given it from its creation and constituting its individual character. It is this that makes each substance represent the entire universe accurately in its own way and according to a definite point of view.

(DM, sec. 33.) We can also see that the perceptions of our senses even when they are clear must necessarily contain certain confused elements, for as all the bodies in the universe are in sympathy, ours receives the impressions of all the others, and while our senses respond to everything, our soul cannot pay attention to every particular. That is why our confused sensations are the result of a variety of perceptions. The variety is infinite. It is almost like the confused murmuring which is heard by those who approach the shore of a sea. It comes from the continual beatings of innumerable waves. If now, out of many perceptions which do not at all fit together to make one, no particular one perception surpasses the others, and if they make impressions about equally strong or equally capable of holding the attention of the soul, they can be perceived only confusedly.

(G VI, 534; Loemker, pp. 557–58; "On the Doctrine of a Universal Spirit" [1702].) In dreams and in unconsciousness nature has given us an example which should convince us that death is not a cessation of all functions but only a suspension of certain more noticeable ones. Elsewhere I have explained an important point whose neglect has led men the more easily to accept the opinion that the soul is mortal. It is that a large number of small perceptions which are equal and balanced among themselves, with nothing to give them relief or distinguish them from each other, are not noticed at all and cannot be remembered. But to conclude from this that the soul is without any function at all would be like the popular belief that there is a void or nothing at all wherever there is no noticeable matter or that the earth does not move because its movement, being uniform and without jerks, is unnoticeable. We have an infinity of little perceptions which we are incapable of distinguishing. A great stupefying roar, as, for example, the murmur of a large assemblage, is composed of all the little murmurs of individual persons which are not noticed at all but of which one must nevertheless have some sensation; otherwise one would not sense the whole. Thus when an animal is deprived of organs capable of giving it sufficiently distinct perceptions, it does not follow that the animal has left no smaller and more uniform perceptions or that it is deprived of all its organs and all its perceptions. Its organs are merely enveloped and reduced to a small volume, but the order of nature requires that everything be developed again sometime and return to a noticeable state and that there be a definite well-regulated progression in its changes which helps to bring things to fruition and perfection.

(Loemker, p. 161; "Paris Notes" [1676].) This operation of the mind seems most remarkable to me. It seems that when I think of myself thinking and already know, between the thoughts themselves, what I think of my thoughts, and a little later marvel at this triplication of reflection, then I turn upon myself wondering and do not know how to admire this admiration. . . . It sometimes happens that I cannot forget something, but involuntarily think of the same thing for almost an hour, and then think of this difficulty in thinking and stupefy myself into reflections through perpetual reflections, so that I almost begin to doubt that I shall ever think of anything else and begin to fear that this direction of mind has harmed me. . . . Anyone who desires an experience of these matters should begin to think of himself and his thinking sometime in the middle of the night, perhaps when he cannot sleep, and think of the perception of perceptions and marvel at this condition of his, so that he comes gradually to turn more and more within himself or to rise above himself, as if by a succession of spurts of his mind. He will wonder that he has never before experienced this state of mind. We are thus never without other perceptions than sense, for we sense without ourselves this direction of the mind by which we are led back within ourselves and suppress externals. The fatigue which accompanies pure thought certainly often arises from this. I have noticed further that this perception of perception also occurs without characters and therefore that memory does also. For to perceive perception, or to sense that I have sensed, is to remember, as Hobbes says. I do not yet adequately experience how these different acts of the mind take place in this continually reciprocating reflection, as it were, in the intervals between these acts, but they seem to be made by a distinguishing sense of the bodily direction. But if you observe well, this act will merely make you remember that you already had this in mind a little previously, that is, this reflection of reflection, and so you observe it and designate it by a distinct image accompanying it. Therefore it already was in your mind earlier, and so perception of perception goes on perpetually in the mind of infinity. In it consists the existence of the mind per se and the necessity of its continuation.

COMMENTARY

For Leibniz, perception is an extraordinarily broad conception: "the representation of multiplicity in unity, within a single substance." The conscious perceptions of higher animals (not to speak of the self-conscious *apperception* of which we humans are capable) are very special cases.

Members of the Cartesian school held that all those organisms that cannot reason (plants and animals alike) are strictly mechanical contrivances or "living automata." Excluded from the domain of the rational, thinking substances, subhuman animals thus fall into the realm of extended substances as strictly physical mechanisms. Leibniz strongly opposed this Cartesian idea that all mental life must be conscious. Unconscious perceptions that lie beneath the threshold of conscious awareness (the so-called minute perceptions, *petites perceptions*) are a crucial instrumentality of his thought. For Leibniz, perception is not the capacity of a specific kind of being but pervades nature throughout.

For the explanation of the idea of *entelechies*, see section 18 below. Monads of all three levels (*entelechies* = created monads in general, *souls* = ruling monads in animals, *spirits* = ruling monads in rational creatures) are all practitioners of perception. But souls can be conscious, and apperception—self-consciousness—occurs in spirits alone. (This tripartite scheme is set out more fully in secs. 19 and 23–30.)

On the tendency to confuse the hibernation of souls ("a prolonged stupor") with their death see also sections 21 and 73. The latter is a matter of ceasing to exist, the former a matter of operating at lesser levels of capacity, which the higher level monads generally do much of the time.

KEY WORDS:

simple substance/*substance simple*
monad/*monade*
perception/*perception*
apperception/*apperception*
consciousness/*conscience*
souls/*âmes*

spirits/*esprits*
beasts/*bêtes*
entelechies/*entéléchies*
mortality/*mortalité*
death/*mort*

PERSONS

the Cartesians

SECTION 15

15. The action of the internal principle which brings about the change or the passage from one perception to another may be called *appetition*. It is true that appetite cannot always attain altogether the whole perception to which it tends, but it always obtains some part of it, and so attains new perceptions.

15. L' Action du principe interne qui fait le changement ou le passage d'une perception à une autre, peut être appellé Appetition: il est vray, que l'appetit ne sçauroit tousjours parvenir entièrement à toute la perception où il tend, mais il en obtient tousjours quelque chose, et parvient à des perceptions nouvelles.

(*Theodicy*, sec. 393.) What does not act does not deserve the name of substance.

(PNG, sec. 2.) It follows that one monad by itself and at a single moment cannot be distinguished from another except by its internal qualities and actions, and these can only be its *perceptions*—that is to say, the representations of the compound, or of that which is without, in the simple—and its *appetitions*, that is to say, its tendencies from one perception to another, which are the principles of change.

(PNG, sec. 3.) The perceptions in the monad arise from each other according to the laws of the appetites or of the *final causes of good and evil*, which consist in observable perceptions, whether regulated or unregulated, in the same way that bodily changes and external phenomena arise from each other according to the laws of *efficient causality*, that is, of motions.

(NE, p. 189.) <Happiness consists in a> progress towards greater goods. Such progress is inevitably accompanied by desire or at least by constant disquiet, but of the kind I have just explained: it does not amount to discomfort, but is restricted to the elements or rudiments of suffering, which we cannot be aware of in themselves but which suffice to act as spurs and to stimulate the will. That is what a healthy man's appetite does, unless it amounts to that discomfort which unsettles us and gives us a tormenting obsession with the idea of whatever it is that we are without. These "appetitions," whether small or large, are what the Scholastics call *motus primo primi*, and they are truly the first steps that nature makes us take; not so much towards happiness as towards joy, since in them one looks only to the present; but experience and reason teach us to govern and moderate them so that they can lead us to happiness. I have already said something about this (I.ii.3). Appetitions are like a stone's endeavor to follow the shortest but not always the best route to the center of the earth; it cannot foresee that it will collide with rocks on which it will shatter, whereas it would have got closer to its goal if it had had the wit and the means to swerve aside. In the same way, by rushing straight at a present pleasure we sometimes fall into the abyss of misery. That is why reason opposes appetition with images of greater goods or evils to come, and with a firm policy and practice of thinking before acting and then standing by whatever is found to be best. . . .

(NS, p. 14.) Being constrained, then, to admit that it is impossible for the soul or any other true substance to receive something from without, except by the divine omnipotence, I was led insensibly to an opinion which surprised me, but which seems inevitable, and which has in fact very great advantages and very significant beauties. This is that we must say that God has originally created the soul, and every other real unity, in such a way that everything in it must arise from its own nature by a perfect *spontaneity* with regard to itself, yet by a perfect *conformity* to things without. And thus, since our internal sensations, that is, those which are in the soul itself and not in the brain or in the subtle parts of the body, are merely phenomena which follow upon external events or better, are really appearances or like well-ordered dreams, it follows that these perceptions internal to the soul itself come to it through its own original constitution, that is to say, through its representative nature, which is capable of expressing entities outside of itself in agreement with its organs— this nature having been given it from its creation and constituting its individual character. It is this that makes each substance represent the entire universe accurately in its own way and according to a definite point of view. And the perceptions or expressions of external things reach the soul at the proper time by virtue of its own laws, as in a world apart, and as if there existed nothing but God and itself (to make use of the expression of a person of exalted mind and renowned piety). So there will be a perfect accord between all these substances which produces the same effect that would be noticed if they all communicated with each other by a transmission of species or of qualities, as the common run of philosophers imagine.

(G II, 256; to de Volder [1703].) I recognize monads that are active *per se*, and in them nothing can be conceived except perception, which in turn involves action.

COMMENTARY

The complex internal state (*détail*) of a monad at any given temporal juncture consists in the *perceptions* by which it represents its whole environing world. The internally programmed drive or *nisus* (*tendance*) from one family of perceptions toward the others that are its temporal successors is called *appetition*. For Spinoza what is basic in things is an impetus of self-preservation (*conatus se preservandi*) which preserves the existing condition of things; for Leibniz it is an impetus to self-development (appetition) which strives to bring new features to actualization—a sort of *conatus se realizandi*. (In sec. 60, Leibniz holds that the monads' appetitive drive to new perceptions is always a matter of its striving to a self-aggrandizement of souls, namely to getting a fuller view of the universe as a whole.) Of appetition Leibniz says that "even as *motion* carries matter from one configuration to another, so *appetite* carries the soul from one image to another" (G III, 347).

The most crucial word of this section is the *internal* of "internal principle." For the whole history of a monad's state-changes (perceptions) is pre-specified by its defining conception, and, so to speak, programmed into its very nature as the individual it is. Leibniz often says that this internal principle of change or appetition functions according to a "law of the series" of monadic states that specifies their unfolding. (It is the fact that an agent's free actions unfold "from within," from its own inherent nature, that makes room for the possibility of free agency in Leibniz's system of predetermination.)

The drive or *force* represented by monadic appetition is the basis of all change and all novelty. This appetitive transit from one set of perceptions to another is what constitutes monadic activity and is the definitive feature of any substance. For Leibniz, the terms *substance* and *agent* are effectively co-extensive.

The manuscript reveals that the brief sentence of section 11 was originally followed by another, subsequently deleted by Leibniz, which characterized the "internal principle" of monadic change as a force (*force*). (Compare sec. 11.) But as the present section indicates, he now prefers to characterize it more specifically as *appetition*.

In the inner adjustment of states, each substance of these best of possible worlds accommodates itself to the others as best it can. But the inherent intractability of their limited nature restricts perfection in this regard, as will emerge more explicitly in section 42.

KEY WORDS:

internal principle (of change)/*principe interne (du changement)*
appetition/*appétition*
perception/*perception*
novel perceptions/*perceptions nouvelles*

SECTION 16

16. We ourselves experience multiplicity in a simple substance when we find that the slightest thought of which we are conscious in ourselves enfolds a variety in its object. Accordingly, all who recognize that the soul is a simple substance must also recognize this multiplicity within the monad, and Monsieur Bayle ought nowise to have found difficulty in this, as he did in his *Dictionary* article "Rorarius."

16. Nous experimentons nous mêmes une multitude dans la substance simple, lorsque nous trouvons que la moindre pensée dont nous nous appercevons, enveloppe une variété dans l'objet. Ainsi tous ceux, qui reconnoissent que l'Ame est une substance simple doivent reconnoitre cette multitude dans la Monade; et Monsieur Bayle ne devoit point y trouver de la difficulté, comme il a fait dans son Dictionnaire article Rorarius.

(PNG, sec. 2.) The simplicity of a substance does not prevent the plurality of modifications which must necessarily be found together in the same simple substance; and these modifications must consist of the variety of relations of correspondence which the substance has with things outside. In the same way there may be found, on one *center* or point, though it is perfectly simple, an infinity of angles formed by the lines which meet in it.

(G II, 45; Ariew & Garber, p. 75; for Arnauld [1686].) In order to judge of the notion of an individual substance, it is well to consult that which I have of myself, as we must consult the specific notion of the sphere to judge of its properties.

(G II. 317; to des Bosses [1706].) A universal is one in many, or the similarity of many; but when we perceive a particular, many are expressed in one, namely in the percipient. You see how far apart these are.

(G III, 247; to Burnett [1699].) I believe that we have a clear but not a distinct idea of substance, which comes in my opinion from the fact that we have the internal feeling of it in ourselves, who are substances.

(G IV, 550; "Remarks on Bayle" [1702].) I have already shown more than once that the soul does many things without knowing how it does them, when it acts by means of confused perceptions and insensible inclinations or appetitions, of which there is always so very great a number that it is impossible for the soul to be conscious of them or to separate them distinctly.

COMMENTARY

According to Leibniz, multiplicity in unity is something we ourselves experience, since our minds are self-conscious substances. It lies in the very nature of consciousness to effect a unity of thought amongst a variegated multiplicity of content (of thought-objects). Even the simplest thought (even "red here") is always complex, always relational ("red," "here"). And these relations to further items run off indefinitely, beyond the range of the commonly unchangeable. The integration of diversity in a single, unified substance is thus something experientially familiar that should cause no difficulties for theoreticians.

In all of Leibniz's expositions of his philosophy, the human person is the paradigm of a substance. Indeed it is only at this level that we humans can gain a cognitive grip on the realm of monads; in all other contexts, *individual* monads lie entirely outside the realm of our experience and knowledge.

Leibniz's contemporary Pierre Bayle (1647–1706)—professor of philosophy first at Sedan and then in Rotterdam—was an important and influential philosopher who sought to extend and reapply the views of the sceptical tradition. His *Historical and Critical Dictionary (Dictionnaire historique et critique)*— first published in Rotterdam in two volumes in 1695 and 1697 and soon reprinted—was a work of great influence, in which he harked back to the sceptics of classical antiquity and adumbrated the enlightenment outlook of Voltaire.

In the article on Hieronymus Rorarius (a theologian who lived 1485–1556 and maintained [in a treatise entitled *Quod animalia bruta saepe ratione utantur melius homine*] that animals make better use of their cognitive abilities than humans do), Bayle undertook an extensive critical discussion of Leibniz's philosophy, basing himself principally on the *Système nouveau* essay published by Leibniz in the *Journal des Savants* in 1695. Leibniz repeatedly took account of Bayle's conclusions, most extensively in the *Theodicy*. Even in the brief *Monadology*, Leibniz keeps Bayle firmly in view. (See also secs. 59, 71.) The article on Rorarius is translated in *Pierre Bayle: Historical and Critical Dictionary* trans. R. H. Popkin (New York: Basic Books, 1965), pp. 239ff.

KEY WORDS:

simple substance/*substance simple*
thought/*pensée*
multiplicty/*multitude*
variety/*variété*
apperception/*apperception*

PERSONS

Pierre Bayle
Hieronymus Rorarius

SECTION 17

17. Furthermore, one is obliged to admit that *perception* and what depends upon it is *inexplicable on mechanical principles*, that is, by figures and motions. In imagining that there is a machine whose construction would enable it to think, to sense, and to have perception, one could conceive it enlarged while retaining the same proportions, so that one could enter into it, just like into a windmill. Supposing this, one should, when visiting within it, find only parts pushing one another, and never anything by which to explain a perception. Thus it is in the simple substance, and not in the composite or in the machine, that one must look for perception. Moreover, there is nothing besides this— besides perceptions and their changes—that one could possibly find in a simple substance. It is also in this alone that all the *internal actions* of simple substances can consist.

17. *On est obligé d'ailleurs de confesser que la* Perception *et ce qui en dépend, est* inexplicable par des raisons mecaniques, c'est à dire, par les figures et par les mouvemens. Et feignant qu'il y ait une Machine, dont la structure <la> fasse penser, sentir, avoir perception, on pourra la concevoir aggrandie en conservant les mêmes proportions, en sorte qu'on y puisse entrer comme dans un moulin. Et cela posé, on ne trouvera en la visitant audedans, que des pieces qui se poussent les unes les autres, et jamais de quoi expliquer une perception. Ainsi c'est dans la substance simple, et non dans le composé ou dans la Machine, qu'il la faut chercher. Aussi n'y a-t-il que cela qu'on puisse trouver dans la substance simple, c'est à dire, les perceptions et leurs changemens. C'est en cela seul aussi que peuvent consister toutes les Actions internes des substances simples.*

(*Theodicy*, Preface [G VI, 40].) I have endeavored to make clear that in reality mechanism is sufficient to produce the organic bodies of animals, without any need of other plastic natures, provided there be added thereto the *preformation* already completely organic in the seeds of the bodies that come into existence, contained in those of the bodies whence they spring, right back to the primary seeds. This could only proceed from the Author of things, infinitely powerful and infinitely wise, who, creating all in the beginning in due order, had *pre-established* there all order and artifice that was to be. There is no chaos in the inward nature of things and there is organism everywhere in a matter whose disposition proceeds from God. . . . The body is prompted by its original constitution to carry out with the help of external things all that it does in accordance with the will of the soul.

(*Theodicy*, sec. 40.) We do not form our ideas because we will to do so, they form themselves within us, they form themselves through us, not in consequence of our will, but in accordance with our nature and that of things. The foetus forms itself in the animal, and a thousand other wonders of nature are produced by a certain *instinct* that God placed there, that is by virtue of *divine preformation*, which had made these admirable automata, adapted to produce mechanically such beautiful effects. Even so it is easy to believe that the soul is a spiritual automaton still more admirable, and that it is through divine preformation that it produces these beautiful ideas, wherein our will has no part and to which our art cannot attain. The operation of spiritual automata, that is of souls, is not mechanical, but it contains in the highest degree all that is beautiful in mechanism. The movements which are developed in bodies are concentrated in the soul by representation as in an ideal world which is in God, that most of the perceptions in the other substances are only confused.

(NE, pp. 66–67.) Thought. . . . cannot be an intelligible modification of matter and be comprehensible and explicable in terms of it. That is, a sentient or thinking being is not a mechanical thing like a watch or a mill: one cannot conceive of sizes and shapes and motions combining mechanically to produce something which thinks, and senses too, in a mass where <formerly> there was nothing of the kind—something which would likewise be extinguished by the machine's going out of order. So sense and thought are not something which is natural to matter, and there are only two ways in which they could occur in it: through God's combining it with a substance to which thought is natural, or through his putting thought into it by a miracle. On this topic I am therefore entirely in agreement with the Cartesians, except that I include the beasts and believe that they too have sense, and souls which are properly described as immaterial and are as imperishable as atoms are according to Democritus and Gassendi; whereas the Cartesians have been needlessly perplexed over the souls of beasts. Not knowing what to do about them if they are preserved (since they have failed to hit on the idea of the preservation of the animal in miniature), they have been driven to deny—contrary to all appearances and to the general opinion of mankind—that beasts have sense. But if someone said that God could at least join the faculty of thought to a machine which was made ready <for it>, I should reply that if that were done, and if God added this faculty to matter without at the same time infusing into it a substance in which this same faculty inhered (which is how I conceive it)—i.e. without joining an immaterial soul to it—the matter would have had to be miraculously exalted in order to receive a power of which it is not naturally capable. Similarly some Scholastics claim that God exalts fire to the point where it is able, without any intermediary, to burn spirits separated from bodies, which would be a sheer miracle. Suffice it to say that we cannot maintain that matter thinks unless we put into it either an imperishable soul or a miracle; and thus that the immortality of our souls follows from what is natural, since we can only maintain their extinction by means of a miracle, whether through the exaltation of matter or through the annihilation of the soul.

(PNG, sec. 3.) The perceptions in the monad arise from each other according to the laws of the appetites or of the *final causes of good and of evil*, which consist in observable perceptions, whether regulated or unregulated, in the same way that bodily changes and external phenomena arise from each other according to the laws of *efficient causality*, that is, of motions.

(G IV, 558–59; Loemker, p. 577; "Reply to Bayle" [1702].) When we recognize that things are determined or inclined to what they ought to do, all the strangeness found in my view completely disappears. Everything which ambition or any other passion makes the soul of Caesar do is represented in his body as well, and the movements of these passions all come from impressions of objects joined to internal movements. The body is made in such a way that the soul never makes any resolutions to which the movements of the body do not correspond; even the most abstract reasonings play their part in this by means of the characters which represent them to the imagination. In a word, so far as the details of phenomena are concerned, everything takes place in the body as if the evil doctrine of those who believe, with Epicurus and Hobbes, that the soul is material were true, or as if man himself were only a body or an automaton. These materialists have thus extended to man as well what the Cartesians have held regarding all other animals. . . . Those who point out to the Cartesians that their way of proving that beasts are only automatons tends at length to support the view that it is possible, metaphysically speaking, for all other men except themselves also to be simple automatons, have said exactly and precisely what I need in order to prove the half of my hypothesis which concerns the body. But in addition to the general principles which establish the monads of which compound things are merely the results, internal experience refutes the Epicurean doctrine. This experience is the consciousness within us of this Ego which perceives the things occurring in the body. And since this perception cannot be explained by figures and movements, it establishes the other half of my hypothesis and makes us recognize an indivisible substance in ourselves which must itself be the source of its phenomena. According to this second half of my hypothesis, therefore, everything occurs in the soul as if there were no body, just as everything occurs in the body as if there were no soul, according to the first half.

(G VI, 507; Loemker, p. 552; Ariew & Garber, p. 192; "On What is Independent of Science and Matter" [1702].) Perception, too, cannot be explained by any mechanism, whatever it may be. We can conclude then that there is also something immaterial everywhere in created beings, and particularly in us, where this force is accompanied by a fairly distinct perception, and even by that light of which I have spoken above, which makes us resemble God in miniature not only through our knowledge of order but also through the order which we can ourselves impart to the things within our grasp, in imitation of that which God imparts to the universe. It is in this, also, that our *virtue* and perfection consist, as our *felicity* consists in the pleasure which we take in it.

(G IV, 521–22; Loemker, p. 495 [1698].) I have compared the soul with a clock only with regard to the regulated precision of its changes, which is but imperfect even in the best clocks, but which is perfect in the works of God. And one can say that the soul is a most exact immaterial automaton. When it is said that a simple being will always act uniformly, a distinction needs to be made. If to act uniformly is to follow perpetually the same law of order or of succession, as in a certain scale or series of numbers, I agree that in this sense every simple being and even every composite being acts uniformly. But if uniformly means similarly, I do not agree. To explain the difference this meaning makes by means of an example, a movement in a parabolic path is uniform in the former sense but not in the latter, for the parts of the parabolic curve are not similar to each other as are the parts of a straight line.

(G VII, 328–29 [1710].) If in that which is organic there is nothing but mechanism, that is, bare matter, having differences of place, magnitude and figure; nothing can be deduced and explained from it, except mechanism, that is, except such differences as I have just mentioned. For from anything taken by itself nothing can be deduced and explained, except differences of the attributes which constitute it. Hence we may readily conclude that in no mill or clock as such is there to be found any principle which perceives what takes place in it; and it matters not whether the things contained in the "machine" are solid or fluid or made up of both. Further we know that there is no essential difference between coarse and fine bodies, but only a difference of magnitude. Whence it follows that, if it is inconceivable how perception arises in any coarse "machine," whether it be made up of fluids or solids, it is equally inconceivable how perception can arise from a finer "machine"; for if our senses were finer, it would be the same as if we were perceiving a coarse "machine," as we do at present.

COMMENTARY

Aristotle, and St. Thomas Aquinas after him, opposed the atomists' idea that sense perception rests on physical transmission. They looked to an exchange on the side of *form* ("sensible species") rather than *matter* to explain cognition. (Compare sending signals by throwing pebbles as opposed to sending waves across a medium that largely remains in place.) But from antiquity to the seventeenth century, species transmission theorists never managed to get a firm grip on the mechanism of the transmission process. Leibniz (like Berkeley) cut the Gordian knot by doing away with transmission in favor of coordination.

Leibniz's clever windmill example is designed to show that perception cannot be understood on mechanical principles. For Leibniz the physical and the psychological realms are absolutely separate. No Cartesian interaction between the two is possible, since they are merely different aspects of the same thing (as in Spinoza). Perception is not a physical process and is not, consequently, explicable in terms of efficient causality. Its proper understanding and explanation must proceed in the order of final causality, as is the case with mental processes in general. But the perfect harmony between the mental order and the physical order within nature means that the perceptual and the physical/mechanical orders will wholly accord with one another. In view of this, the fact that perception is all that is to be found within single substances means that the whole of the operations of the substantial realm is ultimately dictated by considerations of final causality.

KEY WORDS:

perception/*perception*
mechanical principles/*raisons mécaniques*
machine/*machine*
motions/*mouvements*
internal action/*action interne*
simple substance/*substance simple*
composite/*composé*

SECTION 18

18. One could give the name *entelechies* to all simple substances or created monads. For they all have in them a certain perfection (*echousi to enteles*); there is a certain self-sufficiency (*autarkeia*) that makes them sources of their own internal actions and, so to speak, incorporeal automata. (See *Theodicy*, sec. 87.)

*18. On pourroit donner le nom d'Entelechies à toutes les substances simples, ou Monades creées, car elles ont en elles une certaine perfection (echousi to enteles), il y a une suffisance (autarkeia) qui les rend sources de leurs actions internes et pour ainsi dire, des Automates incorporels. (*Théodicée, sec. 87.)

(*Theodicy*, sec. 87.) <There is a long-standing> philosophic dispute on *the origin of forms.* Aristotle and scholastic philosophy after him called *Form* that which is a principle of action and is found in that which acts. This inward principle is either substantial, being then termed "Soul," when it is in an organic body, or accidental, and customarily termed "Quality." The same philosopher gave to the soul the generic name of "Entelechy" or *Act.* This word "Entelechy" obviously takes its origin from the Greek word signifying "perfect," and hence the celebrated Hermolaus Barbarus expressed it literally in Latin by *perfectihabia:* for Act is a realization of potency . . . Aristotle supposes that there are two kinds of Act, the permanent act and the successive act. The permanent or lasting act is nothing but the Substantial or Accidental Form: the substantial form (as for example the soul) is altogether permanent, at least according to my judgment, and the accidental is only so for a time. But the altogether momentary act, whose nature is transitory, consists in action itself. I have shown elsewhere that the notion of Entelechy is not altogether to be scorned, and that, being permanent, it carries with it not only a mere faculty for action, but also that which is called "force," "effort," "conatus," from which action itself must follow if nothing prevents it. Faculty is only an *attribute,* or rather sometimes a mode; but force, when it is not an ingredient of substance itself (that is, force which is not primitive but derivative), is a *quality,* which is distinct and separable from substance. I have shown also how one may suppose that the soul is a primitive force which is modified and varied by derivative forces or qualities, and exercised in actions.

(PNG, sec. 3.) Each simple substance or individual monad . . . forms the center of a compound substance (such as an animal, for example), and is the principle of its uniqueness, being surrounded by a mass composed of an infinity of other monads which constitute the body belonging to this central monad, corresponding to the affections by which it represents, as in a kind of center, the things which are outside of it. This body is *organic* when it forms a kind of automaton or natural machine, which is a machine not only as a whole but also in its smallest observable parts.

(PNG, sec. 14.) The perceptions or expressions of external things reach the soul at the proper time by virtue of its own laws, as in a world apart, and as if there existed nothing but God and itself (to make use of the expression of a person of exalted mind and renowned piety). So there will be a perfect accord between all these substances which produces the same effect that would be noticed if they all communicated with each other by a transmission of species or of qualities, as the common run of philosophers imagine.

(DM, sec. 30.) God foresees from all time that there will be a certain Judas, and in the concept or idea of him which God has, is contained this future free act. The only question, therefore, which remains is why this certain Judas, the betrayer who is possible only because of the idea of God, actually exists. To this question, however, we can expect no answer here on earth excepting to say in general that it is because God has found it good that he should exist notwithstanding that sin which he foresaw. This evil will be more than overbalanced. God will derive a greater good from it, and it will finally turn out that this series of events in which is included the existence of this sinner, is the most perfect among all the possible series of events.

(NS, sec. 3.) At first, after freeing myself from bondage to Aristotle, I accepted the void and the atoms, for it is these that best satisfy the imagination. But in turning back to them after much thought, I perceived that it is impossible to find *the principles of a true unity* in matter alone or in what is merely passive, since everything in it is but a collection or aggregation of parts to infinity. Now a multitude can derive its reality only from the *true unities*, which have some other origin and are entirely different from points, for it is certain that the continuum cannot be compounded of points. To find these *real unities*, therefore, I was forced to have recourse to a formal atom, since a material being cannot be at the same time material and perfectly indivisible, or endowed with true unity. It was thus necessary to restore and as it were, to rehabilitate the *substantial forms* which are in such disrepute today, but in a way which makes them intelligible and separates their proper use from their previous abuse. I found then that their nature consists of force and that there follows from this something analogous to sense and appetite, so that we must think of them in terms similar to the concept which we have of *souls*. But just as the soul ought not to be used to explain the details of the economy of the animal's body, so I concluded that one ought not to use these forms to explain the particular problems of nature, though they are necessary to establish its true general principles. Aristotle calls them *first entelechies*. I call them, more intelligibly perhaps, *primitive forces*, which contain not only the *actuality* or the *completion* of possibility but an original *activity* as well.

(NS, sec. 14.) God has originally created the soul, and every other real unity, in such a way that everything in it must arise from its own nature by a perfect *spontaneity* with regard to itself, yet by a perfect *conformity* to things without. And thus, since our internal sensations . . . are merely phenomena which follow upon external events or better, are really appearances or like well-ordered dreams, it follows that these perceptions internal to the soul itself come to it through its own original constitution, that is to say, through its representative nature, which is capable of expressing entities outside of itself in agreement with its organs—this nature having been given it from its creation and constituting its individual character. It is this that makes each substance represent the entire universe accurately in its own way and according to a definite point of view. And the perceptions or expressions of external things reach the soul at the proper time by virtue of its own laws, as in a world apart, and as if there existed nothing but God and itself (to make use of the expression of a person of exalted mind and renowned piety). So there will be a perfect accord between all these substances which produces the same effect that would be noticed if they all communicated with each other by a transmission of species or of qualities, as the common run of philosophers imagine. Furthermore, the organized mass in which the point of view of the soul is found is itself expressed more immediately by the soul and is in turn ready to act by itself following the laws of the corporeal mechanism, at the moment at which the soul wills but without either disturbing the laws of the other, the animal spirits and the blood taking on, at exactly the right moment, the motions required to correspond to the passions and the perceptions of the soul. It is this mutual agreement, regulated in advance in every substance of the universe, which produces what we call their communication and which alone constitutes the union of soul and body. This makes it clear how the soul has its seat in the body by an immediate presence which could not be closer, since the soul is in it as a unity is in the resultant of unities which is a multitude.

(G II, 54; Loemker, p. 335; to Arnauld [1686].) I said that the presupposition from which all human events could be deduced, was not that of the creation of an undetermined Adam but of the creation of a certain Adam determined in all circumstances, selected out of an infinity of possible Adams. In regard to this you [Arnauld] make two important remarks, the one against the plurality of Adams and the other against the reality of substances which are merely possible. In regard to the first point, you say with good reason that it is as little possible to think of several possible Adams, taking Adam for a particular nature, as to conceive of several me's. I agree, but in speaking of several Adams I do not take Adam for a determined individual but for a certain person conceived *sub ratione generalitatis* under the circumstances which appear to us to determine Adam as an individual but which do not actually determine him sufficiently. As if we should mean by Adam the first man, whom God set in a garden of pleasure whence he went out because of sin, and from whose side God fashioned a woman. All this would not sufficiently determine him and there might have been several Adams separately possible or several individuals to whom all that would apply. This is true, whatever finite number of predicates incapable of determining all the rest might be taken, but that which determines a certain Adam ought to involve absolutely all his predicates. And it is this complete concept which determines the particular individual.

(G IV, 522; Loemker, p. 495 [1698].) I have compared the soul to a clock only as regards the regulated precision of its changes, which is but imperfect even in the best of clocks, but which is perfect in the works of God. And one can say that the soul is a most exact immaterial automaton. When it is said that a simple being will always act uniformly, a distinction needs to be made. If to act uniformly is to follow perpetually the same law of order or of succession, as in a certain scale or series of numbers, I agree that in this sense every simple being and even every composite being acts uniformly. But if uniformly means similarly, I do not agree. . . . The soul, though it is perfectly simple, has always a feeling composed of several perceptions at once; and this is as much to our purpose as if it were composed of pieces, like a machine. For each preceding perception influences those which follow, according to a law which there is in perceptions as in motions.

COMMENTARY

The term *entelechy* is taken from Aristotle, who, as Leibniz understands him, uses it to designate the soul as principle of activity (*energeia*, process) toward the immensely fuller and more perfect realization of a being's self-incorporated teleological end-state (*telos*). Leibniz uses *entelechy* to characterize the basic substance (monad) as an existing agent that functions appetitively to bring its own full nature to realization. He generally confines *monad* to the existing substances of this actual world (though other possible worlds will also comprise other possible substances, albeit in idea only). As Leibniz sees it, the term *entelechy* is ideally suited for possible substances because they all internalize their own developmental principles in their appetitive "programs," these internal principles of change in accordance with their complete individual concepts.

Since matter is divisible *in infinitum*, every substance, however lowly, is dominant over an entourage of others. Each, accordingly, has a coordinated "body" of sorts for which it is the dominant "soul," an entelechy with a function or telos of its own. All of nature is thus organic. Even those objects we deem inorganic, such as rocks, have cells in their crystalline substructure which renders them organic on the level of very small constitutive components. All of these "organic" substances embody principles of operation that exfoliate their development over time even as an acorn is pre-ordained to develop "automatically" into an oak tree. The individual monads themselves, which constitute bodies, are "incorporeal automata" striving to bring their own particular nature to increasingly fuller actualization. (On monads as automata compare sec. 64 below.) Unlike the *autarkeia* of the Stoics and Epicurus, which leads to stability or rest (*ataraxia*), the *suffisance* of Leibniz is the dispositional basis for its appetition, the unfolding of a characteristic mode of activity.

Leibniz standardly contrasts the inner action of his organic automata (monads) with the mechanical action under external prime movers represented by physical machinery, which must be understood on mechanical principles of efficient causality rather than organic principles of final (teleological) causality.

KEY WORDS:

simple substance/*substance simple*
created monads/*monades créées*
entelechy/*entéléchie*

perfection/*perfection*
self-sufficiency/*suffisance*
internal action/*action interne*
incorporeal automata/*automates incorporels*

SECTION 19

19. If we are willing to call *soul* anything that has *perceptions* and *appetites* in the general sense I have just explained, then all simple substances or created monads could be called souls. But as sentience is something more than a mere perception, I hold that the generic name of *monads* or *entelechies* suffices for simple substances which have nothing but this <viz. mere perception>, and that one should call *souls* only those whose perception is more distinct and accompanied by memory.

19. Si nous voulons appeler Ame tout ce qui a perceptions et appetis dans le sens general que je viens d'expliquer, toutes les substances simples ou Monades créées pourroient être appelées Ames; mais comme le sentiment est quelque chose de plus qu'une simple perception, je consens que le nom general de Monades et d'Entelechies suffise aux substances simples qui n'auront que cela; et qu'on appelle Ames seulement celles dont la perception est plus distincte et accompagnée de memoire.

(PNG, sec. 4.) Together with a particular body, each monad makes a living substance.... But when the monad has organs so adjusted that by means of them the impressions which are received, and consequently also the perceptions which represent these impressions, are heightened and distinguished (as, for example, when rays of light are concentrated by means of the shape of the humors of the eye and act with greater force), then this may amount to *sentiment*, that is to say, to a perception accompanied by *memory*—a perception of which there remains a kind of echo for a long time, which makes itself heard on occasion. Such a living being is called an *animal*, as its monad is called a *soul*.

(NE, p. 54.) We become so accustomed to the motion of a mill or a waterfall, after living beside it for a while, that we pay no heed to it. Not that this motion ceases to strike on our sense-organs, or that something corresponding to it does not still occur in the soul because of the harmony between the soul and the body; but these impressions in the soul and the body, lacking the appeal of novelty, are not forceful enough to attract our attention and our memory, which are applied only to more compelling objects. Memory is needed for attention: when we are not alerted, so to speak, to pay heed to certain of our own present perceptions, we allow them to slip by unconsidered and even unnoticed. But if someone alerts us to them straight away, and makes us take note, for instance, of some noise which we have just heard, then we remember it and are aware of just having had some sense of it.

(DM, sec. 34.) The immortality which is required in morals and in religion does not consist merely in this perpetual existence, which pertains to all substances, for if in addition there were no remembrance of what one had been, immortality would not be at all desirable. Suppose that some individual could suddenly become King of China on condition, however, of forgetting what he had been, as though being born again, would it not amount to the same practically, or as far as the effects could be perceived, as if the individual were annihilated, and a king of China were the same instant created in his place? The individual would have no reason to desire this.

(G II, 372; Loemker, p. 599; to des Bosses [1709].) Many years ago, when my philosophy was still too immature, I located souls in points and thus thought that the multiplication of souls could be explained through traduction, since many points can be made out of a single point, as the vertices of many triangles can be made through division from the vertex of one. But having grown more circumspect, I grasped that we were not only led into innumerable difficulties in this way but also that this contains a certain confusion of classes, so to speak. Properties pertaining to extension are not to be assigned to souls, and their unity and multitude are not to be derived from this category of quantity but from the category of substance, that is, not from points but from the primitive force of action. But the action proper to the soul is perception, and the nexus of perceptions, according to which subsequent ones are derived from preceding ones, makes up the unity of the percipient.

(G VII, 529; to R. C. Wagner [1710].) You next ask my definition of *soul*. I reply, that *soul* may be employed in a broad and in a strict sense. Broadly speaking, *soul* will be the same as life or vital principle, to wit, the principle of internal action existing in the simple thing or monad, to which external action corresponds. And this correspondence of internal and external, or representation of the external in the internal, of the composite in the simple, of multiplicity in unity, really constitutes perception. But in this sense soul is attributed not only to animals, but also to all other percipient beings. In the strict sense, *soul* is employed as a nobler species of life, or sentient life, where there is not only the faculty of perceiving, but in addition that of feeling, inasmuch, indeed, as attention and memory are added to perception.

COMMENTARY

Perception is *conscious* when it is "distinct and accompanied by memory." Accordingly, Leibniz sees memory as the correlate of *conscious* perception: perception with sufficient clarity and distinctness ("force and vivacity") to be both *noted and remembered*. (Compare secs. 24–25.) Leibniz designates such conscious perception as *sentience* (*sentiment*).

Leibniz envisions a three-level hierarchy of substances:

1. *simple or bare monads* (or entelechies), which have unconscious perception and lack memory and awareness;
2. *souls*, which are monads that also have consciousness (sentience as reflected in distinct perception and memory);
3. *minds or spirits*, which are souls capable also of self-consciousness (apperception) and of reason. (These are not discussed until later, in secs. 29–30.)

The substances of each successive level add certain capacities and capabilities to those of the preceding one (perception, apperception, self-awareness). But the differences are differences in degree and not in kind. Here too Leibniz sees nature as a continuum, in line with his Principle of Continuity.

The strongly hierarchical nature of Leibniz monadological system unquestionably reflects that of his social environment.

KEY WORDS:

monads/*monades*
simple substance/*substance simple*
entelechy/*entéléchie*
soul/*âme*
sentience/*sentiment*
perception/*perception*
appetite/*appétit*
distinct perception/*perception distincte*
memory/*mémoire*

SECTION 20

20. For we experience in ourselves a state where we remember nothing and have no distinct perception, as when we fall into a swoon or when we are overcome by a deep and altogether dreamless sleep. In this state <of total unconsciousness> the soul does not differ noticeably from a simple monad. But as this state is not at all durable, and the soul emerges from it, the soul is something more <than a simple monad>. (See *Theodicy*, sec. 64.)

*20. Car nous experimentons en nous mêmes un Etat, où nous ne nous souvenons de rien et n'avons aucune perception distinguée; comme lorsque nous tombons en defaillance, ou quand nous sommes accablés d'un profond sommeil sans aucun songe. Dans cet état l'ame ne diffère point sensiblement d'une simple Monade; mais comme cet état n'est point durable, et qu'elle s'en tire, elle est quelque chose de plus. (*Théodicée, sec. 64.)*

(*Theodicy*, sec. 64.) For there is in the soul not only an order of distinct perception, forming its dominion, but also a series of confused perceptions and passions, forming its knowledge; and there is no need for astonishment at that; the soul would be a Divinity if it had none but clear perceptions.

(PNG, sec. 4.) It is true that animals are sometimes in the condition of simple living beings, and their souls in the condition of simple monads, namely, when their perceptions are not distinct enough so that they can be remembered. This happens in a deep sleep without dreams or in a swoon.

(NE, p. 162.) We always have an infinity of minute perceptions without being aware of them. We are never without perceptions, but necessarily we are often without *awareness*, namely when none of our perceptions stand out.

COMMENTARY

Monads are always active: they always have perceptions of some sort and are ever in process of an appetitive movement from old to new. We ourselves (i.e., our minds) are monads of the highest order (namely spirits), and accordingly have cognitive access to the order of substance in our own experience. Often, however, even monads of the higher order function at lower levels, so that even a rational being's unifying spirit (our own individual "dominant monads") sometimes functions at the level of a mere soul and sometimes perhaps even at that of a simple, lowest-grade monad. Nevertheless, our own unifying monad is one of the highest order (a spirit) because (1) it always has the potential of functioning at that level, and (2) it does actually do so on certain occasions.

KEY WORDS:

to experience/*expérimenter*
distinct perception/*perception distinguée*
sleep/*sommeil*
souls/*âmes*
state/*état*
simple monads/*monades simples*

SECTION 21

21. But it by no means follows from this that a simple substance is now wholly without perception. This is even impossible for the aforementioned reasons. <See Secs. 8–14.> For a substance cannot perish, nor can it subsist without some affection, which is nothing other than its perception. But when there is a large multiplicity of minute perceptions where there is nothing distinct, one is stupefied, as when we turn continually in the same direction several times in succession, whence arises a dizziness which can make us faint and which lets us distinguish nothing. Death can give this state for a time to animals.

21. *Et il ne s'ensuit point qu'alors la substance simple soit sans aucune perception. Cela ne se peut pas même, par les raisons susdites; car elle ne sçauroit périr, elle ne sçauroit aussi subsister sans quelque affection,* qui n'est autre chose que sa perception: mais quand il y a une grande multitude de petites perceptions, où il n'y a rien de distingué, on est étourdi; comme quand on tourne continuellement d'un même sens plusieurs fois de suite, où il vient un vertige qui peut nous faire evanouir et qui ne nous laisse rien distinguer. Et la mort peut donner cet état pour un temps aux animaux.*
<*Leibniz originally wrote* variation *here. Compare sec. 13.*>

(*Theodicy*, sec. 403.) Every simple substance embraces the whole universe in its confused perceptions or sensations, and the succession of these perceptions is regulated by the particular nature of this substance, but in a manner which always expresses all the nature in the universe; and every present perception leads to a new perception, just as every movement that it represents leads to another movement. But it is impossible that the soul can know clearly its whole nature, and perceive how this innumerable number of minute perceptions, piled up or rather concentrated together, shapes itself there: to that end it would need to know completely the whole universe which is embraced by them, that is, it must be a God.

(NE, pp. 54–55.) To give a clearer idea of these minute perceptions which we are unable to pick out from a crowd, I like to use the example of the roaring noise of the sea which impresses itself on us when we are standing on the shore. To hear this noise as we do, we must hear the parts which make up this whole, that is the noise of each wave, although each of these little noises makes itself known only when combined confusedly with all the others, and would not be noticed if the wave which made it were by itself. We must be affected slightly by the motion of this wave, and have some perception of each of these noises, however faint they may be; otherwise there would be no perception of a hundred thousand waves, since a hundred thousand nothings cannot make something. Moreover, we never sleep so soundly that we do not have some feeble and confused sensation; and the loudest noise in the world would never waken us if we did not have some perception of its start, which is small, just as the strongest force in the world would never break a rope unless the least force strained it and stretched it slightly, even though that little lengthening which is produced is imperceptible. . . . These insensible perceptions also indicate and constitute the same individual, who is characterized by the vestiges or expressions which the perceptions preserve from the individual's former states. . . . It is also through insensible perceptions that I account for that marvellous pre-established harmony between the soul and the body, and indeed amongst all the monads.

(NE, p. 113) Something remains of all our past thoughts, none of which can ever be entirely wiped out. When we are in dreamless sleep, or when we are dazed by some blow or a fall or a symptom of an illness or other mishap, an infinity of small, confused sensations occur in us. Death itself cannot affect the souls of animals in any way but that; they must certainly regain their distinct perceptions sooner or later, for in nature everything is orderly.

(PNG, sec. 4.) It is true that animals are sometimes in the condition of simple living beings, and their souls in the condition of simple monads, namely, when their perceptions are not distinct enough so that they can be remembered. This happens in a deep sleep without dreams or in a swoon. But perceptions which have become completely confused must be developed again in animals, for reasons which I shall give below in Section 12. So it is well to make a distinction between *perception*, which is the inner state of the monad representing external things, and *apperception*, which is consciousness or the reflective knowledge of this inner state itself and which is not given to all souls or to any soul all the time.

(PNG, sec. 13.) One could learn the beauty of the universe in each soul if one could unravel all that is rolled up in it but that develops perceptibly only with time. But since each distinct perception of the soul includes an infinity of confused perceptions which envelop the entire universe, the soul itself does not know the things which it perceives until it has perceptions which are distinct and heightened.

COMMENTARY

Leibnizian "perceptions" need not be conscious or noticed in any way, and are accordingly something of a range far broader than *sensation*. For, as he sees it, our experience is replete with "minute" perceptions that are too small, as it were, to rise above the threshold of conscious awareness. Multiplied, however, they can produce something distinct. Such minute, subliminal perceptions figure for us humans not only in relation to unconsciousness and death, but also in "peripheral" perception (peripheral vision) and in "aggregate" perception (as when the individual waves contribute to the pounding of the surf that we hear from a distance). The perceptions of each and every monad reach out to embrace the entire universe. (See sec. 62.)

Note that for monads we have a thoroughgoing, one-on-one coordination between "qualities" and "affections" and "perceptions," all of which are simply different aspects of the same condition of things. The qualities of monads all reflect or represent the various ways in which it perceives its world and is affected by the diverse substances that compose it.

The idea of a large multiplicity of individually unnoticeable perceptions producing a noticeable result goes back to the "heap" argumentation (*sorites* from *sôros*), introduced in antiquity by the Stoics (see Cicero, *Academica*, II, 29 and 49) and extensively criticized by Sextus Empiricus. The main forms of the argumentation are: (1) if one grain of sand is not a heap, and a non-heap cannot be turned into a heap by adding but a single further grain, then how can a heap ever be produced? and (2) if the loss of a single hairy person does not make the hairy man bald, and the loss of a single further hair cannot render bald someone who is not, then how can a person ever be bald?

KEY WORDS:

perception/*perception*
simple substance/*substance simple*
to perish/*périr*
affection (i.e., property)/*affection*
minute perception/*petites perceptions*
multiplicity/*multitude*
distinct/*distingué*
unconsciousness/*étourdissement*
death/*la mort*
dizziness/*vertige*
state/*état*
animals/*animaux*

SECTION 22

22. And as every present state of a simple substance is a natural consequence of its preceding state, so is its present pregnant with the future. (See *Theodicy*, sec. 360.)

22. *Et comme tout present état d'une substance simple est naturellement une suite de son état precedent, tellement le present y est gros de l'avenir.* (Théodicée, *sec. 360.*)

(*Theodicy*, sec. 360.) It is one of the rules of my system of general harmony, that the present is big with the future, and that he who sees all sees in that which is that which shall be. What is more, I have proved conclusively that God sees in each portion of the universe the whole universe, owing to the perfect connection of things. He is infinitely more discerning than Pythagoras, who judged the height of Hercules by the size of his footprint. There must therefore be no doubt that effects follow their causes determinately, in spite of contingency and even of freedom, which nevertheless coexist with certainty or determination.

(PNG, sec. 13.) For everything has been regulated in things, once for all, with as much order and agreement as possible; the supreme wisdom and goodness cannot act except with perfect harmony. The present is big with the future; the future could be read in the past; the distant is expressed in the near.

(DM, sec. 13.) The concept of an individual substance includes once for all everything which can ever happen to it and . . . in considering this concept one will be able to see everything which can truly be said concerning the individual, just as we are able to see in the nature of a circle all the properties which can be derived from it.

(DM, sec. 14.) Nothing can happen to us but thoughts and perceptions, and all our future thoughts and perceptions are only consequences, though contingent ones, of our previous thoughts and perceptions, so much so that if I were capable of considering distinctly all that happens or appears to me at the present time, I could see in it all that will happen or appear to me for ever; which would not fail, and would happen to me just the same, if all that is outside of me were destroyed, provided only that God and I remained.

(G I, 382–83; to Foucher [1686].) I believe that every individual substance expresses the whole universe in its own way, and that its following state is a consequence (though often a free one) of its preceding state, as if there were nothing but God and it in the world; but as all substances are a continual production of the sovereign Being, and express the same universe or the same phenomena, they agree exactly with each other.

(G II, 136; Loemker, p. 360; to Arnauld [1690].) Each of these substances contains in its nature the law of the continuing series of its own operations and of all that has happened and will happen to it. All its actions come from its own nature, except for its dependence upon God.

(G IV, 557; Loemker, p. 576, "Reply to Bayle" [1702].) For everything is so controlled and bound together that these infallible machines of nature, which are comparable to ships that would arrive at port by themselves in spite of all obstacles and storms, ought not to be considered any stranger than a rocket which glides along a string or a liquid which runs through a tube. Furthermore, since bodies are not atoms but are divisible, and are indeed divided to infinity, and everything is full of them, it follows that the very smallest body receives some impression from the slightest change in all the others, however distant and small they may be, and must thus be an exact mirror of the universe. The result is that a sufficiently penetrating spirit could, in the measure of his penetration, see and foresee in each corpuscle everything which has happened and will happen everywhere both within and outside of the corpuscle. So nothing happens to it, not even by the impact of surrounding bodies, which does not follow from what is already internal to it and which can disturb its order.

COMMENTARY

The thesis that "the present is pregnant with the future" (*le présent es gros de l'avenir*) is a pet phrase of Leibniz. The entire history of each substance is internally programmed in its natural make-up, so that each state unfolds from its antecedents in a fixed, inexorable succession (like a computing machine grinding through its "program"). The actions and activities of each substance accordingly produce their successors with an inexorable inevitability that inheres in the very constitution of the substance at issue, so that the present state somehow embodies with (relative or conditional) necessity the future that is to evolve. Since all monadic change results from the programmed exfoliation of an "internal principle," the entire history of each substance is fully pre-determined, wholly contained in its complete individual concept.

KEY WORDS:

state/*état*
simple substance/*substance simple*
a natural consequence/*une suite naturelle*
the present/*le présent*
pregnant with the future/*gros de l'avenir*

SECTION 23

23. Therefore, since when reawakened from unconsciousness one *apperceives* <that is, becomes reflexively aware of> one's perceptions, it must be that one had some of them immediately before, although one was not at all aware of them. For a perception can come naturally only from another perception, just as one motion can come naturally only from another motion. (See *Theodicy*, secs. 401, 403.)

23. Donc puisque reveillé de l'étourdissement on s'apperçoit de ses perceptions, il faut bien qu'on en ait eu immediatement auparavant, quoiqu'on ne s'en soit point apperçû; car une perception ne sçauroit venir naturellement que d'une autre perception, comme un mouvement ne peut venir naturellement que d'un mouvement. (Théodicée, secs. 401, 403.)

(*Theodicy*, sec. 401.) We have the experience every day that the ideas we would fain recall do not come, and that they appear of themselves when we are no longer thinking of them. If that does not prevent us from thinking that we are their efficient cause, what reliance shall one place on the proof of feeling, which to M. Jacquelot appears so conclusive? Does our authority over our ideas more often fall short than our authority over our volitions? If we were to count up carefully, we should find in the course of our life more velleities than volitions, that is more evidences of the servitude of our will than of its dominion. How many times does one and the same man not experience an inability to do a certain act of will (for example, an act of love for a man who had just injured him; an act of scorn for a fine sonnet that he had composed; an act of hatred for a mistress; an act of approval of an absurd epigram.)

(*Theodicy*, sec. 403.) What necessity is there for one always to be aware how that which is done is done? Are salts, metals, plants, animals and a thousand other animate or inanimate bodies aware how that which they do is done, and need they be aware? Must a drop of oil or of fat understand geometry in order to become round on the surface of water? Sewing stitches is another matter: one acts for an end, one must be aware of the means. But we do not form our ideas because we will to do so, they form themselves within us, they form themselves through us, not in consequence of our will, but in accordance with our nature and that of things. The foetus forms itself in the animal, and a thousand other wonders of nature are produced by a certain *instinct* that God has placed there, that is by virtue of *divine preformation*, which has made these admirable automata, adapted to produce mechanically such beautiful effects. Even so it is easy to believe that the soul is a spiritual automaton still more admirable, and that it is through divine preformation that it produces these beautiful ideas, wherein our will has no part and to which our art cannot attain. The operation of spiritual automata, that is of souls, is not mechanical, but it contains in the highest degree all that is beautiful in mechanism. The movements which are developed in bodies are concentrated in the soul by representation as in an ideal world, which expresses the laws of the actual world and their consequences, but with this difference from the perfect ideal world which is in God, that most of the perceptions in the other substances are only confused. For it is plain that every simple substance embraces the whole universe in its confused perceptions or sensations, and that the succession of these perceptions is regulated by the particular nature of this substance, but in a manner which always expresses all the nature in the universe; and every present perception leads to a new perception, just as every movement that it represents leads to another movement. But it is impossible that the soul can know clearly its whole nature, and perceive how this innumerable number of minute perceptions, piled up or rather concentrated together, shapes itself there. . . .

(PNG, sec. 4.) So it is well to make a distinction between *perception*, which is the inner state of the monad representing external things, and *apperception*, which is consciousness or the reflective knowledge of this inner state itself and which is not given to all souls or to any soul all the time. It is for lack of this distinction that the Cartesians have made the mistake of disregarding perceptions which are not themselves perceived, just as people commonly disregard imperceptible bodies. It is this too which has made these same Cartesians think that only spirits are monads and that there is no soul in beasts, still less other *principles of life*. And after having defied the everyday opinion of men too much in denying that beasts have feeling, they adjusted their views too far to popular prejudices, on the other hand, when they confused a *long stupor* coming from a great confusion of perceptions with *death* in the rigorous sense, in which all perception would cease.

(NE, pp. 56–57.) Insensible perceptions are as important to pneumatology as insensible corpuscles are to natural science, and it is as just to reject the one as the other on the pretext that they are beyond the reach of our senses. Nothing takes place suddenly, and it is one of my great and best confirmed maxims that *nature never makes leaps*. I called this the Law of Continuity when I discussed it formerly in the *Nouvelles de la république des lettres* ("Letter on a general principle useful in explaining the laws of nature"). There is much work for this law to do in natural science. It implies that any change from small to large, or vice versa, passes through something which is, in respect of degrees as well as of parts, in between; and that no motion ever springs immediately from a state of rest, or passes into one except through a lesser motion; just as one could never traverse a certain line or distance without first traversing a shorter one. Despite which, until now those who have propounded the laws of motion have not complied with this law, since they have believed that a body can instantaneously receive a motion contrary to its preceding one. All of which supports the judgment that noticeable perceptions arise by degrees from ones which are too minute to be noticed.

(G IV, 561–62; Loemker, pp. 578–79; "Reply to Bayle" [1702].) The state of the soul, like that of the atom, is a state of change, a tendency. The atom tends to change its place, the soul to change its thoughts; each changes by itself in the simplest and most uniform way which its state permits. Then how does it come, I will be asked, that there is such simplicity in the change of the atom, and such variety in the changes of the soul? It is because the atom (as it is assumed to be, although there is no such thing in nature), though it has parts, has nothing which causes some variety in its tendency, because we assume that its parts do not change their relations. The soul, on the other hand, though entirely indivisible, involves a composite tendency, that is to say, a multitude of present thoughts, each of which tends to a particular change according to what it involves and what is found in it at the time by virtue of its essential relationship to all the other things in the world. Among other things, it is also their lack of this relationship which bans the atoms of Epicurus from nature. For each thing or part of the universe must point to all the rest, in such a way that the soul, as concerns the variety of its modifications, must be compared, not with a material atom, but with the universe which it represents according to its point of view—and in some ways even with God himself, whose infinity it represents finitely because of its confused and imperfect perception of the infinite. . . . And the reason for the change of thoughts in the soul is the same as that of the change of things in the universe which it represents. The mechanical reasons which are developed in the bodies are united and concentrated, so to speak, in the souls or entelechies; indeed, they have their source there. It is true that not all the entelechies are, like our soul, images of God, for they are not all made to be members of a society or of a state of which he is the head. But they are always images of the universe. They are after their manner worlds in abridged form, fruitful simplicities, substantial unities, but virtually infinite by the multitude of their modifications, centers which express an infinite circumference.

(Loemker, p. 114; "A Fragment on Dreams" [ca. 1670].) To wake up is nothing but to recollect one's self, to begin to connect to your present state with the rest of your life or with you yourself. Hence we have this criterion for distinguishing the experience of dreaming from that of being awake—we are certain of being awake only when we remember why we have come to our present position and condition and see the fitting connection of the things which are appearing to us, to each other, and to those that preceded. In dreams we do not grasp this connection when it is present nor are surprised when it is absent.

COMMENTARY

The particular sort of "heightened" presentation that is accompanied by reflexive self-awareness—consciousness of oneself as such—is Leibnizian *apperception*. This is something episodic and intermittent. Only on the basis of unconscious perceptions can the continuity of our mental life be assured. Otherwise our sensations and perceptions could come ex nihilo. As Leibniz sees it, those unconscious, "minute" perceptions are indispensable to a coherent account of our experience. Since the basis or occasion for a perception can only be another perception, the basis or occasion for our conscious perceptions must be unnoticed, unconscious perceptions.

Leibniz's reasoning here is predicated on his Principle of Continuity for natural processes. (See sec. 10.) As he sees it, each state of a monad is implicitly contained in every earlier state via an implicit developmental "law of the series" that provides for the continuous unfolding of all its features. Our conscious and our unconscious mental life, our dreaming and our waking, are accordingly continuous experiences rather than altogether separate.

KEY WORDS:

unconsciousness/*étourdissement*
perception/*perception*
awareness/*apperception*
naturally/*naturellement*
movement/*mouvement*

SECTION 24

24. One sees from this that if we had in our perceptions nothing distinct and, so to speak, heightened and of an enhanced flavor, we should always remain in unconsciousness. And this is the state of the [simples] totally bare monads.

24. L'on voit par là que, si nous n'avions rien de distingué et pour ainsi dire de relevé, et d'un plus haut goût dans nos perceptions, nous serions toujours dans l'étourdissment. Et c'est l'état des [simples] Monades toutes nues.

(PNG, sec 4.) But when the monad has organs so adjusted that by means of them the impressions which are received, and consequently also the perceptions which represent these impressions, are heightened and distinguished (as, for example, when rays of light are concentrated by means of the shape of the humors of the eye and act with greater force), then this may amount to *sentience* that is to say, to a perception accompanied by memory—a perception of which there remains a kind of echo for a long time, which makes itself heard on occasion.

(NE, pp. 117–18.) Anything which is noticeable must be made up of parts which are not. . . . It is impossible that we should always reflect explicitly on all our thoughts; for if we did, the mind would reflect on each reflection, *ad infinitum*, without ever being able to move on to a new thought.

COMMENTARY

Consciousness, for Leibniz, consists in the *distinctness* or, as it were, the Humean *vivacity* of certain of the perceptions of higher-order monads. Thus a conscious perception differs from an unconscious one not so much in its *content* as in its *force*; what is at issue is a difference in degree rather than in kind. Note the tripartite hierarchy of:

1. perception
2. sentience (= conscious [distinct] perception + memory)
3. apperception (= reflexive [self-conscious] perception + reason)

At each level something new emerges: with sentience comes distinctness of perception, and apperception adds self-consciousness.

It is somewhat puzzling why Leibniz here speaks of "entirely bare monads" (*monades toutes nues*). As the revision shows, he of course means monads of the lowest grade, mere simple substances or entelechies as contrasted with the higher-grade souls and spirits. But even the lowest-grade monads that are part of inanimate nature—say of a rock or a bit of metal—are always members of an organized structure and are never wholly "bare" and lacking a body of some sort. (See sec. 62.) Leibniz would thus have done better to speak here of a *simple* monad, as in section 20.

KEY WORDS:

distinct perception/*perception distingué*
unconsciousness/*étourdissement*
bare monads/*monades nues*
state/*état*

SECTION 25

25. We see too that nature has given heightened perceptions to animals by the care she has taken to furnish them with organs which collect many rays of light or many vibrations of air to make them more effective through their unification. There is something similar in smell, taste, and touch, and perhaps in many other senses that are unknown to us. And I shall explain presently <in secs. 61–62> how what happens in the soul represents what happens in the organs.

25. Aussi, voyons nous que la Nature a donné des perceptions relevées aux animaux, par les soins qu'elle a pris de leur fournir des organes qui ramassent plusieurs rayons de lumière ou plusieurs ondulations de l'air pour les faire avoir plus d'efficace par leur union. Il y a quelque chose d'approchant dans l'odeur, dans le goût et dans l'attouchement, et peut-être dans quantité d'autres sens, qui nous sont inconnûs. Et j'expliqueray tantôt, comment ce qui se passe dans l'Ame represente ce qui se fait dans les organes.

(PNG, sec. 4.) When the monad has organs so adjusted that by means of them the impressions which are received, and consequently also the perceptions which represent these impressions, are heightened and distinguished (as, for example, when rays of light are concentrated by means of the shape of the humors of the eye and act with greater force), then this may amount to *sentience*, that is to say, to a perception accompanied by *memory*—a perception of which there remains a kind of echo for a long time, which makes itself heard on occasion. Such a living being is called an *animal*, as its monad is called a *soul*. When this soul is raised to the level of *reason*, it is something more sublime and is counted among the *spirits*, as will be explained presently.

COMMENTARY

The perceptual heightening discussed in section 24 usually happens through the *combination* of minute, unconscious perceptions into a single more massive collective result. This confluence results from the mutual reinforcement of smaller separate effects when these are combined in our sense organs. Since the "heightened" perception of animals is simply a matter of the aggregation of monadic perceptions, the difference involved is merely one of degree rather than one of kind.

Leibniz's mathematics provides him with a model for his theory of perception. For he views the process of aggregating unnoticeably small units into a discernible larger whole as paralleling the way in which the integral calculus combines infinitesimals into large-scale, measurable quantities.

KEY WORDS:

heightened perception/*perception relevée*
unification/*union*
represent/*représenter*
organs/*organes*

SECTION 26

26. Memory provides a kind of *connectedness* (*consécution*) to souls which resembles reason but must be distinguished from it. For we see that animals which have a perception of something that strikes them and of which they have previously had a similar perception expect, from the representation in their memory, that which has been conjoined in that previous perception, and are thus led to sensations similar to those they have had before. For example, when one shows a stick to dogs, they recall the pain that it has caused them and whine and run off. (See *Theodicy*, Preliminary Discourse, sec. 65.)

26. La memoire fournit une espece de consecution *aux ames, qui imite la raison, mais qui en doit être distinguée. C'est que nous voyons que les animaux, ayant la perception de quelque chose qui les frappe et dont ils ont eu perception semblable auparavant, s'attendent par la representation de leur memoire à ce qui y a été joint dans cette perception precedente et sont portés à des sentimens semblables à ceux qu'ils avoient pris alors. Par exemple: quand on montre le bâton aux chiens, ils se souviennent de la douleur, qu'il leur a causé et crient et fuyent. (*Théodicée, Discours préliminaire, sec. 65.)*

(*Theodicy*, Preliminary Discourse, sec. 65.) The *external* senses, properly speaking, do not deceive us. It is our inner sense which often makes us go too fast. That occurs also in brute beasts, as when a dog barks at his reflection in the mirror: for beasts have *consecutions* of perception which resemble reasoning, and which occur also in the inner sense of men, when their actions have only an empirical quality. But beasts do nothing which compels us to believe that they have what deserves to be properly called a *reasoning* sense, as I have shown elsewhere. Now when the understanding uses and follows the false decision of the inner sense (as when the famous Galileo thought that Saturn had two handles) it is deceived by the judgement it makes upon the effect of appearances, and it infers from them more than they imply. For the appearances of the senses do not promise us absolutely the truth of things, any more than dreams do. It is we who deceive ourselves by the use we make of them, that is, by our consecutions.

(PNG, sec. 5.) There is a connection between the perceptions of animals which has some resemblance to reason, but it is grounded only on the memory of *facts* or effects and not on the knowledge of *causes*. Thus a dog runs away from the stick with which he has been beaten, because his memory represents to him the pain which the stick had caused him.

(NE, p. 52) We are not always aware of our acquired dispositions (*habitude*) or of the contents of our memory, and they do not even come to our aid whenever we need them, though often they come readily to mind when some idle circumstance reminds us of them, as when hearing the opening words of a song is enough to bring back the rest. . . . Memory is needed for attention: when we are not alerted, so to speak, to pay heed to certain of our own present perceptions, we allow them to slip by unconsidered and even unnoticed. But if someone alerts us to them straight away, and makes us take note, for instance, of some noise which we have just heard, then we remember it and are aware of just having had some sense of it. Thus, we were not straight away aware of these perceptions, and we became aware of them only because we were alerted to them after an interval, however brief. To give a clearer idea of these minute perceptions which we are unable to pick out from the crowd, I like to use the example of the roaring noise of the sea which impresses itself on us when we are standing on the shore.

(NE, p. 143.) Beasts pass from one imagining to another by means of a link between them which they have previously experienced. For instance, when his master picks up a stick the dog anticipates being beaten. In many cases children, and for that matter grown men, move from thought to thought in no other way but that. This could be called "inference" or "reasoning" in a very broad sense. But I prefer to keep the accepted usage, reserving these words for men and restricting them to the knowledge of some *reason* for perceptions' being linked together. Mere sensations cannot provide this: all they do is to cause one naturally to expect once more that same linking which has been observed previously, even though the reasons may no longer be the same. Hence those who are guided only by their senses are frequently disappointed.

(NE, p. 238.) A present or immediate memory, the memory of what was taking place immediately before—or in other words, the consciousness or reflection which accompanies inner activity—cannot naturally deceive us. If it could, we would not even be certain that we are thinking about such and such a thing; . . . if immediate inner experience is not certain, we cannot be sure of any truth of fact.

(NE, p. 239.) An immaterial being cannot "be stripped of all" perception of its past existence. It retains impressions of everything which has previously happened to it, and it even has presentiments of everything which will happen to it; but these states of mind are mostly too minute to be distinguishable and for one to be aware of them, although they may perhaps grow some day. It is this continuity and interconnection of perceptions which make someone really the same individual. . . . So it is unreasonable to suppose that memory should be lost beyond any possibility of recovery, since insensible perceptions, whose usefulness I have shown in so many other important connections, serve a purpose here too—preserving the seeds of memory.

(G IV, 300; to Molanus [ca. 1680].) The immortality of the soul, as it is established by Descartes, is of no use and can give us no kind of consolation. For, granting that the soul is a substance and that no substance perishes, the soul then will not be lost, as, indeed, nothing is lost in nature; but, like matter, the soul will change in appearance and, as the matter of which a man is made has at other times belonged to plants and animals, in the same way the soul may be immortal, indeed, but it will pass through innumerable changes and will have no recollection of its former states. But this immortality without recollection is ethically quite useless; for it is inconsistent with reward and punishment. What good, sir, would it do you to become king of China, on condition that you forget what you have been? Would it not be the same as if God, at the moment He destroyed you, were to create a king in China?

COMMENTARY

The higher animals have a "psychological" dimension. They have dominant monads of a higher grade (souls, *âmes*) which provide them with memory. This provides also for the operation of a principle of *association*, enabling such animals to display a capacity which, while akin to reason—in leading from a premise ("the stick is present") to a conclusion ("a beating impends")—is nevertheless carried on by an automatic process associative of thought-transition rather than any actual reasoning. (For this, a universal premise would be needed as a link, namely the "inductive" judgment "Whenever he takes the stick into hand, the master is about to beat me," which is unavailable to mere animals.) The rational capacity for *universalization* requires self-consciousness (rather than merely association) and thus lies outside the cognitive range of mere animals. All the same, the continuity and uniformity of their experience in an orderly world provides higher animals with something of an approximation to reason.

The compresence of "which strikes them" (*qui les frappe*) in sentence 2 with the dog-beating example of the next sentence could hardly have been unintentional. And this would make it one of the very few instances of a Leibnizian joke, one which he apparently liked well enough to carry over into section 27.

KEY WORDS:

memory/*mémoire*
connectedness/*consécution*

association/*association*
representation/*représentation*
sensations/*sentiments*
perception/*perception*
animals/*animaux*

SECTION 27

27. The potent imaging that strikes and moves them <namely, souls (*âmes*), when making associations> comes either from the size or from the number of the <kindred> preceding perceptions. For often a <single> strong impression has at one blow the effect of a long-formed *habit*, or that of a great many repeated perceptions of modest size.

27. Et l'imagination forte, qui les frappe et emeut, vient ou de la grandeur ou de la multitude des perceptions precedentes. Car souvent une impression forte fait tout d'un coup l'effect d'une longue habitude, ou de beaucoup de perceptions mediocres reiterées.

(G VI, 500; Loemker, p. 548; Ariew & Garber, p. 187; "On What is Independent of Sense and Matter" [1702].) Since therefore our soul compares the numbers and the shapes of colors, for example, with the numbers and shapes discovered by touch, there must be an *internal sense* where the perceptions of these different external senses are found united. This is called the *imagination*, which comprises at once the *concepts of particular senses*, which are *clear* but *confused*, and the *concepts of the common sense*, which are clear and distinct.

COMMENTARY

The "principle of association" is critically important in Leibniz' conception of mental phenomena, although he does not call it by that name, but views it simply as part of the natural mechanism of imagination. For Leibniz, as for Descartes and Locke, the imagination is a faculty that re-produces earlier sense-images or impressions. The vividness with which it can do this depends both on the intensity and on the frequency of those earlier impressions. As section 26 indicates, Leibniz takes imagination and association to constitute a lower-level approximation to reason and inference.

KEY WORDS:

imagination (imaging)/*imagination*
perception/*perception*
impression (of a perception)/*impression (d'une perception)*
habit/*habitude*

SECTION 28

28. Men function like beasts <i.e., lower animals> insofar as the connections among their perceptions come about only on the basis of memory, resem-

bling empirical physicians who have mere practice without theory. We are all mere empirics in three-quarters of our actions. For example, when one expects a sunrise tomorrow, one acts as an empiric, seeing that this has always been so heretofore. Only the astronomer judges this by reason. (See *Theodicy*, Preliminary Discourse, sec. 65.)

28. *Les hommes agissent comme les bêtes en tant que les consecutions de leurs perceptions ne se font que par le principe de la memoire, ressemblants aux Medecins Empiriques, qui ont une simple practique sans theorie; et nous ne sommes qu'Empiriques dans les trois quarts de nos Actions. Par exemple, quand on s'attend qu'il y aura jour demain, on agit en Empirique, parce que cela s'est tousjours fait ainsi jusqu'ici. Il n'y a que l'Astronome, qui le juge par raison.* (Théodicée, Discours préliminaire, sec. 65.)

(*Theodicy*, Preliminary Discourse, sec. 65.) Beasts have *consecutions* of perception which resemble reasoning, and which occur also in the inner sense of men, when their actions have only an empirical quality. But beasts do nothing which compels us to believe that they have what deserves to be properly called a *reasoning* sense. . . .

(PNG, sec. 5) Men too, insofar as they are empirics, that is to say, in three-fourths of their actions, act only like beasts. For example, we expect day to dawn tomorrow because we have always experienced this to be so; only the astronomer predicts it with reason, and even his prediction will ultimately fail when the cause of daylight, which is by no means eternal, stops. But *reasoning* in the *true* sense depends on necessary or eternal truths, as are those of logic, number, and geometry, which make the connection of ideas indubitable and their conclusions infallible. Animals in which such consequences cannot be observed are called beasts, but those who know these necessary truths are the ones properly called *rational animals*, and their souls are called *spirits*.

(Loemker, p. 283 [ca. 1684].) Just as there is a twofold way of reasoning from experiments, one leading to the application, the other to the cause, so there is also a twofold way of discovering causes, the one *a priori* (theoretical), the other *a posteriori* (empirical), and each of these may be either certain or conjectural. The *a priori* method is certain if we can demonstrate from the known nature of God that structure of the world which is in agreement with the divine reasons and from this structure can finally arrive at the principles of things. This method is of all the most excellent and hence does not seem to be entirely impossible. For our mind is endowed with the concept of perfection, and we know that God works in the most perfect way. I admit, however, that, though this way is not hopeless, it is certainly difficult and that not everyone should undertake it; besides, it is perhaps too long to be traversed by men. For sensible effects are too greatly compounded to be readily reduced to their first causes. Yet superior geniuses should enter upon this (*a priori*) way, even without the hope of arriving at particulars by means of it, in order that we may have true concepts of the universe, the greatness of God, and the nature of the soul, through which the mind can be most perfected, for this is the most important end of contemplation. Yet we believe the absolute use of this method is conserved for a better life.

(G IV, p. 502; Loemker, p. 549; Ariew & Garber, p. 188; "On What is Independent of Sense and Matter" [1702]). *Being* itself and *truth* are not understood completely through the senses. For it would not at all be impossible for a created being to have long and orderly dreams which resemble our lives, such that everything that it thought it perceived through the senses would be nothing but mere appearances. Something is thus needed beyond the senses, by which to distinguish the true from the apparent. But the truth of the demonstrative sciences is free of such doubts and must even serve to judge the truth of sensible things.

COMMENTARY

Leibniz here adverts to the precedent of the empirical school of ancient Greek physicians who, contemptuous of all theorizing, proceeded wholly on the basis of experiential precedents. This school of thought fell into increasing disrepute as know-nothings who despised all theoretically informed study and innovation and trusted simply to experience, tradition, and "the way it has always been done." The mere empiric bases his expectations solely on prior experience imprinted on the memory. He judges by association and through analogy alone—through assimilating the currently envisioned case to earlier, similar ones. Leibniz regards this as crude and "unscientific." To be sure, predictive guidance can come from experience, but *understanding* requires theory. Only through reason can we achieve a solid knowledge of facts—even merely impersonal facts. The theoretician alone can reason from general principles. The rustic expects the moon to go through its phases by habit; the astronomer understands why this happens because he can explain it through its causes. Only at this point can rational understanding be reached. This capacity to reason by subsuming particular cases under general laws separates the spirits from mere souls and is associated with apperception or self-consciousness.

KEY WORDS:

connection/*consécution*
memory/*mémoire*
practice/*pratique*
theory/*théorie*
empirics/*empiriques*
physicians/*médécins*
astronomers/*astronomes*
reason/*raison*
men/*hommes*
beasts/*bêtes*
perception/*perception*

SECTION 29

29. But the knowledge of necessary and eternal truths is what distinguishes us from mere animals and provides us with *reason* and the sciences, elevating

us to a knowledge of ourselves and of God. And it is this within us that is called the rational soul or *spirit*.

29. Mais la connoissance des vérités necessaires et éternelles est ce qui nous distingue des simples animaux et nous fait avoir la Raison et les sciences, en nous élevant à la connoissance de nous-mêmes et de Dieu. Et c'est ce qu'on appelle en nous Ame Raisonnable, ou Esprit.

(PNG, sec. 4.) When this soul ⟨of an animal⟩ is raised to the level of *reason*, it is something more sublime and is counted among the *spirits*

(PNG, sec. 5.) *Reasoning* in the *true* sense depends on necessary or eternal truths, as are those of logic, number, and geometry, which make the connection of ideas indubitable and their conclusions infallible. Animals in which such consequences cannot be observed are called beasts, but those who know these necessary truths are the ones properly called *rational animals*, and their souls are called *spirits*. These souls are capable of performing acts of reflection and of considering what is called "I," "substance," "soul," "spirit"—in a word, things and truths which are immaterial. It is this which makes us capable of the sciences or of demonstrative knowledge.

(DM, sec. 34.) Not being able to reason, they <mere souls, unlike spirits> are unable to discover necessary and universal truths. It is also because they do not reflect regarding themselves that they have no moral qualities, whence it follows that undergoing a thousand transformations, as we see a caterpillar change into a butterfly, the result from a moral or practical standpoint is the same as if we said that they perished in each case, and we can indeed say it from the physical standpoint in the same way that we say bodies perish in their dissolution. But the intelligent soul, knowing that it is and having the ability to say that word "I" so full of meaning, not only continues and exists, meta-physically far more certainly than do the others, but it remains the same from the moral standpoint, and constitutes the same personality, for it is its memory or knowledge of this ego which renders it open to punishment and reward.

(DM, secs. 35–36.) Spirits are the most perfect of substances and best express the divinity. Since all the nature, purpose, virtue and function of substances is, as has been sufficiently explained, to express God and the universe, there is no room for doubting that those substances which give the expression, knowing what they are doing and which are able to understand the great truths about God and the universe, do express God and the universe incomparably better than do those natures which are either brutish and incapable of recognizing truths, or are wholly destitute of sensation and knowledge. The difference be-tween intelligent substances and those which are not intelligent is quite as great as between a mirror and one who sees. As God is himself the greatest and wisest of spirits it is easy to understand that the spirits with which he can, so to speak, enter into conversation and even into social relations by communi-cating to them in particular ways his feelings and his will so that they are able to know and love their benefactor, must be much nearer to him than the rest of created things which may be regarded as the instruments of spirits. In the same way we see that all wise persons consider far more the condition of a man than of anything else however precious it may be; and it seems that the greatest satisfaction which a soul, satisfied in other respects, can have is to see itself loved by others. However, with respect to God there is this difference that his glory and our worship can add nothing to his satisfaction, the recognition of creatures being nothing but a consequence of his sovereign and perfect felicity and being far from contributing to it or from causing it even in part. Nevertheless, that which is reasonable in finite spirits is found eminently in him and as we praise a king who prefers to preserve the life of a man before that of the most precious and rare of his animals, we should not doubt that the most enlightened and most just of all monarchs has the same preference. . . . Spirits are of all substances the most capable of perfection, and their perfections are different in this that they interfere with one another the least, or rather they aid one another the most, for only the most virtuous can be the most perfect friends. Hence it follows that God who in all things has the greatest perfection will have the greatest care for spirits and will give not only to all of them in general, but even to each one in particular the highest perfection which the universal harmony will permit.

COMMENTARY

Leibniz takes rational spirits of humans to differ from the more primitive souls characteristic of lower animals through the possession of a capacity for conceptual thinking with its concomitant access to knowledge of universal generalizations and truths of reason—especially the "eternal truths" of logic and mathematics. The capacity for abstract thinking (through which self-knowledge becomes possible) endows these higher-level creatures with an ability to perform inductive and deductive reasoning, and also enables them to make evaluative assessments. Thus while mere soul-endowed animals can have consciousness, sensation, memory, association, anticipation, and affection/aversion, it transpires that only the apperceptively self-conscious spirits can attain to the theoretical knowledge and rational evaluation, which involve conceptualization and universal judgment. They alone are capable of *science* and of *morality*.

KEY WORDS:

knowledge/*connaissance*
necessary truths/*vérités nécessaires*
eternal truths/*vérités éternelles*
rational soul/*âme raisonnable*
reason/*raison*
the sciences/*les sciences*
men/*hommes*
animals/*animaux*
spirit/*esprit*

SECTION 30

30. It is also through the knowledge of necessary truths and through their abstraction <from merely sensuous matters> that we are raised to *Reflexive Acts*, which enable us to think of what is called *I* and to consider that this or

that lies within *ourselves*. And, it is thus that in thinking of ourselves we think of being, of substance, of the simple and compound, of the immaterial, and of God himself, by conceiving that what is limited in us is unlimited in him. And these reflexive acts furnish the principal objects of our <present metaphysical> reasonings. (See *Theodicy*, Preface.)

30. *C'est aussi par la connoissance des vérités necessaires et par leurs abstractions que nous sommes élevés aux* Actes Reflexifs, *qui nous font penser à ce qui s'appelle* Moy *et a considérer que ceci ou cela est en nous: et c'est ainsi qu'en pensant à nous, nous pensons à l'Etre, à la Substance, au simple et au composé, à l'immateriel et à Dieu même; en concevant que ce qui est borné en nous, est en lui sans bornes. Et ces Actes Reflexifs fournissent les objects principaux de nos raisonnemens. (*Théodicée, Préface, *4a.)*

(*Theodicy*, Preface [G VI, 27].) The perfections of God are those of our souls, but he possesses them in boundless measure; he is an Ocean, whereof to us only drops have been granted; there is in us some power, some knowledge, some goodness, but in God they are all in their entirety. Order, proportions, harmony delight us; painting and music are samples of these: God is all order; he always keeps truth of proportions, he makes universal harmony; all beauty is an effusion of his rays.

(PNG, sec. 5) Animals . . . who know these necessary truths are the ones properly called *rational animals*, and their souls are called *spirits*. These souls are capable of performing acts of reflection and of considering what is called "I," "substance," "soul," "spirit"—in a word, things and truths which are immaterial. It is this which makes us capable of the sciences or of demonstrative knowledge.

(NE, pp. 51–52) There is a great deal that is innate in our minds, since we are innate to ourselves, so to speak, and since we include Being, Unity, Substance, Duration, Change, Action Perception, Pleasure, and hosts of other objects of our intellectual ideas. And since these objects are immediately related to our understanding and always present to it (although our distractions and needs prevent our being always aware of them), is it any wonder that we say that these ideas, along with what depends on them, are innate in us? I have also used the analogy of a veined block of marble, as opposed to an entirely homogeneous block of marble, or to a blank tablet—what the philosophers call a *tabula rasa*. For if the soul were like such a blank tablet then truths would be in us as the shape of Hercules is in a piece of marble when the marble is entirely neutral as to whether it assumes this shape or some other. However, if there were veins in the block which marked out the shape of Hercules rather than other shapes, then that block would be more determined to that shape and Hercules would be innate in it, in a way, even though labour would be required to expose the veins and to polish them into clarity, removing everything that prevents their being seen. This is how ideas and truths are innate in us—as inclinations, dispositions, tendencies, or natural potentialities, and not as actions; although these potentialities are always accompanied by certain actions, often insensible ones, which correspond to them.

(NE, p. 84.) The nature of things and the nature of mind work together. . . . [Q]uite often a "consideration of the nature of things" is nothing but the knowledge of the nature of our mind and of these innate ideas, and there is no need to look for them outside oneself. . . . Intellectual ideas or ideas of reflection are derived from our own mind; and I should like very much to know how we could obtain the idea of being, were it not that we ourselves are beings and thus find being in ourselves.

(NE, p. 111.) Someone will confront me with this accepted philosophical axiom, that there is nothing in the soul which does not come from the senses. "Nothing is in the intellect that has not been in a sense organ, except for one thing, the intellect itself" (Nihil est in intellectu quod non fuerit in sensu, excipe: nisi ipse intellectus). Now the soul includes being, substance, one, same, cause, perception, reasoning, and many other notions which the senses cannot provide.

(DM, sec. 34.) Supposing that the bodies which constitute a *unum per se*, as human bodies, are substances, and have substantial forms, and supposing that animals have souls, we are obliged to grant that these souls and these substantial forms cannot entirely perish, any more than can the atoms or the ultimate elements of matter, according to the position of other philosophers; for no substance perishes, although it may become very different. Such substances (i.e., souls) also express the whole universe, although more imperfectly than do spirits. The principal difference, however, is that they do not know that they are, nor what they are. Consequently, not being able to reason, they <mere souls, unlike spirits> are unable to discover necessary and universal truths. It is also because they do not reflect regarding themselves that they have no moral qualities, whence it follows that undergoing a thousand transformations, as we see a caterpillar change into a butterfly, the result from a moral or practical standpoint is the same as if we said that they perished in each case, and we can indeed say it from the physical standpoint in the same way that we say bodies perish in their dissolution. But the intelligent soul, knowing that it is and having the ability to say that word "I" so full of meaning, not only continues and exists, metaphysically far more certainly than do the others, but it remains the same from the moral standpoint, and constitutes the same personality, for it is its memory or knowledge of this ego which renders it open to punishment and reward. Also the immortality which is required in morals and in religion does not consist merely in this perpetual existence, which pertains to all substances, for if in addition there were no remembrance of what one had been, immortality would not be at all desirable. Suppose that some individual could suddenly become King of China on condition, however, of forgetting what he had been, as though being born again, would it not amount to the same practically, or as far as the effects could be perceived, as if the individual were annihilated, and a king of China were the same instant created in his place? The individual would have no reason to desire this.

(G VI, 502; Loemker, p. 549; Ariew & Garber, p. 188; "On What is Independent of Sense and Matter" [1702].) This thought of *myself*, who perceive sensible objects, and of my own action which results from it, adds something to the objects of sense. To think of some color and to consider that I think of it—these two thoughts are very different, just as much as color itself differs from the ego who thinks of it. And since I conceive that there are other beings who also have the right to say "I," or for whom this can be said, it is by this that I conceive what is called *substance* in general. It is the consideration of myself, also, which provides me with other concepts in *metaphysics*, such as those of cause, effect, action, similarity, etc., and even with those of *logic* and *ethics*. Thus it may be said that there is nothing in the understanding which has not come from the senses, except the understanding itself, or the one who understands.

COMMENTARY

Leibniz regards the grasp of abstract, general truths as the springboard to a knowledge of the necessary. Maintaining unity throughout a diversified plurality is the central facet of the conception of a substance and is something that we thinking beings experience within ourselves. And this conception of substance that is grounded in the awareness of reflexive self-knowledge—or apperception—is also the means by which we reach all of the characteristic ideas of metaphysics. Reflexive acts alone furnish us with the ideas of substance and attribute, being and unity, perception and representation, action and passion, necessity and contingency, etcetera, that constitute the materials for metaphysical reflection. In forming the basic conceptions of metaphysics we can thus draw on our own experience. (Compare sec. 16.)

Note that Leibniz coordinates *self*-consciousness with reason. As he sees it, self-awareness, abstract thought, and the capacity for conceiving rational connections all go hand in hand.

KEY WORDS:

knowledge/*connaissance*
necessary truths/*vérités nécessaires*
reflexive acts (of knowledge)/*actes réflexifs*
I/*moi*
ourselves/*nous (mêmes)*
being/*être*
substance/*substance*
composite/*composé*
limits/*bornes*
immaterial (substance)/*l'immatériel*
God/*Dieu*
reasoning/*raisonnement*

SECTION 31

31. Our reasonings are founded on *two great principles*, <First> *that of Contradiction*, in virtue of which we judge to be *false* that which contains this <viz. contradiction>, and to be *true* that which is opposed or contradictory to the false. (See *Theodicy*, secs. 44, 169.)

31. Nos raisonnemens sont fondés sur deux grands principes, celuy de la contradiction *en vertu duquel nous jugeons* faux, *ce qui en enveloppe, et* vrai *ce qui est opposé ou contradictoire au faux.* (Théodicée, *secs. 44, 169.*)

(*Theodicy*, sec. 44.) We must take into account that there are two great principles of our arguments. The one is the principle of contradiction, stating that of two contradictory propositions the one is true, the other false; the other principle is that of the determinant reason. . . .

(*Theodicy*, sec. 169.) Epicurus, to preserve freedom and to avoid an absolute necessity, maintained, after Aristotle, that contingent futurities were not susceptible of determinate truth. For if it was true yesterday that I should write to-day, it could therefore not fail to happen, it was already necessary; and, for that same reason, it was from all eternity. Thus all that which happens is necessary, and it is impossible for anything different to come to pass. But since that is not so it would follow, according to him, that contingent futurities have no determinate truth. To uphold this opinion, Epicurus went so far as to deny the first and the greatest principle of the truths of reason, he denied that every assertion was either true or false. Here is the way they confounded him: "You deny that it was true yesterday that I should write to-day; it was therefore false." The good man, not being able to admit this conclusion, was obliged to say that it was neither true nor false. After that, he needs no refutation. . . .

(NE, pp. 362–63.) Stated generally, the principle of contradiction is: *a proposition is either true or false*. This contains two assertions: first, that truth and falsity are incompatible in a single proposition, i.e. that *a proposition cannot be both true and false at once*; and second, that the contradictories or negations of the true and the false are not compatible, i.e. that there is nothing intermediate between the true and the false, or better that *it cannot happen that a proposition is neither true nor false*. Now, all of that holds true in application to every proposition one can imagine, such as *What is A cannot be non-A*, and *AB cannot be non-A*, and *An equilateral rectangle cannot be non-rectangular*, and *It is true that every man is an animal so it is false that there is some man who is not an animal*. We can provide many variations on these assertions and apply them to hypotheticals, conjunctions, disjunctions, and others. As for "disparities," these are propositions which say that the object of one idea is not the object of another idea; for instance *Warmth is not the same thing as colour*, *Man and animal are not the same* although every man is an animal. All these can be established with certainty, without any proof, i.e. without bringing them down to an opposition (i.e. down to the principle of contradiction), when the ideas are well enough understood not to need any analysis at this point. When that is not the case one is liable to error: someone who said *The triangle and the trilateral are not the same* would be wrong, since if we consider it carefully we find that three sides and three angles always go together. And if he said *The quadrilateral rectangle and the rectangle are not the same* he would be wrong again, since it turns out that only a four-sided figure can have all its angles right angles. However, one can still say in the abstract that *triangularity is not trilaterality*, or that the formal causes of the triangle and of the trilateral are not the same, as the philosophers put it. They are different aspects of one and the same thing. Someone who has been listening patiently so far to what I have just been saying will finally lose patience and say that I am wasting time on trivial assertions and the identities are all useless. But this verdict would result from not having thought enough about these matters. The inferences of logic, for example, are demonstrated by means of identities, and geometers need the principle of contradiction for their demonstrations by *reductio ad absurdum*.

(G III, 400; to Coste [1707].) A truth is necessary when the opposite implies contradiction; and when it is not necessary it is called contingent. That God exists, that all right angles are equal to each other, are necessary truths; but it is a contingent truth that I exist, or that there are bodies which show an actual right angle.

(G VII, 299; "Principles" [ca. 1696].) I assume that every judgment (i.e., affirmation or negation) is either true or false and that if the affirmation is true the negation is false, and if the negation is true the affirmation is false; that what is denied to be true—truly, of course—is false, and what is denied to be false is true; that what is denied to be affirmed, or affirmed to be denied, is to be denied; and what is affirmed to be affirmed and denied to be denied is to be affirmed. Similarly, that it is false that what is false should be true or that what is true should be false; that it is true that what is true is true, and what is false, false. All these are usually included in one designation, the *principle of contradiction*.

(G VII, 355; to Clarke II [1715].) The great foundation of mathematics is the principle of contradiction, or identity, that is, a proposition cannot be true and false at the same time. . . . And this principle alone suffices for proving all Arithmetic and all Geometry, that is, all mathematical principles. But in order to proceed from mathematics to natural philosophy another principle is requisite, as I have observed in my *Theodicy:* I mean the principle of a sufficient reason.

COMMENTARY

As Leibniz construes it, the Principle of Contradiction states that whatever proposition engenders a contradiction (through a *finite* process of analytical reasoning) is thereby necessarily false. Moreover, Leibniz accepts the logical principle that the *denial* of a false statement is true. Thus, whatever is true on the basis of the Principle of Contradiction alone is necessarily true. On this basis, Leibniz holds that once we have definitions in hand, so that the analysis of propositions becomes feasible, then this suffices to establish the whole domain of *necessary* truth, preeminently including logic, mathematics, and metaphysics.

Leibniz formulates the Principle of Contradiction as encompassing two claims: the theses "If C(p) then F(p)" ("we judge to be false that which contains a contradiction") and "If F(p) then T(~p)" ("we judge to be true that which is opposed or contradictory to the false"). Putting these together we obtain: If C(p) then T(~p), or, equivalently, If C(~p) then T(p). On this basis, we obtain a criterion of truth through a determination of self-contradiction. Observe, however, that Leibniz does not say that self-contradictoriness is the *sole* route to truth. He does *not* maintain that *only* contradiction-engendering propositions are false—that there are no contingent falsehoods. (These matters of contingency fall under yet another controlling principle, and not that of contradiction.)

KEY WORDS:

reasonings/*raisonnements*
contradiction/*contradiction*
false/*faux*
true/*vrai*

SECTION 32

32. And <second> *that of Sufficient Reason,* in virtue of which we consider that no fact can be real or actual, and no proposition true, without there being a sufficient reason for its being so and not otherwise, although most often these reasons just cannot be known by us. (See *Theodicy*, secs. 44, 196.)

32. *Et* celui de la Raison Suffisante, *en vertu duquel nous considerons qu'aucun fait ne sçauroit se trouver vrai, ou existent, aucune Enonciation veritable, sans qu'il y ait une raison suffisante pour quoi il en soit ainsi et non pas autrement, quoi que ces raisons le plus souvent ne puissent point nous être connues.* (Théodicée, *secs. 44, 196.)*

(*Theodicy*, sec. 44.) The other principle is that of the *determinant reason:* it states that nothing ever comes to pass without there being a cause or at least a reason determining it, that is, something to give an *a priori* reason why it is existent rather than non-existent, and in this wise rather than in any other. This great principle holds for all events, and a contrary instance will never be supplied: and although more often than not we are insufficiently acquainted with these determinant reasons, we perceive nevertheless that there are such. Were it not for this great principle we could never prove the existence of God, and we should lose an infinitude of very just and very profitable arguments whereof it is the foundation; moreover, it suffers no exception, for otherwise its force would be weakened. Besides, nothing is so weak as those systems where all is unsteady and full of exceptions. That fault cannot be laid to the charge of the system I approve, where everything happens in accordance with general rules that at most are mutually restrictive.

(*Theodicy*, sec. 196.) God is incapable of acting without reason. . . . It is as if one were to suppose that God had decreed to make a material sphere, with no reason for making it of any particular size. This decree would be useless, it would carry with it that which would prevent its effect. It would be quite another matter if God decreed to draw from a given point one straight line to another given straight line, without any determination of the angle, either in the decree or in its circumstances. For in this case the determination would spring from the nature of the thing, the line would be perpendicular, and the angle would be right, since that is all that is determined and distinguishable.

(PNG, sec. 7.) So far we have been speaking simply as *natural scientists;* now we must rise to *metaphysics* and make use of the great, but not commonly used, *principle* that *nothing takes place without a sufficient reason;* in other words, that nothing occurs for which it would be impossible for someone who has enough knowledge of things to give a reason adequate to determine why the thing is as it is and not otherwise. This principle having been stated, the first question which we have a right to ask will be, "Why is there something rather than nothing?" For nothing is simpler and easier than something. Further, assuming that things must exist, it must be possible to give a reason *why they should exist as they do and not otherwise.*

(NE, p. 179) If we do not always notice the reason which determines us, or rather by which we determine ourselves, it is because we are as little able to be aware of all the workings of our mind and of its usually confused and imperceptible thoughts as we are to sort out all the mechanisms which nature puts to work in bodies. If by "necessity" we understood a man's being inevitably determined, as could be foreseen by a perfect Mind provided with a complete knowledge of everything going on outside and inside that man, then, since thoughts are as determined as the movements which they represent, it is certain that every free act would be necessary; but we must distinguish what is necessary from what is contingent though determined. Not only are contingent truths not necessary, but the links between them are not always absolutely necessary either; for it must be admitted that when one thing follows from another in the contingent realm, the kind of determining that is involved is not the same as when one thing follows from another in the realm of the necessary. Geometrical and metaphysical "followings" necessitate, but physical and moral ones incline without necessitating. There is even a moral and voluntary element in what is physical, through its relation to God, since the laws of motion are necessitated only by what is best. God chooses freely, even though he is determined to choose the best. But since bodies do not choose for themselves, God having chosen for them, they have come to be called "necessary agents" in common usage. I have no objection to this, provided that no one confounds the necessary with the determined and goes on to suppose that free beings act in an undetermined way—an error which has prevailed in certain minds, and destroys the most important truths, even the fundamental axiom that *nothing happens without reason*, without which the existence of God and other great truths cannot be properly demonstrated.

(G VII, 199 [ca. 1690].) In demonstration I use two principles, of which one is that what implies contradiction is false, the other is that a reason can be given for every truth (which is not identical or immediate), *i.e.* that the notion of the predicate is always expressly or implicitly contained in the notion of its subject, and that this holds good no less in extrinsic than in intrinsic denominations, no less in contingent than in necessary truths.

(G VII, 364; to Clarke, III.6 [1716].) Supposing anyone should ask why God did not create everything a year sooner, and the same person should infer from thence that God has done something concerning which it is not possible there should be a reason why he did it so and not otherwise; the answer is that his inference would be right if time was anything distinct from things existing in time. For it would be impossible there should be any reason why things should be applied to such particular instants rather than to others, their succession continuing the same. But then the same argument proves that instants, considered without the things, are nothing at all and that they consist only in the successive order of things, which order remaining the same, one of the two states, viz., that of a supposed anticipation, would not at all differ, nor could be discerned from the other which now is.

(G VII, 364–65; to Clarke, III.7 [1716].) It appears from what I have said, that my axiom has not been well understood; and that the author [Clarke] denies it, though he seems to grant it. '*Tis true*, says he, *that there is nothing without a sufficient reason*, but he adds, that *this sufficient reason is often the simple or mere will of God.* . . . But this is plainly maintaining that God wills something, without any sufficient reason for his will: against the axiom, or general rule of whatever happens. This is falling back into the loose indifference, which

I have confuted at large, and contrary to the wisdom of God, as if he could operate without acting by reason.

(G VII, 372; to Clarke, IV.4–5 [1716].) There is no such thing as two individuals indiscernible from each other. An ingenious gentleman of my acquaintance, discoursing with me, in the presence of Her Electoral Highness the Princess Sophia, in the garden of Herrenhausen, thought he could find two leaves perfectly alike. The Princess defied him to do it, and he ran all over the garden a long time to look for some; but it was to no purpose. Two drops of water, or milk, viewed with a microscope, will appear distinguishable from each other. This is an argument against atoms; which are confuted as well as a vacuum, by the principles of true metaphysics. Those great principles of a *sufficient reason*, and of the *identity of indiscernibles*, change the state of metaphysics. That science becomes real and demonstrative by means of these principles; whereas before, it did generally consist in empty words.

(Couturat, *Opuscules*, p. 519; Loemker, p. 268; Ariew & Garber, pp. 32–32; "First Truths" [ca. 1685].) There is nothing without a reason, or no effect without a cause. . . . It follows also that there cannot be two individual things in nature which differ only numerically. For surely it must be possible to give a reason why they are different, and this must be sought in some differences within themselves. Thus the observation of Thomas Aquinas about separate intelligences, which he declared never differ in number alone, must be applied to other things also. Never are two eggs, two leaves, or two blades of grass in a garden to be found exactly similar to each other. So perfect similarity occurs only in incomplete and abstract concepts, where matters are conceived, not in their totality but according to a certain single viewpoint, as when we consider only figures and neglect the figured matter. So geometry is right in studying similar triangles, even though two perfectly similar material triangles are never found. And although gold or some other metal, or salt, and many liquids, may be taken for homogeneous bodies, this can be admitted only as concerns the senses and not as if it were true in an exact sense.

COMMENTARY

The Principle of Sufficient Reason asserts that there is always, in theory, at least, a process of "analysis" to validate the truth of any proposition that indeed is true, thereby furnishing a grounding rationale for its being so rather than otherwise. In the case of necessarily true propositions, this validating sufficient reason is provided by the operation of the principle of contradiction in that the denial of such truths leads to contradiction. In the case of *contingently true* propositions, however, this sufficient reason is provided via the *perfection* of God in a manner whose discussion is postponed until sections 36–41, where it eventuates that the sufficient reason of all contingent truth lies in God's choice of the best. (Leibniz thus refers to the Principle of Contingency as *le principe du meilleur*, the principle of the best, as well as the *Principle of Perfection*.)

Accordingly, what is actually at issue overall are *three* principles:

1. the *Principle of Sufficient Reason*, which states that all truths whatsoever have a sufficient reason for being as they are,
2. the *Principle of Contradiction*, which specifies the sufficient reason for necessary truths (as inhering in the self-contradictoriness of their denial), and

3. the *Principle of Perfection* which specifies the sufficient reason for contingent truth (as inhering in a contradiction between their denial and God's commitment to the perfection of his creation)

The idea of a *sufficient* reason is geared to the conception of reasons of different degrees of merit or weight. A proposition affords a *sufficient* reason for another if it presents a pro-reason for this conclusion that is not outweighed by any con-reason:

rSp = For some x, r is a weight-x reason for p and there is no reason
for not-p whose weight exceeds x.

For Leibniz, the Principle of Sufficient Reason is not a principle of explicability, and it is certainly not an epistemic principle of cognitive competency to the effect that everything that is the case can (in principle) be explained by us. Rather, in its application to this world—to the domain of contingent truth—it is an *ontological* principle that asserts (in Hegelian language) the rationality of the real. It is an affirmation of *optimality*, asserting that that possibility among possible alternatives actually is the case whose reasons for being the case (the pro-reasons) outweigh the reasons against (the con-reasons). After all, how—in the Leibnizian framework—is God to make a world; that is, in effect, to decide which world-descriptive propositions to make true? He cannot do it via truths (these are not yet available) but has to do it via truth-determinative reasons, which, in the end, must relate to the issue of comparative perfection. The following somewhat more technical remarks may be helpful to readers versed in formal logic.

In general effect, the Principle of Sufficient Reason asserts that if a proposition is true, then there exists a sufficient reason for its being so:

If $T(p)$, then $(Er)(rSp)$

To convert this into a *criterion* of truth, we may reason as follows:
   1. By contraposition we obtain:

If $(Ar) \sim (rSp)$, then $\sim T(p)$

   2. By the Principle of Excluded Middle, "if $\sim T(p)$, then $T(\sim p)$," we obtain:

If $(Ar) \sim (rSp)$, then $T(\sim p)$

   3. By substituting $\sim p$ for p, and noting the equivalency of p with $\sim \sim p$ and A with $\sim E \sim$, we now obtain:

If $\sim (Er)(rS \sim p)$, then $T(p)$

That is, a thesis p will be true if within the entire domain of available reasons nothing is to be found weighty enough to validate its denial, not-p. But note that the utilization of *this* principle for establishing contingent (i.e., non-necessary) truth requires a search through the entire domain of reasons, an infinitistic process which we imperfect humans cannot expect to carry out. As regards its implementability, the envisioned truth-criterion thus stands on a very different footing from the straightforward "If $C(\sim p)$, then $T(p)$" of section 31 which provides for establishing necessary truth. The demonstration of contingent truths proceeds *ad infinitum* through the need for a potentially infinite search. Leibniz resumes the elaboration of these ideas in section 46.

Leibniz maintains a Principle of the Identity of Indiscernibles as one of the prime consequences of the Principle of Sufficient Reason. He explicitly considers the assumption of two perfectly indiscernible things and insists that "that supposition is false, and contrary to the grand principle of reason." It should be remarked, however, that, while this Principle of the Identity of Indiscernibles is necessarily applicable to all *substances*, it need not, and should not, be taken as applicable to *phenomena*. That two like objects might be indistinguishable to humans operating with limited means for observational discrimination could readily be granted by Leibniz as unproblematic for his system. The crux is that substances are *distinguishable*—discriminable, in the final analysis, by God, who alone knows the definitive complete individual concepts at issue.

KEY WORDS:

fact/*fait*
proposition/*énonciation*
sufficient reason/*raison suffisante*
true/*vrai*
actual (i.e., existent)/*existent*
to know/*connaître*

SECTION 33

33. There are two kinds of truths, those of *reasoning* and those of *fact*. Truths of reasoning are necessary and their opposite is impossible, while those of fact are contingent and their opposite is possible. When a truth is necessary one can find its <sufficient> reason through <finite> analysis, resolving it into ever more simple ideas and truths until one reaches primitives. (See *Theodicy*, secs. 170, 174, 189, 280–82, 367; Abridgment, obj. 3.)

33. Il y a deux sortes des Verités, *celles de* Raisonnement *et celles de* Fait. *Les verités de Raisonnement sont necessaires et leur opposé est impossible, et celles de fait sont contingentes et leur opposé est possible. Quand une verité est necessaire, on en peut trouver la raison par l'analyse, la resolvant en idées et en verités plus simples jusqu'à ce qu'on vienne aux primitives. (*Théodicée, *secs. 170, 174, 189, 280–82, 367; Abrégé, obj. 3.)*

(*Theodicy*, sec. 170.) The possibility of things that do not happen <must be maintained>. <The necessity of the actual is not an absolute but a merely *ex hypothesi* necessity.> . . . It is open to question whether the past is any more necessary than the future. . . . The <merely> hypothetical necessity of both is the same: the one cannot be changed, the other will not be.

(*Theodicy*, sec. 174.) He <Bayle> confuses here what is impossible because it implies contradiction with what cannot happen because it is not fit to be chosen. It is true that there would have been no contradiction in the supposition that Spinoza died in Leyden and not at The Hague; there would have been nothing so possible: the matter was therefore indifferent in respect of the power of God. But one must not suppose that any event, however small it be, can be regarded as indifferent in respect of his wisdom and his goodness. Jesus Christ has said divinely well that everything is numbered, even to the hairs of our head. Thus the wisdom of God did not permit that this event whereof M. Bayle speaks should happen otherwise than it happened, not as if by itself it would have been more deserving of choice, but on account of its connexion with that entire sequence of the universe which deserved to be given preference.

(*Theodicy*, sec. 189.) <Pierre Bayle> seems to fear lest people may take advantage against us of the perfect regularity of the eternal verities. Since this regularity springs only from nature and necessity of things, without being directed by any cognition, M. Bayle fears that one might with Strato thence infer that the world also could have become regular through a blind necessity. But it is easy to answer that. In the region of the eternal verities are found all the possibles, and consequently the regular as well as the irregular: there must be a reason accounting for the preference for order and regularity, and this reason can only be found in understanding. Moreover these very truths can have no existence without an understanding to take cognizance of them; for they would not exist if there were no divine understanding wherein they are realized, so to speak. Hence Strato does not attain his end, which is to exclude cognition from that which enters into the origin of things.

(*Theodicy*, sec. 280.) Speaking generally, it appears more reasonable and more fitting to say that obedience to God's precepts is always *possible*, even for the unregenerate; that the grace of God is always *resistible*, even in those most holy, and that *freedom* is exempt not only from *constraint* but also from *necessity*, although it be never without infallible *certainty* or without inclining *determination*.

(*Theodicy*, sec. 281.) Nevertheless there is on the other hand a sense wherein it would be permitted to say, in certain conjunctures, that the *power* to do good is often lacking, even in the just; that sins are often *necessary*, even in the regenerate; that it is *impossible* sometimes for one not to sin; that grace is *irresistible*; that freedom is not exempt from *necessity*. But these expressions are less exact and less pleasing in the circumstances that prevail about us today.

(*Theodicy*, sec. 282.) It is therefore only necessary to understand fully some distinctions, such as that I have very often urged between the necessary and the certain, and between metaphysical necessity and moral necessity. It is the same with possibility and impossibility, since the event whose opposite is possible is contingent, even as that whose opposite is impossible is necessary. A distinction is rightly drawn also between a proximate potency and a remote potency; and, accordingly to these different senses, one says now that a thing may be and now that it may not be. It may be said in a certain sense that it is necessary that the blessed should not sin; that the devils and the damned should sin; that God himself should choose the best; that man should follow the course which after all attracts him most. But this necessity is not opposed to contingency; it is not of the kind called logical, geometrical or metaphysical, whose opposite implies contradiction.

(*Theodicy*, sec. 367.) Indeed, confusion springs, more often than not, from ambiguity in terms, and from one's failure to take trouble over gaining clear ideas about them. That gives rise to these eternal, and usually mistaken, contentions on necessity and contingency, on the possible and the impossible. But provided that it is understood that necessity and possibility, taken metaphysically and strictly, depend solely upon this question, whether the object in itself or that which is opposed to it implies contradiction or not; and that one takes into account that contingency is consistent with the inclinations, or reasons which contribute towards causing determination by the will; provided also that one knows how to distinguish clearly between necessity and determination or certainty, between metaphysical necessity, which admits of no choice, presenting only one single object as possible, and moral necessity, which constrains the wisest to choose the best; finally, provided that one is rid of the chimera of complete indifference, which can only be found in the books of philosophers, and on paper (for they cannot even conceive the notion in their heads, or prove its reality by an example in things) one will easily escape from a labyrinth whose unhappy Daedalus was the human mind.

(*Theodicy*, Abridgment, obj. 3.) <As regards voluntary actions,> their prevision and predetermination is not absolute, but it presupposes will: if it is certain that one will do them, it is no less certain that one will will to do them. These voluntary actions and their results will not happen whatever one may do and whether one will them or not; but they will happen because one will do, and because one will will to do, that which leads to them. That is involved in prevision and predetermination, and forms the reason thereof. The necessity of such events is called conditional or hypothetical, or again necessity of consequence, because it presupposes the will and the other requisites. But the necessity which destroys morality, and renders punishment unjust and reward unavailing, is found in the things that will be whatever one may do and whatever one may will to do: in a word, it exists in that which is essential. This it is which is called an absolute necessity. Thus it avails nothing with regard to what is necessary absolutely to ordain interdicts or commandments, to propose penalties or prizes, to blame or to praise; it will come to pass no more and no less. In voluntary actions, on the contrary, in what depends upon them, precepts, armed with power to punish and to reward, very often serve, and are included in the order of causes that make action exist.

(G VI, 414; "On the Origin of Evil" [1710].) For it may in a manner be said that these two principles <of Sufficient Reason and of Contradiction> are included in the definition of the true and the false. Nevertheless when, by analyzing a suggested truth, we see that it depends upon truths whose opposite involves a contradiction, we can say that it is absolutely necessary. But when, carrying our analysis as far as we like, we can never reach elements of the given truth, it must be said to be contingent, and to have its origin in a prevailing reason, which inclines without necessitating.

COMMENTARY

The "truths of reason" are necessary truths, whose negation issues in contradiction. Their status as truths is demonstrable in that a finite process of "analysis" (of replacement of definable terms by their definitions) suffices to reduce them to self-repetitive tautologies ("identities"), so that their negation is patently and explicitly absurd. (Thus, for example, "All men are rational" results in an immediate tautology given the definitional equivalence: "Man = rational animal.") The "truths of fact" on the other hand are not finitely analyzable. Their status as truths hinges on God's choice of the best, so that while the truths of reason pivot on the Principle of Contradiction as regards their sufficient reason, the truths of fact pivot on the Principle of Perfection as regards theirs. (This latter theme is deferred until sec. 36.)

In his influential 1936 book on *The Great Chain of Being* (Cambridge, MA: Harvard University Press, 1936), Arthur O. Lovejoy maintained (p. 173) that Leibniz cannot, given his own principles, escape from the force of the following reasoning (where "A-necessity" is absolutely necessity, "absolute logical determinism" as Lovejoy calls it).

A-Necessary: God chooses the best world for actualization
A-Necessary: This world is the best

Therefore: A-Necessary: God chooses this world for actualization

This imputation chooses to ignore Leibniz's repeated and explicit insistence that the initial premise is *not* absolutely necessary (A-necessary), but, rather, is merely *metaphysically* necessary (M-necessary). And Leibniz insists that M-necessity is not reducible to A-necessity unconditionally, but only conditionally or relatively, subject to the idea that moral necessity is absolute necessity *given* (i.e., conditional upon) certain facts about God. That is, we have the principle:

M-necessary p = (Ef) [f is a fact about God that is *already* pre-established as M-necessary, and p is A-necessary given f].

Accordingly, M-necessity can only be coordinated with A-necessity through the intervention of a (prior) M-necessary contention. Thus a "reduction" of M-necessity to A-necessity is possible only in a conditional or "relative" manner, proceeding in a way that involves an infinite regress. One may not *like* the subtle way in which Leibniz distinguishes the two modes of necessitation, but one cannot simply *ignore* it. And it creates a position where an M-necessary proposition does not admit any absolute (categorical) demonstration, but can only be established by an infinitistic process of reasoning that cannot in fact be carried out in a conclusive way (by any finite intelligence, at any rate). For Leibniz, the crucial consideration is that truths of fact cannot be analyzed finitistically but only admit of an infinitistic sort of demonstrative validation that proceeds via the infinite inner complexity of the nature of God.

In characterizing truths of fact as non-necessary in the absolute mode, and (thereby) contingent, Leibniz denies to them a certain logical feature (viz., necessity) and a certain ontological character (viz., independence of the will of God). But these considerations do not in his view prevent them from being *certain* and *determined*. It is just that such certainty does not constitute necessity, nor such determination a predetermination of a sort that renders contingency inevitably independent of human choices (since God can will into existence a being that, through the exercise of its own will, makes certain particular choices).

KEY WORDS:

truths of reason/*vérités de raison* (or *de raisonnement*)
truth of fact/*vérités de fait*

necessary/*nécessaire*
impossible/*impossible*
(sufficient) reason/*raison* (*suffisante*)
contingent/*contingent*
analysis/*analyse*
the simple/*le simple*
primitives/*primitives*

SECTION 34

34. This <sequential resolution into primitives> is how, among mathematicians, theoretical *theorems* and practical *rules* are reduced by analysis to definitions, axioms, and postulates.

34. C'est ainsi que chez Mathematiciens, les Theoremes *de speculation et les* Canons *de practique sont reduits par l'Analyse aux Definitions, Axiomes et Demandes.*

(NE, p. 360.) You must understand that geometers do not derive their proofs from diagrams. . . . It is universal propositions, i.e. definitions and axioms and theorems which have already been demonstrated, that make up the reasoning, and they would sustain it even if there were no diagram.

(NE, pp. 361–62.) The primary truths which we know by "intuition" are of two sorts, as are the derivative ones. They are either truths of reason or truths of fact. Truths of reason are necessary, and those of fact are contingent. The primary truths of reason are the ones to which I give the general name "identities," because they seem to do nothing but repeat the same thing without telling us anything. They are either affirmative or negative. Examples of affirmative ones are: *What is, is; Each thing is what it is,* and as many others as you want: *A is A; B is B.* . . . *An equilateral rectangle is a rectangle.* . . . *If a regular four-sided figure is an equilateral rectangle then this figure is a rectangle.* . . . *If A is non-B it follows that A is non-B.*

(G VII, 300; "Principles" [ca. 1696].) Identical propositions are the primary propositions of all, and are incapable of proof and thus true per se, for of course nothing can be found to serve as a middle term to connect something with itself, so as a result, truths are virtually identical which can be reduced to formal or explicit identities through an analysis of their terms, if we substitute for the original term either an equivalent concept or a concept included in it. It is obvious that all necessary propositions, or propositions which have eternal truth, are virtual identities and can be demonstrated or reduced to primary truths by ideas or definitions alone, that is, by the analysis of terms, so that it is made clear that their opposite implies a contradiction and conflicts with some identity or primary truth. Hence the Scholastics also observed that truths which are absolute or have metaphysical necessity can be proved by their terms alone, since the opposite involves a contradiction.

In general, every true proposition which is not identical or true in itself can be proved a priori with the help of axioms or propositions that are true in themselves and with the help of definitions or ideas. For no matter how often a predicate is truly affirmed of a subject, there must be some real connection between subject and predicate, such that in every proposition whatever, such as *A* is *B* (or *B* is truly predicated of *A*), it is true that *B* is contained in *A*, or its concept is in some way contained in the concept of *A* itself. And this must be either by absolute necessity, in propositions which contain eternal truth; or by a kind of certainty which depends upon the supposed decree of a free substance in contingent matters, a decree, however, which is never entirely arbitrary and free from foundation, but for which some reason can always be given. This reason, however, merely inclines and does not truly necessitate. Such truth could itself be deduced from the analysis of concepts, if this were always within human power, and will certainly not escape the analysis of an omniscient substance who sees everything a priori from ideas themselves and from his decrees. It is certain, therefore, that all truths, even contingent ones, have a proof a priori or some reason why they are rather than are not. And this is what is commonly asserted: that nothing happens without a cause, or there is nothing without a reason. Yet however strong this reason may be—though whatever kind it is, it is enough to effect a greater inclination in one direction or the other—even if it establishes certainty in a predicting being, it does not place necessity in the thing itself, because its contrary would still remain possible per se and implies no contradiction. Otherwise what we call contingent would rather be necessary or of eternal truth.

(Couturat, *Opuscules*, pp. 518–19; Loemker, pp. 267–68; Ariew & Garber, pp. 30–31; "Primary Truths" [ca. 1685].) *Primary Truths* are those which predicate something of itself or deny the opposite of its opposite. For example, *A* is *A*, or *A* is not non-*A*; if it is true that *A* is *B* or that *A* is non-*B*. Likewise, everything is what it is; everything is similar or equal to itself; nothing is greater or less than itself. These and other truths of this kind though they may have various degrees of priority, can nevertheless all be grouped under the one name of *identities*.

All other truths are reduced to primary truths with the aid of definitions or by the analysis of concepts; in this consists *proof* a priori which is independent of experience. I shall give as example this proposition which is accepted as an axiom by mathematicians and all other people alike: the whole is greater than its part, or the part is less than the whole. This is very easily demonstrated from the definition of less or greater, with the addition of a primitive axiom or identity. For that is *less* which is equal to a part of another thing (the *greater*). This definition is very easily understood and is consistent with the general practice of men, when they compare things with each other and measure the excess by subtracting an amount equal to the smaller from the greater. Hence one may reason as follows. A part is equal to a part of the whole (namely, to itself, by the axiom of identity, according to which each thing is equal to itself). But what is equal to a part of a whole is less than the whole (by the definition of less). Therefore the part is less than the whole.

The predicate or consequent therefore always inheres in the subject or antecedent. And as Aristotle, too, observed, the nature of truth in general or the connection between the terms of a proposition consists in this fact. In identities this connection and the inclusion of the predicate in the subject are explicit; in all other propositions that are implied and must be revealed through the analysis of the concepts, which constitutes a demonstration a priori.

This is true, moreover, in every affirmative truth, universal or singular, necessary or contingent, whether its terms are intrinsic or extrinsic denominations. Here lies hidden a wonderful secret which contains that nature of contingency or the essential distinction between necessary and contingent truths and which removes the difficulty involved in a fatal necessity determining even free things.

COMMENTARY

Resuming the line of thought that necessary propositions are reducible to primary ones through a (finite) process of analysis, this section surveys the several kinds of available primitives—viz., definitions, axioms, and postulates. Leibniz sees the process of reductive analysis for necessary truths as issuing ultimately in identicals, once full use has been made of explicit definitions and definitional stipulations on the order of axioms and postulates. Mathematics is, for Leibniz, our best source of clear and characteristic examples of the domain of necessary truths.

KEY WORDS:

theorems/*théorèmes*
rules/*canons*
mathematics/*mathématique*
analysis/*analyse*
definitions/*définitions*
axioms/*axiomes*
postulates/*demandes*

SECTION 35

35. There are, ultimately, simple ideas of which no definition can be given. And there are also axioms and postulates, or, in a word *primitive principles*, which cannot be proved and have no need of it, either. And these are the *identical propositions*, whose opposite contains an explicit contradiction.

35. Et il y a enfin des idées simples dont on ne sçauroit donner la définition; il y a aussi des Axiomes et Demandes ou en <un> mot, des principes primitifs, qui ne sçauroient être prouvés et n'en ont point besoin aussi; et ce sont les Énonciations identiques, dont l'opposé contient une contradiction expresse.

(NE, p. 367.) As for primary truths of fact, these are inner experiences which are immediate with the *immediacy of feeling*. This is where the first truth of the Cartesians and St. Augustine belongs: *I think, therefore I am*. That is, *I am a thing which thinks*. But . . . not only is it immediately evident to me that *I think*, but it is just as evident that *I think various thoughts*. . . . Thus the Cartesian principle is sound, but it is not the only one of its kind.

(NE, p. 411.) One can always say that the proposition *I exist* is evident in the highest degree, since it cannot be proved through any other—indeed, that it is an "immediate truth." To say *I think therefore I am* is not really to prove existence from thought, since *to think* and *to be thinking* are one and the same, and to say *I am thinking* is already to say *I am*. Still, there is some reason for your not including this proposition among the axioms: it is a proposition of fact, founded on immediate experience, and is not a necessary proposition whose necessity is seen in the immediate agreement of ideas. On the contrary, only God can see how these two terms, *I* and *existence*, are connected—that is, why I exist.

(NE, p. 434.) The immediate awareness of our existence and of our thoughts provides us with the first *a posteriori* truths or truths of fact, i.e. *the first experiences*; while identical propositions embody the first *a priori* truths or truths of reason. Neither kind admits of proof, and each can be called "immediate"—the former because nothing comes between the understanding and its object, the latter because nothing comes between the subject and the predicate.

(G IV, 423; Loemker, p. 292; Ariew & Garber, p. 24; "Meditations on Knowledge, Truth, and Ideas" [1684].) When everything that is included in a distinct idea is itself distinctly known in its turn, or when an analysis has been carried out completely, knowledge is *adequate*. I do not know whether we humans can ever provide a perfect instance of this; our idea of numbers, however, closely approaches it.

(Couturat, *Opuscules*, p. 361; "General Inquisitions" [1686].) Concerning concepts of the extended and of thinking in particular it is problematical whether they are simple; in fact many judge that these are concepts which may be conceived per se and do not require further analysis. Yet the extended appears to be a continuum having co-existing parts. Also, the term "thinking" seems not to be integral, for there is reference to some object which is being thought. Nevertheless there is contained in thinking itself some absolute reality which is difficult to explain in words.

COMMENTARY

In general, the truth of propositions admits of a proof by an analysis that consists in a reduction to primitives (a process finite and exact with truths of reason and infinite and approximative with truths of fact). But in the case of the primitive propositions themselves, no further demonstration is possible (let alone necessary), for they are express tautologies and their negations are explicit contradictions. Accordingly, Leibniz is concerned to refute John Locke's view that identities (or tautologous propositions) are empty and trivial, because he sees them as playing a crucial foundational role within the larger domain of necessary truth.

The idea of a *calculus of reasoning* based on a formalized language (the "universal characteristic") which would render the truth-test of (at least) necessary propositions into an automatic and mechanical process was a lifelong dream of Leibniz, and represents a project to which he devoted essays and studies throughout virtually the whole of his working life.

In sections 33–35, then, we have Leibniz the logician expounding his theory of truth as a central element of his wider philosophizing.

KEY WORDS:

simple ideas/*idées simples*
definition/*définition*
axiom/*axiomes*
postulates/*demandes*
to prove/*prouver*
primitive principles/*principes primitifs*
identical propositions/*énonciations identiques*
contradiction/*contradiction*

SECTION 36

36. But a *sufficient reason* must also be present in *contingent truths* or *truths of fact*, that is to say, in the sequence of things dispersed through the universe of created beings. Here the resolution into particular reasons can go on into endless detail, because of the immense variety of things in nature and the *ad infinitum* division of bodies. There is an infinity of shapes and motions, present and past, that enter into the efficient cause of my present writing, and there is an infinity of minute inclinations and dispositions of my soul, present and past, that enter into its final cause. (See *Theodicy*, secs. 36, 37, 44, 45, 49, 52, 121, 122, 337, 340, 344.)

36. Mais la raison suffisante se doit trouver aussi dans les verités contingentes ou de fait, c'est à dire, dans la suite des choses repandues par l'univers des creatures; où la resolution en raisons particulières pourroit aller à un detail sans bornes, à cause de la variété immense des choses de la Nature et de la division des corps à l'infini. Il y a une infinité de figures et de mouvemens presents et passés qui entrent dans la cause efficiente de mon ecriture presente, et il y a une infinité de petites inclinations et dispositions de mon ame presentes et passées qui entrent dans sa cause finale. (Théodicée, secs. 36, 37, 44, 45, 49, 52, 121, 122, 337, 340, 344.)

(*Theodicy*, sec. 36.) Philosophers agree to-day that the truth of contingent futurities is determinate, that is to say that contingent futurities are future, or that they will be, that they will happen: for it is as sure that the future will be, as it is sure that the past has been. It was true already a hundred years ago that I should write to-day, as it will be true after a hundred years that I have written. Thus the contingent is not, because it is future, any the less contingent; and *determination*, which would be called certainty if it were known, is not incompatible with contingency.

(*Theodicy*, sec. 37.) This determination [of contingencies] comes from the very nature of truth, and cannot injure freedom. . . . This truth which states that I shall write to-morrow is not of that nature, it is not necessary. Yet supposing that God foresees it, it is necessary that it come to pass; that is, the consequence is necessary, namely, that it exist, since it has been foreseen; for God is infallible. This is what is termed a *hypothetical* necessity. But our concern is not this necessity: it is an *absolute necessity* that is required, to be able to say that an action is necessary, that it is not contingent, that it is not the effect of a free choice. Besides it is very easily seen that foreknowledge in itself adds nothing to the determination of the truth of contingent futurities, save that this determination is known: and this does not augment the determination or the "futurition" (as it is termed) of these events, that whereon we agreed at the outset.

(*Theodicy*, sec. 44.) Nevertheless, objective certainty or determination need not bring about the necessity of the determinate truth. All philosophers acknowledge this, asserting that the truth of contingent futurities is determinate, and that nevertheless they remain contingent. The thing indeed would imply no contradiction in itself if the effect did not follow; and therein lies contingency. The better to understand this point, we must take into account that there are two great principles of our arguments. . . .

(*Theodicy*, sec. 45.) We must therefore not imagine with some Schoolmen, whose ideas tend towards the chimerical, that free contingent futurities have the privilege of exemption from this general rule of the nature of things <that is, the principle of sufficient reason>. There is always a prevailing reason which prompts the will to its choice, and for the maintenance of freedom for the will it suffices that this reason should incline without necessitating. That is also the opinion of all the ancients, of Plato, of Aristotle, of St. Augustine. The will is never prompted to action save by the representation of the good, which prevails over the opposite representations. This is admitted even in relation to God, the good angels and the souls in bliss: and it is acknowledged that they are none the less free in consequence of that. God fails not to choose the best, but he is not constrained so to do: nay, more, there is no necessity in the object of God's choice, for another sequence of things is equally possible. For that very reason the choice is free and independent of necessity, because it is made between several possibles, and the will is determined only by the preponderating goodness of the object.

(*Theodicy*, sec. 49.) In consequence of this, the case also of Buridan's ass between two meadows, impelled equally towards both of them, is a fiction that cannot occur in the universe, in the order of Nature. . . . Neither the parts of the universe nor the viscera of the animal are alike nor are they evenly placed on both sides of this vertical plane. There will therefore always be many things in the ass and outside the ass, although they be not apparent to us, which will determine him to go on one side rather than the other. And although man is free, and the ass is not, nevertheless for the same reason it must be true that in man likewise the case of a perfect equipoise between two courses is impossible. Furthermore it is true that an angel, or God certainly, could always account for the course man has adopted, by assigning a cause or a predisposing reason which has actually induced him to adopt it: yet this reason would often be complex and incomprehensible to ourselves, because the concatenation of causes linked together is very long.

(*Theodicy*, sec. 52.) All is therefore certain and determined beforehand in man, as everywhere else, and the human soul is a kind of *spiritual automaton*, although contingent actions in general and free action in particular are not on that account necessary with an absolute necessity, which would be truly incompatible with contingency. Thus neither futurition in itself, certain as it is, nor the infallible prevision of God, nor the predetermination either of causes or of God's decrees destroys this contingency and this freedom.

(*Theodicy*, sec. 121.) God, in truth, knows no other judge that can compel him . . . to turn to evil; he is not like Jupiter who fears the Styx. . . . But his own wisdom is the greatest judge that he can find, there is no appeal from its judgements: they are the decrees of destiny. The eternal verities, objects of his wisdom, are more inviolable than the Styx. These laws and this judge do not constrain: they arc stronger, for they persuade. Wisdom only shows God the best possible exercise of his goodness: after that, the evil that occurs is an inevitable result of the best. I will add something stronger: To permit the evil, as God permits it, is the greatest goodness. . . . When God does leave it to a man, it has belonged to him since before his existence; it was already in the idea of him as still merely possible, before the decree of God which makes him to exist.

(*Theodicy*, sec. 122.) God has care for men, he loves the human race, he wishes it well, nothing so true. . . . If in spite of all that someone is wicked and unhappy, it behooved him to be so. God (so they say) could have given happiness to all, he could have given it promptly and easily, and without causing himself any inconvenience, for he can do all. But should he? . . . <To do so would be to give> good things in order that he may cause more affliction than by taking them away. That would be trifling with God in perpetual anthropomorphisms, representing him as a man who must give himself up completely to one particular business, whose goodness must be chiefly exercised upon those objects alone which are known to us, and who lacks either aptitude or good will. God is not lacking therein, he could do the good that we would desire; he even wishes it, taking it separately, but he must not do it in preference to other greater goods which are opposed to it.

(*Theodicy*, sec. 337.) God is incapable of being indeterminate in anything whatsoever: he cannot be ignorant, he cannot doubt, he cannot suspend his judgement; his will is always decided, and it can only be decided by the best. God can never have a primitive particular will, that is, independent of laws or general acts of will; such a thing would be unreasonable. He cannot determine upon Adam, Peter, Judas or any individual without the existence of a reason for this determination; and this reason leads of necessity to some general proposition. The wise mind always acts *according to principles*, always *according to rules*, and never *according to exceptions*, save when the rules come into collision through opposing tendencies, where the strongest carries the day: or else, either they will stop one another or some third course will emerge as a result. In all these cases one rule serves as an exception to the other, and there are never any *original exceptions* with one who always acts in a regular way.

(*Theodicy*, sec. 340.) <Bayle falls into grave error> in relation to the laws of the realm of Nature: he believes them to be arbitrary and indifferent, and he objects that God could better have attained his end in the realm of grace if he had not clung to these laws, if he had more often dispensed with their observance, or even if he had made others. He believed this especially with regard to the law of the union between the soul and the body. For he is persuaded, with the modern Cartesians, that the ideas of the perceptible qualities that God gives (according to them) to the soul, occasioned by movements of the body, have nothing representing these movements or resembling them. Accordingly it was a purely arbitrary act on God's part to give us the ideas of heat, cold, light and other qualities which we experience, rather than to give us quite different ideas occasioned in the same way.

(*Theodicy*, sec. 344.) Mr. Bayle holds that "<If> God was constrained by supreme wisdom to establish the laws that he has established, there we have neither more nor less than the *Fatum* of the Stoics. Wisdom will have marked out a way for God, the abandonment whereof will have been as impossible to him as his own self-destruction." This objection has been sufficiently overthrown: it is only a moral necessity; and it is always a happy necessity to be bound to act in accordance with the rules of perfect wisdom.

(DM, sec. 13.) We have said that the concept of an individual substance includes once for all everything which can ever happen to it and that in considering this concept one will be able to see everything which can truly be said concerning the individual, just as we are able to see in the nature of a circle all the properties which can be derived from it. But does it not seem that in this way the difference between contingent and necessary truths will be destroyed, that there will be no place for human liberty, and that an absolute fatality will rule as well over all our actions as over all the rest of the events of the world? To this I reply that a distinction must be made between that which is certain and that which is necessary. Every one grants that future contingencies are assured since God foresees them, but we do not say just because of that that they are necessary. But it will be objected, that if any conclusion can be deduced infallibly from some definition or concept, it is necessary; and now since we have maintained that everything which is to happen to anyone is already virtually included in his nature or concept, as all the properties are contained in the definition of a circle, therefore, the difficulty remains. In order to meet the objection completely, I say that the connection or sequence is of two kinds; the one, absolutely necessary, whose contrary implies contradiction, occurs in the eternal verities like the truths of geometry; the other is necessary only *ex hypothesi*, and so to speak by accident, and in itself it is contingent since the contrary is not implied. This latter sequence is not founded upon ideas wholly pure and upon the pure understanding of God, but upon his free decrees and upon the processes of the universe. Let us give an example. Since Julius Caesar will become perpetual Dictator and master of the Republic and will overthrow the liberty of Rome, this action is contained in his concept, for we have supposed that it is the nature of such a perfect concept of a subject to involve everything, in fact so that the predicate may be included in the subject *ut possit inesse subjecto*. We may say that it is not in virtue of this concept or idea that he is obliged to perform this action, since it pertains to him only because God knows everything. But it will be insisted in reply that his nature or form responds to this concept, and since God imposes upon him this personality, he is compelled henceforth to live up to it. I could reply by instancing the similar case of the future contingencies which as yet have no reality save in the understanding and will of God, and which, because God has given them in advance this form, must needs correspond to it. But I prefer to overcome a difficulty rather than to excuse it by instancing other difficulties, and what I am about to say will serve to clear up the one as well as the other. It is here that must be applied the distinction in the kind of relation, and I say that that which happens conformably to these decrees is assured, but that it is not therefore necessary, and if anyone did the contrary, he would do nothing impossible in itself, although it is impossible *ex hypothesi* that that other happen. For if anyone were capable of carrying out a complete demonstration by virtue of which he could prove this connection of the subject, which is Caesar, with the predicate, which is his successful enterprise, he would bring us to see in fact that the future dictatorship of Caesar had its basis in his concept or nature, so that one would see there a reason why he resolved to cross the Rubicon rather than to stop, and why he gained instead of losing the day at Pharsalus, and that it was reasonable and by consequence assured that this would occur, but one would not prove that it was necessary in itself, nor that the contrary implied a contradiction, almost in the same way in which it is reasonable and assured that God will always do what is best although that which is less perfect is not thereby implied. For it would be found that this demonstration of this predicate as belonging to Caesar is not as absolute as are those of numbers or of geometry, but this predicate presupposes a sequence of things which God has shown by his free will. This sequence is based on the first free decree of God which was to do always that which is the most perfect and upon the decree which God made following the first one, regarding human nature, which is that men should always do, although freely, that which appears to be the best. Now every truth which is founded upon this kind of decree is contingent, although certain, for the decrees of God do not change the possibilities of things and, as I have already said, although God assuredly chooses the best, this does not prevent that which is less perfect from being possible in itself. Although it will never happen, it is not its impossibility but its imperfection which causes him to reject it. But nothing is necessitated whose opposite is possible. One will then be in a position to satisfy these kinds of difficulties, however great they may appear (and in fact they have not been less vexing to all other thinkers who have ever treated this matter), provided that he considers well that all contingent propositions have reasons why they are thus, rather than otherwise, or indeed (what is the same thing) that they have proof *a priori* of their truth, which render them certain and show that the connection of the subject and the predicate in these propositions has its basis in the nature of the one and of the other, but he must further remember that such contingent propositions have not the demonstrations of necessity, since their reasons are founded only on the principle of contingency or of the existence of things, that is to say, upon that which is, or which appears to be the best among several things equally possible. Necessary truths, on the other hand, are founded upon the principle of contradiction, and upon the possibility or impossibility of the essences themselves, without regard here to the free will of God or of creatures.

(Foucher de Careil, *Nouvelles lettres et opuscules*, p. 179; Loemker, pp. 263–64; Ariew & Garber, p. 95; "On Freedom" [ca. 1689?].) Having thus recognized the contingency of things, I raised the further questions of a clear concept of truth, for I had a reasonable hope of throwing some light from this upon the problem of distinguishing necessary from contingent truths. For I saw that in every true affirmative proposition, whether universal or singular, necessary or contingent, the predicate inheres in the subject or that the concept of the predicate is in some way involved in the concept of the subject. I saw too that this is the principle of infallibility for him who knows everything a priori. But this very fact seemed to increase the difficulty, for, if at any particular time the concept of the predicate inheres in the concept of the subject, how can the predicate ever be denied of the subject without contradiction and impossibility, or without destroying the subject concept? A new and unexpected light arose at last, however, where I least expected it, namely, from mathematical considerations of the nature of the infinite.

(Foucher de Careil, *Nouvelles lettres et opuscules*, p. 180; Loemker, pp. 264–65; Ariew & Garber, p. 96; "On Freedom" [1689?].) Some immediate truths can be reduced to primary truths <by a finite process of analysis>; the others can be reduced in an infinite progression. The former are necessary; the latter, contingent. A necessary proposition is one whose contrary implies a contradiction; such are all identities and all derivative truths reducible to identities. To this genus belong the truths said to be of metaphysical or geometrical necessity. For to demonstrate is merely, by an analysis of the terms of a proposition and the substitution of the definition or a part of it, for the thing defined, to show a kind of equation or coincidence of predicate and subject in a reciprocal proposition, or, in other cases, at least an inclusion of the one in the other, so that what was concealed in the proposition or was contained in it only potentially, is rendered evident or explicit by demonstration. . . . In contingent truths, however, though the predicate inheres in the subject, we can never demonstrate this, nor can the proposition ever be reduced to an equation or an identity, but the analysis proceeds to infinity, only God being able to see, not the end of the analysis indeed, since there is no end, but the nexus of terms or the inclusion of the predicate in the subject, since he sees everything which is in the series. Indeed, this truth itself arises in part from his intellect and in part from his will and so expresses his infinite perfection and the harmony of the entire series of things, each in its own particular way.

(Couturat, *Opuscules*, p. 19; "Necessary and Contingent Truths" [ca. 1686].) Thus, even if one could know the entire series of the universe (*tota series universi*) one could not give its sufficient reason unless a comparison has been made of it with all other possibilities. Whence it becomes clear why no demonstration can be found for a contingent proposition, no matter how far the resolution of concepts is continued.

COMMENTARY

Contingent truths on the order of "Leibniz wrote section 36 of the Monadology with a quill pen" involve an infinitistic resolution into particular causes, regardless of whether we look to causes in the order of physical causation (of efficient causes or motions) or in the order of psychic causation (final causes or reasons).

Contingent truths too—"Caesar crossed the Rubicon," for example—are accordingly also "analytic," albeit in their own (infinitistic) way. For there will always be a line of reasoning to establish how it is better that things are arranged as is rather than otherwise. But any such explanation, which requires discerning the whole interrelated complexity of endless detail regarding the arrangement of things in this world and comparing this with possible alternatives, is always a reasoning of literally unending (i.e., infinite) ramifications that can be carried through by God alone.

Leibniz connects the infinite analysis of contingent truths with the "endless detail" of the world and the "ad infinitum division" of all bodies in nature. (Note that sec. 65 tells us that "each bit of matter is not merely infinitely divisible, but is even actually endlessly subdivided.") Explaining why any of the world's facts are as they are involves showing how this is for the best with *everything* taken into account—that is, with all its involvement with everything else duly considered. Truth coordinates with optimality and demonstrations of optimality require going "into endless detail." (The endless complexity of a contingent truth is akin to that of a statement like "The integer 5 occurs with greater relative frequency in the decimal expansion of pi than it does in that of the square root of 2.") The presentation of the sufficient reason for a contingent truth of fact thus always involves an infinite process of analysis.

But while all truths must, for Leibniz, rest on a sufficient reason of some sort (a sufficient reason that is provided in the case of necessary truths via the principle of contradiction, as per sec. 31), the issue of the operative principle with respect to *contingent truths* still remains unaddressed until this present section. The issue sets the stage for the next few sections, and ultimately finds its resolution in section 46 with the contention that *the principle of contingent truth is that of fitness or of God's choice of the best.* The infinite process involved is one of optimality-determination across an infinite comparison range. The inherent infinitude of the quest for perfection is the key to contingency. Leibniz relies on Aristotle's distinction between "efficient" and "final" causes. Efficient causes operate in the order of natural causality, of physical lawfulness; final causes operate in the order of ends, goals, and purposes. And Leibniz construes the latter in terms of the reasons that govern God's creation choice which, in the final analysis, pivots the issue on the *perfection* of the creation.

KEY WORDS:

sufficient reason/*raison suffisante*
contingent truths/*vérités contingentes*
truth of fact/*vérités de fait*
the universe/*l'univers*
created beings/*créatures*
nature/*nature*
analysis/*analyse* or *résolution en raisons*
variety/*variété*
division (of bodies)/*division* (des corps)
figure/*figure*
motion/*mouvement*
minute inclinations/*petites inclinations*
minute dispositions/*petites dispositions*
series of things/*suite des choses*
particular reasons/*raisons particulières*
detail/*détail*
efficient cause/*causes efficientes*
final cause/*causes finales*
infinity/*infinité*

SECTION 37

37. **And as all this** *detail* **only contains other prior, or yet more detailed contingents each of which also requires a similar analysis to provide its reason, one is no further ahead. The sufficient or final reason must lie outside of the <entire> sequence or** *series* **of this detail of contingencies, however infinite it may be.**

37. *Et comme tout ce* detail *n'enveloppe que d'autres contingens anterieurs ou plus detaillés, dont chacun a encore besoin d'une Analyse semblable pour en rendre raison, on n'en est pas plus avancé: et il faut que la raison suffisante ou dernière soit hors de la suite ou* series *de ce detail des contingences, quelqu'infini qu'il pourroit être.*

(*Theodicy*, sec. 225.) The infinity of possibles, however great it may be, is not greater than that of the wisdom of God, who knows all possibles. One may even say that if this wisdom does not exceed the possibles extensively, since the objects of the understanding cannot go beyond the possible, which in a sense is alone intelligible, then it exceeds them intensively, by reason of the infinitely infinite combinations it makes thereof, and of its many deliberations concerning them.

(PNG, sec. 8.) Now this sufficient reason for the existence of the universe cannot be found in the series of contingent things, that is to say, of bodies and their representations in souls. For since matter is in itself indifferent to motion rather than to another, one cannot find in it a reason for motion and still less for some particular motion. Although the present motion in matter arises from preceding motion, and that in turn from motion which preceded it, we do not get further however far we may go, for the same question always remains. The sufficient reason, therefore, which needs no further reason, must be outside of this series of contingent things and is found in a substance which is the cause of this series or which is a necessary being bearing the reason for its existence within itself; otherwise we should not yet have a sufficient reason with which to stop. This final reason for things is called *God*.

(G VII, 200; "On Demonstrations" [ca. 1690].) The difference between *necessary* and *contingent truths* is indeed the same as that between commensurable and incommensurable numbers. For just as commensurable numbers can be resolved into common factors, so necessary truths can be demonstrated, that is, reduced to identical propositions. Moreover: in surd (irrational) ratios the resolution proceeds *in infinitum* and a common measure cannot be attained; yet a certain series is obtained, though it be endless. Analogously, contingent truths require an infinite analysis which can be performed only by God, so that he alone can know them *a priori* and with certainty. . . . Hence, any truth which is not susceptible of analysis and cannot be demonstrated by reason, but receives its ultimate reason and certainty from the divine mind alone, is not a necessary truth. All the truths of this kind I call *truths of fact*. This is the root of contingency, and so far as I know, no one has hitherto explained it.

(G VII, 302; Loemker, p. 486; "On the Radical Origination of Things" [1697].) For the dominant One of the universe not only rules the world but fabricates or makes it; it is superior to the world and, so to speak, extramundane, and hence is the ultimate reason for things. For a sufficient reason for existence cannot be found merely in any one individual thing or even in the whole aggregate and series of things. Let us imagine the book on the *Elements of Geometry* to have been eternal, one copy always being made from another; then it is clear that though we can give a reason for the present book based on the preceding book from which it is copied, we can never arrive at a complete reason, no matter how many books we may assume in the past, for one can always wonder why such books should have existed at all times; why there should be books at all, and why they should be written in this way. What is true of books is true also of the different states of the world; every subsequent state is somehow copied from the preceding one (although according to certain laws of change). No matter how far we may have gone back to earlier states, therefore, we will never discover in them a full reason why there should be a world at all, and why it should be such as it is.

Even if we should imagine the world to be eternal, therefore, the reason for it would clearly have to be sought elsewhere, since we would still be assuming nothing but a succession of states, in any one of which we can find no sufficient reason, nor can we advance the slightest toward establishing a reason, no matter how many of these states we assume. For even though there be no cause for eternal things, there must yet be understood to be a reason for them. . . . These considerations show clearly that we cannot escape an ultimate extramundane reason of things, that is to say, God, even if we suppose the eternity of the world.

(G VII, 320; Loemker, p. 364; "On the Method for Distinguishing Real from Imaginary Phenomena" [ca. 1690].) But this criterion ⟨of real existence⟩ can be referred back to another general class of tests drawn from preceding phenomena. The present phenomenon must be coherent with these if, namely, it preserves the same consistency or if a reason can be supplied for it from preceding phenomena or if all together are coherent with the same hypothesis, as if with a common cause. But certainly a most valid criterion is a consensus with the whole sequence of life, especially if many others affirm the same thing to be coherent with their phenomena also, for it is not only probable but certain, as I will show directly, that other substances exist which are similar to us. Yet the most powerful criterion of the reality of phenomena, sufficient even by itself, is success in predicting future phenomena from past and present ones, whether that prediction is based upon a reason, upon a hypothesis that was previously successful, or upon the customary consistency of things as observed previously.

(Couturat, *Opuscules*, p. 18; "Necessary and Contingent Truths" [ca. 1686].) There is something which had perplexed me for a long time—how it is possible for the predicate of a proposition to be contained in (*inesse*) the subject without making the proposition necessary. But the knowledge of Geometrical matters, and especially of infinitesimal analysis, lit the lamp for me, so that I came to see that notions too can be resolvable *in infinitum*.

(Grua, p. 302; "Reflections on Bellarmin" [ca. 1682].) But you ask whether the opposite, namely that God does not choose the most perfect thing, involves a contradiction. I say it does not involve a contradiction unless God's will is posited already. For God wills to will the most perfect thing, and He wills to will to will it, and so on to infinity, because this reflexive infinity of choices falls on God, and it does not, to be sure, fall on created things. In this, therefore, lies the whole secret, for God not only decides to do the most perfect thing, but He also decides to decide. . . . For in general it is established that nothing is a decree which God has not previously decreed by another decree, from the nature of perfect freedom, outside of which there is no reason.

(Foucher de Caveil, *Nouvelles lettres et opuscules*, p. 180; Loemker, p. 264; Ariew & Garber, p. 95; "On Freedom" [ca. 1679].) At length some new and unexpected light appeared from a direction I least expected—from mathematical considerations regarding the nature of the infinite. In truth there are two labyrinths in the human mind, one concerning the composition of the continuum, the other concerning the nature of freedom. And both of these spring from exactly the same source—the infinite.

(Foucher de Careil, *Nouvelles lettres et opuscules*, p. 180; Loemker, p. 264; Ariew & Garber, p. 95; "On Freedom" [ca. 1689?].) It must be understood, then, that all created beings have a certain mark of the divine infinity impressed upon them and that this is the source of many wonderful matters which astound the human mind. For example, there is no portion of matter, however tiny, in which there is not a world of creatures, infinite in number. And there is no created substance, however imperfect, which does not act upon all the others and suffer action from all the others, and whose complex concept as this exists in the divine mind does not contain the whole universe, with all that ever is, has been, and will be. And there is no truth of fact or of individual things which does not depend upon an infinite series of reasons, though God alone can see everything that is in this series. This is the cause, too, why only God knows the contingent truths a priori and sees their infallibility otherwise than by experience.

COMMENTARY

The series or regress of grounds does not suffice for the complete explanation of a thing because even if we were to have this whole series, this still does not settle the synoptic question of why the series is as it is. This ground of the overall series of grounds must itself lie outside the series. Accordingly, the ultimately sufficient reason for any aspect of the real must lie beyond and outside the causal order of the world's processes. Leibniz's reasoning here is akin to that of Aristotle's prime mover argument at *Physics*, VIII, v and *Metaphysics*, XII, vi-vii.

The fact that the endeavor to provide the sufficient reasons for contingent truths must always run off into an infinite regress (albeit one of an ultimately convergent nature) means that for Leibniz the root of contingency lies in the infinite (*radix contingentiae est in infinitum*). In the best of possible worlds everything must be attuned to everything else in a way that requires an endless attention to detail.

KEY WORDS:

contingents/*contingents*
detail/*détail (des contingences)*
analysis/*analyse*
infinite/*infini*
sequence (of things)/*suite (des choses)*
sufficient reason/*raison suffisante*
series of contingencies/*série des contingences*

SECTION 38

38. And so the ultimate reason of things must be in a necessary substance in which the detail of the changes is present only eminently, as in its source. It is this that we call *God*. (See *Theodicy*, sec. 7.)

38. Et c'est ainsi que la dernière raison des choses doit être dans une sub-stance necessaire, dans laquelle le detail des changemens ne soit qu'eminem-ment, comme dans la source: et c'est ce que nous appelons Dieu. (Théodicée, sec. 7.)

(*Theodicy*, sec. 7.) God is the first reason of things: for such things as are bounded, as all that which we see and experience, are contingent and have noth-ing in them to render their existence necessary, it being plain that time, space and matter, united and uniform in themselves and indifferent to everything, might have received entirely other motions and shapes, and in another order. Therefore one must seek the reason for the existence of the world, which is the whole assemblage of contingent things, and seek it in the substance which car-ries with it the reason for its existence, and which in consequence is necessary and eternal.

(PNG, sec. 8.) Now this sufficient reason for the existence of the universe cannot be found in the series of contingent things, that is to say, of bodies and their representations in souls. For since matter is in itself indifferent to motion rather than to another, one cannot find in it a reason for motion and still less for some particular motion. Although the present motion in matter arises from preceding motion, and that in turn from motion which preceded it, we do not get further however far we may go, for the same question always remains. The <ultimate> sufficient reason, therefore, which itself needs no further reason, must be outside of this series of contingent things and is found in a substance which is the cause of this series or which is a necessary being bearing the reason for its existence within itself; otherwise we should not yet have a sufficient reason with which to stop. This final reason for things is called *God*.

(PNG, sec. 9.) This simple primary substance must include eminently the perfections contained <formally> in the derivative substances which are its effects. Thus it will have perfect power, knowledge, and will; that is to say, it will have omnipotence, omniscience, and sovereign goodness. And since jus-tice, taken in its most general sense, is nothing but goodness conforming with wisdom, there is also necessarily a sovereign justice in God. The reason which has made things exist through him has also made them depend on him for their existence and operation, and they are continually receiving from him that which causes them to have some perfection. But whatever imperfection re-mains with them comes from the essential and original limitation of the created beings.

COMMENTARY

With Leibniz, a *necessary* substance is one whose very conception carries within itself the reality of its own existence—and which accordingly must exist if this is possible at all (that is, if its conception involves no self-contradiction). With such a substance the move from possibility to actuality is accordingly (uniquely) possible. God alone is a necessary substance in this sense. (Compare sec. 44.)

Regarding God, Laplace declared, "I had no need of that hypothesis" (*Je n'a-vois pas besoin de cette hypothèse*). But for Leibniz, the situation is the very reverse. God is the engine that makes the entire machinery go—the prime mover of the monadic system. In this sense, Leibniz is a true child of the era of Descartes, Spinoza, and Berkeley.

God has been mentioned before in our text in more or less incidental asides (in secs. 29 and 30, and by implication, when created monads were spoken of in sec. 19). But now he comes explicitly on to the stage as the causal source of the monads and "the final reason of things."

As Leibniz sees it, whatever is must have a "final" or *ultimate* sufficient reason, and he holds that the reason for an existent must always lie in something that is itself existent. The final reason of an existent must accordingly be a necessary existent because, were it to depend on some further reason, then it could not itself be final, contrary to hypothesis. However, this ultimate reason for what exists—namely God—is said (in the philosophical terminology of the day) to *"contain"* what exists only in the explanatory order of reasons ("eminently") and *not* in the conceptual order of its substantial make-up or composition ("formally"). One thing is contained "formally" in another if it is physically present as a part or aspect (as the engine is contained in the car or the power in the engine). It is contained "eminently" in another if it is present there not in a physical but rather in an explanatory sense, as the skill of the builder is contained in a structure or the plan of a general in the battle.

In the *Principles of Nature and Grace* (sec. 8) Leibniz insists: "The sufficient reason [of contingent existence] . . . must be outside this series of contingent things, and *must reside in a substance which is the cause of this series.*" Such a view—which goes back to Aristotle—amounts to a thesis of genetic homogeneity maintaining (on analogy with the old, but now rather obsolete, principle that "life must come from life"), that "things must come from things," or "stuff must come from stuff," or "substance must come from substance." But, despite its appeal, this conception has its problems. It presupposes that there must be a type-homogeneity between cause and effect on the lines of the ancient Greek principle that "like must come from like." This highly dubious idea has taken hard knocks in the course of modern science. (Matter can come from energy, and living organisms from complexes of inorganic molecules.) If the homogeneity doctrine fails with matter and life, need it hold for substance as such? Must substance inevitably arise from *substance?* Is it indeed true that only *things* can engender things? Why need a ground of change always inhere in a *thing* rather than in a nonsubstantival "condition of things-in-general"? Why, for example, can processes or principles not be causally operative—as already contemplated by Plato and the Presocratics? (Think, for example, of the love and strife of Empedocles.) To be sure facts must room in facts, and all fact-explanations must have factual inputs (*all* explanations must). But why thing-existential ones: why must the explanation of facts rest in the operation of *things?* A clearly problematic bit of metaphysics is involved here.

KEY WORDS:

detail/*détail*
the ultimate reason/*la dernière raison*
necessary substance/*substance nécessaire*
eminently or finally/*éminemment ou finalement*
God/*Dieu*

SECTION 39

39. Now as this substance is a sufficient reason of all this detail, which is also interconnected throughout, *there is only one God and this God is all-sufficient.*

39. *Or cette Substance étant une raison suffisante de tout ce detail, lequel aussi est lié partout; il n'y a qu'un Dieu et ce Dieu suffit.*

(G VII, 302–03; Loemker, p. 487; Ariew & Garber, p. 150; "On the Radical Origin of Things" [1697].) The reasons for the world therefore lie in something extramundane, different from the chain of states or series of things whose aggregate constitutes the world. And so we must go from physical or hypothetical necessity, which determines later things in the world from earlier ones, to something which has absolute or metaphysical necessity, for which no reason can be given. The present world is necessary in a physical or hypothetical sense, not absolutely or metaphysically. That is, once it is established to be such as it is, it follows that things such as they are will come into being. Therefore, since there must be an ultimate root in something which has metaphysical necessity, and since there is no reason for an existing thing except in another existing thing, there must necessarily exist some one being of metaphysical necessity, or a being to whose essence belongs existence. So there must exist something which is distinct from the plurality of beings, or from the world, which, as we have admitted and shown, has no metaphysical necessity.

COMMENTARY

Two sorts of universal interconnectedness (*liaison universelle*) among substances is operative in the monadic system of Leibniz. The first is their *logical interrelation* operative in view of the fact that the complete individual concept of each substance takes account of all the rest through its inherent completeness. (See sec. 14.) The second is the *lawful harmony* that makes the world into an orderly cosmos whose processes conform to simple laws. (See secs. 56–57.) The former is a logically necessary feature of *every* possible world, the latter a contingent feature of the *actual* world as the best possible.

The qualitative variation (detail) of things is endless, and is an aspect of their own nature. But the world's being a system—a single lawfully coordinated and coherent whole—demands the existence of God in the order of sufficient reasons.

Since God is the sufficient reason that explains all of existence as a whole, it follows that he must be unique. For if there were several separate Gods, which divide the explanatory labor between them, there would have to be a further explanation for this partitioning—a still more ultimate super-explanation to account for this splintering of explanatory responsibilities. This would impede that explanatory ultimacy of God which—with Leibniz—is of necessity a definitive aspect of his nature.

KEY WORDS:

necessary substance/*substance nécessaire*
sufficient reason/*raison suffisante*
detail/*détail*
to link/*lier*
God/*Dieu*
universal interlinkage/*liaison universelle*

SECTION 40

40. One can also conclude that this Supreme Substance, which is unique, universal, and necessary—having nothing outside it that is independent of it, and being a direct consequence of merely being possibile—must be incapable of limits and must contain as much reality as is possible.

40. On peut juger aussi que cette Substance Supreme qui est unique, universelle et necessaire, n'ayant rien hors d'elle qui en soit independant, et étant une suite simple d'être possible; doit être incapable de limites et contenir tout autant de realité qu'il est possible.

(PNG, sec. 9.) This simple primary substance must include eminently the perfections contained <formally> in the derivative substances which are its effects. Thus it will have perfect power, knowledge, and will; that is to say, it will have omnipotence, omniscience, and sovereign goodness. And since justice, taken in its most general sense, is nothing but goodness conforming with wisdom, there is also necessarily a sovereign justice in God. The reason which has made things exist through him has also made them depend on him for their existence and operation, and they are continually receiving from him that which causes them to have some perfection. But whatever imperfection remains with them comes from the essential and original limitation of the created beings.

(NE, p. 438.) God is the greatest or (as Descartes says) the most perfect of beings; which is to say that he is a being whose greatness or perfection is supreme, containing within himself every degree of it. That is the notion of God. Now here is how existence follows from that notion. Existing is something more than not existing, i.e. existence adds a degree to the greatness or to the perfection—as Descartes puts it, existence is itself a perfection. So this degree of greatness and perfection (or rather this perfection) which consists in existence is in that wholly great and wholly perfect supreme being; for otherwise he would be lacking in some degree, which is contrary to his definition. And so it follows that this supreme being exists. The Scholastics, including even their Angelic doctor, held this argument in low esteem, regarding it as fallacious [Thomas Aquinas, *Summa Theologica*, Ia.ii.I ad 2um]; but this was a great mistake on their part, and M. Descartes, having studied scholastic philosophy for a good while at the Jesuit College of La Flèche, was quite right to revive the argument. It is not fallacious, but it is an incomplete demonstration which assumes something which should also be proved in order to render the argument mathematically evident. The point is that it is tacitly assumed that this idea of a wholly great or wholly perfect being is possible and does not imply a contradiction. Even that remark enables us to prove something, namely that *If God is possible, he exists*—a privilege which only the Divinity possesses.

(DM, sec. 1) The conception of God which is the most common and the most full of meaning is expressed well enough in the words: God is an absolutely perfect being. The implications, however, of these words fail to receive sufficient consideration. For instance, there are many different kinds of perfection, all of which God possesses, and each one of them pertains to him in the highest degree. We must also know what perfection is. One thing which can surely be affirmed about it is that those forms or natures which are not susceptible of it to the highest degree, say the nature of numbers or of figures, do not permit of perfection. This is because the number which is the greatest of all (that is, the sum of all the numbers), and likewise the greatest of all figures, imply contradictions. The greatest knowledge, however, and omnipotence contain no impossibility. Consequently power and knowledge do admit of perfection, and in so far as they pertain to God they have no limits. Whence it follows that God who possesses supreme and infinite wisdom acts in the most perfect manner not only metaphysically, but also from the moral standpoint.

(G III, 572; to Bourget [1714].) I agree that the idea of possibles also involves necessarily that of the existence of a being who can produce the possible. But the idea of possibles does not involve the actual existence of this being, as it seems, Sir, that you take it, when you add: "If there were not such a being, nothing would be possible." For it suffices that a being who would produce the thing should be possible, in order that a being may be possible, it suffices that its efficient cause be possible; I except the supreme efficient cause, which must actually exist. But this is for another reason, because nothing would be possible if the necessary Being did not exist.

(G IV, 406; "On the Ontological Argument" [1701].) If the necessary Being is possible, he exists. For the necessary Being and the Being by his essence are one and the same thing. . . . If the Being through self is impossible, all beings through others are so too, since they only are, in the end, through the Being through self; and thus nothing could exist. . . . If there is no necessary Being, there is no possible being.

COMMENTARY

God is "universal" in being all-sufficient—in being the ultimate sufficient reason for all that exists and the ontological basis of all that is possible. (Compare sec. 43.) In this sense (and in this sense only) is Leibniz a pantheist who sees God as omnipresent in that his power is operative everywhere.

Leibniz follows the lead of St. Anselm's ontological argument for the necessary existence of God, who thus stands forth as *the necessary being* whose actual existence is "a direct consequence of its merely being possible." (Compare secs. 38, 44.) This self-necessitated existent that is the ultimate ground of all that exists contingently is maximally real because—in Leibniz's view—the degree of reality of a substance stands coordinate with its inner exigency to existence. (Compare sec. 54.) Accordingly, an existent whose existence is a matter of metaphysical necessity is thereby automatically maximal in point of its "degree of reality."

KEY WORDS:

supreme substance/*substance suprême*
necessary substance/*substance nécessaire*
possible substance/*substance possible*
independent/*indépendent*
limitless/*incapable de limites*
reality/*réalité*

SECTION 41

41. From this it follows that God is absolutely perfect, *perfection* **being noth-ing but the amount of positive reality taken separately, putting aside the limits or bounds in the things that have them. And where there are no bounds at all, namely in God, perfection is absolutely infinite. (See** *Theodicy,* **Preface, sec. 22.)**

41. D'où il s'ensuit que Dieu est absolument parfait; la perfection *n'étant autre chose que la grandeur de la realité positive prise precisément, en mettant à part les limites ou bornes dans les choses qui en ont. Et là, où il n'y a point de bornes, c'est à dire, en Dieu, la perfection est absolument infinie. (*Théo-dicée, Préface, *4a; sec. 22.)*

(*Theodicy,* Preface [G VI, 27].) To love God it suffices to contemplate his perfections, a thing easy indeed, because we find the ideas of these within our-selves. The perfections of God are those of our souls, but he possesses them in boundless measure; he is an ocean, whereof to us only drops have been granted; there is in us some power, some knowledge, some goodness, but in God they are all in their entirety. Order, proportions, harmony delight us; painting and music are samples of these: God is all order; he always keeps truth of propor-tions, he makes universal harmony; all beauty is an effusion of his rays.

(*Theodicy,* sec. 22.) In this sense it may be said that God tends to all good, as good, *ad perfectionem simpliciter simplicem,* to speak like the Schoolmen, and that by an antecedent will.

COMMENTARY

Leibniz conceives of God as the primordial and all-originating substance (see sec. 47). But while God is the prime monad (existing substance), he has a totally non-standard character. For, unlike all other substances, he has no environing entourage to constitute a body of some sort (sec. 72) and lacks any passive as-pect—any *materia prima* or prime matter (sec. 49). And, being changeless, he lacks any sort of appetition as well (sec. 14); among substances he alone is al-together atemporal and unchanging.

Leibniz coordinates the *ontological perfection* of a thing—the lack of limits or limitations in its inherent nature—with its potential to existence, and thus with its degree of reality. God's own nature contains nothing to countervail against the realization of this potential, and so he necessarily exists. So here, uniquely, the transition from essence to existence characteristic of St. Anselm's ontological argument is feasible. With other (contingent) things, their (non-maximal) perfections merely establish *a claim to consideration* by God whose weight he takes account of in his decision to create. Here, then the transition from conceptual perfection to active existence is mediated by the benevolent will of God.

KEY WORDS:

God/*Dieu*
perfection/*perfection*
absolutely perfect/*absolument parfait*
positive reality/*réalité positive*
limits/*bornes*
absolutely infinite/*absolument infinie*

SECTION 42

42. It follows also that created beings owe their perfections to the influence of God, but owe their imperfections to their own nature, which is incapable of being without limits. For it is in this that they differ from God. [This *original imperfection* of created beings expresses itself in the *inherent inertia* of bodies.] (See *Theodicy*, secs. 20, 27–31, 153, 167, 377–78, 380; Abridgment, obj. 5.)

42. *Il s'ensuit aussi que les creatures ont leurs perfections de l'influence de Dieu, mais qu'elles ont leurs imperfections de leur nature propre, incapable d'être sans bornes. Car c'est en cela qu'elles sont distinguées de Dieu.* [*Cette* imperfection originale *des creatures se remarque dans* l'inertie naturelle *des corps.*] (Théodicée, *secs. 20, 27–31, 153, 167, 377–78, 380; Abrégé, obj.5.*)

(*Theodicy*, sec. 20.) The ancients attributed the cause of evil to *matter*, which they believed to be uncreated and independent of God: but we, who derive all being from God, where shall we find the source of evil? The answer is, that it must be sought in the ideal nature of the creature, in so far as this nature is contained in the eternal verities which are in the understanding of God, independent of his will. For we must consider that there is an *original imperfection in the creature* before sin, because the creature is limited in its essence; whence ensues that it cannot know all, and that it can deceive itself and commit other errors.

(*Theodicy*, sec. 27.) Someone will perhaps bring up the objection that it is God himself who acts and who effects all that is real in the sin of the creature. This objection leads us to consider the *physical co-operation* of God with the creature, after we have examined the *moral co-operation* <which must be distinguished from it>.

(*Theodicy*, sec. 28.) The objection will be made that God therefore now creates man a sinner, he that in the beginning created him innocent. But here it must be said, with regard to the moral aspect, that God being supremely wise cannot fail to observe certain laws, and to act according to the rules, as well physical as moral, that wisdom has made him choose. And the same reason that has made him create man innocent, but liable to fall, makes him re-create man when he falls; for God's knowledge causes the future to be for him as the present, and prevents him from rescinding the resolutions made.

(*Theodicy*, sec. 30.) Let us suppose that the current of one and the same river carried along with it various boats, which differ among themselves only in the cargo, some being laden with wood, others with stone, and some more, the others less. That being so, it will come about that the boats most heavily laden will go more slowly than the others, provided it be assumed that the wind or the oar, or some other similar means, assist them not at all. It is not, properly speaking, weight which is the cause of this retardation, since the boats are going down and not upwards; but it is the same cause which also increases the weight in bodies that have greater density, which are, that is to say, less porous and more charged with matter that is proper to them: for the matter which passes through the pores, not receiving the same movement, must not be taken into account. It is therefore matter itself which originally is inclined to slowness or privation of speed; not indeed of itself to lessen this speed, having once received it, since that would be action, but to moderate by its receptivity the effect of the impression when it is to receive it. Consequently, since more matter is moved by the same force of the current when the boat is more laden, it is necessary that it go more slowly; and experiments on the impact of bodies, as well as reason, show that twice as much force must be employed to give equal speed to a body of the same matter but of twice the size. But that indeed would not be necessary if the matter were absolutely indifferent to repose and to movement, and if it had not this natural inertia whereof we have just spoken to give it a kind of repugnance to be moved. Let us now compare the force which the current exercises on boats, and communicates to them, with the action of God, who produces and conserves whatever is positive in creatures, and gives them perfection, being and force: let us compare, I say, the inertia of matter with the natural imperfection of creatures, and the slowness of the laden boat with the defects to be found in the qualities and the action of the creature; and we shall find that there is nothing so just as this comparison. The current is the cause of the boat's movement, but not of its retardation; God is the cause of perfection in the nature and the actions of the creature, but the limitation of the receptivity of the creature is the cause of the defects there are in its action. . . . And God is no more the cause of sin than the river's current is the cause of the retardation of the boat. Force also in relation to matter is as the spirit in relation to the flesh; the spirit is willing and the flesh is weak, and spirits act. . . .

(*Theodicy*, sec. 31) There is, then, a wholly similar relation between such and such an action of God, and such and such a passion or reception of the creature, which in the ordinary course of things is perfected only in proportion to its "receptivity," such is the term used. And when it is said that the creature depends upon God in so far as it exists and in so far as it acts, and even that conservation is a continual creation, this is true in that God gives ever to the creature and produces continually all that in it is positive, good and perfect, every perfect gift coming from the Father of lights. The imperfections, on the other hand, and the defects in operations spring from the original limitation that the creature could not but receive with the first beginning of its being, through the ideal reasons which restrict it. For God could not give the creature all without making of it a God; therefore there must needs be different degrees in the perfection of things, and limitations also of every kind.

(*Theodicy*, sec. 153.) I have already shown how privation is enough to cause error and malice, and how God is prompted to permit them, despite that there be no malignity in him. Evil comes from privation; the positive and action spring from it by accident. . . .

(*Theodicy*, sec. 167.) Some imagine despotism in God, and demand that man be convinced, without reason, of the absolute certainty of his election, a course that is liable to have dangerous consequences. But all those who acknowledge that God produces the best plan, having chosen it from among all possible ideas of the universe; that he there finds man inclined by the original imperfection of creatures to misuse his free will and to plunge into misery; that God prevents the sin and the misery in so far as the perfection of the universe, which is an emanation from his, may permit it: those, I say, show forth more clearly that God's intention is the one most right and holy in the world; that the creature alone is guilty, that his original limitation or imperfection is the source of his wickedness, that his evil will is the sole cause of his misery; that one cannot be destined to salvation without also being destined to the holiness of the children of God, and that all hope of election one can have can only be founded upon the good will infused into one's heart by the grace of God.

(*Theodicy*, sec. 377.) Since . . . every action of the creature is a change of its modifications, it is obvious that action arises in the creature in relation to the limitations or negations which it has within itself, and which are diversified by this change.

(*Theodicy*, sec. 378.) I have already pointed out more than once in this work that evil is a consequence of privation, and I think that I have explained that intelligibly enough. . . . Doubtless God is its author, when the moral evil is assumed to be already in existence; but speaking generally, one might assert that God permitted physical evil by implication, in permitting moral evil which is its source.

(*Theodicy*, sec. 380.) Aristotle was right in rejecting chaos: but it is not always easy to disentangle the conceptions of Plato, and such a task would be still less easy in respect of some ancient authors whose works are lost. Kepler, one of the most excellent of modern mathematicians, recognized a species of imperfection in matter, even when there is no irregular motion: he calls it its "natural inertia," which gives it a resistance to motion, whereby a greater mass receives less speed from one and the same force. There is soundness in this observation, and I have used it to advantage in this work, in order to have a comparison such as should illustrate how the original imperfection of the creatures sets bounds to the action of the Creator, which tends towards good. But as matter is itself of God's creation, it only furnishes a comparison and an example, and cannot be the very source of evil and of imperfection. I have already shown that this source lies in the forms or ideas of the possibles, for it must be eternal, and matter is not so. Now since God made all positive reality that is not eternal, he would have made the source of evil, if that did not rather lie in the possibility of things or forms, that which alone God did not make, since he is not the author of his own understanding.

(*Theodicy*, Abridgment, obj. 5.) I have therefore been well pleased to point out that every imperfection comes from limitation, that is, from the privative: for to limit is to withhold extension, or the more beyond. Now God is the cause of all perfections, and consequently of all realities, when they are regarded as purely positive. But limitations or privatives result from the original imperfection of creatures which restricts their receptivity. It is as with a laden boat, which the river carries along more slowly or less slowly in proportion to the weight that it bears: thus the speed comes from the river, but the retardation which restricts this speed comes from the load. Also I have shown in the present work how the creature, in causing sin, is a deficient cause; how errors and evil inclinations spring from privation; and how privation is efficacious accidentally. . . . If God had willed to do more here he must needs have produced either fresh natures in his creatures or fresh miracles to change their natures, and this the best plan did not allow. It is just as if the current of the river must needs be more rapid than its slope permits or the boats themselves be less laden, if they had to be impelled at a greater speed. So the limitation or original imperfection of creatures brings it about that even the best plan of the universe cannot admit more good, and cannot be exempted from certain evils, these, however, being only of such a kind as may tend towards a greater good. There are some disorders in the parts which wonderfully enhance the beauty of the whole, just as certain dissonances, appropriately used, render harmony more beautiful.

(DM, sec. 30.) God inclines our souls without necessitating them . . . [so] that we must not ask why Judas sinned because this free act is contained in his concept, the only question being why Judas the sinner is admitted to existence, preferably to other possible persons. . . . Regarding the action of God upon the human will there are many quite different considerations which it would take too long to investigate here. Nevertheless the following is what can be said in general. God in cooperating with ordinary actions only follows the laws which he has established, that is to say, he continually preserves and produces our being so that the ideas come to us spontaneously or with freedom in that order which the concept of our individual substance carries with itself. In this concept they can be foreseen for all eternity. Furthermore, by virtue of the decree which God has made that the will shall always seek the apparent good in certain particular respects (in regard to which this apparent good always has in it something of reality expressing or imitating God's will), he, without at all necessitating our choice, determines it by that which appears most desirable.

(PNG, sec. 10.) It follows from the supreme perfection of God that he has chosen the best possible plan in producing the universe, a plan which combines the greatest variety together with the greatest order; with situation, place, and time arranged in the best way possible; with the greatest effect produced by the simplest means; with the most power, the most knowledge, the greatest happiness and goodness in created things which the universe could allow. For as all possible things have a claim to existence in God's understanding in proportion to their perfections, the result of all these claims must be the most perfect actual world which is possible. Without this it would be impossible to give a reason why things have gone as they have rather than otherwise.

(Loemker, p. 146; to Magnus Wedderkopf [1671].) Pilate is condemned. Why? Because he lacks faith. Why does he lack it? Because he lacks the will to attention. Why this? Because he has not understood the necessity of the matter (the utility of attending to it). Why has he not understood it? Because the causes of understanding were lacking. For it is necessary to refer everything to some reason, and we cannot stop until we have arrived at a first cause—or it must be admitted that something can exist without a sufficient reason for its existence, and this admission destroys the demonstration of the existence of God and of many philosophical theorems. Yet what is the ultimate reason for the divine will? The divine intellect. For God wills the things which he understands to be best and most harmonious and selects them, as it were, from an infinite number of all possibilities. Yet what provides the reason for the divine intellect? The harmony of things. What the reason for the harmony of things? Nothing. For example, no reason can be given for the ratio of 2 to 4 being the same as that of 4 to 8, not even in the divine will. This depends on the essence itself, or the idea of things. For the essences of things are numbers, as it were, and contain the possibility of beings which God does not make as he does existence, since these possibilities or ideas of things coincide rather with God himself. Since God is the most perfect mind, however, it is impossible for him not to be affected by the most perfect harmony, and thus to be necessitated to do the best by the very ideality of things. But this in no way detracts from freedom. For it is the highest freedom to be impelled to the best by a right reason.

(Couturat, *Opuscules*, pp. 23–24; "Necessary and Contingent Truths" [ca. 1686].) God first considers a mind as possible before he decrees that it should actually exist. For the possibility or notion of a created mind does not involve existence. But while God considers it as possible, and knows perfectly in it all future events as possible but as connected with it (connected with it contingently, yet infallibly), at that very moment he understands, that is he knows perfectly, all that which will follow its existence. Further, whilst he understands perfectly the notion of this individual substance, still considered as possible, by that very fact he also understands his own decrees, similarly considered as possible; for just as necessary truths involve only the divine intellect, so contingent truths involve the decrees of the will. God sees that he can create things in infinite ways, and that a different series of things will come into existence if he chooses different laws of the series, i.e. other primitive decrees. And so, whilst he considers this mind, which involves in itself this series of things, by that very act he also considers the decree which this mind and this series involve. But he considers each of them as possible, for he has not yet decided to make a decree; or, he has not yet decreed what special decrees of the series, both general decrees and the special decrees connected with them, he is to choose. But when God chooses one of the series, and this particular mind (to be endowed in future with these events) which is involved in it, by that very fact he also decrees concerning all that is involved in it, and so concerning his possible decrees or laws which are to be transferred from possibility to actuality. . . . We can now understand that God is far from decreeing absolutely that Judas must become a traitor; rather, he sees from the notion of Judas, independently of his actual decree, that he will be a traitor. God, therefore, does not decree that Judas must be a traitor. All that he decrees is that Judas, who he foresees will be a traitor, must nevertheless exist, since with his infinite wisdom he sees that this evil will be counterbalanced with an immense gain in greater goods, nor can things be better in any way. The act of betrayal itself God does not will, but he allows it in his decree that Judas the sinner shall now exist, and in consequence he also makes a decree that when the time of betrayal arrives the concourse of his actual predetermination is to be accommodated to this. But this decree is limited to what there is of perfection in this evil act; it is this very notion of the creature, in so far as it involves limitation (which is the one thing that it does not have from God) that drags the act towards badness. And so I believe that if we hold to these two points—that all perfection in creatures is from God, and all imperfection from their own limitation—all other opinions can, after being carefully considered, be reconciled in the last analysis.

COMMENTARY

Leibniz equates passivity with imperfection. This passivity/imperfection has two sides, a physical and (in spirits only) a moral one. Physical imperfection represents the *material* side of substances, moral imperfection their *spiritual* side, as it were.

All created substances have a passive side that incorporates their limited and imperfect nature—an inherent "inertia" that represents their "material" aspect (*materia prima*). This "original imperfection" is included in the inevitable constitution of their defining characterization—the individualized make-up that constitutes them as the individuals they are. (God alone is *actus purus*, wholly active, without any admixture of passivity or imperfection. Compare sec. 47.)

As Leibniz sees it, God does not constrain agents to act as they do: they act as their individual concepts indicate they must. God simply decides what concept to instantiate and does thus with a vow to the best overall advantage of the whole, based on the infinite analysis that implements the principle of perfection. The properties and actions of created substances are thus not determined through the choices of God but lie wholly in their own nature—in their own individually characterizing conception. And it lies in the nature of created beings as such that they are imperfect. God in effecting his creation choice with respect to alternative possible worlds looks to the overall balance of good versus bad. His concern is to maximize the perfection of the whole. Imperfection or evil is only tolerated as the price that must unavoidably be paid to assure an optimal overall balance of positivities over negativities.

For reconciling free agency with divine foreknowledge, Leibniz in effect adopts the conception of middle knowledge (*scientia media*) deployed by the Spanish theologian Luis Molina (1535–1600). The idea is that God knows conditional truths of the form "In circumstances C, the agent X will freely prefer action A" independently of any categorical knowledge of what he will actually create. This sort of conditional knowledge is, as Molina (and his precursor, Pedro Fonseca [1528–92]) saw it, something intermediate between God's "*intuitive* knowledge" of what he actually wills to create and his "knowledge *by mere understanding*" of what sorts of things are possible.

KEY WORDS:

created beings/*créatures*
God/*Dieu*
perfections/*perfections*

imperfection/*imperfection*
limits/*bornes*
inherent inertia/*inertie naturelle*
bodies/*corps*

SECTION 43

43. It is true also that in God lies not only the source of existences, but also that of essences, insofar as they are real, or of whatever is real in possibility. This is because God's understanding is the realm of eternal truths or of the [possible essences <or>] ideas on which they depend. And without him there would be nothing real in possibilities, and not only nothing existent but even nothing possible. (See *Theodicy*, sec. 20.)

43. Il est vrai aussi qu'en Dieu est non seulement la source des existences, mais encor celle des essences, en tant que réelles, ou de ce qu'il y a de réel dans la possibilité. C'est parce que l'Entendement de Dieu est la region des verités éternelles, ou des [essences possibles] idées dont elles dependent, et que sans lui il n'y auroit rien de réel dans les possibilités, et non seulement rien d'existant, mais encore rien de possible. (Théodicée, sec. 20.)

(*Theodicy*, sec. 20.) Plato said in the *Timaeus* that the world originated in order. . . . This can be given a reasonable meaning. God will be the Understanding; and the Necessity, that is, the essential nature of things, will be the object of the understanding, in so far as this object consists in the eternal verities. But this object is inward and abides in the divine understanding. And therein is found not only the primitive form of good, but also the origin of evil: the Region of the Eternal Verities must be substituted for matter when we are concerned with seeking out the source of things.

(*Theodicy*, sec. 184.) We ought not to say, with some Scotists, that the eternal truths would subsist, even if there were no understanding, not even God's. For, in my opinion, it is the divine understanding that makes the reality of eternal truths: although his Will have no part in it. Every reality must be founded in something existent. It is true that an atheist may be a geometer. But if there were no God, there would be no object of Geometry. And without God, not only would there be nothing existent, but there would be nothing possible.

(G II, 41; Ariew & Garber, p. 72; for Arnauld [1686].) Every individual substance of this universe expresses in its concept the universe into which it has entered. Not only the supposition that God has resolved to create this Adam but also any other individual substance that may be, involves the resolves for all the rest because this is the nature of an individual substance, namely, to have so complete a concept that from it may be deduced all that can be attributed to it, and even the whole universe, because of the inter-connection between things; nevertheless, to speak more strictly, it must be said that it is not so much because God has resolved to create this Adam that he made all his other resolutions, but because the resolutions which he made in regard to Adam together with those he made in regard to other particular things, are consequences of the resolve which he made in regard to the whole universe.

(G VII, 305; Loemker, p. 489; Ariew & Garber, p. 152; "On the Ultimate Origin of Things" [1697].) We therefore have the ultimate reason for the reality of essences as well as existences in one being, which must necessarily be greater, higher, and prior to the world but also all possibilities have their reality through it. But because of the interconnection of all these things, this ultimate reason can be found only in a single source. It is evident, however, that existing things are continuously issuing from this source and are being produced and have been produced by it, since no reason appears why one state of the world should issue from it rather than another, that of yesterday rather than today's. It is clear, too, how God acts not merely physically but freely as well and how there is in him not only the efficient but the final cause of the world. Thus we have in him the reason not merely for the greatness and power in the world mechanism as already established, but also for the goodness and wisdom exerted in establishing it.

(G VII, 310; "On Nature's Secrets" [ca. 1690].) A necessary being, if it be possible, exits. This . . . makes possible the transition from essences to existences, from hypothetical to absolute truths, from ideas to the world. . . . If there were no eternal substance, there would be no eternal truths; thus God is also deduced hence, who is the root of possibility, for his mind is itself the region of ideas or truths. But it is very erroneous to suppose that eternal truths and the goodness of things depend on the divine will, since all will presupposes the judgment of the intellect as to goodness, unless some one by a change of names would transfer all judgment from the intellect to the will, though even then no one could say that the will is the cause of truths, since the judgment is not their cause either. The reason of truths lies in the ideas of things, which are involved in the divine essence itself, and who would dare to say that the truth of God's existence depends upon the divine will?

(G. Math. III, 574; to John Bernoulli [1699].) Possible things are those which do not imply a contradiction; actual things are nothing but the best of possibles, everything considered. And so things that are less perfect are not therefore impossible, for we must distinguish between the things which God can do and those which he wills to do; he can do all things, but he wills the best. When I say that God elects out of infinite possibilities, I mean the same as you when you say that he has elected from eternity.

COMMENTARY

For Leibniz, anything that is free from internal self-contradiction is thereby *possible*. And all possibilities exist *in idea*—that is, in the conception that represents them in the mind of an all-knowing God. It is this circumstance that provides even mere possibilities with a reality of sorts, namely an ideal conceptual reality in whose absence their status of being possible would be abrogated.

Thus for Leibniz, even mere possibilities do have and, if they are to be genuine possibilities, must have an existential basis. There is—and must be—a realm where they exist as such, that is, as possibilities (*sub ratione possibilitatis*), namely the mind of God. Here, then, we have yet another proof of God's existence, an argument from possibilities distinct from the argument from ultimate grounding given in section 38. (The argument is not original with Leibniz. Compare J. B. Bossuet, *Traité de la connaissance de Dieu et de soi-même* [Paris, 1680], chap. IV, sec. 5.)

Leibniz connects his theory of the mind of God as "the region of possibilities" with Plato's doctrine of ideas. He regarded the Platonic realm of ideas as one of "Plato's many most beautiful doctrines" and viewed it as adumbrating the conception that "there is in the divine mind an intelligible world, which I too am accustomed to call the realm of ideas (*regio idearum*)" (Erdmann, 445b [1707]).

KEY WORDS:

God/*Dieu*
possibility/*la possibilité*
real/*réel*
source of existence/*source des existences*
source of essence/*source des essences*
God's understanding/*l'entendement de Dieu*
realm of eternal truths/*région des vérités éternelles*
realm of possibilities/*région des possibles*

SECTION 44

44. For it must be that, if there is a reality in essences or possibilities, or indeed in eternal truths, this reality be founded in something existent and actual, and consequently in the existence of the Necessary Being, in whom essence includes existence, or in whom being possible suffices for being actual. (See *Theodicy*, secs. 184, 189, 335.)

44. Car il faut bien que, s'il y a une realité dans les Essences ou possibilités, ou bien dans les verités éternelles, cette realité soit fondée en quelque chose d'Existant et d'Actuel; et par consequent dans l'Existence de l'Etre necessaire, dans lequel l'Essence renferme l'Existence, ou dans lequel il suffit d'être possible pour être Actuel. (Théodicée, secs. 184, 189, 335.)

(*Theodicy*, sec. 184.) It is, in my judgement, the divine understanding which gives reality to the eternal verities, although God's will has no part therein. All reality must be founded on something existent. It is true that an atheist may be a geometrician: but if there were no God, geometry would have no object. And without God, not only would there be nothing existent, but there would be nothing possible.

(*Theodicy*, sec. 189.) In the region of the eternal verities are found all the possibles, and consequently the regular as well as the irregular: there must be a reason accounting for the preference for order and regularity, and this reason can only be found in understanding. Moreover these very truths can have no existence without an understanding to take cognizance of them; for they would not exist if there were no divine understanding wherein they are realized, so to speak.

(*Theodicy*, sec. 335.) Evil springs rather from the *Forms* themselves in their detached state, that is, from the ideas that God has not produced by an act of his will, any more than he thus produced numbers and figures, and all possible essences which one must regard as eternal and necessary; for they are in the ideal region of the possibles, that is, in the divine understanding. God is therefore not the author of essences in so far as they are only possibilities. But there is nothing actual to which he has not decreed and given existence; and he has permitted evil because it is involved in the best plan existing in the region of possibles, a plan which supreme wisdom could not fail to choose. This notion satisfies at once the wisdom, the power and the goodness of God, and yet leaves a way open for the entrance of evil. God gives perfection to creatures in so far as it is possible in the universe.

(G VII, 311, "On Nature's Secrets" [ca. 1690].) If the Eternal Substance did not exist, there would be no eternal truths; whence God is also proved, being the root source of possibility (*radix possibilitatis*), for his mind exactly is the region of ideas or of truths.

COMMENTARY

Leibniz is an "existentialist" in the sense of maintaining that existence precedes essence. As he sees it, everything that has any sort of reality whatsoever—even that which exists only as a possibility—has this status in view of its presence in or connection with something that actually exists. Thus even mere unactualized possibilities have a domain in which they "subsist," as it were—namely in the thoughts of God. The mind of God is the domain of the possible: if—*per impossibile*—God did not exist, then the whole realm of the possible would be abolished—and the sphere of the necessary would vanish with it. (The mere fact that there are necessary, timeless truths speaks for the existence of a necessary, timeless being to provide an existential underpinning for them.)

Leibniz is thus caught up in a bind of circularity: God's existence is a consequence of his possibility (sec. 40). And this possibility depends for its own being in God's mind as the domain of the possible. But in the setting of his system such circularity is not vicious: it is simply a matter of the reciprocal coordination of the several facets of "the *necessary* being."

KEY WORDS:

reality/*réalité*
essence/*essence*
existence/*existence*
possibilities/*possibilités*
eternal truths/*vérités éternelles*
necessary being/*l'Etre nécessaire*
the actual/*l'actuel*

SECTION 45

45. Thus only God, or the Necessary Being, has this privilege, that he must exist if he is possible. And since nothing can prevent the possibility of that which contains no limits and no negation, and consequently no contradiction,

this by itself suffices to establish the existence of God *a priori*. And we have also proved this <in sec. 43> through the reality of the eternal truths.

But we have also just proved it *a posteriori* <in sec. 38>, since some contingent beings exist, which can have their final or sufficient reason only in a necessary being that has the reason of its existence within itself.

45. *Ainsi Dieu seul ou l'Etre Nécessaire a ce privilege, qu'il faut qu'il existe, s'il est possible. Et comme rien ne peut empecher la possibilité de ce qui n'enferme aucunes bornes, aucune négation, et par consequent aucune contradiction, cela seul suffit pour connoître l'Existence de Dieu a priori. Nous l'avons prouvée aussi par la realité des verités éternelles.*

Mais nous venons de la prouver aussi a posteriori *puisque des êtres contingens existent, lesquels ne sçauroient avoir leur raison derniere ou suffisante que dans l'être nécessaire, qui a la raison de son existence en luy-même.*

(G IV, 294–96; to Duchess Sophia [ca. 1680].) There is assuredly reason to doubt whether the idea of the greatest of all beings is not uncertain, and whether it does not involve some contradiction. For I quite understand, for instance, the nature of motion and velocity, and what "the greatest" is. But I do not understand whether these are compatible, and whether it is possible to combine them into the one idea of the greatest velocity of which motion is capable. In the same way, although I know what "being" is, and what the "greatest" and the "most perfect" are, nevertheless I do not therefore know that there is not a hidden contradiction involved in combining these together, as there actually is in the instances I have just given. . . . Yet I admit that God has here a great advantage over all other things. For, in order to prove that He exists, it is sufficient to prove that He is possible, which is not the case with regard to anything else that I know of. . . . Simple forms <i.e. living principles> are the source of things. Now I maintain that all simple forms are compatible with one another. . . . If this be granted, it follows that the nature of God, which contains all simple forms taken absolutely, is possible. Now we have shown above that God exists, provided He is possible. Therefore He exists.

(G IV, 401; "Against Descartes on the Existence of God" [1700].) The Geometers, who are the past masters of the art of reasoning, have realized that in order that proofs based on definitions be valid one must show, or at least postulate, that the notion comprised in any of the definitions used is possible. . . . The same precaution is necessary in every type of reasoning, and above all in the demonstration due to Anselm, Archbishop of Canterbury (*in libro contra insipientem*), which proves that since God is the greatest or most perfect being, He possesses also that perfection termed *existence*, and that consequently He exists; an argument which was subjected to scrutiny by Saint Thomas and other Scholastics, and which was revived by M. Descartes. Regarding this it must be said that the argument is quite valid, providing that the supremely perfect being or that which comprises all perfections is possible. Just this is the privilege of the divine nature—that its essence contains its existence, i.e., that God exists provided only that He is possible. And even omitting all reference to perfection, one can say: *If the Necessary Being is possible, He exists*—doubtless the most beautiful and important proposition of the doctrine of modalities, since it furnishes a passage from possibility to actuality, and it is here and here alone that *a posse ad esse valet consequentia.*

(G IV, 424 ; Loemker, p. 293; Ariew & Garber, p. 25; "Meditations on Knowledge, Truth, and Ideas" [1684].) If God is possible, it follows that He exists. Yet we cannot safely use definitions in order to reach a conclusion, until we know that these definitions are real or that they involve no contradiction. The reason of this is that from notions which involve a contradiction opposite conclusions may be drawn at the same time, which is absurd. To illustrate this I usually take the instance of the swiftest possible motion, which involves an absurdity. For, suppose a wheel to revolve with the swiftest possible motion, is it not evident, that if any spoke of the wheel be made longer its extremity will move more swiftly than a nail on the circumference of the wheel; wherefore the motion of the circumference is not the swiftest possible, as was supposed by the hypothesis. Yet at first sight it may appear that we have an idea of the swiftest possible motion; for we seem to understand what we are saying, and nevertheless we have no idea of impossible things.

(G VII, 261; "That the Most Perfect Being Exists" [1676].) I call a *perfection* every simple quality which is positive and absolute, and expresses without any limits whatever it does express. Now since such a quality is simple, it is also irresolvable or indefinable, for otherwise it will either not be one simple quality, but an aggregate of several, or, if it is one, it will be circumscribed by limits, and will therefore be conceived by a negation of further progress, contrary to the hypothesis, for it is assumed to be purely positive. Hence it is not difficult to show that *all perfections are compatible inter se*, or can be in the same subject. For let there be such a proposition as

A and B are incompatible

(understanding by A and B two such simple forms or perfections—the same holds if several are assumed at once), it is obvious that this cannot be proved without a resolution of one or both of the terms A and B; for otherwise their nature would not enter into the reason, and the incompatibility of any other things could be shown just as well as theirs. But (by hypothesis) they are irresolvable. Therefore this proposition cannot be proved concerning them. But it could be proved concerning them if it were true, for it is not true *per se*; but all necessarily true propositions are either demonstrable, or known *per se*. Therefore this proposition is not necessarily true. In other words, since it is not necessary that A and B should not be in the same subject, they can therefore be in the same subject; and since the reasoning is the same as regards any other assumed qualities of the same kind, therefore all perfections are compatible. There is, therefore, or there can be conceived, a subject of all perfections, or most perfect Being. Whence it follows also that he exists, for existence is among the number of the perfections. . . .

(G VII, 310; "On Nature's Secrets" [ca. 1690].) A necessary being, if it be possible, exists. This makes possible a transition from essences to existences, from hypothetical to absolute truths, from ideas to the world. . . . If there were no eternal substance, there would be no eternal truths; thus God is also deduced hence, who is the root of possibility, for his mind is itself the region of ideas or truths. But it is very erroneous to suppose that eternal truths and the goodness of things depend on the divine will, since all will presupposes the judgment of the intellect as to goodness, unless some one by a change of names would transfer all judgment from the intellect to the will, though even then no one could say that the will is the cause of truths, since the judgment is not their cause either. The reason of truths lies in the ideas of things, which are involved in the divine essence itself. And who would dare to say that the truth of God's existence depends upon the divine will?

COMMENTARY

Overall, Leibniz's *Monadology* thus rehearses three arguments for the existence of God: (1) the currently contemplated ontological argument as modified by his own special proviso concerning possibility, (2) the aforementioned argument from eternal truths (compare sec. 43), which he regards as an important innovation, and (3) the cosmological argument (compare sec. 38), to which he assigned a subsidiary status because of its *a posteriori* character. The possibility proviso of (1) hinges on the fact that in Leibniz's view simple, unanalyzable perfection-predicates (being knowledgeable or good, say)—unlike standard predicates (being round or square)—are bound to be compatible with one another, since they represent "positive and absolute" qualities. An important role is played in Leibniz's thought by the idea that if (*per impossibile*) the necessary existent did not exist, then nothing else could exist either—and indeed nothing would even be *possible* (compare sec. 43).

KEY WORDS:

God/*Dieu*
the Necessary Being/*l'être nécessaire*
possibility/*possibilité*
contingent beings/*êtres contingents*
limit/*borne*
negation/*négation*
contradiction/*contradiction*
a priori a *posteriori*
existence/*existence*
eternal truths/*verités éternelles*
final reason/*raison dernière (ou suffisante)*

SECTION 46

46. However, we must not imagine, as some do, that the eternal truths, being dependent on God, are arbitrary and depend upon his will, as Descartes seems to have held, and Monsieur Poiret after him. That is true only of contingent truths, whose principle is *fitness* or the choice of *the best*. Instead, the necessary truths depend solely on God's understanding, and are its internal object. (See *Theodicy*, secs. 180–84, 185, 335, 351, 380.)

46. Cependant, il ne faut point s'imaginer avec quelques-uns, que les verités éternelles, étant dependantes de Dieu, sont arbitraires et dependent de sa volonté, comme Des-Cartes paroist l'avoir pris et puis Monsieur Poiret. Cela n'est veritable que des Verités contingentes, dont le principe est la convenance ou le choix du meilleur: au lieu que les Verités necessaires dépendent uniquement de son entendement, et en sont l'objet interne. (Théodicée, secs. *180–84, 185, 335, 351, 380.)*

(*Theodicy*, sec. 180.) I find also that M. Bayle combats admirably the opinion of those who assert that goodness and justice depend solely upon the arbitrary choice of God; who suppose, moreover, that if God had been determined by the goodness of things themselves to act, he would be entirely subjected to necessity in his actions, a state incompatible with freedom. That is confusing metaphysical necessity with moral necessity. . . . [Moreover] it opens the door to the most exaggerated Pyrrhonism: for it leads to the assertion that this proposition, three and three makes six, is only true where and during the time when it pleases God; that it is perhaps false in some parts of the universe; and that perhaps it will be so among men in the coming year.

(*Theodicy*, sec. 181) To say that God, having resolved to create man just as he is, could not but have required of him piety, sobriety, justice and chastity, because it is impossible that the disorders capable of overthrowing or disturbing his work can please him, that is to revert in effect to the common opinion. Virtues are virtues only because they serve perfection or prevent the imperfection of those who are virtuous, or even of those who have to do with them. And they have that power by their nature and by the nature of rational creatures, before God decrees to create them. To hold a different opinion would be as if someone were to say that the rules of proportion and harmony are arbitrary with regard to musicians because they occur in music only when one has resolved to sing or to play some instrument. But that is exactly what is meant by being essential to good music: for those rules belong to it already in the ideal state, even when none yet thinks of singing, since it is known that they must of necessity belong to it as soon as one shall sing. In the same way virtues belong to the ideal state of the rational creature before God decrees to create it; and it is for that very reason we maintain that virtues are good by their nature.

(*Theodicy*, sec. 182.) <Some theologians> exempt the will of God from any kind of reason: *ubi stat pro ratione voluntas.* But, as I have observed already on various occasions, Calvin himself acknowledged that the decrees of God are in conformity with justice and wisdom, although the reasons that might prove this conformity in detail are unknown to us.

(*Theodicy*, sec. 183.) God saw from all eternity and in all necessity the essential relations of numbers, and the identity of the subject and predicate in the propositions that contain the essence of each thing. He saw likewise that the term just is included in these propositions: to esteem what is estimable, be grateful to one's benefactor, fulfil the conditions of a contract, and so on, with many others relating to morals. One is therefore justified in saying that the precepts of natural law assume the reasonableness and justice of that which is enjoined, and that it would be man's duty to practice what they contain even though God should have been so indulgent as to ordain nothing in that respect. Pray observe that in going back with our visionary thoughts to that ideal moment when God has yet decreed nothing, we find in the ideas of God the principles of morals under terms that imply an obligation. We understand these maxims as certain, and derived from the eternal and immutable order: it beseems the rational creature to conform to reason; a rational creature conforming to reason is to be commended, but not conforming thereto is blameworthy.

You would not dare to deny that these truths impose upon man a duty in relation to all acts which are in conformity with strict reason, such as these: one must esteem all that is estimable; render good for good; do wrong to no man; honour one's father; render to every man that which is his due, etc. Now since by the very nature of things, and before the divine laws, the truths of morality impose upon man certain duties, Thomas Aquinas and Grotius were justified in saying that if there were no God we should nevertheless be obliged to conform to natural law.

(*Theodicy*, sec. 184.) One must not say, with some Scotists, that the eternal verities would exist even though there were no understanding, not even that of God. For it is, in my judgement, the divine understanding which gives reality to the eternal verities, albeit God's will have no part therein. All reality must be founded on something existent. It is true that an atheist may be a geometrician: but if there were no God, geometry would have no object. And without God, not only would there be nothing existent, but there would be nothing possible. That, however, does not hinder those who do not see the connexion of all things one with another and with God from being able to understand certain sciences, without knowing their first source, which is in God.

(*Theodicy*, sec. 185.) Yet the same M. Bayle, who says so much that is admirable in order to prove that the rules of goodness and justice, and the eternal verities in general, exist by their nature, and not by an arbitrary choice of God, has spoken very hesitatingly about them in another passage. . . . Is it possible that <this gifted man had> the power to believe that two contradictories never exist together for the sole reason that God forbade them to, and, moreover, that God could have issued them an order to ensure that they always walked together? There is indeed a noble paradox!

(*Theodicy*, sec. 335.) <Chrysippus> is right in saying that vice springs from the original constitution of some minds. He was met with the objection that God formed them, and he could only reply by pointing to the imperfection of matter, which did not permit God to do better. This reply is of no value, for matter in itself is indifferent to all forms, and God made it. Evil springs rather form the *Forms* themselves in their detached state, that is, from the ideas that God has not produced by an act of his will, any more than he thus produced numbers and figures, and all possible essences which one must regard as eternal and necessary; for they are in the ideal region of the possibles, that is, in the divine understanding. God is therefore not the author of essences in so far as they are only possibilities. But there is nothing actual to which he has not decreed and given existence; and he has permitted evil because it is involved in the best plan existing in the region of possibles, a plan which supreme wisdom could not fail to choose.

(*Theodicy*, sec. 351.) The ternary number <of the dimensions of space> is determined for it not by the reason of the best, but by a geometrical necessity, because the geometricians have been able to prove that there are only three straight lines perpendicular to one another which can intersect at one and the same point. Nothing more appropriate could have been chosen to show the difference there is between the moral necessity that accounts for the choice of wisdom and the brute necessity of Strato and the adherents of Spinoza, who deny to God understanding and will, than a consideration of the difference existing between the reason for the laws of motion and the reason for the ternary number of the dimensions: for the first lies in the choice of the best and the second in a geometrical and blind necessity.

(*Theodicy*, sec. 380.) <The ultimate source of evil and of imperfection lies not in matter but> in the forms or ideas of the possibles, for it must be eternal, and matter is not so. Now since God made all positive reality that is not eternal, he would have made the source of evil, if that did not rather lie in the possibility of things or forms, that which alone God did not make, since he is not the author of his own understanding.

(DM, sec. 2) I am far removed from the opinion of those who maintain that there are no principles of goodness or perfection in the nature of things, or in the ideas which God has about them, and who say that the works of God are good only through the formal reason that God has made them. If this position were true, God knowing that he is the author of things, would not have to regard them afterwards and find them good, as the Holy Scripture witnesses. Such anthropomorphic expressions are used only to let us know that excellence is recognized in regarding the works themselves, even if we do not consider their evident dependence on their author. This is confirmed by the fact that it is in reflecting upon the works that we are able to discover the one who wrought. They must therefore bear in themselves his character. I confess that the contrary opinion seems to me extremely dangerous and closely approaches that of recent innovators who hold that the beauty of the universe and the goodness which we attribute to the works of God are chimeras of human beings who think of God in human terms. In saying, therefore, that things are not good according to any standard of goodness, but simply by the will of God, it seems to me that one destroys, without realizing it, all the love of God and all his glory; for why praise him for what he has done, if he would be equally praiseworthy in doing the contrary? Where will be his justice and his wisdom if he has only a certain despotic power, if arbitrary will takes the place of reasonableness, and if in accord with the definition of tyrants, justice consists in that which is pleasing to the most powerful? Besides it seems that every act of willing supposes some reason for the willing and this reason, of course, must precede the act. This is why, accordingly, I find so strange those expressions of certain philosophers who say that the eternal truths of metaphysics and Geometry, and consequently the principles of goodness, of justice, and of perfection, are effects only of the will of God. To me it seems that all these follow from his understanding, which does not depend upon his will any more than does his essence.

(G VII, 390; to Clarke, V, 9 [1716].) But to say that God can only choose what is best, and to infer from thence that what He does not choose is impossible, this, I say, is a confounding of terms: 'tis blending power and will, metaphysical necessity and moral necessity, essences and existences. For what is [strictly or metaphysically] necessary is so by its essence, since its opposite implies a contradiction. But a contingent which exists owes its existence to the principle of what is best (*principe du meilleur*), which is a sufficient reason for the existence of things. And therefore I say that <morally necessitating> motives incline without necessitating <metaphysically>; and that there is a certainty and infallibility, but not an absolute necessity in contingent things.

COMMENTARY

The distinction between the necessary truths of reasoning and the contingent truths of fact harks back to sections 32–33.

When a factual claim is perfection-maximizing it is, in virtue of this very fact, such that any reason against it can be outweighed by a still more weighty reason for it, so that no reason against it can be sufficient. Thus

$$\text{If P-max}(p), \text{ then } \sim(\text{E}r)rS\text{-}p.$$

When this principle is adjoined to the truth-criterion of section 32, we obtain

$$\text{If P-max}(p), \text{ then } T(p).$$

It is this principle to the effect that perfection-maximizing propositions are *ipso facto* true which affords the criteriological rule for *contingent* truths (that for necessary truths being given by the Law of Contradiction's principle that, "If $C(\text{-}p)$, then $T(p)$" of sec. 31).

Contingent truths—unlike necessary ones—are ultimately grounded in the will of God. They hinge upon his creation-choice of one particular set of possibilities for actualization in preference to all others, namely the *optimal*, the objectively best, those which maximize perfection. And this outcome itself turns on God's free decision to subscribe to the *perfection* of potential creatures as a ruling standard of choice. But the necessary or eternal truths, though dependent on the *intellect* of God for their ontological foothold in the real, are totally independent of the *will* of God as regards their nature. He *finds* rather than *makes* them as they are.

Leibniz thus pivots the totality of contingent truth regarding the world on God's will—specifically on his free choice among available alternatives over whose composition as such God has no control. This choice is governed by the "principle of fitness" or "of the choice of the best" (*principe de la convenance ou du choix du meilleur*). And it is this principle that resolves the problem, set in section 36, of providing "a sufficient reason for contingent truths or truths of fact." (Compare also sec. 54.)

Leibniz often criticizes and opposes the position of Descartes that: "The metaphysical truths which you (Mersenne) call eternal have been established by God and are entirely dependent upon him. . . ." (*Lettre au Père Mersenne*, in *Oeuvres*, ed. V. Cousin, Vol. VI (Paris: Didot, 1826), p. 109). Descartes held that God was perfectly free to make it untrue that the three angles of a plane triangle should come to two right angles. The question of the dependency of logico-mathematical truth on the will of God was much discussed among the Scholastics. Descartes' view accords with that of Duns Scotus, Leibniz's with that of St. Thomas Aquinas.

As Leibniz sees the matter, moreover, it will not do to consider those things that depend on God's will as being strictly (i.e., more than "metaphysically") *necessitated* thereby. For Leibniz emphatically rejects the voluntaristic necessitarianism of Abailard's dictum "Whatever God wills he *must* necessarily will." For Leibniz, God freely choses the perfectionism that guides his will—doing otherwise would be compatible with his metaphysical, albeit not with his moral, nature.

The fact that contingent truths depend on God's will renders them *certain*, but not *strictly necessary* (i.e., non-contingent). And their certainty makes them foreknowable, albeit without thereby abolishing freedom of the will. In his 1585 treatise on free will (*De Liberi arbitrii*), the Spanish Jesuit Luis Molina (1535–1600) developed his doctrine of a "middle knowledge" by which God foreknows and foresees what free choices free agents will freely make, so that foreknowledge does not imply a freedom-excluding predetermination. By (purely) intellectual knowledge (*scientia intellectus*) God knows the things that are possible; by his intuitive knowledge (*scientia visionis*) he knows the things that are necessary (e.g., eclipses and the conjunctions of planets); but by a special middle knowledge (*scientia media*) halfway between the two he knows the free choices of people that are conditional upon the operation of the will and are thus more than mere possibilities, while yet existing without any necessitation. God thus foresees the results of any free choices without thereby anywise necessitating them, leaving such acts unconstrained yet certain, so that human free will is reconciled with divine foreknowledge. Leibniz in effect accepts this theory of Molina's, albeit with some qualifications of his own. (See *Theodicy*, secs. 39ff.)

In its emphasis on God's role in furnishing the basis of contingency, this section bears closely on Leibniz's argument for God's existence as the ultimate ground of things. (See sec. 38.)

Pierre Poiret (1646–1719) was a French Calvinist minister who settled in Germany. At first a Cartesian, he later became a theosophistic mystic in the tradition of Jacob Boehme and turned into an ardent critic of Cartesianism. He maintained that God creates the realm of ideas freely, although they are, in view of God's nature, for the best. (See his *Économie divine* [Amsterdam, 1687], treatise I, chap. 3.) His *Cogitationum rationalium de Deo, anima, et malo* (1677) was criticized in Bayle's *Dictionary*.

KEY WORDS:

God/*Dieu*
arbitrary/*arbitraire*
will (of God)/*volonté (de Dieu)*
eternal truths/*vérités éternelles*
contingent truths/*vérités contingentes*
necessary truths/*vérités nécessaires*
principle of fitness/*principe de la convenance*
choice of the best/*le choix du meilleur*
God's understanding/*l'entendement de Dieu*

PERSONS:

René Descartes
Pierre Poiret

SECTION 47

47. Accordingly, God alone is the primary unity or the original simple substance, of which all the created or derivative monads are products. They originate, so to speak, through continual fulgurations of the divinity from moment to moment, limited by the receptivity of the created being, to which it is essential to be limited. (See *Theodicy*, secs. 382–91, 395, 398.)

47. Ainsi Dieu seul est l'Unité primitive, * ou la substance simple originaire, dont toutes les Monades creées ou derivatives sont des productions, et naissent, pour ainsi dire, par des Fulgurations continuelles de la Divinité de moment à moment, bornées par la receptivité de la creature, à laquelle il est essentiel d'être limitée. (*Théodicée, secs. 382–91, 395, 398.)*

<* Leibniz initially wrote: *la substance Simple ou Monade primitive*>.

(*Theodicy*, sec. 201.) If we could understand the structure and the economy of the universe, we should find that it is made and directed as the wisest and most virtuous could wish it, since God cannot fail to do thus. This necessity nevertheless is only of a moral nature: and I admit that if God were forced by a metaphysical necessity to produce that which he makes, he would produce all the possibles, or nothing . . . and in this sense M. Bayle's conclusion would be fully correct. . . . But as all the possibles are not compatible together in one and the same world-sequence, for that very reason all the possibles cannot be produced, and it must be said that God is not forced, metaphysically speaking, into the creation of this world. One may say that as soon as God has decreed to create something there is a struggle between all the possibles, all of them laying claim to existence, and that those which, being united, produce most reality, most perfection, most significance carry the day. It is true that all this struggle can only be ideal, that is to say, it can only be a conflict of reasons in the most perfect way, and consequently to choose the best. Yet God is bound only by a moral necessity, to make things in such a manner that there can be nothing better.

(*Theodicy*, sec. 382.) He <Bayle> places too great reliance especially on that doctrine accepted of the Schoolmen, that conservation is a continued creation.

(*Theodicy*, sec. 383.) It does not follow *of necessity* that, because I am, I shall be; but this follows *naturally*, nevertheless, that is, of itself, *per se*, if nothing prevents it. It is the distinction that can be drawn between the essential and the natural. For the same movement endures naturally unless some new cause prevents it or changes it, because the reason which makes it cease at this instant, if it is no new reason, would have already made it cease sooner.

(*Theodicy*, sec. 384.) To establish continual creation it would be necessary to prove that the creature always emerges from nothingness and relapses thither forthwith. In particular it must be shown that the privilege of enduring more than a moment by its nature belongs to the necessary being alone.

(*Theodicy*, sec. 385.) What can be said for certain on the present subject is that the creature depends continually upon divine operation, and that it depends upon that no less after the time of its beginning than when it first begins. This dependence implies that it would not continue to exist if God did not continue to act; in short, that this action of God is free. For if it were a necessary emanation, like that of the properties of the circle, which issue from its essence, it must then be said that God in the beginning produced the creature by necessity; or else it must be shown how in creating it once, he imposed upon himself the necessity of conserving it. Now there is no reason why this conserving action should not be called production, and even creation, if one will.

(*Theodicy*, sec. 388.) Let us assume that the creature is produced anew at each instant; let us grant also that the instant excludes all priority of time, being indivisible; but let us point out that it does not exclude priority of nature, or what is called anteriority *in signo rationis*, and that this is sufficient. The production, or action whereby God produces, is anterior by nature to the existence of the creature that is produced; the creature taken in itself, with its nature and its necessary properties, is anterior to its accidental affections and to its actions; and yet all these things are in being in the same moment. God produces the creature in conformity with the exigency of the preceding instants, according to the laws of his wisdom; and the creature operates in conformity with that nature which God conveys to it in creating it always. The limitations and imperfections arise therein through the nature of the subject, which sets bounds to God's production; this is the consequence of the original imperfection of creatures. Vice and crime, on the other hand, arise there through the free inward operation of the creature, in so far as this can occur within the instant, repetition afterwards rendering it discernible.

(*Theodicy*, sec. 390.) When God produces the thing he produces it as an individual and not as a universal of logic (I admit); but he produces its essence before its accidents, its nature before its operations, following the priority of their nature, and *in signo anteriore rationis*. Thus one sees how the creature can be the true cause of the sin. . . .

(*Theodicy*, sec. 391.) I concede therefore that the creature does not co-operate with God to conserve himself (in the sense in which I have just explained conservation). But I see nothing to prevent the creature's co-operation with God for the production of any other thing: and especially might this concern its inward operation, as in the case of a thought or a volition, things really distinct from the substance.

(*Theodicy*, sec. 395.) As for the so-called creation of the accidents, who does not see that one needs no creative power in order to change place or shape, to form a square or a column, or some other parade-ground figure, by the movement of the soldiers who are drilling; or again to fashion a statue by removing a few pieces from a block of marble; or to make some figure in relief, by changing, decreasing or increasing a piece of wax? The production of modifications has never been called creation, and it is an abuse of terms to scare the world thus. God produces substances from nothing, and the substances produce accidents by the changes of their limits.

(*Theodicy*, sec. 398.) I am, however, of the same opinion as Father Malebranche, that, in general, creation properly understood is not so difficult to admit as might be supposed, and that it is in a sense involved in the notion of the dependence of creatures. "How stupid and ridiculous are the Philosophers," (he exclaims, in his *Christian Meditations*, 9, No. 3), "They assume that Creation is impossible, because they cannot conceive how God's power is great enough to make something from nothing. But can they any better conceive how the power of God is capable of stirring a straw?"

(DM, sec. 14.) Now it is first of all very evident that created substances depend upon God who preserves them and can produce them continually by a kind of emanation just as we produce our thoughts. For when God turns his mind, so to say, on all sides and in all fashions, there results the general system of phenomena which he finds it good to produce for the sake of manifesting his glory. And when he regards all the aspects of the world in all possible manners, since there is no relation which escapes his omniscience, the result of each view of the universe as seen from a different position is a substance which expresses the universe conformably to this view.

(DM, sec. 32.) The thoughts which we have just explained and particularly the great principle of the perfection of God's operations and the concept of substance which includes all its changes with all its accompanying circumstances . . . serve to dissipate great difficulties, to inflame souls with a divine love and to raise the mind to a knowledge of incorporeal substances much more than the present-day hypotheses. For it appears clearly that all other substances depend upon God just as our thoughts emanate from our own substances; that God is all in all and that he is intimately united to all created things, in proportion however to their perfection . . . .[Thus] it may be said in metaphysical strictures that God alone acts upon me and he alone causes me to do good or ill, other substances contributing only because of his determinations; because God, who takes all things into consideration, distributes his bounties so as to compel created beings to accommodate themselves to one another. Thus God alone constitutes the relation or communication between substances. It is through him that the phenomena of the one meet and accord with the phenomena of the others, so that there may be a reality in our perceptions. In common parlance, however, an action is attributed to particular causes in the sense that I have explained above because it is not necessary to make continual mention of the universal cause when speaking of particular cases. It can be seen also that every substance has a perfect spontaneity (which becomes liberty with intelligent substances). Everything which happens to it is a consequence of its idea or its being and nothing determines it except God only. It is for this reason that a person of exalted mind and revered saintliness may say that the soul ought often to think as if there were only God and itself in the world.

COMMENTARY

As Leibniz sees it, "God is the primary center from which all else that exists emanates" (G IV, 533). He does not constantly re-create the world at each moment—as in Descartes's theory of "continuous creation"—but *sustains* it in continuous existence through "continual fulgurations" (*fulgurations continuelles*) that are reminiscent of the emanation theory of Plotinus. (Here too, then, Leibniz is something of a neo-Platonist.) These fulgurations or emanations simply consist in the continual operation of God's will in sustaining the monads in existence, thereby providing them with the opportunity of allowing their own pre-programmed nature to unfold itself.

The idea of "continual fulgurations of the divinity from moment to moment" associates Leibniz with the continuous creation (*creatio continua*) theorists tracing back to St. Augustine. Leibniz repeatedly suggests that God's mind produces *things* in much the same way as our minds produce *thoughts:* for Leibniz, God sustains the world by *thinking* of it in a particular sort of way. (If he were to fall asleep—which cannot happen—the world would cease to exist.) However, while Leibniz assumes a God who is "on duty" 24 hours a day, every day, to assure THAT the world keeps on existing, he precludes an *intervening* God who readjusts WHAT is going on. The course of world history is settled by a once-and-for-all creation-choice and there is no possibility and no need of God's having any "second thoughts" on the matter. In the correspondence with Samuel Clarke, Leibniz emphatically and scornfully rejects any idea of a "hands-on" God who needs to readjust or rewind the universe on the pattern of an imperfect clockmaker who has made a defective timepiece.

Leibniz thus regards God as the creator and sustainer of all things—in all of their aspects, imperfections included. But these imperfections lie in their own nature (in the complete individual concepts of the monads involved). And in creating a world—even the best of possible worlds—God has to take the bad with the good. Leibniz accordingly reemphasizes the inherent *limited receptivity of the created beings* of which he earlier spoke (in sec. 42) as "the imperfections of their nature."

KEY WORDS:

God/*Dieu*
primary unity/*l'unité primitive*
original simple substance/*substance simple originaire*
created or derivative monads/*monades créées ou dérivatives*
continual fulgurations/*fulgurations continuelles*
created being/*créature*
limits/*bornes* or *limites*
receptivity/*réceptivité*

SECTION 48

48. There is in God *Power*, which is the source of all, and also *Knowledge*, which contains the detail (*détail*) of the ideas <of things>, and finally *Will*, which effects changes or products according to the *principle of the best*. (See *Theodicy*, secs. 7, 48, 149, 150.)

This <triad> corresponds in created monads to the subject or basis, the perceptive faculty, and the appetitive faculty. But in God these attributes are absolutely infinite or perfect, while in the created monads or entelechies (or *perfectihabies* <"perfection-havers">, as Hermolaus Barbarus rendered this word) they are mere imitations, <authentic only> to the extent that there is perfection. (See *Theodicy*, secs. 48, 87.)

48. Il y a en Dieu la Puissance, *qui est la source de tout, puis la* Connoissance, *qui contient le detail des idées, et enfin la* Volonté, *qui fait les changemens ou productions selon le principe du Meilleur. (See* Theodicy, *secs. 7, 48, 149, 150.)*

Et c'est ce qui répond à ce qui dans les Monades creées fait le Sujêt ou la

Base, la Faculté Perceptive et la Faculté Appetitive. Mais en Dieu ces attributs sont absolument infinis ou parfaits; et dans les Monades creées ou dans les Entelechies (ou perfectihabies, *comme Hermolaus Barbarus traduisoit ce mot) ce n'en sont que des imitations, à mesure qu'il y a de la perfection. (*Théodicée, *secs. 48, 87.)*

(*Theodicy,* sec. 7.) *God is the first reason of things:* for such things as are bounded, as all that which we see and experience, are contingent and have nothing in them to render their existence necessary, it being plain that time, space and matter, united and uniform in themselves and indifferent to everything, might have received entirely other motions and shapes, and in another order. Therefore one must seek the reason for the existence of the world, which is the whole assemblage of *contingent* things, and seek it in the substance which carries with it the reason for its existence, and which in consequence is *necessary* and eternal. Moreover, this cause must be intelligent: for this existing world being contingent and an infinity of other worlds being equally possible, and holding, so to say, equal claim to existence with it, the cause of the world must needs have had regard or reference to all these possible worlds in order to fix upon one of them. This regard or relation of an existent substance to simple possibilities can be nothing other than the understanding which has the ideas of them, while to fix upon one of them can be nothing other than the act of the *will* which chooses. It is the power of this substance that renders its will efficacious. Power relates to being, wisdom or understanding to *truth,* and will to good. And this intelligent cause ought to be infinite in all ways, and absolutely perfect in *power,* in *wisdom* and in *goodness,* since it relates to all that which is possible. Furthermore, since all is connected together, there is no ground for admitting more than *one.* Its understanding is the source of *essences,* and its will is the origin of *existences.* There in few words is the proof of one only God with his perfections, and through him of the origin of things.

(*Theodicy,* secs. 45–48.) The will is never prompted to action save by the representation of the good, which prevails over the opposite representations. This is admitted even in relation to God, the good angels and the souls in bliss: and it is acknowledged that they are nonetheless free in consequence of that. God fails not to choose the best, but he is not constrained so to do: nay, more, there is no necessity in the object of God's choice, for another sequence of things is equally possible. For that very reason the choice is free and independent of necessity, because it is made between several possibilities, and the will is determined only by the preponderating goodness of the object. This is therefore not a defect where God and the saints are concerned: on the contrary, it would be a great defect, or rather a manifest absurdity, were it otherwise, even in men here on earth, and if they were capable of acting without any inclining reason. There is therefore a freedom of contingency or, in a way, of indifference, provided that by "indifference" is understood that nothing necessitates us to one course or the other; but there is never any *indifference of equipoise,* that is, where all is completely even on both sides, without any inclination towards either. The Molinists were much embarrassed by this false idea of an indifference of equipoise. They were asked not only how it was possible to know in what direction a cause absolutely indeterminate would be determined, but also how it was possible that there should finally result therefrom a determination for which there is no source.

(*Theodicy*, sec. 87.) Aristotle and scholastic philosophy after him called *Form* that which is a principle of action and is found in that which acts. This inward principle is either substantial, being then termed "Soul," when it is in an organic body, or accidental, and customarily termed "Quality." The same philosopher gave to the soul the generic name of "Entelechy" or *Act*. This word "Entelechy" obviously takes its origin from the Greek word signifying "perfect," and hence the celebrated Hermolaus Barbarus expressed it literally in Latin by *perfectihabia:* for *Act* is a realization of potency. He had no need to consult the Devil, as people say he did, in order to learn that.

(*Theodicy*, sec. 149.) There are in truth two principles, but they are both in God, to wit, his understanding, and his will. The understanding furnishes the principle of evil, without being sullied by it, without being evil; it represents natures as they exist in the eternal verities; it contains within it the reason wherefore evil is permitted: but the will tends only towards good. Let us add a third principle, namely power; it precedes even understanding and will, but it operates as the one displays it and as the other requires it.

(*Theodicy*, sec. 150.) Some (like Campanella) have called these three perfections of God the three primordialities. Many have even believed that there was therein a secret connexion with the Holy Trinity: that power relates to the Father, that is, to the source of Divinity, wisdom to the Eternal Word, which is called *logos* by the most sublime of the Evangelists, and will or Love to the Holy Spirit. Well-nigh all the expressions or comparisons derived from the nature of the intelligent substance tend that way.

(PNG, sec. 9.) This simple primary substance must include eminently the perfections contained in the derivative substances which are its effects. Thus it will have perfect power, knowledge, and will; that is to say, it will have omnipotence, omniscience, and sovereign goodness. And since justice, taken in its most general sense, is nothing but goodness conforming with wisdom, there is also necessarily a sovereign justice in God. The reason which has made things exist through him has also made them depend on him for their existence and operation, and they are continually receiving from him that which causes them to have some perfection. But whatever imperfection remains with them comes from the essential and original limitation of the created beings.

(DM, sec. 1.) The conception of God which is the most common and the most full of meaning is expressed well enough in the words: God is an absolutely perfect being. The implications, however, of these words fail to receive sufficient consideration. For instance, there are many different kinds of perfection, all of which God possesses, and each one of them pertains to him in the highest degree. We must also know what perfection is. One thing which can surely be affirmed about it is that those forms or natures which are not susceptible of it to the highest degree, say the nature of numbers or of figures, do not permit of perfection. This is because the number which is the greatest of all (that is, the sum of all the numbers), and likewise the greatest of all figures, imply contradictions. The greatest knowledge, however, and omnipotence contain no impossibility. Consequently power and knowledge do admit of perfection, and insofar as they pertain to God they have no limits. Whence it follows that God who possesses supreme and infinite wisdom acts in the most perfect manner not only metaphysically, but also from the moral standpoint.

COMMENTARY

Leibniz here envisions the following parallelism:

God	Monads
power	reality (being)
knowledge	perception
will	appetition

But while in God these three capacities are present limitlessly and infinitely, in creatures they are present only finitely in a limited way. Still, as Leibniz sees it, the difference is one of degree and not one of kind. These three "perfections" of substance are present in *all* substances, divine or created alike, albeit in the latter to a lower or lesser extent. The principle of the best assures the maximization of perfection all right, but of course only within the limits of the feasible.

Hermolaus Barbarus (1454–93) was a Venetian humanist, diplomatist, and scholar devoted to the study and translation of Aristotle's works. He tried to discern Aristotle's original meaning beneath the varnish of Scholastic interpretations. Bayle's *Dictionary* devotes a substantial article to him. See also Garrett Mattingly, *Renaissance Diplomacy* (London: Jonathan Cape, 1955), chapter XI.

KEY WORDS:

God/*Dieu*
detail/*détail (des idées)*
power/*puissance*
knowledge/*connaissance*
will/*volonté*
change/*changement*
created monads/*monades créées*
the subject or basis/*le sujet ou la base*
perceptive faculty/*faculté perceptive*
appetitive faculty/*faculté appétitive*
perfection/*perfection*
principle of the best/*principe du meilleur*
entelechies/*entéléchies*
infinite attributes/*attributs infinis*
perfect attributes/*attributs parfaits*

PERSONS:

Hermolaus Barbarus

SECTION 49

49. A created being is said *to act* externally insofar as it has perfection, and *to react* to <or "suffer" by> another insofar as it is imperfect. Thus *action* is attributed to the monad insofar as it has distinct perceptions and *reaction* (*passion*) insofar as it has confused ones. (See *Theodicy*, secs. 32, 66, 386.)

49. *La Creature est dite* agir *au dehors en tant qu'elle a de la perfection, et patir d'une autre, en tant qu'elle est imparfaite. Ainsi l'on attribue l'*Action *à la Monade en tant qu'elle a des perceptions distinctes, et la* Passion *en tant qu'elle en a de confuses. (*Théodicée, *secs. 32, 66, 386.)*

(*Theodicy*, sec. 32.) This consideration will serve also to satisfy some modern philosophers who go so far as to say that God is the only agent. It is true that God is the only one whose action is pure and without admixture of what is termed "to suffer": but that does not preclude the creature's participation in actions, since the action of the creature is a modification of the substance, flowing naturally from it and containing a variation not only in the perfections that God has communicated to the creature, but also in the limitations that the creature, being what it is, brings with it.

(*Theodicy*, sec. 66.) In so far as the soul has perfection and distinct thoughts, God has accommodated the body to the soul, and has arranged beforehand that the body is impelled to execute its order. And in so far as the soul is imperfect and as its perceptions are confused, God has accommodated the soul to the body, in such sort that the soul is swayed by the passions arising out of corporeal representations. This produces the same effect and the same appearance as if the one depended immediately upon the other, and by the agency of a physical influence. Properly speaking, it is by its confused thoughts that the soul represents the bodies which encompass it. The same thing must apply to all that we understand by the actions of simple substances upon one another. For each one is assumed to act upon the other in proportion to its perfection, although this be only ideally, and in the reasons of things, as God in the beginning ordered one substance to accord with another in proportion to the perfection or imperfection that there is in each. (Withal action and passion are always reciprocal in creatures, because one part of the reasons which serve to explain clearly what is done, and which have served to bring it into existence, is in the one of these substances, and another part of these reasons is in the other, perfections and imperfections being always mingled and shared.) Thus it is we attribute *action* to the one, and *passion* to the other.

(*Theodicy*, sec. 386.) <A recent author says:> "If God creates me in this instant, and one says that afterwards he produces with me my actions, it will be necessary to imagine another instant for action: for before acting one must exist. Now that would be two instants where we only assume one. It is therefore certain in this hypothesis that creatures have neither more connexion nor more relation with their actions than they had with their production at the first moment of the first creation." The author . . . draws thence very harsh conclusions which one can picture to oneself; and he testifies at the end that one would be deeply indebted to any man that should teach those who approve this system how to extricate themselves from these frightful absurdities.

(*Theodicy*, sec. 400.) In my system every simple substance (that is, every true substance) must be the true immediate cause of all its actions and inward passions; and, speaking strictly in a metaphysical sense, it has none other than those which it produces. Those who hold a different opinion, and who make God the sole agent, are needlessly becoming involved in expressions whence they will only with difficulty extricate themselves without offence against religion; moreover, they unquestionably offend against reason.

(DM, sec. 15.) It is sufficient for reconciling the language of metaphysics with that of practical life to remark that we preferably attribute to ourselves, and with reason, the phenomena which we express the most perfectly, and that we attribute to other substances those phenomena which each one expresses the best. Thus a substance, which is of an infinite extension insofar as it expresses all, becomes limited in proportion to its more or less perfect manner of expression. It is thus then that we may conceive of substances as interfering with and limiting one another, and hence we are able to say that in this sense they act upon one another, and that they, so to speak, accommodate themselves to one another. For it can happen that a single change which augments the expression of the one may diminish that of the other. Now the virtue of a particular substance is to express well the glory of God, and the better it expresses it, the less it is limited. Everything when it expresses its virtue or power, that is to say, when it acts, changes to better, and expands just insofar as it acts. When therefore a change occurs by which several substances are affected (in fact every change affects them all) I think we may say that those substances, which by this change pass immediately to a greater degree of perfection, or to a more perfect expression, exert power and act, while those which pass to a lesser degree disclose their weakness and suffer.

(NS, sec. 17.) Ordinary ways of speaking can still be preserved. For one may say that when the particular disposition of one substance provides a reason for a change occurring in an intelligible manner, in such a way that we can conclude that the other substances have been adapted to it on this point from the beginning according to the order of the divine decree, then that substance should be thought of as *acting* upon the others in this sense. Further, the action of one substance upon another is not an emission or a transplanting of some entity, as is commonly supposed; and it can be understood reasonably only in the way just shown. It is true that we can easily conceive of both the emission and the reception of parts in matter and can in this way reasonably explain all the phenomena of physics mechanically.

(G I, 382–83; to Foucher [1686].) I believe that every individual substance expresses the whole universe in its manner and that its following state is a consequence (though often free) of its previous state, as if there were only God and it in the world; but since all substances are a continual production of the sovereign Being, and express the same universe and the same phenomena, they agree with each other entirely, and that makes us say that the one acts on the other, because the one expresses more distinctly than the other the cause or reason of the changes, rather in the way we attribute motion to the vessel rather than to the whole of the sea.

COMMENTARY

For Leibniz, the degree of monadic perfection stands coordinate with *action*. And the more perfect substances demand (in God's thoughts) that the others be adjusted to them. A monad thus *acts* on another insofar as the reasons for what the latter does lie in the former—and thus is simply a matter of the former's clearer and prior apprehension of the changes that pervade their common world. (Compare sec. 5.) Thus action, clarity of perception, and substantial perfection all correspond with one another. Leibniz holds that perfection (in the contingent realm, at any rate) is measured by clear *perception* even as for Spinoza it is measured by clear *conception*. (*Mens nostra . . . quatenus adaequatas habet ideas, eatenus . . . agit, et quatenus ideas habet inaequatas, eatenus . . . patitur.* [*Ethics*, Bk. III, prop. 1].) Leibniz's approach to action/passion is thus simply a more generalized version of Spinoza's.

Strictly speaking, of course, monads do not really act upon one another. But their mutual accommodation means that we can plausibly speak of *action* which is indeed there, in net effect and "for all practical purposes." As Latta helpfully observes: "This is merely Leibniz' explanation of what we mean when we speak of outward action, just as the Copernican system explains what we mean when we speak of 'sunrise' or 'sunset,' though the sun never 'rises' nor 'sets'" (Latta, p. 245n.).

KEY WORDS:

created being/*créature*
to act/*agir*
to react/*patir*
action/*l'action*
perfection/*perfection*
monad/*monade*
distinct or confused perception/*perception distincte ou confusé*

SECTION 50

50. And one created being is more perfect than another insofar as one finds within it that which provides an *a priori* reason for what happens in the other. And it is because of this that one says that it *acts* upon the other.

50. Et une creature est plus parfaite qu'une autre en ce qu'on trouve en elle ce qui sert à rendre raison a priori de ce qui se passe dans l'autre, et c'est par là qu'on dit qu'elle agit sur l'autre.

(G VII, 194 [ca. 1680].) Absolutely first truths are, among truths of reason, those which are identical, and among truths of fact this, from which all experiments can be proved *a priori*, namely: *Everything possible demands that it should exist*, and hence will exist unless something else prevents it, which also demands that it should exist and is incompatible with the former; and hence it follows that that combination of things always exists by which the greatest possible number of things exists; as, if we assume *A,B,C,D*, to be equal as regards essence, i.e. equally perfect, or equally demanding existence, and if we assume that *D* is incompatible with *A* and with *B*, while *A* is compatible with any except *D*, and similarly as regards *B* and *C*; it follows that the combination *ABC*, excluding *D*, will exist; for if we wish *D* to exist, it can only coexist with *C*, and hence the combination *CD* will exist, which is more imperfect than the combination *ABC*. And hence it is obvious that things exist in the most perfect way. This proposition, that everything possible demands that it should exist, can be proved *a posteriori*, assuming that something exists; for either all things exist, and then every possible so demands existence that it actually exists; or some things do not exist, and then a reason must be given otherwise than from a general reason of essence or possibility, assuming that the possible demands existence in its own nature, and indeed in proportion to its possibility or according to the degree of its essence. Unless in the very nature of Essence there were some inclination to exist, nothing would exist; for to say that some essences have this inclination and others not, is to say something without a reason, since existence seems to be referred generally to every essence in the same way. But it is as yet unknown to men, whence arises the incompossibility of diverse things, or how it can happen that diverse essences are opposed to each other, seeing that all purely positive terms seem to be compatible *inter se.*

(G VII, 303; Loemker, p. 487; Ariew & Garber, p. 150; "On the Radical Origination of Things" [1697].) Perfection is nothing but quantity of essence.

COMMENTARY

For Leibniz, *X* exerts causal influence on *Y* if *X* is involved in the sufficient reason for some fact about *Y*—that is, is part of what impels God toward actualizing *Y*. Leibniz thus grounds agency in perfection. The harmonious attunement of substances in the world means that each must be accommodated to all the rest. As Leibniz sees it, God, in selecting a particular substance over against its alternatives for actualization, recognizes in more perfect substances an entitlement to be predominant—to have others accommodated to their needs. The more imperfect substances are as they are because they need to be so in order to accommodate the requirements of the more perfect—in relation to which they are, accordingly, the active agents. The inherent rationality of God's choice of the best thus coordinates perfection and active agency by embedding the latter in the former. (Note the equation: quantity of essence = degree of perfection = claim on God for actualization = agency.)

His coordination of perfection with agency means that, for Leibniz, the order of *causes* (of active agency) and that of *reasons* of (rational explanation) stand in perfect coordination with one another. The causal agency of the world's processes finds its basis in the rational structure of God's choices: things act as they do (operatively) because this conduces to the best (normatively). In Leibniz's system all causality is ultimately teleological.

Leibniz's doctrine here is the antithesis of Hume's: for Hume, reason has no foothold in the causal order (causal connection being a matter of experienced-based expectation where reason has no role). For Leibniz, the causal order operates throughout on reason-legislated principles, the laws of nature reflecting divinely chosen regularities. To be sure, Hume considers the matter from the angle of human reason, Leibniz from the angle of God's.

KEY WORDS:

created being/*créature*
perfection/*perfection*
reason/*raison*
a priori/*a priori*
to act/*agir*

SECTION 51

51. But in simple substances there is only an ideal influence of one monad on another, which can have its effect only through the intervention of God, insofar in the ideas of God one monad demands with good reason that God should have regard for it in regulating the others from the very beginning of things. For, since one created monad cannot have any physical influence on the inner make-up of another, it is in this way alone that the one can be dependent on the other. (See *Theodicy*, secs. 9, 54, 65, 66, 201; Abridgment, obj. 3.)

*51. Mais dans les substances simples ce n'est qu'une influence idéale d'une Monade sur l'autre, qui ne peut avoir son effect, que par l'intervention de Dieu, en tant que dans les Idées de Dieu une Monade demande avec raison, que Dieu en reglant les autres dès le commencement des choses, ait égard à elle. Car, puisqu'une Monade creée ne sçauroit avoir une influence physique sur l'interieur de l'autre, ce n'est que par ce moyen, que l'une peut avoir de la dependance de l'autre. (*Théodicée, secs. 9, 54, 65, 66, 201; Abrégé, obj. 3.)*

(*Theodicy,* sec. 9.) For it must be known that all things are *connected* in each one of the possible worlds: the universe, whatever it may be, is all of one piece, like an ocean: the least movement extends its effect there to any distance whatsoever, even though this effect becomes less perceptible in proportion to the distance. Therein God has ordered all things beforehand once for all, having foreseen prayers, good and bad actions, and all the rest; and each thing *as an idea* has contributed, before its existence, to the resolution that has been made upon the existence of all things; so that nothing can be changed in the universe (any more than in a number) save its essence or, if you will, save its *numerical individuality.* Thus, if the smallest evil that comes to pass in the world were missing in it, it would no longer be this world; which, with nothing omitted and all allowance made, was found the best by the Creator who chose it.

(*Theodicy,* sec. 54.) It will be said also that, if all is ordered, God cannot then perform miracles. But one must bear in mind that the miracles which happen in the world were also enfolded and represented as possible in this same world considered in the state of mere possibility; and God, who has since performed them, when he chose this world had even then decreed to perform them. Again the objection will be made that vows and prayers, merits and demerits, good and bad actions avail nothing, since nothing can be changed. This objection causes most perplexity to people in general, and yet it is purely a sophism. These prayers, these vows, these good or bad actions that occur to-day were already before God when he formed the resolution to order things. . . . The prayer or the good action were even then an *ideal cause* or *condition,* that is, an inclining reason able to contribute to the grace of God, or to the reward, as it now does in reality. Since, moreover, all is wisely connected together in the world, it is clear that God, foreseeing that which would happen freely, ordered all other things on that basis beforehand, or (what is the same) he chose that possible world in which everything was ordered in this fashion.

(*Theodicy,* sec. 65.) And now, to bring to a conclusion this question of spontaneity, it must be said that, on a rigorous definition, the soul has within it the principle of all its actions, and even of all its passions, and that the same is true in all the simple substances scattered throughout Nature, although there be freedom only in those that are intelligent. In the popular sense notwithstanding, speaking in accordance with appearances, we must say that the soul depends in some way upon the body and upon the impressions of the senses: much as we speak with Ptolemy and Tycho in everyday converse, and think with Copernicus, when it is a question of the rising and the setting of the sun.

(*Theodicy*, sec. 66.) One may however give a true and philosophic sense to this *mutual dependence* which we suppose between the soul and the body. It is that the one of these two substances depends upon the other *ideally*, in so far as the reason of that which is done in the one can be furnished by that which is in the other. This had already happened when God ordered beforehand the harmony that there would be between them. Even so would that automaton, that should fulfil the servant's function, depend upon me ideally, in virtue of the knowledge of him, who foreseeing my future orders, would have rendered it capable of serving me at the right moment all through the morrow. The knowledge of my future intentions would have actuated this great craftsman, who would accordingly have fashioned the automaton: my influence would be objective and his physical. For in so far as the soul has perfection and distinct thoughts, God has accommodated the body to the soul, and has arranged beforehand that the body is impelled to execute its orders. And in so far as the soul is swayed by the passions arising out of corporeal representations. This produces the same effect and the same appearance as if the one depended immediately upon the other, and by the agency of a physical influence. Properly speaking, it is by its confused thoughts that the soul represents the bodies which encompass it. The same thing must apply to all that we understand by the actions of simple substances one upon another. For each one is assumed to act upon the other in proportion to its perfection, although this be only ideally, and in the reasons of things, as God in the beginning ordered one substance to accord with another in proportion to the perfection or imperfection that there is in each. (Withal action and passion are always reciprocal in creatures, because one part of the reasons which serve to explain clearly what is done, and which have served to bring it into existence, is in the one of these substances, and another part of these reasons is in the other, perfections and imperfections being always mingled and shared.) Thus it is we attribute *action* to the one, and *passion* to the other.

(*Theodicy*, sec. 201.) It may be said that, if we could understand the structure and the economy of the universe, we should find that it is made and directed as the wisest and most virtuous could wish it, since God cannot fail to do thus. This necessity nevertheless is only of a moral nature: and I admit that if God were forced by a metaphysical necessity to produce that which he makes, he would produce all the possibles, or nothing; and in this sense M. Bayle's conclusion would be fully correct. But as all the possibles are not compatible together in one and the same world-sequence, for that very reason all the possibles cannot be produced, and it must be said that God is not forced, metaphysically speaking, into the creation of this world. One may say that as soon as God has decreed to create something there is a struggle between all the possibles, all of them laying claim to existence, and that those which, being united, produce most reality, most perfection, most significance carry the day. It is true that all this struggle can only be ideal, that is to say, it can only be a conflict of reasons in the most perfect understanding, which cannot fail to act in the most perfect way, and consequently to choose the best. Yet God is bound by a moral necessity, to make things in such a manner that there can be nothing better: otherwise not only would others have cause to criticize what he makes, but, more than that, he would not himself be satisfied with his work, he would blame himself for its imperfection; and that conflicts with the supreme felicity of the divine nature.

(*Theodicy*, Abridgment, obj. 3.) Not only pains and effort but also prayers are effective, God having had even these prayers in mind before he ordered things, and having made due allowance for them. . . . So the predetermination of events by their causes is precisely what contributes to morality instead of destroying it, and the causes incline the will without necessitating it. For this reason the determination we are concerned with is not a necessitation. It is certain (to him who knows all) that the effect will follow this inclination; but this effect does not follow thence by a consequence which is necessary, that is, whose contrary implies contradiction; and it is also by such an inward inclination that the will is determined, without the presence of necessity.

(PNG, sec. 10.) For all possible things have a claim to existence in God's understanding in proportion to their perfections, the result of all these claims must be the most perfect actual world which is possible. Without this it would be impossible to give a reason why things have gone as they have rather than otherwise.

(NS, sec. 14.) Being constrained, then, to admit that it is impossible for the soul or any other true substance to receive something from without, except by the divine omnipotence, I was led insensibly to an opinion which surprised me, but which seems inevitable, and which has in fact very great advantages and very significant beauties. This is that we must say that God has originally created the soul, and every other real unity, in such a way that everything in it must arise from its own nature by a perfect *spontaneity* with regard to itself, yet by a perfect *conformity* to things without. And thus, since our internal sensations, that is, those which are in the soul itself and not in the brain or in the subtle parts of the body, are merely phenomena which follow upon external events or better, are really appearances or like well-ordered dreams, it follows that these perceptions internal to the soul itself come to it through its own original constitution, that is to say, through its representative nature, which is capable of expressing entities outside of itself in agreement with its organs— this nature having been given it from its creation and constituting its individual character.

(DM, sec. 14.) The perceptions and expressions of all substances intercorrespond, so that each one following independently certain reasons or laws which he has noticed meets others which are doing the same, as when several have agreed to meet together in a certain place on a set day, they are able to carry out the same phenomena, this does not bring it about that their expressions are exactly alike. It is sufficient if they are proportional. As when several spectators think they see the same thing and are agreed about it, although each one sees or speaks according to the measure of his vision. It is God alone, (from whom all individuals emanate continually, and who sees the universe not only as they see it, but besides in a very different way from them) who is the cause of this correspondence in their phenomena and who brings it about that that which is particular to one, is also common to all, otherwise there would be no relation. In a way, then, we might properly say, although it seems strange, that a particular substance never acts upon another particular substance nor is it acted upon by it. That which happens to each one is only the consequence of its complete idea or concept, since this idea already includes all the predicates and expresses the whole universe. In fact nothing can happen to us except thoughts and perceptions, and all our thoughts and perceptions are but the consequence, contingent it is true, of our precedent thoughts and perceptions, in such a way that were I able to consider directly all that happens or appears to me at the present time, I should be able to see all that will happen to me or that will ever appear to me. This future will not fail me, and will surely appear to me even if all that which is outside of me were destroyed, save only that God and myself were left.

(DM, sec. 15.) Without entering into a long discussion it is sufficient for reconciling the language of metaphysics with that of practical life to remark that we preferably attribute to ourselves, and with reason, the phenomena which we express the most perfectly, and that we attribute to other substances those phenomena which each one expresses the best. Thus a substance, which is of an infinite extension insofar as it expresses all, becomes limited in proportion to its more or less perfect manner of expression. It is thus then that we may conceive of substances as interfering with and limiting one another, and hence we are able to say that in this sense they act upon one another, and that they, so to speak, accommodate themselves to one another. For it can happen that a single change which augments the expression of the one may diminish that of the other. Now the virtue of a particular substance is to express well the glory of God, and the better it expresses it, the less is it limited. Everything when it expresses its virtue or power, that is to say, when it acts, changes to better, and expands just insofar as it acts. When therefore a change occurs by which several substances are affected (in fact every change affects them all) I think we may say that those substances, which by this change pass immediately to a greater degree of perfection, or to a more perfect expression, exert power and act, while those which pass to a lesser degree disclose their weakness and suffer.

(DM, sec. 28.) The only immediate object of our perceptions which exists outside of us is God, and in him alone is our light. For in the strictly metaphysical sense no external cause acts upon us excepting God alone, and he is in immediate relation with us only by virtue of our continual dependence upon him. Whence it follows that there is absolutely no other external object which comes into contact with our souls and directly excites perceptions in us. We have in our souls ideas of everything, only because of the continual action of God upon us, that is to say, because every effect expresses its cause and therefore the essences of our souls are certain expressions, imitations or images of the divine essence, divine thought and divine will, including all the ideas which are there contained. We may say, therefore, that God is for us the only immediate external object, and that we see things through him. For example, when we see the sun or the stars, it is God who gives to us and preserves in us the ideas and whenever our senses are affected according to his own laws in a certain manner, it is he, who by his continual concurrence, determines our thinking.

(DM, sec. 32.) For it appears clearly that all other substances depend upon God just as our thoughts emanate from our own substances; that God is all in all and that he is intimately united to all created things, in proportion however to their perfection; that it is he alone who determines them from without by his influence, and if to act is to determine directly, it may be said in metaphysical language that God alone acts upon me and he alone causes me to do good or ill, other substances contributing only because of his determinations; because God, who takes all things into consideration, distributes his bounties and compels created beings to accommodate themselves to one another. Thus God alone constitutes the relation or communication between substances. It is through him that the phenomena of the one meet and accord with the phenomena of the others, so that there may be a reality in our perceptions. In common parlance, however, an action is attributed to particular causes in the sense that I have explained above because it is not necessary to make continual mention of the universal cause when speaking of particular cases. It can be seen also that every substance has a perfect spontaneity (which becomes liberty with intelligent substances). Everything which happens to it is a consequence of its idea or its being and nothing determines it except God only. It is for this reason that a person of exalted mind and revered saintliness may say that the soul ought often to think as if there were only God and itself in the world.

(NS, sec. 17.) For one may say that when the particular disposition of one substance provides a reason for a change occurring in an intelligible manner, in such a way that we can conclude that the other substances have been adapted to it on this point from the beginning according to the order of the divine decree, then that substance should be thought of as *acting* upon the others in this sense. Further, the action of one substance upon another is not an emission or a transplanting of some entity, as is commonly supposed; and it can be understood reasonably only in the way just shown.

(G II, 57–58; Loemker, p. 337; to Arnauld [1686].) Thus every individual substance or complete being is, as it were, a world apart, independent of everything else excepting God . . . . This independence however does not prevent the interactivity of substances among themselves, for, as all created substances are a continual production of the same sovereign Being according to the same designs and express the same universe of the same phenomena, they agree with one another exactly; and this enables us to say that one acts upon another because the one expresses more distinctly than the other the cause or reason for the changes,—somewhat as we attribute motion rather to a ship than to the whole sea; and this with reason, although, if we should speak abstractly, another hypothesis of motion could be maintained, that is to say, the motion in itself and abstracted from the cause could be considered as something relative. It is thus, it seems to me, that the inter-activities of created substances among themselves must be understood, and not as though there were a real physical influence or dependence. The latter idea can never be distinctly conceived of.

(G II, 264; to de Volder [1704].) There is only one case of one substance acting immediately upon another: the action, namely, of infinite substance upon finite substances—an action which consists in continuously producing or constituting them. For there must necessarily be a cause why these finite substances exist and correspond with each other, and this must necessarily arise from the infinite substance which is necessary per se. But if it is claimed that substances do not remain the same but that different substances which follow upon prior ones are always produced by God, this would be to quarrel about a word, for there is no further principle in things by which such a controversy can be decided. The succeeding substance will be considered the same as the preceding as long as the same law of the series or of simple continuous transition persists, which makes us believe in the same subject of change, or the monad. The fact that a certain law persists which involves all of the future states of that which we conceive to be the same—this is the very fact, I say, which constitutes the enduring substance.

(G VI, 593; Loemker, p. 627; Ariew & Garber, p. 268; "Conversation of Philarète and Ariste" [ca. 1712].) I am convinced that God is the only immediate external object of souls, since there is nothing except him outside of the soul which acts immediately upon it. Our thoughts with all that is in us, insofar as it includes some perfection, are produced without interruption by his continuous operation. So, inasmuch as we receive our finite perfections from his which are infinite, we are immediately affected by them. And it is thus that our mind is affected immediately by the eternal ideas which are in God, since our mind has thoughts which are in correspondence with them and participate in them. It is in this sense that we can say that our mind sees all things in God.

(Loemker, p. 269; Ariew & Garber, p. 33; "First Truths" [ca. 1685].) *All individual created substances, indeed, are different expressions of the same universe* and of the same universal cause, God. But these expressions vary in perfection as do different representations or perspectives of the same city seen from different vantage points. *Every created individual substance exerts physical action and passion on all others.* For if a change occurs in one, some corresponding change results in all others, because their denomination is changed. This is confirmed by our experience of nature, for we observe that in a vessel full of liquid (the whole universe is such a vessel) a motion made in the middle is propagated to the edges, though it may become more and more insensible as it recedes farther from its origin. It can be said that, speaking with metaphysical rigor, *no created substance exerts a metaphysical action or influence upon another.* For to say nothing of the fact that it cannot be explained how anything can pass over from one thing into the substance of another it has already been shown that all the future states of each thing follow from its own concept. What we call causes are in metaphysical rigor only concomitant requisites. This is illustrated by our experiences of nature, for bodies in fact recede from other bodies by force of their own elasticity and not by any alien force, although another body has been required to set the elasticity (which arises from something intrinsic to the body itself) working.

COMMENTARY

Various analogy-models for causality among the world's substances can be conceived:

• transfer of physical impetus (the billiard-ball atomism of Hobbes, Gassendi, etc.)
• emanation (Cambridge neo-Platonism)
• communicative information transmission from premises to conclusions (Berkeley)

• deductive/inferential information transfer (Spinoza)
• re-creation (Occasionalism)

Leibniz rejects all of these in favor of simple coordination—the unfolding of events in a pre-programmed way through a mathematics-reminiscent coordination ("law of series"). All causal interaction is thus something "merely ideal" that exists in appearance only (much as is the case in a film strip).

For Leibniz, the only causality in nature is an ideal causality, one that results from God's concern for the mutual accommodation of things to one another in an orderly and perfection-manifesting world. Since all substances have a fixed and unchanging nature—one that is programatically pre-determined by their complete defining concepts—this quasi-causality of mutual accommodation is the only causality there is. The "causally active" substance is the one in whose favor, as it were, God proceeded to adjust the remainder of the substantial manifold. Causal agency thus mirrors rational explanation. It is a matter of the weight of a substance's claims to have others be adjusted to it in the interests of the overall perfection of the whole system. (Sec. 52 elaborates this theme.) The coordination of substances is thus geared to the harmonization of the whole.

In the monadic system, the only "causality" is the accommodation of one substance's make-up to the greater claims of another. So there is no *interaction* among monads, but only an elaborate *co-ordination* among them in virtue of their co-existence in the best of possible worlds. (Compare sec. 56.) This co-ordination creates a quasi causality that serves every bit as effectively in interconnecting the comportment monads as would the real thing.

KEY WORDS:

simple substance/*substance simple*
monad/*monade*
ideal influence/*influence idéale*
intervention of God/*intervention de Dieu*
reason/*raison*
ideas of God/*idées de Dieu*
physical influence/*influence physique*
inner make-up/*intérieur*
dependence/*dépendence*
creation/*le commencement des choses*

SECTION 52

52. And it is in this way that among created beings actions and reactions <or "passions"> are reciprocal. For God, comparing two simple substances, finds in each reasons which oblige him to accommodate the other to it, and consequently that which is in certain regards active is passive from another point of consideration. It is *active* insofar as what is distinctly known in it provides the reason for what happens in another, and *reactive* (*passive*) insofar as the reason for what happens in it is found in what is distinctly known in another. (See *Theodicy*, sec. 66.)

52. Et c'est par là, qu'entre les Creatures les Actions et Passions sont mutuelles. Car Dieu, comparant deux substances simples, trouve en chacune des raisons, qui l'obligent à y accommoder l'autre; et par consequent ce qui est actif à certains égards, est passif suivant un autre point de consideration: actif en tant que ce qu'on connoît distinctement en lui, sert à rendre raison de ce qui se passe dans un autre; et passif en tant que la raison de ce qui se passe en lui, se trouve dans ce qui se connoît distinctement dans un autre. (Théodicée, sec. 66.)

(*Theodicy*, sec. 66) One may however give a true and philosophic sense to this *mutual dependence* which we suppose between the soul and the body. It is that the one of these two substances depends upon the other ideally, insofar as the reason of that which is done in the one case be furnished by that which is in the other. This had already happened when God ordered beforehand the harmony that there would be between them. Even so would that automaton, that should fulfil the servant's function, depend upon me *ideally*, in virtue of the knowledge of him who, foreseeing my future orders, would have rendered it capable of serving me at the right moment all through the morrow. The knowledge of my future intentions would have actuated this great craftsman, who would accordingly have fashioned the automaton: my influence would be objective, and his physical. For insofar as the soul is imperfect and as its perceptions are confused, God has accommodated the soul to the body, in such sort that the soul is swayed by the passions arising out of corporeal representations. This produces the same effect and the same appearance as if the one depended immediately upon the other, and by the agency of a physical influence. Properly speaking, it is by its confused thoughts that the soul represents the bodies which encompass it. The same thing must apply to all that we understand by the actions of simple substances one upon another. For each one is assumed to act upon the other in proportion to its perfection, although this be only ideally, and in the reasons of things, as God in the beginning ordered one substance to accord with another in proportion to the perfection or imperfection that there is in each. (Withal action and passion are always reciprocal in creatures, because one part of the reasons which serve to explain clearly what is done, and which have served to bring it into existence, is in the one of these substances, and another part of these reasons is in the other, perfections and imperfections being always mingled and shared.) Thus it is we attribute *action* to the one, and *passion* to the other.

(PNG, sec. 4.) Together with a particular body, each monad makes a living substance. Thus not only is there life everywhere, joined to members or organs, but there are also infinite degrees of it in the monads, some of which dominate more or less over others.

(PNG, sec. 11.) The supreme wisdom of God has made him choose especially those *laws of motion* which are best adjusted and most fitted to abstract or metaphysical reasons. There is conserved the same quantity of total and absolute force or of action, also the same quantity of relative force or of reaction, and finally, the same quantity of directive force. Furthermore, action is always equal to reaction, and the entire effect is always equal to its full cause.

(DM, sec. 32.) It must be said in metaphysical strictness that God alone acts upon me and he alone causes me to do good or ill, other substances contributing only because of his determinations; because God, who takes all things into consideration, distributes his bounties and compels created beings to accommodate themselves to one another. Thus God alone constitutes the relation or communication between substances. It is through him that the phenomena of the one meet and accord with phenomena of the others, so that there may be a reality in our perceptions. In common parlance, however, an action is attributed to particular causes . . . because it is not necessary to make continual mention of the universal cause when speaking of particular cases.

COMMENTARY

As Leibniz sees it, substance A is active in relation to substance B, and B passive in relation to A, to exactly the extent that B is being accommodated to meet the conditions of the make-up of A. There is consequently a perfect reciprocity of active and passive. The order of activity stands in coordinative relation with the order of grounding—that is, the weight of reasons for giving the claims of one substance priority over those of another in the interests of assuring the perfection of the entire resulting world. (Compare sec. 54.) Thus activity and perfection are also correlated. (Leibniz sees in these metaphysical considerations the grounding of the physical principle that action equals reaction.)

KEY WORDS:

created being/*créature*
simple substances/*substances simple*
action/*action (l' actif)*
passion (reaction)/*passion (le passif)*
reason/*raison*
to accommodate/*accommoder*
distinct knowledge/*connaisance distincte*
point of consideration/*point de considération*
to know distinctly/*connaître distinctement*

SECTION 53

53. Now, as there is an infinity of possible universes in the ideas of God, and as only one of them can exist, there must be a sufficient reason for God's choice, which determines him to one rather than another. (See *Theodicy*, secs. 8, 10, 44, 173, 196–99, 225, 414–16.)

53. *Or, comme il y a une infinité des univers possibles dans les Idées de Dieu et qu'il n'en peut exister qu'un seul, il faut qu'il y ait une raison suffisante du choix de Dieu, qui le determine à l'un plutôt qu' à l'autre.* (Théodicée, secs. 8, 10, 44, 173, 196 seqq., 225, 414–16.)

(*Theodicy*, sec. 8) Now this supreme wisdom, united to a goodness that is no less infinite, cannot but have chosen the best. For as a lesser evil is a kind of good, even so a lesser good is a kind of evil if it stands in the way of a greater good; and there would be something to correct in the actions of God if it were possible to do better. As in mathematics, when there is no maximum nor minimum, in short nothing distinguished, everything is done equally, or when that is not possible nothing at all is done: so it may be said likewise in respect of perfect wisdom, which is no less orderly than mathematics, that if there were not the best (*optimum*) among all possible worlds, God would not have produced any. I call "world" the whole succession and the whole agglomeration of all existent things, lest it be said that several worlds could have existed in different times and different places. For they must needs be reckoned all together as one world or, if you will, as one Universe. And even though one should fill all times and all places, it still remains true that one might have filled them in innumerable ways, and that there is an infinitude of possible worlds among which God must needs have chosen the best, since he does nothing without acting in accordance with Supreme Reason.

(*Theodicy*, sec. 10.) It is true that one may imagine possible worlds without sin and without unhappiness, and one could make some like Utopian or Sevarambian romances: but these same worlds again would be very inferior to ours in goodness. I cannot show you this in detail. For can I know and can I present infinites to you and compare them together? But you must judge with me from the results since God has chosen this world as it is. We know, moreover, that often an evil brings forth a good whereto one would not have attained without that evil. . . . A general makes sometimes a fortunate mistake which brings about the winning of a great battle. . . .

(*Theodicy*, sec. 44.) We must take into account that there are two great principles of our arguments. The one is the principle of *contradiction*, stating that of two contradictory propositions the one is true, the other false; the other principle is that of the *determinant reason:* it states that nothing ever comes to pass without there being a cause or at least a reason determining it, that is, something to give an *a priori* reason why it is existent rather than non-existent, and in this wise rather than in any other. This great principle holds for all events, and a contrary instance will never be supplied: and although more often than not we are insufficiently acquainted with these determinant reasons, we perceive nevertheless that there are such. Were it not for this great principle we could never prove the existence of God, and we should lose an infinitude of very just and very profitable arguments whereof it is the foundation. . . .

(*Theodicy*, sec. 173.) As far as one can understand him, he <Spinoza> acknowledges no goodness in God, properly speaking, and he teaches that all things exist through the necessity of the divine nature, without any act of choice by God. We will not waste time here in refuting an opinion so bad, and indeed so inexplicable. My own opinion is founded on the nature of the possibles, that is, of things that imply no contradiction. I do not think that a Spinozist will say that all the romances one can imagine exist actually now, or have existed, or will still exist in some place in the universe. Yet one cannot deny that romances . . . are possible. Let us therefore bring up against him these words of M. Bayle, which please me well: "it is to-day," he says, "a great embarrassment for the Spinozists to see that, according to their hypothesis, it was as impossible from all eternity that Spinoza, for instance, should not die at The Hague, as it is impossible for two and two to make six. They are well aware that it is a necessary conclusion from their doctrine, and a conclusion which disheartens, affrights, and stirs the mind to revolt, because of the absurdity it involves, diametrically opposed to common sense. They are not well pleased that one should know they are subverting a maxim so universal and so evident as this one: All that which implies contradiction is impossible, and all that which implies no contradiction is possible."

(*Theodicy*, sec. 196.) It is therefore not a question of a creature, but of the universe; and the adversary will be obliged to maintain that one possible universe may be better than the other, to infinity; but there he would be mistaken, and it is that which he cannot prove. If this opinion were true, it would follow that God had not produced any universe at all: for he is incapable of acting without reason, and that would be even acting against reason. It is as if one were to suppose that God had decreed to make a material sphere, with no reason for making it of any particular size. This decree would be useless, it would carry with it that which would prevent its effect. It would be quite another matter if God decreed to draw from a given point one straight line to another given straight line, without any determination of the angle, either in the decree or in its circumstances. For in this case the determination would spring from the nature of the thing, the line would be perpendicular, and the angle would be right, since that is all that is determined and distinguishable. It is thus one must think of the creation of the best of all possible universes, all the more since God not only decrees to create a universe, but decrees also to create the best of all. For God decrees nothing without knowledge, and he makes no separate decrees, which would be nothing but antecedent acts of will: and these we have sufficiently explained, distinguishing them from genuine decrees.

(*Theodicy*, sec. 199.) I hold . . . that one can reconcile the evil, or the less good, in some parts with the best in the whole. If the Dualists demanded that God should do the best, they would not be demanding too much. They are mistaken, rather, in claiming that the best in the whole should be free from evil in the parts, and that therefore what God has made is not the best.

(*Theodicy*, sec. 225.) The infinity of possibles, however great it may be, is no greater than that of the wisdom of God, who knows all possibles. One may even say that if this wisdom does not exceed the possibles extensively, since the objects of the understanding cannot go beyond the possible, which in a sense is alone intelligible, it exceeds them intensively, by reason of the infinitely infinite combinations it makes thereof, and its many deliberations concerning them. The wisdom of God, not content with embracing all the possibles, penetrates them, compares them, weighs them one against the other, to estimate their degrees of perfection or imperfection, the strong and the weak, the good and the evil. It goes even beyond the finite combinations, it makes of them an infinity of infinites, that is to say, an infinity of possible sequences of the universe, each of which contains an infinity of creatures. By this means the divine Wisdom distributes all the possibles it had already contemplated separately, into so many universal systems which it further compares the one with the other. The result of all these comparisons and deliberations is the choice of the best from among all these possible systems, which wisdom makes in order to satisfy goodness completely; and such is precisely the plan of the universe as it is. Moreover, all these operations of the divine understanding, although they have among them an order and a priority of nature, always take place together, no priority of time existing among them.

(*Theodicy*, sec. 335.) Evil springs rather from the *Forms* themselves in their detached state, that is, from the ideas that God has not produced by an act of his will, any more than he thus produced numbers and figures, and all possible essences which one must regard as eternal and necessary; for they are in the ideal region of the possibilities. But there is nothing actual to which he has not decreed and given existence; and he has permitted evil because it is involved in the best plan existing in the region of possibles, a plan which supreme wisdom could not fail to choose. This notion satisfies at once the wisdom, the power and the goodness of God, and yet leaves a way open for the entrance of evil.

(*Theodicy*, secs. 414–16.) ⟨The mind of God is akin to the mythical palace of the fates.⟩ . . . Here are representations not only of that which happens but also of all that which is possible. Jupiter ⟨the guardian of the palace⟩ having surveyed them before the beginning of the existing world, classified the possibilities into worlds, and chose the best of all. He comes sometimes to visit these places, to enjoy the pleasure of recapitulating things and of renewing his own choice, which cannot fail to please him. I ⟨the Goddess reciting this⟩ have only to speak, and we shall see a whole world that my father might have produced, wherein will be represented anything that can be asked of him; and in this way one may know also what would happen if any particular possibility should attain unto existence. And whenever the conditions are not determinate enough, there will be as many such worlds differing from one another as one shall wish, which will answer differently the same question, in as many ways as possible. You ⟨Theodorus, the auditor⟩ learnt geometry in your youth, like all well-instructed Greeks. You know therefore that when the conditions of a required point do not sufficiently determine it, and there is an infinite number of them, they all fall into what the geometricians call a locus, and this locus at least (which is often a line) will be determinate. Thus you can picture to yourself an ordered succession of worlds, which all contain each and every one the case that is in question, and shall vary its circumstances and its consequences. But if you put a case that differs from the actual world only in one single definite thing and in its results, a certain one of those determinate worlds will answer you. These worlds are all here, that is, in ideas. I will show you some, wherein shall be found, not absolutely the same Sextus as you have seen (that is not possible, he carries with him always that which he shall be) but several Sextuses resembling him, possessing all that you know already of the true Sextus, but not all that is already in him imperceptibly, nor in consequence all that shall yet happen to him. You will find in one world a very happy and noble Sextus, in another a Sextus content with a mediocre state, a Sextus, indeed, of every kind and endless diversity of forms.

(DM, sec. 2.) In saying, therefore, that things are not good according to any standard of goodness, but simply by the will of God, it seems to me that one destroys, without realizing it, all the love of God and all His glory; for why praise Him for what he has done, if he would be equally praiseworthy in doing the contrary? . . . This is why, accordingly, I find so strange those expressions of certain philosophers who say that the eternal truths of metaphysics and geometry, and so also the principles of goodness, of justice, and of perfection, are effects only of the will of God. ⟨We must reject⟩ the extremely dangerous view, almost approaching that of recent innovators, whose opinion is that the beauty of the universe, and the goodness that we attribute to the works of God, are nothing more than the chimeras of men who conceive God after their own fashion . . . [and who] also say that things are not good by any rule of goodness, but only by the will of God, one destroys, it seems to me, without realizing it, all love of God and all God's glory.

(G II, 18–19; to Hessen-Rheinfels [1686].) We must not think of the intention of God to create a certain man Adam as detached from all the other intentions which he has in regard to the children of Adam and of all the human race, as though God first made the decree to create Adam without any relation to his posterity. This, in my opinion, does away with his freedom in creating Adam's posterity as seems best to him, and is a very strange sort of reasoning. We must rather think that God, choosing not an indeterminate Adam but a particular Adam, whose perfect representation is found among the possible beings in the Ideas of God and who is accompanied by certain individual circumstances and among other predicates possesses also that of having in time a certain posterity—God, I, say, in choosing him, has already had in mind his posterity and chooses them both at the same time. I am unable to understand how there is any evil in this opinion. If God should act in any other way he would not act as God.

(G III, 401; Ariew & Garber, p. 194; to Coste [1707].) But I find that we need to be very cautious here so that we do not fall into a chimera which shocks the principles of good sense, namely, what I call an *absolute indifference* or *indifference of equilibrium*, an indifference that some people imagine freedom to involve, and that I believe to be chimerical. We must therefore consider that this interconnection about which I have just spoken is not necessary, absolutely speaking, but that it is certainly true, nevertheless, and that, in general, every time that the circumstances, taken together, tip the balance of deliberation more on one side than on the other, it is certain and infallible that the former side will be chosen. God or a perfectly wise person will always choose the best that they know of, and if one side were not better than the other, they would choose neither the one nor the other. The passions often take the place of reason in other intelligent substances, and we can always assert, with respect to the will in general, that *choice follows the greatest inclination* (by which I understand both passions and reasons, true or apparent).

(Foucher de Careil, *Nouvelles lettres et opuscules*, p. 178; Loemker, p. 263; Ariew & Garber, p. 94; "On Freedom" [1689?].) When I considered that nothing occurs by chance or by accident . . . and that nothing exists unless certain conditions are fulfilled from all of which together its existence at once follows, I found myself very close to the opinions of those who hold everything to be absolutely necessary; believing that when things are not subject to coercion even though they are to necessity, there is freedom, and not distinguishing between the infallible, or what is known with certainty to be true, and the necessary. But I was pulled back from this precipice by considering those possible things never exist, existing things cannot always be necessary; otherwise it would be impossible for other things to exist in their place, and whatever never exists would therefore be impossible. For it cannot be denied that many stories, especially those we call novels, may be regarded as possible, even if they do not actually take place in this particular sequence of the universe which God has chosen—unless someone imagines that there are certain poetic regions in the infinite extent of space and time where we might see wandering over the earth King Arthur of Great Britain, Amadis of Gaul, and the fabulous Dietrich von Bern invented by the Germans. A famous philosopher of our century <Descartes> does not seem to have been far from such an opinion, for he expressly affirms somewhere that matter successively receives all the forms of which it is capable <*Principles of Philosophy*, Part III, Art. 47>. This opinion cannot be defended, for it would obliterate all the beauty of the universe and any choice of matters.

COMMENTARY

This section resumes the theme of the sufficient reason for contingent facts initially broached in section 36. For Leibniz, the key to this lies in the sphere of God's will to perfection and in the infinite comparison involved in its implementation.

Possibility, for Leibniz, is determined through an absence of contradiction. The mind of God serves as the region of possibilities, where all alternative possibilities subsist in idea, *sub ratione possibilitatis*. (See sec. 43.) But alternative possibilities logically exclude one another (at a given juncture, you cannot be both taller and shorter than your father). And when God choses to actualize one rather than another possibility there must be a sufficient determining reason for his choice; the perfect rationality of God's divine wisdom is incompatible with any sort of arbitrariness or randomness. The nature of this sufficient reason is characterized in the very next section as the perfection of the whole system of created beings.

Three distinctions with respect to being (existence, "what actually is") have played a central role throughout the history of metaphysics:

1. *Appearance:* What appears to be versus what actually is
2. *Value:* What ought to be versus what actually is
3. *Possibility:* What is possible versus what actually is

In each instance, important and influential positions have been developed by flatly *denying* the distinction in question, and insisting that "what actually is" in facts consists in and thus embraces its supposed contrast-opposite:

Case 1: Phenomenalism. The domain of appearance is not something apart from and outside that of the actual. For what is actual in fact comprises the appearances and is made up of them. The actual is simply a complex manifold of appearances.

Case 2: Optimism. The domain of "ought to be" should not be distinguished from that of "is": What actually is is just exactly what ought to be. Reality is optimal: this is the best of possible worlds.

Case 3: Determinism. The domain of the possible is just exactly that of the actual. The two coincide. The real *exhausts* the realm of possibility: everything that is really and truly possible in fact exists. Seeing that whatever is is *necessarily* so, it follows that only what is is in fact possible.

Although he is prepared to take the road of phenomenalism and optimism, Leibniz emphatically rejects determinism. The contrast between the actual and the possible is, for him, absolutely indispensable.

KEY WORDS:

infinity/*infinité*
possible universes/*univers possibles*
ideas of God/*idées de Dieu*
to exist/*exister*
sufficient reason/*raison suffisante*
God's choice/*choix de Dieu*
to determine/*déterminer*

SECTION 54

54. And this ⟨sufficient⟩ reason ⟨for the actualization of a contingent possibility⟩ can only be found in *fitness* or in the degrees of perfection that these worlds contain, each possible world having the right to lay claim to existence to the extent of the perfection it enfolds. [Thus nothing is wholly arbitrary.] (See *Theodicy*, secs. 74, 130, 167, 201, 345–47, 350, 352, 354.)

54. Et cette raison ne peut se trouver que dans la convenance ou dans les degrés de perfection que ces Mondes contiennent; chaque possible ayant droit de pretendre à l'existence à mesure de la perfection, qu'il enveloppe. [Ainsi il n'y a rien d'arbitraire entierement.] (Théodicée, secs. 74, 130, 167, 201, 345 seqq. 350, 352, 354.)

(*Theodicy*, sec. 74.) All God's actions are founded on the principle of the fitness of things, which has seen to it that affairs were so ordered that the evil action must bring upon itself a chastisement. There is good reason to believe, following the parallelism of the two realms, that of final causes and that of efficient causes, that God has established in the universe a connexion between punishment or reward and bad or good action, in accordance wherewith the first should always be attracted by the second, and virtue and vice obtain their reward and their punishment in consequence of the natural sequence of things, which contains still another kind of pre-established harmony than that which appears in the communication between the soul and the body. For, in a word all that God does, as I have said already, is harmonious to perfection.

(*Theodicy*, sec. 130.) It is true that God . . . <does> whatever he wills; but he is like a good sculptor, who will make from his block of marble only that which he judges to be the best, and who judges well. God makes of matter the most excellent of all possible machines; he makes of spirits the most excellent of all governments conceivable; and over and above all that, he establishes for their union the most perfect of all harmonies, according to the system I have proposed. Now since physical evil and moral evil occur in this perfect world, one must conclude (contrary to M. Bayle's assurance here) that otherwise a still greater evil would have been altogether inevitable. This great evil would be that God would have chosen ill if he had chosen otherwise than he has chosen. It is true that God is infinitely powerful; but his power is indeterminate, goodness and wisdom combined determine him to produce the best.

(*Theodicy*, sec. 167.) But all those who acknowledge that God produces the best plan, having chosen it from among all possible ideas of the universe; that he there finds man inclined by the original imperfection of creatures to misuse his free will and to plunge into misery; that God prevents the sin and the misery in so far as the perfection of the universe, which is an emanation from his, may permit it: those, I say, show forth more clearly that God's intention is the one most right and holy in the world: that the creature alone is guilty, that his original limitation or imperfection is the source of his wickedness, that his evil will is the sole cause of his misery; that one cannot be destined to salvation without also being destined to the holiness of the children of God and that all hope of election one can have can only be founded upon the good will infused into one's heart by the grace of God.

(*Theodicy*, sec. 201.) As all the possibles are not compatible together in one and the same world-sequence, for that very reason all the possibles cannot be produced, and it must be said that God is not forced, metaphysically speaking, into the creation of this world. One may say that as soon as God has decreed to create something there is a struggle between all the possibles, all of them laying claim to existence, and that those which, being united, produce most reality, most perfection, most significance carry the day. It is true that all this struggle can only be ideal, that is to say, it can only be a conflict of reasons in the most perfect understanding, which cannot fail to act in the most perfect way, and consequently to choose the best.

(*Theodicy*, sec. 208.) The ways of God are those most simple and uniform . . . [being] the most productive in relation to the *simplicity of ways and means*. It is as if one said that a certain house was the best that could have been constructed at a given cost. . . . If the effect were assumed to be greater, but the process less simple, I think one might say, when all is said and done, that the effect itself would be less great, taking into account not only the final effect but also the mediate effect. For the wisest mind so acts, as far as is possible, that the *means* are also *ends* of a sort, i.e., are desirable not only on account of what they do, but on account of what they are.

(*Theodicy*, sec. 345.) I discovered at the same time that the laws of motion actually existing in Nature, and confirmed by experiments, are not in reality absolutely demonstrable, as a geometrical proposition would be; but neither is it necessary that they be so. They do not spring entirely from the principle of necessity, but rather from the principle of perfection and order; they are an effect of the choice and the wisdom of God. I can demonstrate these laws in divers ways, but must always assume something that is not of an absolutely geometrical necessity. Thus these admirable laws are wonderful evidence of an intelligent and free being, as opposed to the system of absolute and brute necessity, advocated by Strato or Spinoza.

(*Theodicy*, sec. 346.) I have found that one may account for these laws by assuming that the effect is always equal in force to its cause, or, which amounts to the same thing, that the same force is conserved always: but this axiom of higher philosophy cannot be demonstrated geometrically. One may again apply other principles of like nature, for instance the principle that action is always equal to reaction, one which assumes in things a distaste for external change, and cannot be derived either from extension or impenetrability; and that other principle, that a simple movement has the same properties as those which might belong to a compound movement such as would produce the same phenomena of locomotion. These assumptions are very plausible, and are successful as an explanation of the laws of motion: nothing is so appropriate, all the more since they are in accord with each other. But there is to be found in them no absolute necessity, such as may compel us to admit them, in the way one is compelled to admit the rules of logic, of arithmetic and geometry.

(*Theodicy,* sec. 347.) <As regards the laws of nature,> there is no geometrical necessity therein. Yet it is this very lack of necessity which enhances the beauty of the laws that God has chosen, wherein divers admirable axioms exist in conjunction, and it is impossible for one to say which of them is the primary.

(*Theodicy,* sec. 350.) M. Bayle . . . fears that, if God is always determinate, Nature could dispense with him and bring about that same effect which is attributed to him, through the necessity of the order of things. That would be true if the laws of motion for instance, and all the rest, had their source in a geometrical necessity of efficient causes; but in the last analysis one is obliged to resort to something depending upon final causes and upon what is fitting. . . . <For example,> when a wicked man exists, God must have found in the region of possibles the idea of such a man forming part of that sequence of things, the choice of which was demanded by the greatest perfection of the universe, and in which errors and sins are not only punished but even repaired to greater advantage, so that they contribute to the greatest good.

(*Theodicy,* sec. 352–53.) Having spoken of the laws of bodies, that is, of the rules of motion, let us come to the laws of the union between body and soul, where M. Bayle believes that he finds again some vague indifference, something absolutely arbitrary. . . . I agree with M. Bayle that God could have so ordered bodies and souls on this globe of earth, whether by ways of nature or by extraordinary graces, that it would have been a perpetual paradise and a foretaste of the celestial state of the blessed. There is no reason why there should not be worlds happier than ours; but God had good reasons for willing that ours should be such as it is.

(*Theodicy,* secs. 354–55.) It is evident that M. Bayle believes that everything accomplished through general laws is accomplished without miracles. But I have shown sufficiently that if the law is not founded on reasons and does not serve to explain the event through the nature of things, it can only be put into execution by a miracle. If, for example, God had ordained that bodies must have a circular motion, he would have needed perpetual miracles, or the ministry of angels, to put this order into execution: for that is contrary to the nature of motion, whereby the body naturally abandons the circular line to continue in the tangent straight line if nothing holds it back. Therefore it is not enough for God to ordain simply that a wound should excite an agreeable sensation: natural means must be found for that purpose. The real means whereby God causes the soul to be conscious of what happens in the body have their origin in the nature of the soul, which represents the bodies, and is so made beforehand that the representations which are to spring up one from another within it, by a natural sequence of thoughts, correspond to the changes in the body.

(PNG, sec. 10.) It follows from the supreme perfection of God that he has chosen the best possible plan in producing the universe, a plan which combines the greatest variety together with the greatest order; with situation, place, and time arranged in the best way possible; with the greatest effect produced by the simplest means; with the most power, the most knowledge, the greatest happiness and goodness in created things which the universe could allow. For as all possible things have a claim to existence in God's understanding in proportion to their perfections, the result of all these claims must be the most perfect actual world which is possible.

(PNG, sec. 11.) The supreme wisdom of God has made him choose especially those *laws of motion* which are best adjusted and most fitted to abstract or metaphysical reasons. There is conserved the same quantity of total and absolute force or of action, also the same directive force. Furthermore, action is always equal to reaction, and the entire effect is always equal to its full cause. It is surprising that no reason can be given for the laws of motion which have been discovered in our own time, and part of which I myself have discovered, by a consideration of *efficient causes* or of matter alone. For I have found that we must have recourse to *final causes* and that these laws do not depend upon the *principle of necessity*, as do the truths of logic, arithmetic, and geometry, but upon the *principle of fitnesss*, that is to say, upon the wisdom.

(DM, sec. 6.) God has chosen <to create> that world which is the most perfect, that is to say, which is at the same time the simplest in its hypotheses <i.e., its laws> and the richest in phenomena.

(DM, sec. 13.) The demonstration of this predicate of Caesar <that he resolved to cross the Rubicon> is not as absolute as those of numbers or of geometry, but presupposes the series of things which God has chosen freely, and which is founded on the first free decree of God, namely, to do always what is most perfect, in regard to human nature, which is that man will always do (though freely) what appears best. Now every truth which is founded on decrees of this kind is contingent, although it is certain. . . . All contingent propositions have reasons for being as they are rather than otherwise, or (what is the same thing) they have *a priori* proofs of their truth, which render them certain, and show that the relation between subject and predicate of these prepositions has its foundation in the nature of the one and the other. But they do not have demonstrations of necessity, since these reasons are only founded on the principle of contingency, or of the existence of things, i.e. on what is or appears the best among several equally possible things.

(DM, sec. 31.) In regard to that great and ultimate question why it has pleased God to choose him among so great a number of possible persons, it is surely unreasonable to demand more than the general reasons which we have given. The reasons in detail surpass our ken. Therefore, instead of postulating an absolute decree, which being without reason would be unreasonable, and instead of postulating reasons which do not succeed in solving the difficulties and in turn have need themselves of reasons, it will be best to say with St. Paul that there are for God's choice certain great reasons of wisdom and congruity which he follows, which reasons, however, are unknown to mortals and are founded upon the general order, whose goal is the greatest perfection of the world.

(G III, 582; to Bourguet [1715].) Two hypotheses can be formed—one that nature is always equally perfect, the other that it always increases in perfection. If it is always equally perfect, though in variable ways, it is more probable that it had no beginning. But if it always increases in perfection (assuming that it is impossible to give it its whole perfection at once), there would still be two ways of explaining the matter, namely <with or without a beginning>. . . . I do not yet see any way of demonstrating by pure reason which of these we should choose. But though the state of the world could never be absolutely perfect at any particular instant whatever according to the hypothesis of increase, nevertheless the whole actual sequence would always be the most perfect of all possible sequences, because God always chooses the best possible.

(G VII, 303; Loemker, p. 487; Ariew & Garber, pp. 150–51; "On the Radical Origination of Things" [1697].) To explain a little more distinctly, however, how temporal, contingent, or physical truths arise out of truths that are eternal and essential, or if you like, metaphysical, we should first acknowledge that from the very fact that something exists rather than nothing, there is a certain urgency (*exigentia*) toward existence in possible things or in possibility or essence itself—a pre-tension to exist, so to speak—in a word, that essence in itself tends to exist. From this follows further that all possible things, or things expressing an essence or possible reality, are real to the degree of perfection which they have; for perfection is nothing but quantity of essence. Hence it is very clearly understood that out of the infinite combinations and series of possible things, one exists through which the greatest amount of essence or possibility is brought into existence. There is always a principle of determination in nature which must be sought by maxima and minima; namely, that a maximum effect should be achieved with a minimum outlay, so to speak. And at this point time and place, or in a word, the receptivity or capacity to the world, can be taken for the outlay, or the terrain on which a building is to be erected as commodiously as possible, the variety of forms corresponding to the spaciousness of the building and the number and elegance of its chambers. The case is like that of certain games in which all the spaces on a board are to be filled according to definite rules, but unless we use a certain device, we find ourself at the end blocked from the difficult spaces and compelled to leave more spaces vacant than we needed or wished to. Yet there is a definite rule by which a maximum number of spaces can be filled in the easiest way. Therefore, assuming that it is ordered that there shall be a triangle with no other further determining principle, the result is that an equilateral triangle is produced. And assuming that there is to be motion from one point to another without anything more determining the route, that path will be chosen which is easiest or shortest. Similarly, once having assumed that being involves more perfection than nonbeing, or that there is a reason why something should come to exist rather than nothing, or that a transition from possibility to actuality must take place, it follows that even if there is no further determining principle, there does exist the greatest amount possible in proportion to the given capacity of time and space (or the possible order of existence), in much the same way as tiles are laid so that as many as possible are contained in a given area.

(Loemker, p. 146; to Magnus Wedderkopf [1671].) What, therefore, is the ultimate reason for the divine will? The divine intellect.... What then is the reason for the divine intellect? The harmony of things. What the reason for the harmony of things? Nothing. For example, no reason can be given for the ratio of 2 to 4 being the same as that of 4 to 8, not even in the divine will. This depends on the essence itself, or the idea of things. For the essences of things are numbers, as it were, and contain the possibility of beings which God does not make as he does existence, since these possibilities or ideas of things coincide rather with God himself. Since God is the most perfect mind, however, it is impossible for him not to be affected by the most perfect harmony, and thus to be necessitated to do the best by the very ideality of things. This in no way detracts from freedom. For it is the highest freedom to be impelled to the best by a right reason. Whoever desires any other freedom is a fool. Hence it follows that whatever has happened, is happening, or will happen is best, and also necessary, but as I have said, with a necessity which takes nothing away from freedom because it takes nothing from the will and from the use of reason.

(Loemker, p. 158; "Paris Notes" [1676].) <There is> a most perfect mind, or *God.* And this mind is a whole in the whole body of the world; to it is due also the existence of the world. It itself is its own cause. Existence is nothing but that which is the cause of sensations agreeing among themselves. The reason for the world is the aggregate of requisites of all things. . . . That particular minds exist amounts merely to this—that the highest being judges it conducive to harmony that there should be somewhere something that understands, i.e. some intellectual mirror or a reduplication of the world. To exist is nothing other than to be <maximally> harmonious; the mark of existence is organized sensations.

COMMENTARY

Recall that section 48 has already stated that in God and created substance alike power/reality can be equated with degree of perfection ("à mesure qu'il y a de la perfection"). We humans make our choices with a (potentially flawed) view to what *appears* best. God chooses on the basis of what *is* best. This explains why every aspect of the real has a teleological explanation: if some feature of the real were not for the overall best, it would not in fact be there as a feature of the reality. A God who did not make optimality-geared creation choices—whose acts or choices were merely willful or arbitrary—would not be a perfectly rational agent.

The Principle of Perfection (or of Fitness) is Leibniz's supreme principle for the determination of contingent truth. God selected the real world for actualization as one possibility among infinitely many others precisely because it maximizes "perfection," that is, the combination of variety with order. The actual world is accordingly "the best of possible worlds." It is in this metaphysical commitment to perfection as the principle of definiteness for the actualization of possibility in which Leibniz's "optimism" resides. His is ultimately a theologically based position geared to the benevolence of God as manifested in his concern to maximize the good overall.

Note that the only "exigency to existence" that possible substances can exert is via the claims for consideration they are able to make upon God in virtue of the comparative perfection that their defining conception incorporates. Leibniz's occasional metaphor of alternative possibilities *competing* with one another for actualization is just exactly that—a metaphor.

KEY WORDS:

(sufficient) reason/*raison (suffisante)*
fitness/*convenance*
degrees of perfection/*degrés de perfection*
(possible) world/*mondes (possible)*

possible (substance)/*(substance) possible*
existence/*existence*
perfection/*perfection*
arbitrary/*arbitraire*

SECTION 55

55. And this is the cause of the existence of the best: that his wisdom makes it known to God, his goodness makes him chose it, and his power makes him produce it. (See *Theodicy*, secs. 8, 78, 80, 84, 119, 204, 206, 208, and Abridgment, objs. 1, 8.)

*55. Et c'est ce qui est la cause de l'Existence du Meilleur, que sa sagesse <le> fait connoître à Dieu, que sa bonté le fait choisir, et que sa puissance le fait produire. (*Théodicée, secs. 8, 78, 80, 84, 119, 204, 206, 208; Abrégé, objs. 1, 8.)*

(*Theodicy*, sec. 8.) Now this supreme wisdom, united to a goodness that is no less infinite, cannot but have chosen the best. . . . There is an infinitude of possible worlds among which God must needs have chosen the best, since he does nothing without acting in accordance with Supreme Reason.

(*Theodicy*, sec. 78.) God, in designing to create the world, purposed solely to manifest and communicate his perfections in the way that was most efficacious, and most worthy of his greatness, his wisdom and his goodness. But that very purpose pledged him to consider all the actions of creatures while still in the state of pure possibility, that he might form the most fitting plan. He is like a great architect whose aim in view is the satisfaction or the glory of having built a beautiful palace, and who considers all that is to enter into this construction: the form and the materials, the palace, the situation, the means, the workmen, the expense, before he forms a complete resolve. For a wise person in laying his plans cannot separate the end from the means; he does not contemplate any end without knowing if there are means of attaining thereto.

(*Theodicy*, sec. 80.) For it is sufficient to consider that God, as well as every wise and beneficent mind, is inclined towards all possible good, and that this inclination is proportionate to the excellence of the good.

(*Theodicy*, sec. 84.) God, before decreeing anything, considered among other possible sequences of things that one which he afterwards approved. In the idea of this is represented how the first parents sin and corrupt their posterity; how Jesus Christ redeems the human race; how some, aided by such and such graces, attain to final faith and to salvation; and how others, with or without such or other graces, do not attain thereto, continue in sin, and are damned. God grants his sanction to this sequence only after having entered into all its detail, and thus pronounces nothing final as to those who shall be saved or damned without having pondered upon everything and compared it with other possible sequences. Thus God's pronouncement concerns the whole sequence at the same time; he simply decrees its existence. In order to save other men, or in a different way, he must needs choose an altogether different sequence, seeing that all is connected in each sequence. In this conception of the matter, which is that most worthy of the All-wise, all whose actions are connected together to the highest possible degree, there would be only one total decree, which is to create such a world. This total decree comprises equally all the particular decrees, without setting one of them before or after another. Yet one may say also that each particular act of antecedent will entering into the total result has its value and order, in proportion to the good whereto this act inclines. But these acts of antecedent will are not called decrees, since they are not yet inevitable, the outcome depending upon the total result. According to this conception of things, all the difficulties that can here be made amount to the same as those I have already stated and removed in my inquiry concerning the origin of evil.

(*Theodicy*, sec. 119.) All is connected in Nature; and if a skilled artisan, an engineer, an architect, a wise politician often makes one and the same thing serve several ends, if he makes a double hit with a single throw, when that can be done conveniently, one may say that God, whose wisdom and power are perfect, does so always. That is husbanding the ground, the time, the place, the material, which make up as it were his outlay. Thus God has more than one purpose in his projects. The felicity of all rational creatures is one of the aims he has in view; but it is not his whole aim, nor even his final aim.

(*Theodicy*, sec. 204.) It is true that when one wills a thing one wills also in a sense everything that is necessarily attached to it, and in consequence God cannot will general laws without also willing in a sense all the particular effects that must of necessity be derived from them. But it is always true that these particular events are not willed for their own sake, and that is what is meant by the expression that they are not willed by a *particular and direct will*. There is no doubt that when God resolved to act outside himself, he made choice of a manner of action which should be worthy of the supremely perfect Being, that is, which should be infinitely simple and uniform, but yet of an infinite productivity. One may even suppose that this manner of action by *general acts of will* appeared to him preferable—although there must thence result some superfluous events (and even bad if they are taken separately, that is my own addition <to Malebranche's opinion>)—to another manner more composed and more regular.

(*Theodicy*, sec. 206.) As God can do nothing without reasons, even when he acts miraculously, it follows that he has no will about individual events but what results from some general truth or will. Thus I would say that God never has a *particular will* such as this Father Malebranche implies, that is to say, a *particular primitive will*.

(*Theodicy*, sec. 208.) The ways of God are those most simple and uniform: for he chooses rules that least restrict one another. They are also the most *productive* in proportion to the *simplicity of ways and means*. It is as if one said that a certain house was the best that could have been constructed at a certain cost. One may, indeed, reduce these two conditions, simplicity and productivity, to a single advantage, which is to produce as much perfection as is possible. . . . Even if the effect were assumed to be greater, but the process less simple, I think one might say that, when all is said and done, the effect itself would be less great, taking into account not only the final effect but also the mediate effect. For the wisest mind so acts, as far as it is possible, that the *means* are also in a sense *ends*, that is, they are desirable not only on account of what they do, but on account of what they are. The more intricate processes take up too much ground, too much space, too much place, too much time that might have been better employed.

(*Theodicy*, Abridgment, obj. 1.) Among older writers the fall of Adam was termed *felix culpa*, a fortunate sin, because it had been expiated with immense benefit by the incarnation of the Son of God: for he gave to the universe something more noble than anything there would otherwise have been amongst created beings. For the better understanding of the matter I added, following the example of many good authors, that it was consistent with order and the general good for God to grant to certain of his creatures the opportunity to exercise their freedom, even when he foresaw that they would turn to evil: for God could easily correct the evil, and it was not fitting that in order to prevent sin he should always act in an extraordinary way. It will therefore sufficiently refute the objection to show that a world with evil may be better than a world without evil. But I have gone still further in the work, and have even shown that this universe must be indeed better than every other possible universe.

(*Theodicy*, Abridgment, obj. 8.) If the will of God had not as its rule the principle of the best, it would tend towards evil, which would be worst of all; or else it would be indifferent somehow to good and to evil, and guided by chance. But a will that would always drift along at random would scarcely be any better for the government of the universe than the fortuitous concourse of corpuscles, without the existence of divinity. And even though God should abandon himself to chance only in some cases, and in a certain way (as he would if he did not always tend entirely towards the best, and if he were capable of preferring a lesser good to a greater good, that is, an evil to a good, since that which prevents a greater good is an evil) he would be no less imperfect than the object of his choice. Then he would not deserve absolute trust; he would act without reason in such a case, and the government of the universe would be like certain games equally divided between reason and luck. This all proves that this objection which is made against the choice of the best perverts the notions of free and necessary, and represents the best to us actually as evil: but that is either malicious or absurd.

(PNG, sec. 10.) It follows from the supreme perfection of God that he has chosen the best possible plan in producing the universe, a plan which combines the greatest variety together with the greatest order; with situation, place, and time arranged in the best way possible; with the greatest effect produced by the simplest means; with the most power, the most knowledge, the greatest happiness and goodness in created things which the universe could allow. . . . For as all possible things have a claim to existence in God's understanding in proportion to their perfections, the result of all these claims must be the most perfect actual world which is possible.

(NS, sec. 8.) And one can say that everything tends to the perfection not merely of the universe in general but also of these created beings in particular, which are destined for so high a degree of happiness that the universe itself is concerned in it by virtue of the divine goodness which is communicated to each being to the extent which the sovereign wisdom can permit.

(DM, sec. 5.) It is sufficient therefore to have this confidence in God, that he has done everything for the best. . . . One is able to say, therefore, that he who acts perfectly is like an excellent Geometer who knows how to find the best construction for a problem; like a good architect who utilizes his location and the funds destined for the building in the most advantageous manner, leaving nothing which shocks or which does not display that beauty of which it is capable; like a good householder who employs his property in such a way that there shall be nothing uncultivated or sterile; like a clever machinist who makes his production in the least difficult way possible; and like an intelligent author who encloses the most of reality in the least possible compass. . . . When the simplicity of God's way is spoken of, reference is specially made to the means which he employs, and on the other hand when the variety, richness and abundance are referred to, the ends or effects are had in mind. Thus one ought to be proportioned to the other, just as the cost of a building should balance the beauty and grandeur which is expected. It is true that nothing costs God anything, just as there is no cost for a philosopher who makes hypotheses in constructing his imaginary world, because God has only to make decrees in order that a real world come into being; but in matters of wisdom the decrees or hypotheses meet the expenditure in proportion as they are more independent of one another. The reason wishes to avoid multiplicity in hypotheses or principles very much as the simplest system is preferred in Astronomy.

(G VII, 390; to Clarke V. 6–8 [1716].) God, being moved by his supreme reason to choose, among many series of things or worlds possible, that in which free creatures should take such or such resolutions, though not without his concourse, has thereby rendered every event certain and determined once and for all, without derogating thereby from the liberty of those creatures that simple decree of choice, not at all changing but only actualizing their free natures which he saw in his ideas. As for moral necessity, this also does not derogate from liberty. For when a wise being, and especially God who has supreme wisdom, chooses what is best, he is not the less free upon that account; on the contrary, it is the most perfect liberty not to be hindered from acting in the best manner. . . . But good, either true or apparent—in a word, the motive—inclines without necessitating that is, without imposing an absolute necessity. For when God (for instance) chooses the best, what he does not choose, and is inferior in perfection, is nevertheless possible. But if what he chooses was absolutely necessary, any other way would be impossible, which is against the hypothesis. For God chooses among possibles, that is, among many ways none of which implies a contradiction.

(G VII, 305–06; Loemker, p. 489; Ariew & Garber, pp. 152–53; "On the Radical Origination of Things" [1697].) We therefore have the ultimate reason for the reality of essences as well as existences in one being, which must necessarily be greater, higher, and prior to the world itself, since not only the existing things which compose the world but also all possibilities have their reality through it. But because of the interconnection of all these things, this ultimate reason can be found only in a single source. It is evident, however, that existing things are continuously issuing from this source and are being produced and have been produced by it, since no reason appears why one state of the world should issue from it rather than another, that of yesterday rather than today's. It is clear, too, how God acts not merely physically but freely as well, and how there is in him not only the efficient but the final cause of the world. Thus we have in him the reason not merely for the greatness and power in the world mechanism as already established, but also for the goodness and wisdom exerted in establishing it. . . . You may object, however, that we experience the very opposite of this in the world, for often the very worst things happen to the best; innocent beings, not only beasts but men, are struck down and killed, even tortured. In fact, especially if we consider the government of mankind, the world seems rather a kind of confused chaos than something ordained by a supreme wisdom. So it seems at first sight, I admit, but when we look more deeply, the opposite can be established. A priori it is obvious from the principles which I have already given that the highest perfection possible is obtained for all things and therefore also for minds.

COMMENTARY

Evil and imperfection result from the inherent nature of things (as included in their very conceptions). God, who choses for actualization a world that is as perfect as it is possible for a world to be, is thus nowise responsible for imperfection and evil. On the contrary, world-optimization is the underlying operative principle of God's creative activity, and the (relative) perfection of its product is the prime object of his creative concern.

God is committed to optimality, but not by the absolute necessitation of the definitive constitution of his nature, but by his goodness as guided by his wisdom. God's will is ineradicably involved in the matter and his choice of the best is thus a *free* choice, unfailing but not necessitated. The results of this choice—this particular world and its specific features—are accordingly matters of contingency rather than necessity. (Necessitation is averted through the infinite complexity of the choices at issue in the face of infinite alternatives.)

Leibniz was not one of those rosy-visioned theologians who argue that all of the world's evils and imperfections are mere illusions. He was quite prepared to recognize that much is wrong in the world. But such evil as there is is simply unavoidable—all the other possibilities are worse. (Even a half-full barrel can be fuller than all the rest.) Leibniz recognized evil as real. But he saw it as a systemically necessary condition for the greater good. The myth of Sextus at the end of the *Théodicée* illustrates this: "The crime of Sextus serves for great things: it renders Rome free; thence will arise a great empire, which will show noble examples to mankind" (sec. 416). The world's arrangements are systemically interconnected. If we improved something here, even more would come unstruck over there—an "improvement" at one point of the system always has damaging repercussions at another.

KEY WORDS:

cause/*cause*
existence of the best/*l'existence du meilleur*
God/*Dieu*
wisdom/*sagesse*
to chose (the best)/*choisir (le meilleur)*
goodness/*bonté*
power/*puissance*

SECTION 56

56. Now this interlinkage or accommodation of all created things to each other, and of each to all the others, brings it about that each simple substance has relations that express all the others, and is in consequence a perpetual living mirror of the <whole> universe. (See *Theodicy*, secs. 130, 360.)

*56. Or cette liaison ou cet accommodement de toutes les choses creées à chacune et de chacune à toutes les autres, fait que chaque substance simple a des rapports qui expriment toutes les autres, et qu'elle est par consequent un miroir vivant perpetuel de l'univers. (*Théodicée, secs. 130, 360.)*

(*Theodicy*, sec. 130.) It is true that God makes of matter and of spirits whatever he wills; but he is like a good sculptor, who will make from his block of marble only that which he judges to be the best, and who judges well. God makes of matter the most excellent of all possible machines; he makes of spirits the most excellent of all governments conceivable; and over and above all that, he establishes for their union the most perfect of all harmonies, according to the system I have proposed. . . . God cannot establish a system ill-connected and full of dissonances. It is to some extent the nature of souls to represent bodies.

(*Theodicy*, sec. 360.) It is true that God sees all at once the whole sequence of this universe, when he chooses it, and that thus he has no need of the connexion of effects and causes in order to foresee these effects. But since his wisdom causes him to choose a sequence in perfect connexion, he cannot but see one part of the sequence in the other. It is one of the rules of my system of general harmony, that the present is big with the future, and that he who sees all sees in that which is that which shall be. What is more, I have proved conclusively that God sees in each portion of the universe the whole universe, owing to the perfect connection of things. . . . There can therefore be no doubt that effects follow their causes determinately, in spite of contingency and even of freedom, which nevertheless coexist with certainty or determination.

(PNG, sec. 3.) Since everything is connected because of the plenitude of the world, and each body acts on every other one more or less, depending on the distance, and is affected by its reaction, it follows that each monad is a living mirror, or a mirror endowed with an internal action, and that it represents the universe according to its point of view and is regulated as completely as is the universe itself. . . . Thus there is a perfect *harmony* between the perceptions of the monad and the motions of the body, pre-established from the beginning between the system of efficient causes and that of final causes. It is in this that the accord and the physical union of soul and body consist, without either one being able to change the laws of the other.

(DM, sec. 9.) Every substance is like an entire world and like a mirror of God, or indeed of the whole world which it portrays, each one in its own fashion; almost as the same city is variously represented according to the various situations of him who is regarding it. Thus the universe is multiplied in some sort as many times as there are substances, and the glory of God is multiplied in the same way by as many wholly different representations of his works. It can indeed be said that every substance bears in some sort the character of God's infinite wisdom and omnipotence, and imitates him as much as it is able to; for it expresses, although confusedly, all that happens in the universe, past, present and future, deriving thus a certain resemblance to an infinite perception . or power of knowing. And since all other substances express this particular substance and accommodate themselves to it, we can say that it exerts its power upon all the others in imitation of the omnipotence of the creator.

(G II, 95; Ariew & Garber, pp. 84–85; to Arnauld [1687].) To employ a comparison, I will say in regard to this universal concomitance, which I hold to be true, that it is like several bands of musicians or choirs separately taking up their parts and placed in such a way that they neither see nor hear one another, though they nevertheless agree perfectly in following their notes, each one his own, in such a way that he who hears the whole finds in it a wonderful harmony much more surprising than if there were a connection between the performers. It is quite possible also that a person who is close by one of two such choirs could judge from the one what the other was doing, and would form such a habit (particularly if we supposed that he was able to hear his own choir without seeing it and to see the other without hearing it), that his imagination would come to his aid and he would no longer think of the choir where he was, but of the other, and he would take his own for an echo of the other, attributing to his own only certain interludes, in which certain rules of symphony by which he understood the other did not appear, or else attributing to his own certain movements which he caused to be made from his side, according to certain plans that he thought were imitated by the other because of the inter-relationship which he found in the kind of melody, not knowing at all that those who were in the other choir were doing also something which corresponded according to their own plans.

(G II, 112; Loemker, pp. 339–40; to Arnauld [1687].) All substances sympathize with one another and receive some proportional change corresponding to the slightest motion which occurs in the whole universe. These changes, however, may be more or less noticeable, as other bodies have more or less relation with ours. . . . But the slightest movement would have its effect upon neighboring bodies and consequently from body to body to infinity, but in diminishing proportion. Thus, our bodies ought to be affected in some sort by the changes of all others. Now, to all the movements of our bodies certain perceptions or thoughts of our soul, more or less confused, correspond; therefore, the soul also will have some thought of all the movements of the universe, and in my opinion every other soul or substance will have some perception or expression of them. It is true that we do not distinctly perceive all the movements in our body, as for example the movement of the lymph, but to use an example which I have already employed, it is somewhat in the same way that I must have some perception of every wave upon the shore so that I may perceive what results from the whole; that is to say, that great sound which is heard near the sea. In the same way we feel also some indistinct result from all the movements which go on within us, but, being accustomed to this internal motion, we perceive it clearly and noticeably only when there is a considerable change, as at the beginning of an illness.

(G III, 623; to Remond [1714].) Plato . . . considers material objects as unreal, and the Academics put in doubt whether they exist outside us, which can be explained reasonably by saying that they are nothing besides perceptions, and that they have their reality through the agreement among the perceptions of perceivers. This agreement results from the Preestablished Harmony in these substances, because every simple substance is a mirror of the same universe, just as durable and as ample as it is. To be sure, these perceptions of created beings can be distinct only with regard to a few things at any time, and they are differentiated through the relations or, so to speak, the points of view of these mirrors. This has the result that one selfsame universe is multiplied in an infinity of ways through the infinity of living mirrors, each representing it in its own way. One can accordingly say that every simple substance is an image of the entire universe. . . .

COMMENTARY

Returning to the theme of sections 51–52, Leibniz here envisions a grand coordination of all things, a universal interlinkage (*liaison universelle*) which connects the doings of each substance with those of all the others. In his language, each substance "expresses" and "represents" the rest in its own make-up. Though the monads are "windowless" and do not allow of any *causal* influence from without, they are nevertheless "mirrors" whose states reflect the doings of all the rest. Despite the absence of causality there is thus a harmony in which everything in nature is adjusted to everything else through the mutual accommodation of the "programming" of their complete individual concepts in the interest of making for a harmonious whole. Although the real excludes causality, there is an "ideal causality" of sorts.

Note, however, that the harmonious interrelatedness of all substances is a special feature of this actual world that marks its perfection and establishes its claims as the best possible world. It is not an inevitable feature of possible worlds as such, most of which will be substantially chaotic and disorderly.

The mirror analogy which Leibniz introduces here plays a very important role in his thought. (Compare also secs. 63, 77, 83.) Nicholas of Cusa (b. 1401) already taught that "The whole is reflected in all of the parts; all things keep their own inclination [*habitudo*] and analogy [*proportio*] to the whole universe." (*Dialogi de ludo globi*, i, 157a.). Leibniz too espouses this neo-Platonic line of thought.

KEY WORDS:

interlinkage/*liaison (universelle)*
accommodation/*accommodement*
created things/*choses créées*
simple substance/*substance simple*
relations/*rapports*
to express/*exprimer*
living mirror of the universe/*miroir vivant de l'univers*

SECTION 57

57. And as one and the same town viewed from different sides looks altogether different, and is, as it were, *perspectively* multiplied, it similarly hap-

pens that, through the infinite multitude of simple substances, there are, as it were, just as many different universes, which however are only the perspectives of a single one according to the different *points of view* of each monad. (See *Theodicy*, sec. 147.)

57. *Et comme une même ville regardée de differens côtés paroist toute autre, et est comme multipliée perspectivement; il arrive de même que par la multitude infinie des substances simples, il y a comme autant de differens univers, qui ne sont pourtant que les perspectives d'un seul selon les differens* points *de veue de chaque Monade.* (Théodicée, sec. 147.)

(*Theodicy*, sec. 147.) Thus man is there like a little god in his own world or *Microcosm*, which he governs after his own fashion. . . . But he also commits great errors. . . . Man finds himself the worse for this, in proportion to his fault; but God, by a wonderful art, turns all the errors of these little worlds to the greater adornment of his great world. It is as in those devices of perspective, where certain beautiful designs look like mere confusion until one restores them to the right angle of vision or one views them by means of a certain glass or mirror. It is by placing and using them properly that one makes them serve as adornment for a room. Thus the apparent deformities of our little worlds combine to become beauties in the great world, and have nothing in them which is opposed to the oneness of an infinitely perfect universal principle.

(*Theodicy*, sec. 357.) It is true that the same thing may be represented in different ways; but there must always be an exact relation between the representation and the thing, and consequently between the different representations of one and the same thing. The projections in perspective of the conic sections of the circle show that one and the same circle may be represented by an ellipse, a parabola and a hyperbola, and even by another circle, a straight line and a point. Nothing appears so different nor so dissimilar as these figures; and yet there is an exact relation between each point and every other point. Thus one must allow that each soul represents the universe to itself according to its point of view, and through a relation which is peculiar to it; but a perfect harmony always subsists therein. God, if he wished to effect representation of the dissolution of continuity of the body by an agreeable sensation in the soul, would not have neglected to ensure that this very dissolution should serve some perfection in the body, by giving it some new relief, as when one is freed of some burden or loosed from some bond. But organic bodies of such kinds, although possible, do not exist upon our globe, which doubtless lacks innumerable inventions that God may have put to use elsewhere. Nevertheless it is enough that, due allowance being made for the place our world holds in the universe, nothing can be done for it better than what God does. He makes the best possible use of the laws of nature which he has established.

(DM, sec. 9.) Every substance is like an entire world and like a mirror of God, or indeed of the whole world which it portrays, each one in its own fashion; almost as the same city is variously represented according to the various situations of him who is regarding it. Thus the universe is multiplied in some sort as many times as there are substances, and the glory of God is multiplied in the same way by as many wholly different representations of his works. It can indeed be said that every substance bears in some sort the character of God's infinite wisdom and omnipotence, and imitates him as much as it is able to; for it expresses, although confusedly, all that happens in the universe, past, present and future, deriving thus a certain resemblance to an infinite perception or power of knowing. And since all other substances express this particular substance and accommodate themselves to it, we can say that it exerts its power upon all the others in imitation of the omnipotence of the creator.

(Cassirer, *Hauptschriften*, II, 131.) But we cannot see nature's order, because we don't occupy the right point of view, just as a perspectival painting can best be seen from some positions, but does not show itself properly if seen from the side. Only we have put ourselves with the eyes of reason where the eyes of our body do not, cannot stand. For example, if we observe the movements of the stars from our earthly sphere on which we stand the result will be something strangely confused. . . . But after one had finally found that one must put the eye into the sun, in order to observe the sky correctly, and that this makes everything turn out wonderfully well, then one sees that it was due to the supposed disorder and confusion of our understanding and not to nature.

COMMENTARY

The complete overall coordination of the monads of this "best of possible worlds" is so tight that they are simply so many different representations of one single complex world-system, each depicting this common universe from its own point of view. This coordination offsets the fact that the monads "have no windows" (sec. 7). It assures the agreement and consonance of each with all without any actual interaction. All embody the same information—tell the same story, so to speak—but with different emphases and elaborations. It is as though they shone a variable light (with variable obscurities) upon one and the same picture. "Every monad is omniscient, but confused," Leibniz tells us. The monad is a microcosm that encapsulates (albeit imperfectly) the entire universe.

All monads, all actual substances, perceive essentially the same thing—the actual universe as a whole. But they perceive it from different points of view, and accordingly with different degrees of clarity. In this way, the greatest appropriate degree of variety is achieved. And the fact that every possible point of view is actually occupied by a substance makes this world a plenum.

The geometry of perspective painting—and in particular the projective geometry that was devised by Desargues a generation earlier—greatly interested Leibniz as mathematician. The fact that one selfsame object—a box, say, or the bust of a Roman senator—manifests a characteristically different appearance from every possible perspective—all of them duly coordinated by geometric laws—provided Leibniz with yet another of the many guiding analogies of his metaphysical system.

KEY WORDS:

different sides/*différents côtés*
perspective/*perspective*
perspectivally multiplied/*multipliée perspectivement*
infinite multitude/*multitude infinie*
different universes/*différents univers*

simple substances/*substances simples*
points of view/*points de vue*
monad/*monade*

SECTION 58

58. And this is the way to obtain as much variety as possible, but combined with the greatest possible order, that is to say, it is the way to obtain as much perfection as can be. (See *Theodicy*, secs. 120, 124, 214, 241–43, 275.)

*58. Et c'est le moyen d'obtenir autant de varieté qu'il est possible, mais avec le plus grand ordre qui se puisse, c'est à dire, c'est le moyen d'obtenir autant de perfection qu'il se peut. (*Théodicée, secs. 120, 124, 214, 241seqq., 243, 275.)

(*Theodicy*, sec. 120.) <One should reject the> false maxim . . . the happiness of rational creatures is the sole aim of God. If that were so, perhaps neither sin nor unhappiness would ever occur, even by concomitance. God would have chosen a sequence of possibles where all these evils would be excluded. But God would fail in what is due to the universe, that is, in what he owes to himself. If there were only spirits they would be without the required connexion, without the order of time and place. This order demands matter, movement and its laws; to adjust these to spirits in the best possible way means to return to our world. When one looks at things only in the mass, one imagines to be practicable a thousand things that cannot properly take place.

(*Theodicy*, sec. 124.) God's affection for any created thing whatsoever is proportionate to the value of the thing. Virtue is the noblest quality of created things, but it is not the only good quality of creatures. There are innumerable others which attract the inclination of God: from all these inclinations there results the most possible good, and it turns out that if there were only virtue, if there were only rational creatures, there would be less good. Midas proved to be less rich when he had only gold. And besides, wisdom must vary. To multiply one and the same thing only would be superfluity, and poverty too. To have a thousand well-bound Vergils in one's library, always to sing the airs from the opera of Cadmus and Hermione, to break all the china in order only to have cups of gold, to have only diamond buttons, to eat nothing but partridges, to drink only Hungarian or Shiraz wine—would one call that reason? Nature had need of animals, plants, inanimate bodies; there are in these creatures, devoid of reason, marvels which serve for exercise of the reason. What would an intelligent creature do if there were no unintelligent things? What would it think of, if there were neither movement, nor matter, nor sense? If it had only distinct thoughts it would be a God, its wisdom would be without bounds: that is one of the results of my meditations. As soon as there is a mixture of confused thoughts, there is sense, there is matter. For these confused thoughts come from the relation of all things one to the other by way of duration and extent. Thus it is that in my philosophy there is no rational creature without some organic body, and there is no created spirit entirely detached from matter. But these organic bodies vary no less in perfection than the spirits to which they belong. Therefore, since God's wisdom must have a world of bodies, a world of substances capable of perception and incapable of reason; since, in short, it was necessary to choose from all things possible what produced the best effect together, and since vice entered in by this door, God would not have been altogether good, altogether wise if he had excluded it.

(*Theodicy*, sec. 214.) By cutting carefully in parts the squares on the two side of the right-angled triangle, and arranging these parts carefully, one makes from them the square on the hypotenuse; that is demonstrating empirically the 47th proposition of the first book of Euclid. Now supposing that some of these pieces taken from the two smaller squares are lost, something will be lacking in the large square that is to be formed from them; and this defective combination, far from pleasing, will be disagreeably ugly. If then the pieces that remained, composing the faulty combination, were taken separately without any regard to the large square to whose formation they ought to contribute, one would group them together quite differently to make a tolerably good combination. But as soon as the lost pieces are retrieved and the gap in the faulty combination is filled, there will ensue a beautiful and regular thing, the complete large square: this perfect combination will be far more beautiful than the tolerably good combination which had been made from the pieces one had not mislaid alone. The perfect combination corresponds to the universe in its entirety, and the faulty combination that is a part of the perfect one corresponds to some part of the universe, where we find defects which the Author of things has allowed, because otherwise, if he had wished to re-shape this faulty part and make thereof a tolerably good combination, the whole would not then have been so beautiful. For the parts of the faulty combination, grouped better to make a tolerably good combination, could not have been used properly to form the whole and perfect combination.

(*Theodicy*, sec. 241.) One must believe that even sufferings and monstrosities are part of order; and it is well to bear in mind not only that it was better to admit these defects and these monstrosities than to violate general laws, as Father Malebranche sometimes argues, but also that these very monstrosities are in the rules, and are in conformity with general acts of will, though we be not capable of discerning this conformity. It is just as sometimes there are appearances of irregularity in mathematics which issue finally in a great order when one has finally got to the bottom of them: that is why I have already in this work observed that according to my principles all individual events, without exception, are consequences of general acts of will.

(*Theodicy*, sec. 242.) It should be no cause for astonishment that I endeavour to elucidate these things by comparisons taken from pure mathematics, where everything proceeds in order, and where it is possible to fathom them by a close contemplation which grants us an enjoyment, so to speak, of the vision of the ideas of God. One may propose a succession or series of numbers perfectly irregular to all appearance, where the numbers increase and diminish variably without the emergence of any order; and yet he who knows the key to the formula, and who understands the origin and the structure of this succession of numbers, will be able to give a rule which, being properly understood, will show that the series is perfectly regular, and that it even has excellent properties. One may make this still more evident in lines. A line may have twists and turns, ups and downs, points of reflexion and points of inflexion, interruptions and other variations, so that one sees neither rhyme nor reason therein, especially when taking into account only a portion of the line; and yet it may be that one can give its equation and construction, wherein a geometrician would find the reason and the fittingness of all these so-called irregularities. That is how we must look upon the irregularities constituted by monstrosities and other so-called defects in the universe.

(*Theodicy*, sec. 243.) It belongs to the great order that there should be some small disorder. One may even say that this small disorder is apparent only in the whole, and it is not even apparent when one considers the happiness of those who walk in the ways of order.

(*Theodicy*, sec. 275.) Lying or wickedness springs from the Devil's own nature . . . because it was written in the book of the eternal verities, which contains the things possible before any decree of God, that this creature would freely turn toward evil if it were created. It is the same with Eve and Adam; they sinned freely, albeit the Devil tempted them. God gives the wicked over to a reprobate mind (Rom. i. 28), abandoning them to themselves and denying them a grace which he owes them not, and indeed ought to deny to them.

(PNG, sec. 10.) It follows from the supreme perfection of God that he has chosen the best possible plan in producing the universe, a plan which combines the greatest variety together with the greatest order; with situation, place, and time arranged in the best way possible; with the greatest effect produced by the simplest means; with the most power, the most knowledge, the greatest happiness and goodness in created things which the universe could allow. For as all possible things have a claim to existence in God's understanding in proportion to their perfections, the result of all these claims must be the most perfect actual world which is possible. Without this it would be impossible to give a reason why things have gone as they have rather than otherwise.

(DM, sec. 5.) To know in particular, however, the reasons which have moved God to choose this order of the universe, to permit sin, to dispense his salutary grace in a certain manner—this passes the capacity of a finite mind, above all when such a mind has not come into the joy of the vision of God. Yet it is possible to make some general remarks touching the course of providence in the government of things. One is able to say, therefore, that he who acts perfectly is like an excellent Geometer who knows how to find the best construction for a problem; like a good architect who utilizes his location and the funds destined for the building in the most advantageous manner, leaving nothing which shocks or which does not display that beauty of which it is capable; like a good householder who employs his property in such a way that there shall be nothing uncultivated or sterile; like a clever machinist who makes his production in the least difficult way possible; and like an intelligent author who encloses the most of reality in the least possible compass. Of all beings those which are the most perfect and occupy the least possible space, that is to say those which interfere with one another the least, are the spirits whose perfections are the virtues. That is why we may not doubt that the felicity of the spirits is the principal aim of God and that he puts this purpose into execution, as far as the general harmony will permit. . . . When the simplicity of God's way is spoken of, reference is specially made to the means which he employs, and on the other hand when the variety, richness and abundance are referred to, the ends or effects are had in mind. Thus one ought to be proportioned to the other, just as the cost of a building should balance the beauty and grandeur which is expected. It is true that nothing costs God anything, just as there is no cost for a philosopher who makes hypotheses in constructing his imaginary world, because God has only to make decrees in order that a real world come into being; but in matters of wisdom the decrees or hypotheses meet the expenditure in proportion as they are more independent of one another. The reason wishes to avoid multiplicity in hypotheses or principles very much as the simplest system is preferred in Astronomy.

(G VII, 378; to Clarke, IV.PS [1716].) To omit many other arguments against a vacuum and atoms, I shall here mention those which I ground upon God's perfection and upon the necessity of a sufficient reason. I lay it down as a principle that every perfection which God could impart to things without derogating from their other perfections has actually been imparted to them. Now let us fancy a space wholly empty. God could have placed some matter in it without derogating in any respect from all other things; therefore he hath actually placed some matter in that space; therefore there is no space wholly empty; therefore all is full.

(G VII, 279; Loemker, p. 484; "Tentamen anagogicum" [ca. 1696].) Assume the case that nature were obliged in general to construct a triangle and that for this purpose only the perimeter or the sum of the sides were given, and nothing else; then nature would construct an equilateral triangle. This example shows the difference between architectonic and geometric determinations. Geometric determinations introduce an absolute necessity, the contrary of which implies a contradiction, but architectonic determinations introduce only a necessity of choice whose contrary means imperfection. . . . But since nature is governed architectonically, the half-determinations of geometry are sufficient for it to achieve its work; otherwise it would most often have been stopped. And this is particularly true with regard to the laws of nature. . . . [which obtain through] depending on architectonic principles. Nothing seems to me to be more effectual in proving and admiring the sovereign wisdom of the Author of things as shown in the very principles of things themselves.

(Couturat *Opuscules*, p. 530; Loemker, p. 169; for Spinoza [1676].) My principle, namely, is that whatever can exist and is maximally compatible with other things does exist, because the reason for existing in preference to other possibles cannot be limited by any other consideration than that not all things are compatible. Thus there is no other reason for determining existences than that the more perfect shall exist, that is, those things which involve the greatest possible reality.

COMMENTARY

Leibniz standardly construes "*perfection*" as involving the optimal combinative of *variety* with *orderliness*. Neither factor alone is determined. If the world were too orderly—if, for example, it were a perfect sphere of copper—then it would be defective for lack of variety. If it were too variegated—a perpetual kaleidoscope of chaotically varied effects—then it would also be grossly defective disorder. For perfection, a creation needs to realize a situation of ordered variety—exactly as in a baroque church, a composition by Vivaldi, or a formally landscaped garden like that of Versailles. Too simple a world would be uninteresting for an intelligent being; too chaotic a world would lack the requisites for engaging the grasp of a rational mind. It is just this standard of organized complexity that God has in view in selecting the best of possible worlds. God as world-designer is an architect who creates a world of elegance and complexity.

Renaissance thinkers like Paracelsus, Helmont, and Bacon delighted in stressing a degree of complexity and diversity not envisaged by ancient thinkers for whom symmetry and orderliness were paramount. Leibniz followed these moderns in welcoming fecundity, insisting that variety in the world is not just a matter of the number of its substances, but of the infinite multiplicity of the forms or kinds they exemplify. Accordingly, he was positively enthusiastic— as no classically fastidious thinker could have been—about the discovery by the early microscopists of a vast multitude of little squirming organic things throughout nature. A vivid illustration of this welcoming of diversity is Leibniz's insistence that the variety of the world is not just a matter of the number of its substances, but of the infinite multiplicity of the forms or kinds they exemplify. He would not countenance a *vacuum formarum*, but taught that infinite gradations of kind connect any two natural species.

Leibniz sees variety and order as jointly operative and mutually delimiting factors that are conjoined within a single composite standard of the perfection of possible worlds. Its basis of plausibility rests upon a whole network of analogies, three of which are clearly primary:

1. *Art.* Throughout the fine arts an excellent production requires that a variety of effects be combined within a structural unity of workmanship. Think here of the paradigm of baroque music and architecture.

2. *Statecraft.* Excellence can only be achieved in the political organization of affairs when variety (freedom) is duly combined with lawfulness (= order and the rule of law).

3. *Science.* Any really adequate mechanism of scientific explanation must succeed in combining a wide variety of phenomena (fall of apple, tides, moon) within the unifying range of a simple structure of laws (gravitation).

All these diverse paradigms meet and run together in Leibniz's thinking. A true systematizer, he likes to exploit such overarching connections.

KEY WORDS:

variety/*variété*
order/*ordre*
perfection/*perfection*
maximization/*obtenir autant qu'il se peut.*

SECTION 59

59. Further, no hypothesis but this (which I venture to call established) fittingly exalts the greatness of God. Monsieur Bayle recognized this when in his *Dictionary* (article "Rorarius") he made some objections in which he was even inclined to believe that I ascribed too much to God—more than is possible. But he could give no reason why this universal harmony, which makes every sub-

stance express exactly all the others through the relations it has to them, should be impossible.

59. Aussi n'est-ce que cette Hypothèse (que j'ose dire demontrée) qui relève comme il faut la grandeur de Dieu. C'est ce que Monsieur Bayle reconnut, lorsque dans son Dictionnaire (article Rorarius) il y fit des objections, où même il fut tenté de croire que je donnois trop à Dieu, et plus qu'il n'est possible. Mais il ne pût alleguer aucune raison pourquoy cette harmonie universelle, qui fait que toute substance exprime exactement toutes les autres par les rapports qu'elle y a, fut impossible.

(PNG, sec. 13.) For everything has been regulated in things, once for all, with as much order and agreement as possible; the supreme wisdom and goodness cannot act except with perfect harmony. The present is great with the future; the future could be read in the past; the distant is expressed in the near. One could learn the beauty of the universe in each soul if one could unravel all that is rolled up in it but that develops perceptibly only with time.

(NS, sec. 15.) This hypothesis is entirely possible. For why should God be unable to give to substance in the beginning a nature or internal force which enables it to produce in regular order—as in an *automaton that is spiritual or formal but free* in the case of that substance which has a share of reason— everything which is to happen to it, that is, all the appearances or expressions which it is to have, and this without the help of any created being? Especially since the nature of substance necessarily demands and essentially involves progress or change and would have no force of action without it. And since it is the nature of the soul to represent the universe in a very exact way, though with relative degrees of distinctness, the sequence of representations which the soul produces will correspond naturally to the sequence of changes in the universe itself. So the body, in turn, has also been adapted to the soul to fit those situations in which the soul is thought of as acting externally. This is all the more reasonable inasmuch as bodies are made solely for the spirits themselves, who are capable of entering into a society with God and of extolling his glory. Thus as soon as one sees the possibility of this *hypothesis of agreement*, one sees also that it is the most reasonable one and that it gives a wonderful idea of the harmony of the universe and of the perfection of the works of God.

(G VII, 307–308; Loemker, p. 490; Ariew & Garber, p. 154; "On the Radical Origination of Things" [1697].) As for the afflictions, especially of good men, however, we must take it as assured that these lead to their greater good and that this is true not only theologically but also naturally. So a seed sown in the earth suffers before it bears fruit. In general, one may say that, though afflictions are temporary evils, they are good in effect, for they are shortcuts to greater perfection. So in physics the liquids which ferment slowly also are slower to settle, while those in which there is a stronger disturbance settle more promptly, throwing off impurities with greater force. We may well call this backing up the better to spring forward (*qu'on recule pour mieux sauter*). These views must therefore be affirmed not merely as gratifying and comforting but also as most true.

(G VII, 390; to Clarke, V.9.) But to say, that God can only choose what is best; and to infer from thence, that what he does not choose is impossible; this,

I say, is confounding of terms: it is blending power and will, metaphysical necessity and moral necessity, essences and existences. For, what is necessary, is so by its essence, since the opposite implies a contradiction; but a contingent which exists, owes its existence to the principle of what is best, sufficient reason for the existence of things. And therefore I say, that motives incline without necessitating; and that there is a certainty and infallibility, but not an absolute necessity in contingent things.

COMMENTARY

The programmed coordination of all actual substances—all of those that compose this real world of ours—pre-establishes a universal harmony (*harmonie universelle*) within nature, a "pre-established harmony." This coordination is part of this actual world's distinctive perfection; it is not a necessary feature of every possible world but a distinguishing feature of the actual world, the best possible world.

Leibniz firmly rejects Bayle's doubts that a world-system of perfectly programmed substances of this sort is really possible. As he himself sees it—as inventor of one of the earliest forms of calculating machines—Bayle suffers from a lack of vision, and refused to credit the Almighty with powers well within the range of human imagination.

KEY WORDS:

God/*Dieu*
hypothesis/*hypothèse*
greatness of God/*grandeur de Dieu*
universal harmony/*harmonie universelle*
objection/*objection*
reason/*raison*
substance/*substance*
to express/*exprimer*
relations/*rapports*

PERSONS:

Pierre Bayle (see sec. 16)
G. R. Rorarius (see sec. 16)

SECTION 60

60. Moreover, one sees in what I have just discussed the *a priori* reasons why things cannot be otherwise than they are. For in regulating the whole, God has had regard for each part, and in particular for each monad, which, its very nature being representative, is such that nothing can restrict it to representing only one part of things. To be sure, this representation is only confused regarding the detail of the whole universe. It can only be distinct in regard to a small part of things, namely those that are nearest or most extensively related to each monad. Otherwise each monad would be a deity. It is not in their object

<namely the whole universe>, but in the particular mode of knowledge of this object that the monads are restricted. They all reach confusedly to the infinite, to the whole; but they are limited and differentiated by the degrees of their distinct preceptions.

60. *On voit d'ailleurs dans ce que je viens de rapporter, les Raisons a priori pour quoy les choses ne sauroient aller autrement. Parce que Dieu en reglant le tout a eu égard à chaque partie, et particulierement à chaque Monade, dont la nature étant representative, rien ne la sauroit borner à ne representer qu'une partie des choses; quoy qu'il soit vrai que cette representation n'est que confuse dans le detail de tout l'Univers, et ne peut être distincte que dans une petite partie des choses, c'est à dire, dans celles, qui sont ou les plus prochaines ou les plus grandes par rapport à chacune des Monades. Autrement chaque Monade seroit une Divinité. Ce n'est pas dans l'objet, mais dans la modification de la connoissance de l'objet, que les Monades sont bornées. Elles vont toutes confusement à l'infini, au tout; mais elles sont limitées et distinguées par les degrés des perceptions distinctes.*

(PNG, sec. 13.) Since each distinct perception of the soul includes an infinity of confused perceptions which envelop the entire universe, the soul itself does not know the things which it perceives until it has perceptions which are distinct and heightened. And it has perfection in proportion to the distinctness of its perceptions. Each soul knows the infinite, knows everything, but confusedly. Thus when I walk along the seashore and hear the great noise of the sea, I hear the separate sounds of each wave but do not distinguish them; our confused perceptions are the result of the impressions made on us by the whole universe. It is the same with each monad. Only God has a distinct knowledge of everything, for he is the source of everything. It has been very well said that he is everywhere as a center but that his circumference is nowhere, since everything is immediately present to him without being withdrawn at all from this center.

(NE, pp. 374–75.) The truth about sensible things consists only in the linking together of phenomena, this linking (for which there must be a reason) being what distinguishes sensible things from dreams; but that the truth about our existence and about the cause of phenomena is of a different order, since it establishes [the existence of] substances; and that the sceptics were spoiling their good case by pushing it too far, wanting to extend their doubts to immediate experience and truths of geometry. . . . I believe that where objects of the senses are concerned the true criterion is the linking together of phenomena, i.e. the connectedness of what happens at different times and places and in the experience of different men—with men themselves being phenomena to one another, and very important ones so far as this present matter is concerned. And the linking of phenomena which warrants the *truths of fact* about sensible things outside us is itself verified by means of *truths of reason*, just as optical appearances are explained by geometry. It must be acknowledged, though, as you have clearly recognized, that none of this certainty is of the highest degree. For it is not impossible, metaphysically speaking, for a dream to be as coherent and prolonged as a man's life. But this would be as contrary to reason as the fiction of a book's resulting by chance from jumbling the printer's type together. Besides, so long as the phenomena are linked together it does not matter whether we call them dreams or not, since experience shows that we do not go wrong in the practical steps we take on the basis of phenomena, so long as we take them in accordance with the truths of reason.

(G II, 51; Loemker, p. 333; to Arnauld [1686].) There were an infinity of possible ways of creating the world according to the different plans which God might have formed and that each possible world depends on certain principal plans or designs of God that are his own; that is to say, upon certain primary free decrees conceived *sub ratione possibilitatis*, or upon certain laws of the general order of this possible universe with which they agree and whose concept they determine. At the same time they determine the concepts of all individual substances which ought to enter into this same universe. . . . Thus, all human events cannot fail to happen as they have actually happened, supposing that the choice of Adam was made. But this is so, not so much because of the concept of the individual Adam, although this concept involves them, but because of the purposes of God, which also determine the concept of the whole universe. These purposes determine, consequently, as well the other individual substances of this universe, because each individual substance expresses the whole universe, of which it is a part according to a certain relation, through the connection which there is between all things, and this connection is owing to the connection of the resolutions or plans of God.

COMMENTARY

Each monad perceives all the rest; they all perceive the entire universe. But only God knows the detail of the whole universe clearly and distinctly; the monads themselves perceive one another with varying degrees of confusion—variable accuracy of detail. The situation is akin to that of many pictures, each depicting the same overall scene differently, bringing this or that aspect to the fore.

For Leibniz, representation is the inverse of perception; when A "perceives" B then B is (in some way) "represented" in A. Thus each created substance reaches out to the infinite, and represents the whole world in its state. All the monads thus reflect one selfsame object—namely the whole universe—but in very different ways—that is, with different "points of view" which highlight some items far more clearly than others.

Because the monads are interrelated systematically in regard to their points of view, they go to make up a space of sorts in which their relative closeness or distance is reflected in a similarity of their points of view—that is, in the comparative clarity with which they reflect one another's states. Note that for Leibniz perceptual relations are not the consequences of spatial position but rather the very reverse.

How do we know of the existence of an external world—a whole coordinated system of other monads? After all, our intellects, as monads, are self-contained: with each, it is as if only it itself and God existed. But the existence of *any* monad entails the existence of God, its creator; and once God's existence is assured, so is the existence the entire system that constitutes "the best possible world." For Leibniz, it is not just through *perception* that we become assured of the existence of an external world, but through *reason*.

For Leibniz, the reason why *this* world exists (why God has preferred it to other possibilities) lies in its order—so that order stands coordinate with reality both ontologically and epistemologically.

KEY WORDS:

a priori reasons/raisons *a priori*
representation/*representation*
the detail of the whole universe/*le détail de tout l'univers*
distinct perception/*perception distincte*
confused representation/*représentation confuse*
relation/*rapport*
mode of knowledge/*modification de la connaisance*
divinity/*divinité*near/*prochain*
limits/*bornes*
confusion/*confusion*
objects (of knowledge)/*objects (de connaissance)*
the infinite/*l'infini*
degrees of distinct perception/*degrés des perceptions distinctes*

SECTION 61

61. And composites accord with simples in this regard. For as all is a plenum, which renders all matter interconnected, and as in a plenum any motion has some effect on distant bodies in proportion to their distance—so that each body is affected not only by those that touch it, in some way feeling the effects of all that happens to them, but also through their mediation feeling affected by those in contact with the former by which it is directly touched—it follows that this inter-communication extends to any distance, however great. And in consequence, all bodies feel the effects of everything that happens in the universe. Accordingly, someone who sees all could read in each all that happens throughout, and even what has happened or will happen, observing in the present that which is remote, be it in time or in place. *Sympnoia panta* <"all things conspire">, as Hippocrates said. But a soul can read in itself only that which is represented distinctly there; it cannot unfold all-at-once all of its complications, because they extend to infinity.

61. Et les composés symbolisent en cela avec les simples. Car, comme tout est plein, ce qui rend toute la matière liée, et comme dans le plein tout mouvement fait quelque effect sur les corps distans, à mesure de la distance, de sorte que chaque corps est affecté non seulement par ceux qui le touchent, et se ressent en quelque façon de tout ce qui leur arrive, mais aussi par leur moyen se ressent encore de ceux qui touchent les premiers, dont il est touché immediatement: il s'ensuit, que cette communication va à quelque distance que ce soit. Et par consequent tout corps se ressent de tout ce qui se fait dans l'univers; tellement que celuy qui voit tout, pourroit lire dans chacun ce qui se fait partout et même ce qui s'est fait ou se fera; en remarquant dans le present ce qui est éloigné, tant selon les temps, que selon les lieux. Sympnoia panta, disoit Hippocrate. Mais une Ame ne peut lire en elle-même que ce qui y est representé distinctement, elle ne sauroit developper tout d'un coup tous ses replis, car ils vont à l'infini.

(*Theodicy*, sec. 360.) It is one of the rules of my system of general harmony, *that the present is big with the future*, and that he who sees all sees in that which is that which shall be. What is more, I have proved conclusively that God sees in each portion of the universe the whole universe, owing to the perfect connexion of things. He is infinitely more discerning than Pythagoras, who judged the height of Hercules by the size of his footprint. There must therefore be no doubt that effects follow their causes determinately, in spite of contingency and even of freedom, which nevertheless coexist with certainty or determination.

(PNG, sec. 3.) Everything is a plenum in nature. Everywhere there are simple substances actually separated from each other by their own actions, which continually change their relations. And each outstanding simple substance or monad which forms the center of a compound substance (such as an animal, for example), and is the principle of its uniqueness, is surrounded by a mass composed of an infinity of other monads which constitute the body belonging to this central monad, corresponding to the affections by which it represents, as in a kind of center, the things which are outside of it. This body is *organic* when it forms a kind of automaton or natural machine, which is a machine not only as a whole but also in its smallest observable parts. And since everything is connected because of the plentitude of the world, and each body acts on every other one more or less, depending on the distance, and is affected by its reaction it follows that each monad is a living mirror, or a mirror endowed with an internal action, and that it represents the universe according to its point of view and is regulated as completely as is the universe itself.

(PNG, sec. 13.) For everything has been regulated in things, once for all, with as much order and agreement as possible; the supreme wisdom and goodness cannot act except with perfect harmony. The present is great with the future; the future could be read in the past; the distant is expressed in the near. One could learn the beauty of the universe in each soul if one could unravel all that is rolled up in it but that develops perceptibly only with time. But since each distinct perception of the soul includes an infinity of confused perceptions which envelop the entire universe, the soul itself does not know the things which it perceives until it has perceptions which are distinct and heightened. And it has perfection in proportion to the distinctness of its perceptions. Each soul knows the infinite, knows everything, but confusedly. Thus when I walk along the seashore and hear the great noise of the sea, I hear the separate sounds of each wave but do not distinguish them; our confused perceptions are the result of the impressions made on us by the whole universe. It is the same with each monad.

(DM, sec. 9.) Every substance is like an entire world and like a mirror of God, or indeed of the whole world which it portrays, each one in its own fashion; almost as the same city is variously represented according to the various situations of him who is regarding it. Thus the universe is multiplied in some sort as many times as there are substances, and the glory of God is multiplied in the same way by as many wholly different representations of his works.

(NE, p. 55.) These minute perceptions, then, are more effective in their results than has been recognized. They constitute that *je ne sais quoi*, those flavours, those images of sensible qualities, vivid in the aggregate but confused as to the parts; those impressions which are made on us by the bodies around us and which involve the infinite; that connection that each being has with all the rest of the universe. It can even be said that by virtue of these minute perceptions the present is big with the future and burdened as with the past, that all things harmonize—*sympnoia panta*, as Hippocrates put it—and that eyes as piercing as God's could read in the lowliest substance the universe's whole sequence of events.

(G II, 57; Loemker, p. 337; to Arnauld [1686].) This ⟨causal⟩ independence ⟨of monads⟩ however does not prevent the inter-activity of substances among themselves, for, as all created substances are a continual production of the same sovereign Being according to the same designs and express the same universe or the same phenomena, they agree with one another exactly; and this enables us to say that one acts upon another because the one expresses more distinctly than the other the cause or reason for the changes—somewhat as we attribute motion rather to a ship than to the whole sea; and this with reason, although, if we should speak abstractly, another hypothesis of motion could be maintained, that is to say, the motion in itself and abstracted from the cause could be considered as something relative. It is thus, it seems to me, that the inter-activities of created substances among themselves must be understood.

(G II, 112; Loemker, p. 339; to Arnauld [1687].) Because of the continuity and divisibility of all matter, the least motion has its effect upon neighbouring bodies, and consequently upon one body after another *ad infinitum*, in a gradually lessening degree; and thus our body must in some way be affected by the changes in all other bodies. Now, to all the motions of our body there correspond certain more or less confused perceptions of our soul, and accordingly our soul also will have some thought of all the motions in the universe, and in my opinion every other soul or substance will have some perception or expression of them.

(G II, 450; to des Bosses [1715].) I consider the explanation of all phenomena solely through the perceptions of monads functioning in harmony with each other, with corporeal substances rejected, to be useful for a fundamental investigation of things. In this way of explaining things, space is the order of co-existing phenomena, as time is the order of successive phenomena, and there is no spatial or absolute nearness or distance between monads. And to say that they are crowded together in a point or disseminated in space is to use certain fictions of our mind when we seek to visualize freely what can only be understood. In this conception, also, there is involved no extension or composition of the continuum, and all difficulties about points disappear.

(G III, 635–36; to Remond [1715].) There are <within the world> undoubtedly a thousand derangements, a thousand disorders in particular matters. But it is impossible that there should be any in the whole, or even in each monad, since each monad is a living mirror of the universe according to its point of view. It is impossible that the universe as a whole should not be well regulated, since the superiority of its perfection is the reason for the existence of this system of things in preference to any other possible system. Thus the disorders must exist only in parts. Just so there are geometric curves the parts of which are irregular, but, when the entire curve is considered, one finds it to be perfectly regulated according to its equation or general nature. So all these particular disorders are redressed with benefit in the whole, even in each monad.

(G IV, 557; Loemker, p. 576; "Reply to Bayle" [1702].) Everything is so controlled and bound together that these infallible machines of nature, which are comparable to ships that would arrive at port by themselves in spite of all obstacles and storms, ought not to be considered any stranger than a rocket which glides along a string or a liquid which runs through a tube. Furthermore, since bodies are not atoms but are divisible, and are indeed divided to infinity, and everything is full of them, it follows that the very smallest body receives some impression from the slightest change in all of the universe. The result is that a sufficiently penetrating spirit could, in the measure of his penetration, see and foresee in each corpuscle everything which has happened and will happen in that corpuscle and everything which has happened and will happen everywhere both within and outside of the corpuscle. So nothing happens to it, not even by the impact of surrounding bodies, which does not follow from what is already internal to it and which can disturb its order.

COMMENTARY

In saying that composites "accord with" (*symbolisent avec* = be in harmony with) simples, Leibniz invokes the alchemical doctrine of "signs." Compare Emile Boutroux, *Leibniz: La Monadologie*, who quotes (p. 176, n. 2) Ambroise Paré's exposition of the alchemical teaching that the transmutability of substances into one another roots in their harmonization: "Les éléments symbolisent tellement les uns avec les autres, qu'ils se transmuent l'un en l'autre".

Leibniz maintains the universal coordination and connectedness (*liaison universelle*) of all of the activities of all of the substances in the universe. In view of this, anything that happens anywhere is interconnected with and reflective of what happens everywhere else. Both at the level of individual monads and at the level of the composites that they engender, everything happens in overall coordination. This grand orchestration of all substantial activity produces, among much else, the "preestablished harmony" between the states of our mind (our dominant monads) and our bodies. In view of this, every substance "reaches to infinity," and Leibniz thus endorsed in his own way the thesis of Spinoza that every substance is of necessity infinite (*omnis substantia est necessario infinita; Ethics*, Bk. I, prop. 8).

Only at this late stage in the *Monadology* does Leibniz address the unification of composites or aggregates, which has only been touched on incidentally in earlier discussions (see secs. 17, 36). He makes it clear that any such composition is no more than the coordinated functioning of essentially independent simples.

In this section and the next two (i.e., secs. 62–63), Leibniz deals with expression or representation. This concept is central in his philosophizing; he sees it as the genus to which all perception belongs. (Compare the discussions of representation in secs. 25–26.) All of these processes (perception, expression, representation) in the end come down to one and the same thing: the programmed coordination of the monads.

Note also that Leibniz coordinates the spatial proximity of bodies with their interaction: any change of state "has some effect on distant bodies according to their distance." This recourse to a principle akin to Newton's Law enables him to embed spatial relationships in monadic characteristics; and given his theory of action (see secs. 49–52) he therefore need not pre-suppose space as a pre-given container for monads.

Hippocrates of Cos, the famous Greek physician, born around 460 B.C., emphasized both the empirical standing of medicine as a body of knowledge rooted in experience and its holistic nature in having to take all aspects of people's situation (not their bodily make-up alone but their diet, lifestyle, environment, etc.).

KEY WORDS:

compounds/*composés*
simple substances/*substances simples*
plenum/*plein*
matter/*matière*
motion/*mouvement*
distance/*distance*
to feel the effects of/*se ressentir de*
to link/*lier*
communication/*communication*
to be in contact/*toucher*
to represent distinctly/*représenter distinctement*
complications/*replis*
to infinity/*à l'infini*
all things conspire/*sympnoia panta*

PERSONS:

Hippocrates

SECTION 62

62. Thus, although every created monad represents the entire universe, it represents more distinctly the body which is especially bound to it and of which it is the entelechy [and which is always organic so that there should be an order is in the body]. And even as this body expresses the whole universe through the connection of all matter in the plenum, so the soul also represents the entire universe in representing this body, which belongs to it in a special way. (See *Theodicy*, sec. 400.)

62. *Ainsi quoique chaque Monade creée represente tout l'univers, elle represente plus distinctement le corps qui lui est affecté particulièrement et dont elle fait l'Entelechie [et qui est toujours organique afin qu'il y ait un ordre dans le corps]: et comme ce corps exprime tout l'univers par la connexion de toute la matiere dans le plein, l'ame represente aussi tout l'univers en representant ce corps, qui lui appartient d'une manière particulière. (*Théodicée, sec. 400.)*

(*Theodicy*, sec. 400.) I admit that the soul cannot stir the organs by a physical influence; for I think that the body must have been so formed beforehand that it would do in time and place that which responds to the volitions of the soul, although it be true nevertheless that the soul is the principle of the operation. But if it be said that the soul does not produce its thoughts, its sensations, its feelings of pain and of pleasure, that is something for which I see no reason. In my system every simple substance (that is, every true substance) must be the true immediate cause of all its actions and inward passions; and, speaking strictly in a metaphysical sense, it has none other than those which it produces. Those who hold a different opinion, and who make God the sole agent, are needlessly becoming involved in expressions whence they will only with difficulty extricate themselves without offence against religion; moreover, they unquestionably offend against reason.

(NE, p. 146.) This unity of the idea of an aggregate is a very genuine one; but fundamentally we have to admit that this unity that collections have is merely a respect or relation, whose foundation lies in what is the case within each of the individual substances taken alone. So the only perfect unity that these "entities by aggregation" have is a mental one, and consequently their very being is also in a way mental, or phenomenal, like that of the rainbow.

(DM, sec. 33.) We can also see the explanation of that great mystery "the union of the soul and the body," that is to say how it comes about that the passions and actions of the one are accompanied by the actions and passions or else the appropriate phenomena of the other. For it is not possible to conceive how one can have an influence upon the other and it is unreasonable to have recourse at once to the extraordinary intervention of that universal cause in an ordinary and particular case. The following, however, is the true explanation. We have said that everything which happens to a soul or to any substance is a consequence of its concept; hence the idea itself or the essence of the soul brings it about that all of its appearances or perceptions should be born out of its nature and precisely in such a way that they correspond of themselves to that which happens in the universe at large, but more particularly and more perfectly to that which happens in the body associated with it, because it is in a particular way and only for a certain time according to the relation of other bodies to its own body that the soul expresses the state of the universe. This last fact enables us to see how our body belongs to us, without, however, being attached to our essence. I believe that those who are careful thinkers will decide favorably for our principles because of this single reason, viz., that they are able to see in what consists the relation between the soul and the body, a parallelism which appears inexplicable in any other way.

(G VII, 311n; "On Nature's Secrets" [ca. 1690].) Indeed, the multiple finite substances are nothing other than diverse expressions of the same universe according to diverse respects and each with its own limitations. In this way <each substance> has an infinite ichnography <tracing out the whole world>.

COMMENTARY

When Leibniz says that every substance has a body that is "especially bound to it," he does not mean that monads are material—that they have bodies by way of *composition*. Rather, he means that monads from parts of organized complexes and thus acquire bodies by way of *association*. Each created substance has a "body" of certain other substances that are coordinated with it and for which it serves as unifying entelechy. In its role as "dominant" monad it perceives/represents with comparatively greater clarity the environing "body" of other monads that are affiliated to it. And since these perceive/represent the monads in their vicinity, the process continues, by transitivity, to reverberate throughout the whole of nature, albeit with important differences as regards *clarity* of perception, since each monad perceives more clearly those others which are in its proximity. But for Leibniz this proximity or distance does not reflect a placement of substances in a preexistent space, but rather, spatial order itself emerges from the nature of these perceptive interrelations.

Leibniz here returns to a familiar theme of his, the interlinkage of microcosm and macrocosm inherent in the fact that the world's smallest and largest units—its individual substances on the one hand and the entire universe on the other—are duly coordinated and mutually adjusted. There is only one underlying order of reality which is differently represented at different levels of organization, in such a way that there is a smooth coordination between the individual substance, its environing body, and the universe as a whole.

KEY WORDS:

created monad/*monade créée*
universe/*univers*
to represent/*représenter*
to express/*exprimer*
body/*corps*
entelechy/*entéléchie*
organic/*organique*
matter/*matière*
plenum/*plein*
connection/*connexion*

SECTION 63

63. The body belonging to the monad that is its entelechy or soul constitutes with this entelechy what may be called an *organism* <i.e., *living being*>, and with a soul what is called an *animal*. Now the body of an organism or an animal is always organic; for, since every monad is a mirror of the universe in its own way, and the universe is regulated in a perfect order, there must also be an order in the representer—that is, in the perceptions of the soul, and consequently in the body—through which the <whole> universe is represented there. (See *Theodicy*, sec. 403.)

63. Le corps appartenant à une Monade qui en est l'Entelechie ou l'Ame constitue avec l'Entelechie ce qu'on peut appeler un Vivant, et avec l'Ame ce qu'on appelle un Animal. Or ce corps d'un vivant ou d'un animal est tousjours organique; car toute Monade étant un miroir de l'univers à sa mode, et l'univers étant reglé dans un ordre parfait, il faut qu'il y ait aussi un ordre dans le

representant, c'est à dire, dans les perceptions de l'ame, et par consequent dans le corps, suivant lequel l'univers y est representé. (Théodicée, sec. 403.)

(*Theodicy*, sec. 403.) The movements which are developed in bodies are concentrated in the soul by representation as in an ideal world, which expresses the laws of the actual world and their consequences, but with this difference from the perfect ideal world which is in God, that most of the perceptions in the other substances are only confused. For it is plain that every simple substance embraces the whole universe in its confused perceptions or sensations, and that the succession of these perceptions is regulated by the particular nature of this substance, but in a manner which always expresses all the nature in the universe; and every present perception leads to a new perception, just as every movement that it represents leads to another movement. But it is impossible that the soul can know clearly its whole nature, and perceive how this innumberable multitude of small perceptions, piled up or rather concentrated together, shapes itself there: to that end it would have to know completely the whole universe which is embraced by them, that is, it would have to be a God.

(PNG, sec. 3.) And each superior simple substance or monad which forms the center of a compound substance (such as an animal, for example), and is the principle of its uniqueness, is surrounded by a mass composed of an infinity of other monads which constitute the body belonging to this central monad, corresponding to the affections by which it represents, as in a kind of center, the things which are outside of it. This body is *organic* when it forms a kind of automaton or natural machine, which is a machine not only as a whole but also in its smallest observable parts. And since everything is connected because of the plentitude of the world, and each body acts on every other one more or less, depending on the distance, and is affected by its reaction, it follows that each monad is a living mirror, or a mirror endowed with an internal action, and that it represents the universe according to its point of view and is regulated as completely as is the universe.

(PNG, sec. 4.) Together with a particular body, each monad makes a living substance. Thus not only is there life everywhere, joined to members or organs, but there are also infinite degrees of it in the monads, some of which dominate more or less over others.

(PNG, sec. 13.) For everything has been regulated in things, once for all, with as much order and agreement as possible; the supreme wisdom and goodness cannot act except with perfect harmony. The present is great with the future; the future could be read in the past; the distant is expressed in the near. One could learn the beauty of the universe in each soul if one could unravel all that is rolled up in it but that develops perceptibly only with time. But since each distinct perception of the soul includes an infinity of confused perceptions which envelop the entire universe, the soul itself does not know the things which it perceives until it has perceptions which are distinct and heightened. And it has perfection in proportion to the distinctness of its perceptions. Each soul knows the infinite, knows everything, but confusedly.

(NE, p. 58.) I agree with most of the ancients that every Spirit, every soul, every created simple substance is always united with a body and that no soul is ever entirely without one. I have *a priori* reasons for this doctrine, but it will be found to have the further merit of solving all the philosophical difficulties about the state of souls, their perpetual preservation, their immortality, and their mode of operation. Their changes of state never are and never were anything but changes from more to less sensible, from more perfect to less perfect, or the reverse.

(DM, sec. 33) The following, however, is the true explanation <of the relation of soul and body>. We have said that everything which happens to a soul or to any substance is a consequence of its concept; hence the idea itself or the essence of the soul brings it about that all of its appearances or perceptions should be born out of its nature and precisely in such a way that they correspond of themselves to that which happens in the universe at large, but more particularly and more perfectly to that which happens in the body associated with it, because it is in a particular way and only for a certain time according to the relation of other bodies to its own body that the soul expresses the state of the universe. This last fact enables us to see how our body belongs to us.

COMMENTARY

Every created monad has a body of some sort of which it makes a quasi unity through the perceptual linkages that it provides as a unifying entelechy. With a lower degree of unity we have a (mere) *organism;* with a higher degree, an actual *animal.* (See secs. 19–21.)

Leibniz accordingly envisions three hierarchical levels of organic existence among aggregated substances:

1. (mere) organism: an integrated aggregate dominated by an entelechy
2. (mere) animal: an organism dominated by a soul
3. intelligent creature: an animal dominated by a spirit

Organisms have (bare) perceptions; animals have consciousness or feeling; intelligent creatures have self-consciousness. Since all monads have an environing "body" (entourage) of some sort, Leibniz's philosophy is pan-organic. And every one of these organisms is, in its own characteristic (and imperfect) way, a "living mirror of the whole universe." (Compare sec. 60.)

Note that Leibniz discusses the realm of created being at three levels of scale: individual monads, bodies, and the universe as a whole. However, each is simply an element in an all-embracing universal order of coordination.

Leibniz frequently says that all nature is alive and that no created monad is without a body—i.e., lacks some entourage of others that makes up a composite structure whose dominant entelechy it is. Thus every monad is a vital center of an organic structure. But the converse is not the case. That is, not every composite body has a single dominant monad that makes it into a quasi unit. In nature there indeed are "mere aggregates." Latta offers an instructive observation:

> Thus order and organism are conceived by Leibniz under the idea of an infinite series of elements, each differing from its neighbour to an infinitely small extent. The Monad-series of the universe, extending from God to the lowest of Monads, is reflected in the structure of the individual organism, extending from the dominant Monad downwards, and that again is reflected in the series of perceptions within each Monad itself, extending

from the most distinct perceptions to which it has attained down to the most obscure. (P. 253n.)

In his earlier writings of the 1680s and 1690s (especially in the 1686 *Discourse on Metaphysics* and the 1695 *Specimen Dynamicum*), Leibniz was more concerned to stress the aggregative aspect of bodies as against the primitive, immaterial, entelechies or substantial forms that unify them. In his later writings after 1700, the correspondence with des Bosses and de Volder, and—especially—the *Monadology*, Leibniz emphasizes the role of individual substances (monads) as unifiers of aggregative corporeal "substances," which only count as true substances insofar as individual substances endow them with an organic unity. But these differences reflect variant emphases within a single coherent view, rather than representing a change of mind from one view to another, incompatible one.

KEY WORDS:

body/*corps*
entelechy/*entéléchie*
soul/*âme*
organism/*vivant*
animal/*animal*
the universe/*l'univers*
perfect order of the universe/*ordre parfait de l'univers*
mirror of the universe/*miroir de l'univers*
to regulate/*régler*
to represent/*représenter*
perception/*perception*

SECTION 64

64. Thus each organic body of a living being is a kind of divine machine or natural automaton which infinitely surpasses all artificial automata. For a machine made by human artifice is not a machine in each of its parts. For example, the tooth of a brass wheel has parts or pieces which to us are no longer artificial things, and no longer have something recognizably machine-like about them, reflecting the use for which the wheel is intended. But the machines of nature, namely living organisms, are still machines even in their smallest parts, *ad infinitum*. It is this that constitutes the difference between nature and artifice, that is, between divine artifice and ours. (See *Theodicy*, secs. 134, 146, 194, 403.)

64. Ainsi chaque corps organique d'un vivant est une espece de Machine divine, ou d'un Automate Naturel, qui surpasse infiniment tous les Automates artificiels. Parce qu'une Machine faite par l'art de l'homme n'est pas Machine dans chacune de ses parties. Par exemple: la dent d'une roue de [fer] loton <i.e., laiton> a des parties ou fragmens qui ne nous sont plus quelque chose d'artificiel, et n'ont plus rien qui marque de la machine par rapport à l'usage où la roue étoit destinée. Mais les Machines de la Nature, c'est à dire les corps vivans, sont encore des Machines dans leurs moindres parties jusqu'à l'infini.

C'est ce qui fait la difference entre la Nature et l'Art, c'est à dire, entre l'art Divin et le Nôtre. (Théodicée, secs. *134, 146, 194, 403.)*

(*Theodicy*, sec. 134.) God does all the best possible, in accordance with the infinite wisdom which guides his actions. It is true that we have already before our eyes proofs and tests of this, when we see something entire, some whole complete in itself, and isolated, so to speak, among the works of God. Such a whole, shaped as it were by the hand of God, is a plant, an animal, a man. We cannot wonder enough at the beauty and the contrivance of its structure. But when we see some broken bone, some piece of animal's flesh, some sprig of a plant, there appears to be nothing but confusion, unless an excellent anatomist observe it: and even he would recognize nothing therein if he had not before seen like pieces attached to their whole.

(*Theodicy*, sec. 146.) The harmony existing in all the rest allows of a strong presumption that it would exist also in the government of men, and generally in that of Spirits, if the whole were known to us. One must judge the works of God as wisely as Socrates judged those of Heraclitus in these words: What I have understood thereof pleases me; I think that the rest would please me no less if I understood it.

(*Theodicy*, sec. 194.) I have many times wondered that gifted and pious persons should have been capable of setting bounds to the goodness and the perfection of God. For to assert that he knows what is best, that he can do it and that he does it not, is to avow that it rested with his will only to make the world better than it is; but that is what one calls lacking goodness. . . . If some adduce experience to prove that God could have done better, they set themselves up as ridiculous critics of his works. To such will be given the answer given to all those who criticize God's course of action, and who from this same assumption, that is, the alleged defects of the world, would infer that there is an evil God, or at least a God neutral between good and evil. And if we hold the same opinion as King Alfonso, we shall, I say, receive this answer: You have known the world only since the day before yesterday, you see scarce farther than your nose, and you carp at the world. Wait until you know more of the world and consider therein especially the parts which present a complete whole (as do organic bodies); and you will find there a contrivance and a beauty transcending all imagination. Let us thence draw conclusions as to the wisdom and the goodness of the author of things, even in things that we know not. We find in the universe some things which are not pleasing to us; but let us be aware that it is not made for us alone.

(*Theodicy*, sec. 403) The foetus forms itself in the animal, and a thousand other wonders of nature are produced by a certain *instinct* that God has placed there, that is by virtue of *divine reformation*, which has made these admirable automata, adapted to produce mechanically such beautiful effects. Even so it is easy to believe that the soul is a spiritual automaton still more admirable, and that it is through divine preformation that it produces these beautiful ideas, wherein our will has no part and to which our art cannot attain. The operation of spiritual automata, that is of souls, is not mechanical, but it contains in the highest degree all that is beautiful in mechanism.

(PNG, sec. 3.) Everything is a plenum in nature. Everywhere there are simple substances actually separated from each other by their own actions, which continually change their relations. And each outstanding simple substance or monad which forms the center of a compound substance (such as an animal, for example), and is the principle of its uniqueness, is surrounded by a mass composed of an infinity of other monads which constitute the body belonging to this central monad, corresponding to the affections by which it represents, as in a kind of center, the things which are outside of it. This body is *organic* when it forms a kind of automaton or natural machine, which is a machine not only as a whole but also in its smallest observable parts.

(NE, p. 329.) Organic bodies are really machines, although as much superior to the artificial ones which we design as is the Designer of those natural ones to us. For the machines of nature are as imperishable as souls themselves, and the animal together with its soul persists for ever. I can explain my meaning better with the help of a pleasant though very silly example: it is as if someone tried to strip Harlequin on the stage but could never finish the task because he had on so many costumes, one on top of the other; though the infinity of replications of its organic body which an animal contains are not as alike as suits of clothes, and nor are they arranged one on top of another, since nature's artifice is of an entirely different order of subtlety. This all shows that the philosophers were not utterly mistaken when they made so great a separation between artificial bodies and natural bodies endowed with true unity.

(NS, sec. 10.) I am as ready as any man to do justice to the moderns. Yet I find that they have carried reform too far, among other things in confusing natural with artificial matters, because they have not held high enough ideas of the majesty of nature. They think that the difference between natural machines and ours is merely the difference between great and small. This led a very able man, <Fontenelle> the author of the *Conversations on Plurality of Worlds*, to say recently that when we examine nature closely we find it less admirable than has been thought, it being merely like a craftsman's workshop—a conception which I consider neither just enough nor worthy enough of it. It is only our system which shows us, at length, the real and immense distance which lies between the least productions and mechanisms of the Divine Wisdom and the greatest masterpieces of the craft of a finite mind. This difference consists not merely in degree but also in kind. We must recognize that the machines of nature have a truly infinite number of organs, and are so well equipped and so completely proof against all accidents, that it is impossible to destroy them. A natural machine remains a machine even in its smallest parts, and what is more, it always remains the same machine that it has been, being merely transformed through the different foldings which it undergoes, and being now extended, now compressed and, as it were, concentrated, when it is thought to have perished.

(DM, sec. 22.) We recognize and praise the ability of a workman not only when we show what designs he had in making the parts of his machine, but also when we explain the instruments which he employed in making each part, above all if these instruments are simple and ingeniously contrived. God is also a workman able enough to produce a machine still a thousand times more ingenious than is our body, by employing only certain quite simple liquids purposely composed in such a way that ordinary laws of nature alone are required to develop them so as to produce such a marvellous effect.

(G II, 58; Loemker, p. 338; to Arnauld [1686].) Nature must always be explained mathematically and mechanically, provided it be kept in mind that the principles or the laws of mechanics and of force do not depend upon mathematical extension alone but have certain metaphysical causes.

(G IV, 396; Ariew & Garber, p. 253; "Against Descartes" [1702].) Moreover, a natural machine has the great advantage over an artificial machine, that, displaying the mark of an infinite creator, it is made up of an infinity of entangled organs. And thus, a natural machine can never be absolutely destroyed just as it can never absolutely begin, but it only decreases or increases, enfolds or unfolds, always preserving, to a certain extent, the very substance itself and, however transformed, preserving in itself some degree of life (*vitalitas*) or, if you prefer, some degree of primitive activity (*actuositas*). For whatever one says about living things must also be said, analogously, about things which are not animals, properly speaking. However, we must grant that intelligences or higher souls, which are also called spirits, are ruled by God, not only as machines, but also as subjects, and that intelligences are not subject to those radical changes to which other living things are subject.

(G IV, 555; Loemker, p. 575; "Reply to Bayle" [1702].) There is no doubt whatever that a man could make a machine capable of walking about for some time through a city and of turning exactly at the corners of certain streets. A spirit incomparably more perfect, though still finite, could also foresee and avoid an incomparably greater number of obstacles. This is so true that if this world were nothing but a composite of a finite number of atoms which move in accordance with the laws of mechanics, as the hypothesis of some thinkers holds, it is certain that a finite spirit could be so enlightened as to understand and to foresee demonstratively everything which would occur in a determinate time, so that this spirit not only could construct a ship capable of sailing by itself to a designated port, by giving it the needed route, direction, and force at the start, but could also form a body capable of counterfeiting a man. For this involves merely a matter of more or less, which does not alter matters in the realm of possibilities. However great may be the number of functions of a machine, the power and skill of the builder could increase proportionately in such a way that not to see this possibility would be to give insufficient consideration to the degrees of things. It is true that the world is not compounded of a finite number of atoms but is rather like a machine composed in each of its parts of a truly infinite number of forces.

(Foucher de Careil, *Nouvelles lettres et opuscules*, p. 277; to Arnauld [1687].) The machines of nature are machines throughout, however small a part of them we take; or rather the least part of such a machine is itself an infinite world, which even expresses in its own way all that there is in the rest of the universe. That passes our imagination, yet we know that it must be so; and all that infinitely infinite variety is animated in all its parts by a constructive wisdom that is more than infinite. It may be said that there is Harmony, Geometry, Metaphysics, and, so to speak, Ethics everywhere, and (what is surprising) in one sense each substance acts spontaneously as independent of all other created things, while in another sense, all others compel it to adapt itself to them; so that it may be said that all nature is full of miracles, but miracles of reason, miracles which become miracles in virtue of their being rational, in a way which amazes us. For the reasons of things follow one another in an infinite progression, so that our mind while it sees that things must be so, cannot follow so as to comprehend.

COMMENTARY

Leibniz's pan-organic outlook is forcibly expressed in this passage. For him, everything that exists is part of the "machinery of nature," whose organismic character is inherent in the proportion:

machine : human artifice :: organism : divine artifice

The purposeful organization of the parts of an organism into a coherently functioning whole typifies the nature of reality as the product of divine planning. For some 17th century thinkers, God was the great watchmaker, a machinemaker. (Already Copernicus had spoken of the astronomical domain as *machina mundi*, using the machine as a descriptive paradigm.) But God was the great organism-maker for Leibniz, who regarded an organism as the quintessential machine, an *organic* automaton with an inherent teleology—an implicit purposiveness of its own.

Leibniz viewed nature as involving a nested hierarchy of functional complexity that began and ended in metaphysics:

monads/micro-units	substantival metaphysics
mere aggregates	mechanical physics
animals	biology
humans	medicine and human psychology
human communities	politics
astronomical bodies	celestial physics
the whole universe	metaphysics
the realm of possibility	theology: teleological metaphysics (via the mind of God)

The interrelatedness of these various levels means that our knowledge as a whole must be developed as a coordinated *system*. Even as nature is organic, so an adequate knowledge of it must be systematic.

Leibniz's reference in this section to man-made machines with brass wheels is an allusion to his own calculating machine.

KEY WORDS:

organic body/*corps organique*
organism/*vivant*
machine/*machine*
automata/*automates*
nature/*nature*
artifice/*art*
natural/*naturel*
artificial/*artificiel*
wheel/*roue*
to infinity/*à l'infini*

SECTION 65

**65. And the Author of Nature has been able to practice this divine and in-
finitely wonderful artifice because each bit of matter is not merely infinitely
divisible, as the ancients already realized, but is even actually endlessly subdivided, every piece into further pieces, each of which has some motion of its
own. Otherwise it would be impossible that each bit of matter could express
the whole universe. (See *Theodicy*, Preliminary Discourse, sec. 70; sec. 195.)**

*65. Et l'Auteur de la Nature a pû practiquer cet artifice divin et infiniment
merveilleux, parce que chaque portion de la matière n'est pas seulement divisible à l'infini, comme les anciens ont reconnû, mais encore sous-divisée
actuellement sans fin, chaque partie en parties, dont chacune a quelque
mouvement propre: autrement il seroit impossible que chaque portion de la
matière pût exprimer tout l'univers. (*Théodicée, Discours préliminaire, sec. 70;
sec. 195.*)*

(*Theodicy*, Preliminary Discourse, sec. 70.) It seems that M. Descartes con-
fesses also, in a passage of his Principles, that it is impossible to find an answer
to the difficulties on the division of matter to infinity, which he nevertheless
recognizes as actual. . . . But if they ⟨i.e., people who think this⟩ took the trouble
to give to the objections the form these ought to have, they would see that there
are faults in the reasoning, and sometimes false assumptions which cause confusion. Here is an example. A man of parts one day brought up to me an objection in the following form: Let the straight line BA be cut in two equal parts
at the point C, and the part CA at the point D, and the part DA, at the point
E, and so on to infinity; all the halves, BC, CD, DE, etc., together make the
whole BA; therefore there must be a last half, since the straight line BA finishes
at A. But this last half is absurd: for since it is a line, it will be possible again
to cut it in two. Therefore division to infinity cannot be admitted. But I pointed
out to him that one is not justified in the inference that there must be a last
half, although there be a last point A, for this last point belongs to all the halves
of its side. And my friend acknowledged it himself when he endeavoured to
prove this deduction by a formal argument; on the contrary, just because the
division goes on to infinity, there is no last half. And although the straight line
AB be finite, it does not follow that the process of dividing it has any final end.
The same confusion arises with the series of numbers going on to infinity. One
imagines a final end, a number that is infinite, or infinitely small; but that is
all simple fiction. Every number is finite and specific; every line is so likewise,
and the infinite or infinitely small signify only magnitudes that one may take
as great or as small as one wishes, to show that an error is smaller than that
which has been specified, that is to say, that there is no error; or else by the
infinitely small is meant the state of a magnitude at its vanishing point or its
beginning, conceived after the pattern of magnitudes already actualized.

(*Theodicy*, sec. 195.) Someone will say that it is impossible to produce the
best, because there is no perfect creature, and that it is always possible to produce one which would be more perfect. I answer that what can be said of a
creature or of a particular substance, which can always be surpassed by another,
is not to be applied to the universe, which, since it must extend through all

future eternity, is an infinity. Moreover, there is an infinite number of creatures in the smallest particle of matter, because of the actual division of the *continuum* to infinity. And infinity, that is to say, the accumulation of an infinite number of substances, is, properly speaking, not a whole any more than the infinite number itself, whereof one cannot say whether it is even or uneven. That is just what serves to confute those who make of the world a God, or who think of God as the Soul of the world; for the world or the universe cannot be regarded as an animal or as a substance.

(G I, 416; to Foucher [1693].) I am so much in favor of the actual infinite, that rather than agree that nature abhors it, as is commonly said, I hold that nature exemplifies it everywhere, the better to manifest the perfection of her author.

COMMENTARY

The infinite divisibility of matter was maintained by Aristotle against the atomists (*Physics*, 231b10). Leibniz's theory of non-extended monads enables him also to depart from classical atomism and to see matter as infinitely divided—down to the level of the punctiform monads. And this renders possible his Chinese-box organicism, with organisms contained within organisms which contain further organisms in their turn. At every level of substructure, these organisms perceive and represent the entire universe in their own (admittedly imperfect) way, owing to the interconnectedness of all things.

KEY WORDS:

God/*dieu (l'auteur de la nature)*
divine artifice/*artifice divin*
bit of matter/*portion de la matière*
motion/*mouvement*
infinitely divisible/*divisible à l'infini*
express the whole universe/*exprimer tout l'univers*

SECTION 66

66. From this one sees that there is a whole world of creatures—of organisms, animals, entelechies, and souls—even in the least piece of matter.

66. Par où l'on voit, qu'il y a un Monde de creatures, de vivans, d'Animaux, d'Entelechies, d'Ames dans la moindre partie de la matière.

(PNG, sec. 3.) Everywhere there are simple substances actually separated from each other by their own actions, which continually change their relations. And each outstanding simple substance or monad which forms the center of a compound substance (such as an animal, for example), and is the principle of its uniqueness, is surrounded by a mass composed of an infinity of other monads which constitute the body belonging to this central monad, corresponding to the affections by which it represents, as in a kind of center, the things which are outside of it. This body is *organic* when it forms a kind of automaton or natural machine, which is a machine not only as a whole but also in its smallest observable parts.

(G I, 416; to Foucher [1693].) There is no part of matter which is not, I do not say divisible, but actually divided; and consequently the smallest particle must be considered as a world filled with an infinity of different creatures.

COMMENTARY

The combination of cells into plants or the fusion of individuals into co-operative source units (in sponges or even bee-swarms or flocks of birds) make for a unification of separate individuals into a larger whole. Leibniz puts great emphasis on this sort of emergence of higher level composite units through the coordinated and, as it were, collaborative interactions of lower-level ones.

Leibniz's pan-organic view of the world is predicated on the idea that "life is everywhere." The then-recent discovery of the microscope, and the finding that even a single drop of water contains a whole variety of minuscule organisms, were regarded by him as a striking illustration of this position. (Note that when Leibniz thinks of the *physical* aspect of nature, he usually speaks of "the universe" [*l'univers*], but when he thinks of its organic aspect, he usually speaks of "the world" [*le monde*].)

The work of Robert Hooke, Marcello Malpighi, Jan Swammerdam, Anton von Leeuwenhoek, and other early microscopists always interested Leibniz enormously, as did the controversy over the biological theory of the "preformation" of organisms in microscopic seeds. And from his early days in Paris the speculations of Nicholas Malebranche's *Recherche de la vérité* about an infinite descending chain of ever smaller creatures existing within ever-smaller creatures appealed to his fertile imagination. Some contemporary theorists had a sense of insignificance and anomie in the face of the proliferation of life on a cosmic scale (think of Pascal's unease about "how many creatures know us not"). But Leibniz rejoiced in the proliferation of life that signalized God's bounty and the boundless extent of his providential care.

KEY WORDS:
world of creatures/*monde de créatures*
organisms/*vivants*
animals/*animaux*
entelechies/*entéléchies*
souls/*âmes*
piece of matter/*partie de la matière*

SECTION 67

67. Every bit of matter can be conceived as a garden full of plants or a pond full of fish. But each branch of the plant, each member of the animal, each drop of its bodily fluids, is also such a garden or such a pond.

67. *Chaque portion de la matière peut être conçue comme un jardin plein de plantes, et comme un Etang plein de poissons. Mais chaque rameau de la plante, chaque membre de l'Animal, chaque goutte de ses humeurs est encor un tel jardin, ou un tel étang.*

(NS, sec. 10.) <There is> a real and immense distance which lies between the least productions and mechanisms of the Divine Wisdom and the greatest masterpieces of the craft of a finite mind. This difference consists not merely in degree but also in kind. We must recognize that the machines of nature have a truly infinite number of organs, and are so well equipped and so completely proof against all accidents, that it is impossible to destroy them. A natural machine remains a machine even in its smallest parts, and what is more, it always remains the same machine that it has been, being merely transformed through the different foldings which it undergoes, and being now extended, now compressed and, as it were, concentrated, when it is thought to have perished.

(G II, 122; Loemker, p. 345; to Arnauld [1687].) Those who conceive that there is as it were an infinity of small animals in the least drop of water, as Mr. Leeuwenhoek has shown, and who do not find it strange that matter should be filled everywhere with animated substances, will not find it any more strange that there is something animated even in ashes, so that fire can transform an animal and reduce it to small size, instead of destroying it entirely. What can be said of one caterpillar or silkworm can be said of a hundred or a thousand animals. It does not follow that we should see the silkworm arise again from the ashes, for perhaps this is not the order of nature. I know that several people have affirmed that the seminal powers remain in the ashes in such a way that plants can arise from them again, but I do not want to make use of any doubtful experiences.

(G VII, 377; to Clarke, IV.PS [1716].) We would have nature to go no further and to be finite as our minds are; but this is being ignorant of the greatness and majesty of the author of things. The least corpuscle is actually subdivided *in infinitum* and contains a world of other creatures which would be wanting in the universe if that corpuscle was an atom, that is, a body of one entire piece without subdivision.

(Loemker, p. 159; "Paris Notes" [1676].) The whole labyrinth about the composition of the continuum must be unraveled as rigorously as possible. . . . ⟨One must bear in mind the⟩ treatment of the angle of the tangent, for this discussion belongs not to geometry but to metaphysics. We must see whether it can be demonstrated that there is something infinitely small yet not indivisible; from the existence of such a being there follow wonderful things about the infinite; namely if we assume creatures of another, infinitely small world, we will be infinite in comparison with them. Hence we can clearly be assumed to be infinitely small in comparison with another world of infinite magnitude, yet bounded. Hence it is clear that the infinite is other than the unbounded, as we surely assume popularly. . . . Since we see that the hypothesis of infinites and infinitesimals turns out to be consistent in geometry, this also increases the probability that it is true.

COMMENTARY

Here, Leibniz stresses the dialectic of microcosm and macrocosm, of worlds within worlds, mini-universes reflecting macro-universe. The whole of nature is organized in a hierarchical descent of this sort, a sequence that extends "all the way down" (so to speak) toward the level of individual monads.

Leibniz thus continues to give full play to his penchant for explanatory similes. (As chapter 4 of the present book shows, his metaphysics is a network of such expository and explanatory analogies.)

KEY WORDS:

bit of matter/*portion de la matière*
organisms/*êtres vivants* (plantes et animaux)
garden/*jardin*
pond/*étang*
plant/*plante*
animal/*animal*
humor/*humeur*

SECTION 68

68. And though the earth and the air emplaced between the plants of the garden or the water emplaced between the fish of the pond are certainly neither plant nor fish, they contain yet more of them, though mostly of a minuteness imperceptible to us.

68. Et quoyque la terre et l'air interceptés entre les plantes du jardin, ou l'eau interceptée entre les poissons de l'étang, ne soit point plante, ni poisson, ils en contiennent pourtant encore, mais le plus souvent d'une subtilité à nous imperceptible.

(PNG, sec. 1.) There must of necessity be simple substances everywhere, for without simple substances there would be no compounds. As a result, the whole of nature is full of life.

(PNG, sec. 4.) Together with a particular body, each monad makes a living substance. . . . There is life everywhere, joined to members or organs. . . .

(NS, sec. 10.) The machines of nature have a truly infinite number of organs. . . . A natural machine remains a machine even in its smallest parts.

COMMENTARY

This theory that living organisms remain organic in their microscopic and submicroscopic components "all the way down" in the scale of composition, provides Leibniz with yet another natural application for his idea of things so minute as to lie beneath the threshold of perceptibility.

KEY WORDS:

garden/*jardin*
pond/*étang*
organisms/*êtres vivants, plantes et animaux*

minuteness/*subtilité*
imperceptible/*imperceptible*

SECTION 69

69. Thus nothing is fallow, sterile, or dead in the universe; there is no chaos, no disorder save in appearance. It is somewhat like what appears in a distant pond, in which one might see the confused and, so to speak, teeming motion of the pond's fish, without distinguishing the fish themselves. (See *Theodicy*, Preface.)

*69. Ainsi, il n'y a rien d'inculte, de sterile, de mort dans l'univers, point de chaos, point de confusions qu'en apparence; à peu près comme il en paroîtroit dans un étang à une distance dans laquelle on verroit un mouvement confus et grouillement, pour ainsi dire, des poissons de l'étang, sans discerner les poissons mêmes. (*Théodicée, Préface, *** 5b, ****b.)*

(*Theodicy*, Preface, 5b; G VI, 40.) In reality, mechanism is sufficient to produce the organic bodies of animals, without any need of other plastic natures, provided there be added thereto the *preformation* already completely organic in the seeds of the bodies that come into existence, contained in those of the bodies whence they spring, right back to the primary seeds. This could only proceed from the Author of things, infinitely powerful and infinitely wise, who, creating all in the beginning in due order, had *pre-established* there all order and artifice that was to be. There is no chaos in the inward nature of things, and there is organism everywhere in a matter whose disposition proceeds from God. More and more of it would come to light if we pressed closer our examination of the anatomy of bodies; and we should continue to observe it even if we could go on to infinity, like Nature, and make subdivision as continuous in our knowledge as Nature has made it in fact.

Theodicy, Preface; G VI, 44.) <An integrating> connection is displayed in the union of the soul with the body, and in general in the communication of true substances with one another and with material phenomena. But the first takes place in the preformation of organic bodies or rather of all bodies, since there is organism everywhere, although all masses do not compose organic bodies. So a pond may very well be full of fish or of other organic bodies, although it is not itself an animal or organic body, but only a mass that contains them.

(G II, 77; Ariew & Garber, p. 80; to Arnauld [1686].) If I am asked, in particular, what I say of the sun, the globe of the earth, the moon, trees and similar bodies, and even beasts, I could not affirm absolutely that they are animated, or at least that they are substances, or whether they are merely machines or aggregates of several substances. But at least I can say that if there are no corporeal substances such as I want, it follows that bodies will be only true phenomena, like the rainbow. . . . We shall never come to anything of which we can say: "there is truly a being," except when we find animated machines to which their soul or substantial form gives a substantial unity independent of the external union of contact. And if there are none such, it follows that except man there would be nothing substantial in the visible world.

(G VI, 539; Loemker, p. 586; "On Vital Principles and Plastic Nature" [1705].) When I am asked if these [principles of life] are substantial forms, I reply by a distinction: for if this term is taken, as M. Descartes takes it, when he maintains . . . that the reasonable soul is the substantial form of man, I should answer yes. But I should say no, if any one understood the term as those do who imagine that there is a substantial form of a piece of stone, or of some other non-organic body; for principles of life belong only to organic bodies. It is true . . . that there is no portion of matter in which there are not numberless organic and animated bodies . . . but for all this, it must not be said that each portion of matter is animated, just as we do not say that a pond full of fish is an animated body, although a fish is so.

COMMENTARY

A principle of fecundity is operative throughout Leibniz's thought. The universe is an organic whole pervaded through and through by a richness of organic being. Life and fertility are on display everywhere: nothing is altogether inert and sterile. The entire universe is, as it were, an organic plenum. After all, perfection for Leibniz consists in the combination of order with *variety*.

KEY WORDS:

sterility/*le stérile*
dead/*mort*
chaos/*chaos*
pond/*étang*
universe/*l'univers*
motion/*mouvement*
disorder/*confusion*

SECTION 70

70. One sees from this that every living body has a dominant entelechy, which in an animal is the soul. But the members of this living body are themselves full of other organisms—plants or animals—each of which also has its own entelechy or dominant soul.

70. On voit par là, que chaque corps vivant a une Entelechie dominante qui est l'Ame dans l'animal; mais les membres de ce corps vivant sont pleins d'autres vivans, plantes, animaux, dont chacun a encore son Entelechie ou son Ame dominante.

(PNG, sec. 3.) Everything is a plenum in nature. Everywhere there are simple substances actually separated from each other by their own actions, which continually change their relations. And each outstanding simple substance or monad which forms the center of a compound substance (such as an animal, for example), and is the principle of its uniqueness, is surrounded by a mass composed of an infinity of other monads which constitute the body belonging to this central monad, corresponding to the affections by which it represents, as in a kind of center, the things which are outside of it. This body is *organic* when it forms a kind of automaton or natural machine, which is a machine not only as a whole but also in its smallest observable parts.

(PNG, sec. 4.) Together with a particular body, each monad makes a living substance. Thus not only is there life everywhere, joined to members or organs, but there are also infinite degrees of it in the monads, some of which dominate more or less over others.

(NE, p. 58.) I agree with most of the ancients that every Spirit, every soul, every created simple substance is always united with a body and that no soul is ever entirely without one. I have *apriori* reasons for this doctrine, but it will be found to have the further merit of solving all the philosophical difficulties about the state of souls, their perpetual preservation, their immortality, and their mode of operation.

(NE, pp. 328–29.) Organic bodies are really machines, although as much superior to the artificial ones which we design as is the Designer of those natural ones to us. For the machines of nature are as imperishable as souls to themselves, and the animal together with its soul persists for ever. I can explain my meaning better with the help of a pleasant though very silly example: it is as if someone tried to strip Harlequin on the stage but could never finish the task because he had on so many costumes, one on top of the other; though the infinity of replications of its organic body which an animal contains are not as alike as suits of clothes, and nor are they arranged one on top of another, since nature's artifice is of an entirely different order of subtlety.

(G II, 100; to Arnauld; Ariew & Garber, p. 88 [1687].) I maintain that the body apart, without the soul, has only a unity of aggregation, but the reality which remains to it comes from the parts which compose it, and which retain their substantial unity because of the numberless living bodies which are enveloped in them. However, though it is possible for a soul to have a body composed of parts animated by separate souls, the soul or form of the whole is not on that account composed of the souls or forms of the parts.

(G II, 435–36; Loemker, p. 600; to des Bosses [1712].) Either bodies are mere phenomena, in which case extension too will be only a phenomenon and only monads will be real, but the union will be supplied in the phenomenon by the action of the perceiving soul; or . . . substance consists in that unifying reality which adds something absolute and hence substantial, even though fluid, to the things to be united.

(G II, 444; Loemker, p. 602; to des Bosses [1712].) Monads do not constitute a complete composite substance since they will not make up a unity *per se* but merely an aggregate unless some substantial bond *(vinculum substantiale)* is added.

(G VII, 502; to Bierling [1711].) Every created monad is provided with some organic body. . . . Every mass contains innumerable monads, for although every organic body in nature has its corresponding monad, yet it contains in its parts other monads similarly provided with their organic bodies, which are subservient to the primary organic body.

(Couturat, *Opuscules*, p. 522; Loemker, p. 270; Ariew & Garber, p. 32, "First Truths" [ca. 1684].) Hence it follows that *every particle of the universe contains a world with an infinity of creatures.* But a continuum is not divided into points, nor is it divided in all possible ways. It is not divided into points, because points are not parts but limits. It is not divided in all possible ways, because not all creatures are in the same part, but only a certain infinite progression of them. Thus, if you bisect a straight line and then any part of it, you will set up different divisions than if you trisect it.

COMMENTARY

Leibniz holds that hierarchical organization pervades the organic realm. Every organism is a unit of units, each integrated into a single whole through the operation of a dominant monad (or entelechy) that provides for the substantial bonding unit of this unit. This dominant monad perceives (and thereby expresses or represents) with comparatively great clarity what is happening throughout this whole organism and thus constitutes its principle of unity. If it were not for this unifying agency there really would be no composites but mere aggregates whose unity would lie wholly "in the eyes of the observer," like that of a flock of birds. It is this unifying and bonding capacity of monads that entitles them to be called "substantial forms." (See sec. 74.) Thus physical reality, for Leibniz, is like a never-ending set of Chinese boxes, in infinitely descending nesting of macro-units containing further micro-units—each successive unit integrated by a dominant monad that serves as a non-extended principle of substantial unity.

KEY WORDS:

living body/*corps vivant*
dominant entelechy/*entéléchie* (or *âme*) *dominante*
organism/*vivant*
plants and animals/*plantes et animaux*
soul/*âme*

SECTION 71

71. But it must not be imagined, as some have done who misunderstood my thought <viz. Bayle>, that every soul has a bulk or bit of matter of its own that is attached to it forever, and that it consequently possesses other inferior organisms destined always to be at its service. For all bodies are in a perpetual flux, like rivers, and some parts enter into them and some pass out continually.

71. Mais il ne faut point s'imaginer avec quelques uns, qui avoient mal pris ma pensée, que chaque ame a une masse ou portion de la matière propre ou affectée à elle pour toûjours, et qu'elle possède par consequent d'autres vivans inferieurs destinés toûjours à son service. Car tous les corps sont dans un flux perpetuel comme des rivières; et des parties y entrent et en sortent continuellement.

(NE, pp. 231–32.) If there were atoms, i.e. perfectly hard and perfectly unalterable bodies which were incapable of internal change and could differ from one another only in size and in shape, it is obvious that since they could have the same size and shape they would then be indistinguishable in themselves and discernible only by means of external denominations with no internal foundation; which is contrary to the greatest principles of reason. In fact, however, every body is changeable and indeed is actually changing all the time, so that it differs in itself from every other.

(G. II, 368; to des Bosses [1709].) A new entelechy can be created, even if no new part of mass is created; for although mass already has unities everywhere, yet it is always capable of new ones, dominating over many others; as if you were to imagine that God should make an organic body out of a mass which, as a whole, is inorganic, *e.g.* a lump of stone, and should set its soul over it; for there are as many entelechies as there are organic bodies.

(G. VII, 502; to Bierling [1712].) Every created monad is provided with some organic body. . . . Every mass contains innumerable monads, for although every organic body in nature has its corresponding monad, yet it contains in its parts other monads similarly provided with their organic bodies, which are subservient to the primary organic body.

(G. VII, 530; to R. C. Wagner [1710].) To each primitive entelechy or each vital principle there is perpetually united a certain natural machine, which comes to us under the name of organic body: which machine, although it preserves its form in general, consists in a flux, and is, like the ship of Theseus, perpetually repaired. And we cannot be certain that the smallest particle received by us at birth remains in our body. . . . Some animal always remains, although no particular animal ought to be called everlasting.

COMMENTARY

Every monad has a "body"—an entourage of other monads over which it dominates. However, this affiliation of various substances to a dominant one is nothing fixed and stable, but ever-changing in its composition. The unity of an organism is something like the unity of a street-crowd gathered to see a (unifying) performer, with various comings and goings. Pierre Bayle misunderstood Leibniz's position on this point. (See note H of the article "Rorarius" of his *Dictionary* and compare also sec. 16 above.)

Leibniz's reference to "a perpetual flux, like rivers" is an allusion to the pre-Socratic philosopher Heraclitus (b. ca. 540 B.C.) who, as Plato put it, taught "that all things move and nothing remains still, and he likens existence to the current of a river, saying that you cannot step into the same stream twice" (*Cratylus*, 402A).

KEY WORDS:

dominant soul/*âme dominante*
bulk/*masse*
bit of matter/*portion de matière*
organism/*vivant*
body/*corps*
perpetual flux/*flux perpétuel*
part/*partie*

PERSONS:
Pierre Bayle

SECTION 72

72. Thus the soul changes its body only slowly and by degrees, so that it is never laid bare of all its organs all at once. There is often a metamorphosis in animals, but never metempsychosis or transmigration of souls. Nor are there *souls* altogether *separated* <from bodies> or disembodied spirits. God alone is wholly detached from any body. (See *Theodicy*, secs. 90, 124.)

72. Ainsi l'ame ne change de corps que peu à peu et par degrés, de sorte qu'elle n'est jamais depouillée tout d'un coup de tous ses organes; et il y a souvent metamorphose dans les animaux, mais jamais Metempsychose ni transmigration des Ames: il n'y a pas non plus des Ames tout à fait separées, ny de Genies sans corps. Dieu seul en est detaché entierement. (Théodicée, secs. 90, 124.)

(*Theodicy*, sec. 90.) As the formation of organic animate bodies appears explicable in the order of nature only when one assumes a *preformation* already organic, I have thence inferred that what we call generation of an animal is only a transformation and augmentation. Thus, since the same body was already furnished with organs, it is to be supposed that it was already animate, and that it had the same soul: so I assume *vice versa*, from the conservation of the soul when once it is created, that the animal is also conserved, and that apparent death is only an envelopment, there being no likelihood that in the order of nature souls exist entirely separated from all body, or that what does not begin naturally can cease through natural forces.

(*Theodicy*, sec. 124.) Nature had need of animals, plants, inanimate bodies; there are in these creatures, devoid of reason, marvels which serve for exercise of the reason. What would an intelligent creature do if there were no unintelligent things? What would it think of, if there were neither movement, nor matter, nor sense? If it had only distinct thoughts it would be a God, its wisdom would be without bounds: that is one of the results of my meditations. As soon as there is a mixture of confused thoughts, there is sense, there is matter. For these confused thoughts come from the relation of all things one to the other by way of duration and extent. Thus it is that in my philosophy there is no rational creature without some organic body, and there is no created spirit entirely detached from matter. But these organic bodies vary no less in perfection than the spirits to which they belong. Therefore, since God's wisdom must have a world of bodies, a world of substances capable of perception and incapable of reason; since, in short, it was necessary to choose from all the things possible what produced the best effect together, and since vice entered in by this door, God would not have been altogether good, altogether wise if he had excluded it.

(PNG, sec. 6.) The investigations of the moderns have taught us, and reason confirms them, that the living beings whose organs are known to us, that is, plants and animals, do not come from putrefaction or chaos, as the ancients believed, but from *preformed* seeds, and therefore from the transformation of living beings existing prior to them. There are little animals in the seeds of large animals, which assume a new vesture in conception, which they appropriate and which provides them with a method of nourishment and growth, so that they may emerge into a greater stage and propagate the large animal. It is true that the souls of human spermatic animals are not rational and become so only when conception determines them for human nature. Just as animals in general are not completely born in conception or *generation*, moreover, neither do they completely perish in what we call *death*, for it is reasonable that what has no natural beginning also has no end within the order of nature. Thus, abandoning their masks or their rags, they merely return, but to a lesser stage, on which, however, they can be as sensitive and as well ordered as on the larger one. And what has been said about grosser animals takes place also in the generation and death of spermatic animals themselves, that is, they are the enlargements of other smaller spermatic animals, in proportion to which they may be considered large, for everything in nature proceeds to infinity. Not only souls, therefore, but animals as well, cannot be generated or perish; they are only developed, enveloped, reclothed, stripped, transformed. Souls never leave the whole of their bodies and do not pass from one body to another entirely new to them. Thus there is no *metempsychosis*, though there is *metamorphosis*. Animals change, take on, and put off, only parts; in nutrition this takes place little by little and through minute, insensible particles but continually, while in conception or in death, where much is acquired or lost all at once, it occurs suddenly and noticeably but infrequently.

(NE, p. 59.) In my account of things, there is no more difficulty in conceiving the preservation of the soul (or rather, on my view, of the animal) than in conceiving the transformation of a caterpillar into a butterfly, or the preservation of thought during sleep, to which Jesus Christ has sublimely compared death. I have also said already that no sleep could last for ever; and in the case of rational souls it will be of even briefer duration or almost none at all. These souls are destined always to preserve the *persona* which they have been given in the city of God, and hence to retain their memories, so that they may be more susceptible of punishments and rewards. I further add that in general no disruption of its visible organs can reduce an animal to total confusion, or destroy all the organs and deprive the soul of its entire organic body and of the ineradicable vestiges of its previous traces.

(NE, pp. 233–34.) A single individual substance can retain its identity only by preservation of the same soul, for the body is in continual flux and the soul does not reside in certain atoms which are reserved for it or in some little indestructible bone, like the *luz* of the rabbis. However, there is no "transmigration" in which the soul entirely abandons its body and passes into another. Even in death it always retains an organic body, part of its former one although what it retains is always subject to wasting away insensibly and to restoring itself, and even at a given time to undergoing a great change. Thus, instead of transmigration of the soul there is reshaping, infolding, unfolding, and flowing, in the soul's body. M. van Helmont the younger believed that souls pass from body to body, but always within the same species. This implies that there will always be the same number of souls of a given species—the same number of men or of wolves, so that if the wolves have been reduced or wiped out in England they must have correspondingly increased elsewhere. Certain meditations published in France seemed to take the same view <Lannion>. If transmigration is not taken strictly, i.e. if anyone thought that souls remain in the same rarefied bodies and only change their coarse bodies, that would be possible, even to the extent of the same soul's passing into a body of another species in the Brahmin or Pythagorean manner. But not everything which is possible is therefore in conformity with the order of things. If such a transformation did occur, however, and assuming in accordance with rabbinical doctrine that Cain, Ham and Ishmael had the same soul, the question of whether they ought to be called the same man is merely a question of a name. I have noticed that the distinguished author whose opinions you have supported recognizes this and sets it forth very clearly (in the final paragraph of this chapter). There would be identity of substance but, if there were no connection by way of memory between the different *personae* which were made by the same soul, there would not be enough moral identity to say that this was a single person. And if God wished a human soul to pass into the body of a hog and to forget the man and perform no rational acts, it would not constitute a man. But if while in the body of the beast it had the thoughts of a man, and even of the man whom it had animated before the change, like the golden ass of Apuleius, perhaps no one would object to saying that the same Lucius, who had come to Thessaly to see his friends, remained inside the skin of the ass where Photis had inadvertently put him, and wandered from master to master until by eating the roses he was restored to his natural shape.

(NS, sec. 6.) To return to ordinary forms, however, or to material souls, this duration which we must ascribe to them instead of that which was attributed to the atoms could lead us to doubt whether they do not pass from body to body. This would be *metempsychosis*, somewhat like the transmission of motion and of species in which some philosophers have believed. But such a fancy is far from the nature of things. There is no such transfer; at this point the *transformations* of Swammerdam, Malpighi, and Leeuwenhoek, the best of observers of our times, have come to my aid and led me to admit the more readily that animals and all other organized substances do not at all begin when we believe them to and that their apparent generation is merely a development and a form of augmentation. I have noticed, too, that the author of the *Récherche de la vérité* and Mr. Régis, Mr. Hartsoeker, and other able men have held opinions nor far removed from this.

(G II, 99–100; Ariew & Garber, p. 88; to Arnauld [1687].) Every living thing contains a world of diversity in a real unity. Our experience is in favor of this great number of living things; we find that there is a prodigious quantity of them in a drop of water. . . . Now, if these animals have souls, the same must be said of their souls which can probably be said of the animals themselves; namely, that they have been living from the very creation of the world and that they will live to its end, and that birth being apparently only a change consisting in growth, so death is only a change or diminution which causes this animal to re-enter into the engulfing of a world of minute creatures, where perceptions are very limited until the command comes calling them to return to the theater of action. The ancients made the mistake of introducing the transmigration of souls, in place of the transformation of the same animal which always preserves the same soul. They put metempsychoses in place of metaschematisms. Spirits, however, are not subjected to these revolutions, or rather these revolutions of bodies must serve the divine economy for the sake of spirits. God creates them when it is time and he detaches them from the body, at least from the material body by death; since they must always preserve their moral qualities and their memory in order to be perpetual citizens of that universal republic, absolutely perfect, whose monarch is God. This republic can never lose any of its members and its laws are superior to those of the body. I grant that bodies by themselves without the soul have only a unity of aggregation, but the reality which inheres in them comes from the parts which compose them and which retain their substantial unity through living bodies that are included in them without number. Nevertheless, although it is possible that a soul have a body made up of animated parts or of separate souls, the soul or the form of the whole is not, therefore, composed of soul or forms of parts. In regard to an insect which is cut in two, it is not necessary that the two parts shall remain animated, although there may be some movement in them, at least the soul of the whole insect will remain only on one side and as in the formation and in the growth of the insect the soul has already been in a certain part alive from the very start, it will remain also after the destruction of the insect.

(G III, 635; to Remond [1715].) As for metempsychosis, I believe that the universal order does not permit it; it demands that everything should be explicable distinctly and that nothing should take place in a leap. But the passage of the soul from one body to another would be a strange and inexplicable leap. What happens in an animal at present happens in it always; that is, the body is in continuous change like a river, and what we call generation or death is only a greater or quicker change than ordinary, as would be a waterfall or cataract in a river. But these leaps are not absolute and of the kind which I reject, as would be that of a body which went from one position to another without passing through the intervening space. Such leaps are prohibited not only in motion but also in the whole order of things or of truths. . . . But just as there are certain outstanding points in a geometric curve which are called summits, bend points, points of return, or some other thing, and as there are curves which contain an infinity of them, even so there must be conceived in the life of an animal or a person times of extraordinary change which still fall within the general rule—as the distinctive points of a curve can be determined by its general nature or its equation. We can always say of an animal that everything is just as it is now; the difference is only that of more or less.

COMMENTARY

Here Leibniz's pan-organicism comes to the fore. As he sees it, nature is pervasively organic, everywhere replete with organisms and proto-organisms. And nature contains no isolated substances: every monad has a "body" of some sort, an organized (but ever-changing) entourage of other substances affiliated to and coordinated with it. This happens in such a way that souls can acquire new bodies (metamorphosis), but for reasons of "fitness," never in such a way that souls take on the body of an animal of the same type (metempsychosis). Moreover, spirits (here *génies*) never cease to dominate over some body or other—that is, are never reduced to the level of "bare monads," but are always present as dominant members of some non-trivial organism and constantly retain their potential for higher things.

KEY WORDS:
to change by degrees/*changer par degrés*
soul/*âme*
body/*corps*
organs/*organes*
stripped of its organs/dépouillée de ses organes
metamorphosis/*métamorphose*
transmigration/*transmigration*
metempsychosis/*métempsychose*
spirits/*génies*
disembodied/*sans corps*
God/*Dieu*

SECTION 73

73. This also brings it about that there is never either complete birth or complete death, in the strict sense of a separation of the soul <from the body>. What we call *births* are unfoldings and growths; even as what we call *deaths* are enfoldings and diminutions.

73. *C'est ce qui fait aussi qu'il n'y a jamais ni generation entière, ni mort parfaite prise à la rigueur, consistant dans la separation de l'âme. Et ce que nous appellons* Generations *sont des développemens et des accroissemens; comme ce que nous appellons* Morts, *sont des Enveloppemens et des Diminutions.*

(PNG, sec. 12.) Souls, that is to say, the most dominant monads, cannot fail to awake from the state of stupor into which death or some other accident may place them.

(NS, sec. 7.) The greatest question still remained, however: What becomes of the souls or forms at the death of the animal or at the destruction of the individual unit of organized substance? This question is the more difficult, inasmuch as it hardly seems reasonable that souls should remain, useless in a chaos of confused matter. This led me at length to conclude that there is only one reasonable view to take—that of the conservation not only of the soul but also of the animal itself and its organic machine, even though the destruction of its grosser parts may have reduced this machine to a size so small that it escapes our senses just as it did before birth. Moreover, no one can mark exactly the true time of death, which may for a long time be taken to be a simple suspension of observable actions and in the last analysis is never anything but this in the simple animals. Witness the *resuscitation* of flies which have been drowned and then buried under powdered chalk, and a number of similar examples which suffice to show that there would be other resuscitations, in cases much further gone, if men were in a position to restore the mechanism. It seems that the great Democritus spoke of something approaching this, extreme atomist though he was, though Pliny laughed at his opinion. It is natural, then, that animals which have always been living and organized (as people of great penetration are beginning to recognize) will also always remain so. And since an animal has thus no first birth or entirely new generation, it follows that there will be no final extinction or complete death, in a strict metaphysical sense, and that as a result, there is no transmigration of souls but only a transformation of the same animal, as its organs are differently arranged and are more or less developed.

(G II, 116; Loemker, p. 342; to Arnauld [1687].) I proceed to the question of forms or souls, which I hold to be indivisible and indestructible. Parmenides (of whom Plato speaks with veneration), as well as Melissus, maintained that there is no generation nor corruption except in appearance: Aristotle mentions this (De Caelo, bk. III, chap. 2). And the author of the De Diaeta, bk. I (which is attributed to Hippocrates), expressly says that an animal cannot be engendered absolutely (tout de nouveau) nor completely (tout à fait) destroyed.

(G II, 123–24; Loemker, p. 345; to Arnauld [1687].) I learned some time ago that Mr. Leeuwenhoek holds opinions very close to mine, in that he believes that even the largest animals arise through a kind of transformation. I do not venture either to approve or to reject the details of his opinion, but I hold this to be true in general, and Mr. Swammerdam, another great investigator and anatomist, gives enough evidence of also inclining toward it. The opinions of these men in such matters are worth as much as those of many other men. It is true that so far as I have seen, they do not extend this opinion so far as to say that corruption and death itself is also a transformation in the case of living beings devoid of a reasonable soul, as I hold it to be.... Nevertheless, sleep, which is an image of death; and ecstasy; and the envelopment of a silkworm in its cocoon, which can pass for death; the resuscitation of drowned flies by covering them with a certain dry powder (instead of which they would have died completely if left alone); the reviving of swallows which make their winter quarters in the reeds and are found without an appearance of life; and finally, the experiences of men frozen to death, drowned, or strangled, who have been brought to life ... all these things serve to confirm my opinion that these different states differ only in degree. If we do not have the means for bringing about resuscitation in other kinds of death, this is only because we do not know what must be done, or knowing it, our hands, our instruments, and our other remedies are inadequate, especially when the dissolution proceeds at once to the very small parts. Therefore we must not stop with the common conceptions of death or life, since we have both analogies and, what is more, firm arguments which prove the contrary. For I believe I have shown sufficiently that there must be entelechies if there are corporeal substances and that if we grant these entelechies or these souls, we must recognize that they are incapable of generation and destruction.

COMMENTARY

Individual substances are immortal: initiated with the start of cosmic history, they can perish only at its end. (See sec. 6.) But their participatory role in particular organisms is a matter of their programmatic coordination with other substances with which they can cooperate to produce higher-level organisms. But such micro/macro coordination is characteristic not of any system of substances whatsoever, but rather is an aspect of the lawful order of this best of possible worlds.

For Leibniz, the birth and death of organisms are matters of dissolution by way of decreased functional complexity: those higher-order organisms simply fall apart into their more rudimentary constituents. (See sec. 14.) Here, then, we have yet another example of his insistence on the continuity of all natural processes.

KEY WORDS:

birth/*génération*
death/*mort*
soul/*âme*
separation of the soul/ *séparation de l'ame*
growth/*accroissement*
diminution/*diminution*
unfolding/*développement*
enfolding/*enveloppement*

SECTION 74

74. Philosophers have been much perplexed about the origin of ⟨substantial⟩ forms, entelechies, or souls. But today, when we have learned from scientific studies of plants, insects, and animals, that the organic bodies of nature are never products of a chaos or decay, but always grow from seeds in which there was undoubtedly some *pre-formation*, it has been concluded that not only was the organic body already present before conception, but also the soul in this body and, in short, the animal itself, and that through its conception this animal has only been positioned for a great transformation so as to become an animal of a different kind. One even sees something like this apart from birth, as when larvae become flies and caterpillars become butterflies. (See *Theodicy*, Preface; secs. 86, 89, 90, 187, 188, 397, 403.)

74. Les Philosophes ont été fort embarassés sur l'origine des Formes, Entelechies, ou Ames; mais aujourd'huy, lorsqu'on s'est apperçû, par des recherches exactes faites sur les plantes, les insectes et les animaux, que les corps organiques de la nature ne sont jamais produits d'un chaos ou d'une putrefaction; mais toûjours par les semences, dans lesquelles il y avoit sans doute quelque preformation; *on a jugé que non seulement le corps organique y étoit déjà avant la conception, mais encore une Ame dans ce corps et en un mot l'animal même, et que par le moyen de la conception cet animal a été seulement disposé à une grande transformation pour devenir un animal d'une autre espèce. On voit même quelque chose d'approchant hors de la generation, comme lorsque les vers deviennent mouches, et que les chenilles deviennent papillons.* (Théodicée, Préface, ***5b et suiv.; secs. 86, 89, 90, 187, 188, 397, 403.)

(*Theodicy*, Preface; G VI, 40.) Mechanism is sufficient to produce the organic bodies of animals, without any need of other plastic natures, provided there be added thereto the *preformation* already completely organic in the seeds of the bodies that come into existence, contained in those of the bodies whence they spring, right back to the primary seeds. This could only proceed from the Author of things, infinitely powerful and infinitely wise, who, creating all in the beginning in due order, had *pre-established* there all order and artifice that was to be. There is no chaos in the inward nature of things, and there is organism everywhere in a matter whose disposition proceeds from God. More and more of it would come to light if we pressed closer our examination of the anatomy of bodies; and we should continue to observe it even if we could go on to infinity, like Nature, and make subdivision as continuous in our knowledge as Nature has made it in fact.

(*Theodicy,* sec. 86.) <There are> three opinions on the origin of the soul itself. The first is that of the *Pre-existence* of human souls in another world or in another life, where they had sinned and on that account had been condemned to this prison of the human body, an opinion of the Platonists which is attributed to Origen and which even to-day finds adherents. Henry More, an English scholar, advocated something like this dogma in a book written with that express purpose. Some of those who affirm this pre-existence have gone as far as metempsychosis. The younger van Helmont held this opinion, and the ingenious author of some metaphysical *Meditations,* published in 1678 under the name of William Wander, appears to have some leaning towards it. The second opinion is that of *Traduction,* as if the soul of children were engendered (*per traducem*) from the soul or souls of those from whom the body is engendered. St. Augustine inclined to this judgement the better to explain original sin. This doctrine is taught also by most of the theologians of the Augsburg Confession. Nevertheless it is not completely established among them, since the Universities of Jena and Helmstedt, and others besides, have long been opposed to it. The third opinion, and that most widely accepted to-day, is that of *Creation:* it is taught in the majority of the Christian Schools, but it is fraught with the greatest difficulty in respect of original sin.

(*Theodicy,* sec. 89) But traduction and eduction are equally inexplicable when it is a question of finding the origin of the soul. It is not the same with accidental forms, since they are only modifications of the substance, and their origin may be explained by eduction, that is, by variation of limitations, in the same way as the origin of shapes. But it is quite another matter when we are concerned with the origin of a substance, whose beginning and destruction are equally difficult to explain. Sennert and Sperling did not venture to admit the subsistence and the indestructibility of the souls of beasts or of other primitive forms, although they allowed that they were indivisible and immaterial. But the fact is that they confused indestructibility with immortality, whereby is understood in the case of man that not only the soul but also the personality subsists. In saying that the soul of man is immortal one implies the subsistence of what makes the identity of the person, something which retains its moral qualities, conserving the *consciousness,* or the reflective inward feeling of what it is: thus it is rendered susceptible to chastisement or reward. But this conservation of personality does not occur in the souls of beasts: that is why I prefer to say that they are imperishable rather than to call them immortal. Yet this misapprehension appears to have been the cause of a great inconsistency in the doctrine of the Thomists and of other good philosophers: they recognized the immateriality or indivisibility of all souls, without being willing to admit their indestructibility, greatly to the prejudice of the immortality of the human soul.

(*Theodicy*, sec. 90.) I consider that souls and simple substances altogether cannot begin except by creation, or end except by annihilation. Moreover, as the formation of organic animate bodies appears explicable in the order of nature only when one assumes a *preformation* already organic, I have thence inferred that what we call generation of an animal is only a transformation and augmentation. Thus, since the same body was already furnished with organs, it is to be supposed that it was already animate, and that it had the same soul: so I assume vice versa, from the conservation of the soul when once it is created, that the animal is also conserved, and that apparent death is only an enfolding, there being no likelihood that in the order of nature souls exist entirely separated from all body, or that what does not begin naturally can cease through natural forces.

(*Theodicy*, sec. 91.) It is of the essence of God's wisdom that all should be harmonious in his works, and that nature should be parallel with grace. It is thus my belief that those souls which one day shall be human souls, like those of other species, have been in the seed, and in the progenitors as far back as Adam, and have consequently existed since the beginning of things, always in a kind of organic body. On this point it seems that M. Swammerdam, Father Malebranche, M. Bayle, M. Pitcairne, M. Hartsoeker and numerous other very able persons share my opinion. This doctrine is also sufficiently confirmed by the microscope observations of M. Leeuwenhoek and other good observers. But it also for divers reasons appears likely to me that they existed then as sentient or animal souls only, endowed with perception and feeling, and devoid of reason. Further I believe that they remained in this state up to the time of the generation of the man to whom they were to belong, but that then they received reason, whether there be a natural means of raising a sentient soul to the degree of a reasoning soul (a thing I find it difficult to imagine) or whether God may have given reason to this soul through some special operation, or (if you will) by a kind of *transcreation*. This latter is easier to admit, inasmuch as revelation teaches much about other forms of immediate operation by God upon our souls. This explanation appears to remove the obstacles that beset this matter in philosophy or theology. For the difficulty of the origin of forms thus disappears completely; and besides it is much more appropriate to divine justice to give the soul, already corrupted *physically* or on the animal side by the sin of Adam, a new perfection which is reason, than to put a reasoning soul, by creation or otherwise, in a body wherein it is to be corrupted *morally*.

(*Theodicy*, sec. 187.) Strato maintained (according to Cicero's account) that this world had been formed such as it is by Nature or by a necessary cause devoid of cognition. I admit that that might be so, if God had so preformed matter as to cause such an effect by the laws of motion alone. But without God there would not even have been any reason for existence, and still less for any particular existence of things: thus Strato's system is not to be feared.

(*Theodicy*, sec. 188.) Nevertheless M. Bayle is in difficulties over this: he will not admit plastic natures devoid of cognition, which Mr. Cudworth and others had introduced, for fear that the modern Stratonists, that is, the Spinozists, take advantage of it. This has involved him in disputes with M. le Clerc. Under the influence of this error, that a non-intelligent cause can produce nothing where contrivance appears, he is far from conceding to me that *preformation* which produces naturally the organs of animals, and *the system of a harmony pre-established by God* in bodies, to make them respond in accordance with their own laws to the thoughts and the wills of souls. But it ought to have been taken into account that this non-intelligent cause, which produces such beautiful things in the grains and seeds of plants and animals, and effects the actions of bodies as the will ordains them, was formed by the hand of God: and God is infinitely more skilful than a watchmaker, who himself makes machines and automata that are capable of producing as wonderful effects as if they possessed intelligence.

(*Theodicy*, sec. 397.) I have shown already (sec. 86 *seqq.*) that souls cannot spring up naturally, or be derived from one another, and that it is necessary that ours either be created or be pre-existent. I have even pointed out a certain middle way between a creation and an entire pre-existence. I find it appropriate to say that the soul preexisting in the seeds from the beginning of things was only sentient, but that it was elevated to the superior degree, which is that of reason, when the man to whom this soul should belong was conceived, and when the organic body, always accompanying this soul from the beginning, but under many changes, was determined for forming the human body. I considered also that one might attribute this elevation of the sentient soul (which makes it reach a more sublime degree of being, namely reason) to the extraordinary operation of God. Nevertheless it will be well to add that I would dispense with miracles in the generating of man, as in that of the other animals. It will be possible to explain that, if one imagines that in this great number of souls and of animals, or at least organic bodies which are in the seeds, those souls alone which are destined to attain one day to human nature contain the reason that shall appear therein one day, and the organic bodies of these souls alone are preformed and predisposed to assume one day the human shape, while the other small animals or seminal living beings, in which no such thing is pre-established, are essentially different from them and possessed only of an inferior nature. This production is a kind of *traduction*, but more manageable than that kind which is commonly taught: it does not derive the soul from the soul, but only the animate from an animate, and it avoids the repeated miracles of a new creation, which would cause a new and pure soul to enter the body that must corrupt it.

(*Theodicy*, sec. 403.) The foetus forms itself in the animal, and a thousand other wonders of nature are produced by a certain *instinct* that God has placed there, that is by virtue of *divine preformation*, which has made these admirable automata, adapted to produce mechanically such beautiful effects. Even so it is easy to believe that the soul is a spiritual automaton still more admirable, and that it is through divine preformation that it produces these beautiful ideas, wherein our will has no part and to which our art cannot attain. The operation of spiritual automata, that is of souls, is not mechanical, but it contains in the highest degree all that is beautiful in mechanism. The movements which are developed in bodies are concentrated in the soul by representation as in an ideal world, which expresses the laws of the actual world and their consequences, but with this difference from the perfect ideal world which is in God, that most of the perceptions in the other substances embrace the whole universe in its confused perceptions or sensations, and that the succession of these perceptions is regulated by the particular nature of this substance, but in a manner which always expresses all the nature in the universe; and every present perception leads to a new perception, just as every movement that it represents leads to a another movement.

(PNG, sec. 6.) The investigations of the moderns have taught us, and reason confirms them, that the living beings whose organs are known to us, that is, plants and animals, do not come from putrefaction or chaos, as the ancients believed, but from *preformed* seeds, and therefore from the transformation of living beings existing prior to them. There are little animals in the seeds of large animals, which assume a new vesture in conception, which they appropriate and which provides them with a method of nourishment and growth, so that they may emerge into a greater stage and propagate the large animal. It is true that the souls of human spermatic animals are not rational and become so only when conception determines them for human nature.

(G VI, 533; Loemker, p. 557; "On the Doctrine of a Single Universal Spirit" [1702].) Nature shows us the transformation of caterpillars and other insects, for flies too come from worms, to help us grasp that there are transformations everywhere. Our experiments on insects have destroyed the popular notion that these animals are reproduced through nourishment, without propagation. Nature has likewise also given us, in birds, a sample of how all animals are generated by means of eggs, a fact which the new discoveries have now made us accept. There are also microscopic observations which have shown that the butterfly is merely a development of the caterpillar, but especially that seeds already contain the formed plant or animal, although it still needs transformation and nourishment, or growth, to become an animal of the kind which our ordinary senses can observe. And since even the smallest insects reproduce by the propagation of their kind, one must conclude the same to be true for these little seminal animals, that is, that they themselves come from other still smaller seminal animals, and thus have originated only with the world. This agrees well with the Holy Scriptures, which suggest that there were seeds in the beginning.

(G VI, 543–44; Loemker, p. 589; "On Vital Principles and Plastic Natures" [1705].) Very exact observers have noted before now that it is doubtful that an entirely new animal is ever produced but that living animals as well as plants already exist in miniature in the seeds before conception. Assuming this doctrine to be true, we may reasonably conclude that what does not begin to live does not stop living either and that death, like generation, is only the transformation of the same animal, which is sometimes augmented and sometimes diminished. Thus we discover the marvels of divine artifice even where they have never been thought of. For since the mechanisms of nature are mechanisms down to their smallest parts, they are indestructible, since smaller machines are enfolded in greater machines into infinity. Thus one finds himself forced to maintain at the same time both the pre-existence of the soul with that of the animal and also the subsistence of the animal with that of the soul. . . . The laws of mechanism by themselves could not form an animal where there is nothing already organized. I find that he is right in opposing what certain ancients have sensed on the subject, and also Descartes's *Traité de l'homme*, whose man costs so little to form but also so little resembles a true man. I strengthen this opinion of Cudworth's with the consideration that if matter is arranged by divine wisdom, it must be essentially organized throughout and that there must thus be machines in the parts of the natural machine into infinity, so many enveloping structures and so many organic bodies enveloped, one within the other, that one can never produce any organic body entirely anew and without any performation, nor any more destroy entirely an animal which already exists. So I have no need to resort, as does Cudworth, to certain immaterial *plastic natures* . . . because this preformation and this infinitely complex organism provide me with material plastic natures that meet the need. Immaterial plastic natures, by contrast, are as unnecessary as they are incapable of satisfying it. For since animals are never formed naturally from an inorganic mass, the mechanism, though incapable of producing their infinitely varied organs anew, can at least draw them out of pre-existing organic bodies by a process of development and transformation. However, those who make use of plastic natures, whether material or immaterial, by no means weaken the proof for the existence of God drawn from the wonders of nature, which appear with particular force in the structure of animals, assuming that the defenders of immaterial plastic natures add to them a particular guidance by God, and assuming that those who make use, as I do, of a material cause agree that the plastic mechanism supports not only a continual preformation but also an original divine pre-establishment. In whatever way one interprets this, therefore, one cannot escape the divine existence in seeking to explain these wonders which have always been admired, but which have never been shown as well as in my system.

COMMENTARY

The principal exponent of the preformation theory was Leibniz's older contemporary Anton van Leeuwenhoek (1632–1723), the microscopist who discovered spermatozoa. Leibniz, encouraged by these observational investigations, was convinced of the continuity of organic life. He maintained that organisms are never initiated *de novo* but always preexist in some more seminal, rudimentary form. (He thus held on largely metaphysical grounds the thesis that life comes only from life, for which Pasteur provided much empirical evidence.) The biological doctrine of spermatic germination, just like the psychological doctrine of the unconscious, is tailor-made for Leibniz's doctrine of the continuity of all natural process.

Robert Latta explained the historical background as follows.

> Immediately before the time of Leibniz, the origin of life in the individual plant, animal, or man was explained either by a theory of traduction or by a theory of eduction. According to the theory of traduction, the "form" of the offspring comes from the parental "form" or "forms" in the same way as the body of the offspring comes from the parental body or bodies. According to the theory of eduction, on the other hand, life comes from inorganic matter, from "chaos or putrefaction." Eduction thus corresponds to what we now call "spontaneous generation." According to the theory of preformation, adopted by Leibniz, the germ contains in miniature the whole plant or animal, point for point, and accordingly the "form" of the plant or animal exists in the spermatozoon in a contracted or "enveloped" state, and it has existed since the beginning of time. For, as we have seen (in sec. 65), there is no limit to the smallness of things, and even a spermatozoon may contain an indefinite number of other living beings. This theory of preformation, which was based on the microscopic investigations

of Malpighi and Leuwenhoek, has now been entirely abandoned, as the result of more thorough observations. (Latta, p. 260n.)

KEY WORDS:

philosophers/*philosophes*
origin/*origine*
(substantial) forms/*formes*
entelechies/*entéléchies*
souls/*âmes*
body/*corps*
plants and animals/*plantes et animaux*
seeds/*semences*
chaos/*chaos*
decay/*putréfaction*
birth/*génération*
pre-formation/*préformation*
species/*espèce*
organic body/*corps organique*
conception/*conception*
transformation/*transformation*
generation/*génération*

SECTION 75

75. The *animals*, some of which are raised through conception to the level of the highest animals, may be called *spermatics*. But those among them which are more typical, that is, the majority, are born, multiply, and are destroyed just like the higher animals, and it is only a few specially chosen ones (the "elect") that achieve a larger role.

75. Les animaux, *dont quelques uns sont élevés au degré des plus grands animaux, par le moyen de la conception, peuvent être appellés* spermatiques; *mais ceux d'entre eux qui demeurent dans leur espece, c'est à dire la plus part, naissent, se multiplient et sont détruits comme les grands animaux, et il n'y a qu'un petit nombre d'Elûs, qui passe à un plus grand theatre.*

(PNG, sec. 6.) Just as animals in general are not completely born in conception or *generation*, moreover, neither do they completely perish in what we call *death*, for it is reasonable that what has no natural beginning also has no end within the order of nature. Thus, abandoning their masks or their rags, they merely return, but to a finer stage, on which, however, they can be as sensitive and as well ordered as on the larger one. And what has been said about grosser animals takes place also in the generation and death of spermatic animals themselves, that is, they are the enlargements of other smaller spermatic animals, in proportion to which they may be considered large, for everything in nature proceeds to infinity.

(G. Math. III, 565; to John Bernoulli [1699].) Concerning the human soul I dare not assert anything as to its origin nor as to its state after death, because rational or intelligent souls, such as ours is, having been so fashioned that they have a peculiar relation to the image of God, are governed by very different laws from those to which souls without understanding are subject.

COMMENTARY

Some lower organisms arise through asexual cell-division; others reproduce through a conception engendered by sexual fertilization. But all animals, all developed organisms, are regarded by Leibniz as *spermatic* in that all contain in embryo, as it were, the potential for higher things. However, only in the "elect" animals of the highest order, that is, in humans, is the greatest potential of animals realized—the potential for a conscious, reasoning, conceptualizing mind. (Compare sec. 82 regarding the election of those souls that come to play the role of spirits.)

KEY WORDS:

animals/*animaux*
conception/*conception*
spermatics/*spermatiques*
species/*espèce*
to be born/*naître*
to be destroyed/*être détruit*
elect/*élû*

SECTION 76

76. Yet this is only half of the truth. I have therefore concluded that if an animal never begins by natural means, it does not end by natural means either. Not only will there be no real birth, but also no total destruction, nor death in the strict sense. And these reasonings, made *a posteriori* and drawn from experience, agree perfectly with principles deduced *a priori*, as above <in Sect. 73>. (See *Theodicy*, sec. 90.)

76. *Mais ce n'étoit que la moitié de la vérité: j'ai donc jugé que, si l'animal ne commence jamais naturellement, il ne finit pas naturellement non plus; et que non seulement il n'y aura point de generation, mais encore point de destruction entière, ni mort prise à la rigueur. Et ces raisonnemens faits* a posteriori *et tirés des experiences s'accordent parfaitement avec principes deduits* a priori *comme ci-dessus.* (Théodicée, sec. 90.)

(*Theodicy*, sec. 90.) I consider that souls and simple substances altogether cannot begin except by creation, or end except by annihilation. Moreover, as the formation of organic animate bodies appears explicable in the order of nature only when one assumes a *preformation* already organic, I have thence inferred that what we call generation of an animal is only a transformation and augmentation. Thus, since the same body was already furnished with organs, it is to be supposed that it was already animate, and that it had the same soul: so I assume *vice versa*, from the conservation of the soul when once it is created, that the animal is also conserved, and that apparent death is only an enfolding, there being no likelihood that in the order of nature souls exist entirely separated from all body, or that what does not begin naturally can cease through natural forces.

(PNG, sec. 6.) Not only souls, therefore, but animals as well, cannot be generated or perish; they are only developed, enveloped, reclothed, stripped, transformed. Souls never leave the whole of their bodies and do not pass from one body to another entirely new to them. Thus there is no *metempsychosis*, though there is *metamorphosis*. Animals change, take on, and put off, only parts; in nutrition this takes place little by little and through minute, insensible particles, but continually, while in conception or in death, where much is acquired or lost all at once, it occurs suddenly and noticeably but infrequently.

(NS, sec. 6.) We may wonder whether they ⟨i.e., souls⟩ do not pass from body to body. This would be *metempsychosis*, somewhat like the transmission of motion and of species in which some philosophers have believed. But such a fancy is far from the nature of things. There is no such transfer; at this point the *transformations* of Swammerdam, Malpighi, and Leeuwenhoek, the best observers of our times, have come to my aid and led me to admit the more readily that animals and all other organized substances do not at all begin when we believe them to and that their apparent generation is merely a development and a form of augmentation.

(G II, 123; Loemker, p. 345; to Arnauld [1687].) There is nothing more natural than to think that whatever has no beginning will also never perish. When one recognizes that all generation is but the increase and development of an animal which is already formed, it is easy to be persuaded that corruption or death is nothing but the diminution and involution of an animal which does not cease to subsist and to remain alive and organized. It is not as easy, it is true, to make this credible by means of particular observation as is the case in generation, but the reason is obvious; it is because generation proceeds in a natural manner, little by little, so that we have leisure to observe it, but death is a sudden reverse by a leap (*per saltum*), a return all at once to parts which are too small for us, because death ordinarily occurs in too violent a way to permit us to observe the details of the retrogression. . . . Nevertheless, sleep, which is an image of death; and ecstasies; and the envelopment of a silkworm in its cocoon, which can pass for death; the resuscitation of drowned flies by covering them with a certain dry powder (instead of which they would have died completely if left alone); the reviving of swallows which make their winter quarters in the reeds and are found without an appearance of life; and finally, the experiences of men frozen to death, drowned, or strangled, who have been brought back to life, about which a man of discernment has recently written a book in German, giving examples from his own experience and urging people who are confronted with such cases to make greater efforts to revive them than is usually done.

COMMENTARY

Leibniz does not claim that an animal is indestructible as a member of its species; that, say, a dog is immortal as a dog—as the particular animal it is. Rather, it is indestructible *as an organism:* the material of the dog's body will always be organic. And its dominant monad or entelechy will always retain the *potential* of functioning at that higher level.

On the distinction between *a priori* and *a posteriori* see the commentary on section 45. A salient and characteristic feature of his philosophy is reflected in Leibniz's insistence on the harmonization of the metaphysical *a priori* and the empirical *a posteriori*—in that the scientific laws of nature must concretize and illustrate the operation of underlying metaphysical principles.

KEY WORDS:

animal/*animal*
to begin naturally/*commencer naturellement*
to end naturally/*finir naturellement*
generation/*génération*
destruction/*destruction*
death/*mort*
experience/*expérience*
a priori principles/*principes a priori*
a posteriori/*a posteriori*

SECTION 77

77. Thus we can say that not only the soul, that mirror of an indestructible universe, is indestructible, but also the animal itself, although its bodily mechanism may often perish in part, and leave off or take on organic coverings.

77. Ainsi on peut dire que non seulement l'Ame (miroir d'un univers indestructible) est indestructible, mais encore l'animal même, quoi que sa Machine perisse souvent en partie, et quitte ou prenne des depouilles organiques.

(PNG, sec. 6.) Not only souls, therefore, but animals as well, cannot be generated or perish; they are only developed, enveloped, reclothed, stripped, transformed. Souls never leave the whole of their bodies and do not pass from one body to another entirely new to them. Thus there is no *metempsychosis*, though there is *metamorphosis*. Animals change, take on, and put off, only parts; in nutrition this takes place little by little and through minute, insensible particles, but continually, while in conception or in death, where much is acquired or lost all at once, it occurs suddenly and noticeably but infrequently.

(PNG, sec. 12.) It follows also from the perfection of the supreme Author, not only that the order of the entire universe is the most perfect possible, but also that each living mirror which represents the universe according to its own point of view, that is, each *monad* or each substantial center, must have its perceptions and its appetites regulated in the best way compatible with all the rest. From this it also follows that souls, that is to say, the most dominant monads, or rather animals themselves, cannot fail to awake from the state of stupor into which death or some other accident may place them.

(NS, sec. 8.) Rational souls, however, follow much more elevated laws and are exempt from everything which might make them lose the quality of citizens of the society of minds, since God has provided so well that no changes in matter can make them lose the moral qualities of their personality. And one can say that everything tends to the perfection not merely of the universe in general but also of these created beings in particular.

(DM, sec. 9) Furthermore every substance is like an entire world and like a mirror of God, or indeed of the whole world which it portrays, each one in its own fashion; almost as the same city is variously represented according to the various situations of him who is regarding it. Thus the universe is multiplied in some sort as many times as there are substances, and the glory of God is multiplied in the same way by as many wholly different representations of his works. It can indeed be said that every substance bears in some sort the character of God's infinite wisdom and omnipotence, and imitates him as much as it is able to; for it expresses, although confusedly, all that happens in the universe, past, present and future, deriving thus a certain resemblance to an infinite perception or power of knowing.

COMMENTARY

As Leibniz sees it, creatures shed their bodily materials "as a snake casts off its old skin" (G VII, 544). The stuff of an animal's physical body is constantly renewed through the utilization of nourishment and the disposal of wastes. It is the continuing operation of a single dominant monad that assures the ongoing identity of the organism. Any animal's ongoing existence as an organism of some sort is thus assured for all of time.

The word *machine* was standardly used by seventeenth century philosophers to refer to the *bodily mechanism* of an animal (humans included). Leibniz sees the organic materials of animal bodies as transmissible from one to another (for example, when they eat one another), but always only at a lower level of operation. (When one fish eats another, the latter's dominant monad need play no special role in the former's body. Its *potential* for higher-level operation however, remains.)

KEY WORDS:

soul/*âme*
mirror of the universe/*miroir de l'univers*
indestructible/*indestructible*
to perish/*périr*
animal/*animal*
machine (i.e., bodily mechanism)/*machine*
organic coverings/*dépouilles organiques*

SECTION 78

78. These principles have given me a way to explain naturally the union, or rather the conformity of the soul and the organic body. The soul follows its own laws and the body likewise follows its own; and they agree by virtue of the *pre-established harmony* among all substances, because they are all rep-

resentations of one selfsame universe. (See *Theodicy*, Preface; secs. 340, 352, 353, 358.)

78. Ces principes m'ont donné moyen d'expliquer naturellement l'union ou bien la conformité de l'Ame et du corps organique. L'ame suit ses propres loix, et le corps aussi les siennes; et ils se rencontrent en vertu de l'harmonie préétablie entre toutes les substances, puisqu'elles sont toutes des representations d'un même univers. (Théodicée, Préface, ***6; secs. 340,352,353,358.)

(*Theodicy*, Preface; G VI, 40–42.) Unless it be said God forms organic bodies himself by a perpetual miracle, or that he has entrusted this care to intelligences whose power and knowledge are almost divine, we must hold the opinion that God *preformed* things in such sort that new organisms are only a mechanical consequence of a preceding organic constitution. Even so do butterflies come out of silkworms, an instance where M. Swammerdam has shown that there is nothing but development. And I would have added that nothing is better qualified than the preformation of plants and of animals to confirm my System of Pre-established Harmony between the soul and the body. For in this the body is prompted by its original constitution to carry out with the help of external things all that it does in accordance with the will of the soul. So the seeds by their original constitution carry out naturally the intentions of God, by an artifice greater still than that which causes our body to perform everything in conformity with our will. And since M. Bayle himself deems with reason that there is more artifice in the organism of animals than in the most beautiful poem in the world or in the most admirable invention whereof the human mind is capable, it follows that my system of the connexion between the body and the soul is as intelligible as the general opinion on the formation of animals. For this opinion (which appears to me true) states in effect that the wisdom of God has so made Nature that it is competent in virtue of its laws to form animals; I explain this opinion and throw more light upon the possibility of it through the system of preformation. Whereafter there will be no cause for surprise that God has so made the body that by virtue of its own laws it can carry out the intentions of the reasoning soul: for all that the reasoning soul can demand of the body is less difficult than the organization which God has demanded of the seeds. M. Bayle says (*Reply to the Questions of a Provincial*, ch. 182, p. 1294) that it is only very recently that there have been people who have understood that the foundation of living bodies cannot be a natural process. This he could say also (in accordance with his principles) of the communication between the soul and the body, since God effects this whole communication in the system of occasional causes to which this author subscribes. But I admit the supernatural here only in the beginning of things, in respect of the first formation of animals or in respect of the original constitution of pre-established harmony between the soul and the body. Once that has come to pass, I hold that the formation of animals and the relation between the soul and the body are something as natural now as the other most ordinary operations of Nature.

(*Theodicy*, sec. 340.) <M. Bayle> is persuaded, with the modern Cartesians, that the ideas of the perceptible qualities that God gives (according to them) to the soul, occasioned by movements of the body, have nothing representing these movements or resembling them. Accordingly it was a purely arbitrary act on God's part to give us the ideas of heat, cold, light and other qualities which we experience, rather than to give us quite different ideas occasioned in the same way. I have often wondered that people so talented should have been capable of relishing notions so unphilosophic and so contrary to the fundamental maxims of reason. For nothing gives clearer indication of the imperfection of a philosophy than the necessity experienced by the philosopher to confess that something comes to pass, in accordance with his system, for which there is no reason.

(*Theodicy*, sec. 352.) One must then admit that it depended altogether upon God's freedom to combine particular thoughts of our soul with particular modifications of our body, even when he had once established all the laws for the action of bodies one upon another. Whence it results that there is in the universe no portion of matter which by its proximity can harm us, save when God wills it.

(*Theodicy*, sec. 353.) I agree with M. Bayle that God could have so ordered bodies and souls on this globe of earth, whether by ways of nature or by extraordinary graces, that it would have been a perpetual paradise and a foretaste of the celestial state of the blessed. There is no reason why there should not be worlds happier than ours; but God had good reasons for willing that ours should be such as it is. Nevertheless, in order to prove that a better state would have been possible here, M. Bayle had no need to resort to the system of occasional causes: it abounds in miracles and in hypotheses for which their very originators confess there is no justification; and these are two defects such as will most of all estrange a system from true philosophy. It is a cause for surprise, in the first place, that M. Bayle did not bethink himself of the System of Preestablished Harmony which he had examined before, and which for this matter was so opportune. But as in this system all is connected and harmonious, all following from reasons and nothing being left incomplete or exposed to the rash discretion of perfect indifference, it seems that it was not pleasing to M. Bayle: for he was here somewhat biassed in favour of such indifference.

(*Theodicy*, secs. 358–59.) "Why has God established laws that give rise to so many difficulties?" philosophers who are somewhat precise will say. "Could he not have established others of a kind not subject to any defects? And to cut the matter short, how comes it that he has prescribed laws for himself? Why does he not act without general laws, in accordance with all his power and all his goodness?" . . . <However,> the laws God established were the most excellent that could be established. <Were this writer accurate,> he would have acknowledged, at the same time, that God could not have refrained from establishing laws and following rules, because laws and rules are what makes order and beauty; that to act without rules would be to act without reason; and that because God called into action all his goodness the exercise of his omnipotence was consistent with the laws of wisdom, to secure as much good as was possible of attainment.

(PNG, sec. 3.) Each monad is a living mirror, or a mirror endowed with an internal action that represents the universe according to its point of view and is regulated as completely as is the universe itself. The perceptions in the monad arise from each other according to the laws of the appetites or of the *final causes of good and of evil*, which consist in observable perceptions, whether regulated or unregulated, in the same way that bodily changes and external phenomena arise from each other according to the laws of *efficient causality*, that is, of motions. Thus there is a perfect *harmony* between the perceptions of the monad and the motions of the body, pre-established from the beginning between the system of efficient causes and that of final causes. It is in this that the accord and the physical union of soul and body consist, without either one being able to change the laws of the other.

(NE, p. 55.) This is a marvellous pre-established harmony between the soul and the body, and indeed amongst all the monads or simple substances, which takes the place of an untenable influence of one on another and, in the opinion of the author of the finest of dictionaries <i.e., Bayle>, exalts the greatness of divine perfection beyond anything previously conceived.

(NE, p. 440.) I attribute perception to all this infinity of beings: each of them is like an animal, endowed with a soul (or some comparable active principle which makes it a true unity), along with whatever the being needs in order to be passive, and endowed with an organic body. Now, these beings have received their nature which is active as well as passive (i.e. have received both their immaterial and their material features) from a universal and supreme cause; for otherwise, as our author has so well said, their mutual independence would have made it impossible for them ever to have produced this order, this harmony, this beauty that we find in nature. But this argument, which appears to have only moral certainty, is brought to a state of absolute metaphysical necessity by the new kind of harmony. Here is how: each of these souls expresses in its own manner what occurs outside itself, and it cannot do so through any influence of other particular beings (or, to put it a better way, it has to draw up this expression from the depths of its own nature); and so necessarily each soul must have received this nature—this inner source of the expressions of what lies without—from a universal cause, upon which all of these beings depend and which brings it about that each of them perfectly agrees with and corresponds to the others. That could not occur without infinite knowledge and power. And great ingenuity would be needed, especially, to bring about the spontaneous agreement of the machine with the actions of the rational soul; so great, indeed, that a distinguished writer <Bayle> who offered some objections in his wonderful *Dictionary* came close to doubting whether *all possible* wisdom would suffice for the task—for he said that the wisdom of God did not appear to him to be more than was needed for such a result.

(NS, sec. 15.) This hypothesis <of pre-established harmony> is entirely possible. For why should God be unable to give to substance in the beginning a nature or internal force which enables it to produce in regular order—as in an *automaton that is spiritual or formal but free* in the case of that substance which has a share of reason—everything which is to happen to it, that is, all the appearances or expressions which it is to have, and this without the help of any created being? Especially since the nature of substance necessarily demands and essentially involves progress or change and would have no force of action without it. And since it is the nature of the soul to represent the universe in a very exact way, though with relative degrees of distinctness, the sequence of representations which the soul produces will correspond naturally to the sequence of changes in the universe itself. So the body, in turn, has also been adapted to the soul to fit those situations in which the soul is thought of as acting externally. This is all the more reasonable inasmuch as bodies are made solely for the spirits themselves, who are capable of entering into a society with God and of extolling his glory. Thus as soon as one sees the possibility of this *hypothesis of agreement*, one sees also that it is the most reasonable one and that it gives a wonderful idea of the harmony of the universe and of the perfection of the works of God.

(DM, sec. 33.) We can also see the explanation of that great mystery "the union of the soul and the body," that is to say how it comes about that the passions and actions of the one are accompanied by the actions and passions or else the appropriate phenomena of the other. For it is not possible to conceive how one can have an influence upon the other and it is unreasonable to have recourse at once to the extraordinary intervention of the universal cause in an ordinary and particular case. The following, however, is the true explanation. We have said that everything which happens to a soul or to any substance is a consequence of its concept; hence the idea itself or the essence of the soul brings it about that all of its appearances or perceptions should be born out of its nature and precisely in such a way that they correspond of themselves to that which happens in the universe at large, but more particularly and more perfectly to that which happens in the body associated with it, because it is in a particular way and only for a certain time according to the relation of other bodies to its own body that the soul expresses the state of the universe. This last fact enables us to see how our body belongs to us, without, however, being attached to our essence. I believe that those who are careful thinkers will decide favorably for our principles because of this single reason, viz., that they are able to see in what consists the relation between the soul and the body, a parallelism which appears inexplicable in any other way.

(NS, sec. 12.) But when I began to think about the union of the soul with the body, it was like casting me back into the open sea, for I found no way to explain how the body causes anything to take place in the soul, or vice versa, or how one substance can communicate with another created substance. So far as we can know from his writings, Descartes gave up the struggle over this problem. But seeing that the common opinion is inconceivable, his disciples concluded that we sense the qualities of bodies because God causes thoughts to arise in our soul on the occasion of material movements and that when our soul in its turn wishes to move the body, God moves the body for it. And since the communication of motion also seemed inconceivable to them, they believed that God imparts motion to a body on the occasion of the motion of another body. This they call the *System of Occasional Causes*; it has had great vogue as a result of the beautiful reflections of <Malebranche,> the author of the *Récherche de la vérité*. . . . It is quite true that speaking with metaphysical rigor, there is no real influence of one created substance upon another and that all things, with all their reality, are continually produced by the power of God. But problems are not solved merely by making use of a general cause and calling in what is called the *deus ex machina*. To do this without offering any other explanation drawn from the order of secondary causes is, properly speaking, to have recourse to miracle. In philosophy we must try to give a reason which will show how things are brought about by the Divine Wisdom in conformity with the particular concept of the subject in question.

(G I, 382; to Foucher [1686].) I believe that every individual substance expresses the whole universe in its own way, and that its following state is a consequence (though often a free one) of its preceding state, as if there were nothing but God and it in the world; but as all substances are a continual production of the sovereign Being, and express the same universe or the same phenomena, they agree exactly with each other.

(G II, 58; Loemker, p. 338; to Arnauld [1686].) Only the hypothesis of the concomitance or agreement of substances *inter se* explains everything in a manner which is conceivable and worthy of God; it is even demonstrative and inevitable, in my opinion, according to the proposition which we have just established <that in every proposition the notion of the predicate is contained in that of the subject>.... God created the soul from the very start in such a manner that for the ordinary events it has no need of these interventions, and whatever happens to the soul comes from its own being, without any necessity, on its part, of accommodation in the sequence of events to the body, any more than there is of the body's accommodating itself to the soul. Each one follows its laws, the one acts freely, the other without choice, and they accord with one another in the same phenomena. The soul is nevertheless the form of its body, because it expresses the phenomena of all other bodies according to their relation to its own.

(G II, 68; to Hessen-Rheinfels [1686].) The hypothesis of concomitance is a consequence of the notion which I have of substance. For according to me the individual notion of a substance involves all that will ever happen to it.

(G II, 93; to Arnauld [1687].) To make myself better understood I will add that the activities of the mind change nothing at all in the nature of the body, nor the body in that of the mind; and I will also add that neither does God change anything on the occasion of their action except when he performs a miracle. In my opinion, things are so concerted together that the mind never desires anything efficaciously excepting when the body is ready to accomplish it in virtue of its own laws and forces; while, according to the authors of occasional causes, God changes the laws of the body on the occasion of the action of the soul and, *vice versa*.

(G II, 95; to Arnauld [1687].) To employ a comparison, I will say in regard to this universal concomitance, which I hold to be true, that it is like several bands of musicians or choirs separately taking up their parts and placed in such a way that they neither see nor hear one another, though they nevertheless agree perfectly in following their notes, each one his own, in such a way that he who hears the whole finds in it a wonderful harmony much more surprising than if there were a connection between the performers.

(G II, 122; Loemker, p. 345; to Arnauld [1687].) Those who perceive that there is an infinity of small animals in the least drop of water, as the experiments of M. Leewenhoeck have shown, and who do not find it strange that matter should be entirely filled with animated substances, will not find it strange either that there should be something animated in the ashes themselves, and that fire can transform an animal and reduce it, without, however, entirely destroying it.

(G II, 136; to Arnauld [1690].) Each substance expresses the whole universe, but some more distinctly than others, especially each in regard to certain things, and according to its point of view. The union of soul and body, and even the operation of one substance on another, consists only in this perfect mutual agreement, purposely established by the order of the first creation, in virtue of which each substance, following its own laws, falls in with what the others demand, and the operations of the one thus follow or accompany the operation or change of the other.

(G II, 226; to de Volder [1701].) Certainly, in my opinion, there is nothing in the universe of creatures which does not need, for its perfect concept, the concept of every other thing in the universe of things, since everything influences everything else, so that if it were taken away or supposed different, all the things in the world would have been different from those that now are.

(G III, 143; to Basagne [1706].) It is true there is miracle in my system of pre-established Harmony, and that God enters into it extraordinarily, but it is only in the beginning of things, after which everything goes its own way in the phenomena of nature, according to the laws of souls and bodies.

(G III, 144; to Basagne [1706].) It seems to me that I may say that my hypothesis (concerning the pre-established Harmony) is not gratuitous, since I believe I have made it appear that there are only three possible hypotheses <namely, *influxus physicus*, occasionalism, and the pre-established harmony>, and that only mine is at once intelligible and natural; but it can even be proved *a priori*.

(G IV, 498–500; to Basagne [1696].) Imagine two clocks or watches which are in perfect agreement. Now this can happen in *three ways*. The *first* is that of a natural influence. This is the way with which Mr. Huygens experimented, with results that greatly surprised him. He suspended two pendulums from the same piece of wood. The continued strokes of the pendulums transmitted similar vibrations to the particles of wood, but these vibrations could not continue in their own frequency without interfering with each other, at least when the two pendulums did not beat together. The result, by a kind of miracle, was that even when their strokes had been intentionally disturbed, they came to beat together again, somewhat like two strings tuned to each other. The *second* way of making two clocks, even poor ones, agree always is to assign a skilled craftsman to them who adjusts them and constantly sets them in agreement. The *third* way is to construct these two timepieces at the beginning with such skill and accuracy that one can be assured of their subsequent agreement. Now put the soul and the body in the place of these two timepieces. Then their agreement or sympathy will also come about in one of these three ways. The *way of influence* is that of the common philosophy. But since it is impossible to conceive of material particles or of species or immaterial qualities which can pass from one of these substances into the other, this view must be rejected. The *way of assistance* is that of the system of occasional causes. But I hold that this makes a *deus ex machina* intervene in a natural and ordinary matter where reason requires that God should help only in the way in which he concurs in all other natural things. Thus there remains only my hypothesis, that is, the *way of preestablished harmony*, according to which God has made each of the two substances from the beginning in such a way that though each follows only its own laws which it has received with its being, each agrees throughout with the other, entirely as if they were mutually influenced or as if God were always putting forth his hand, beyond his general concurrence. . . . And assuming that God can do it, it is clear that this way is the most beautiful and the most worthy of him.

(G IV, 510; Loemker, p. 503; "On Nature Itself" [1698].) For who will doubt that the mind thinks and wills, that many thoughts and volitions are produced in us and by us, and that there is something spontaneous about us? To doubt this would be to deny human freedom and to thrust the cause of evil back to God but also to contradict the testimony of our internal experience and consciousness, by which we feel that what these opponents have transferred to God without even the appearance of a reason belongs to ourselves. But if we ascribe to our mind an inherent force of producing immanent actions or what is the same thing, of acting immanently, then nothing prevents the same force from residing in other souls or forms or if you prefer, in the natures of other substances. . . . Thus the *intercourse of substances* or of monads namely, arises not from an influence but from a consensus originating in their preformation by God, so that each one is adjusted to the outside while it follows the internal force and laws of its own nature. It is also in this that the *union of soul and body* consists.

(G VII, 311; "On Nature's Secrets" [ca. 1690].) Every substance has something of the infinite, in so far as it involves its cause, namely God; that is, it has some trace of omniscience and omnipotence. For in the perfect notion of each individual substance there are contained all its predicates, alike necessary and contingent, past, present, and future; nay each substance expresses the whole universe according to its situation and aspect, in so far as other things are referred to it; and hence it is necessary that some of our perceptions, even if they be clear, should be confused, since they involve things which are infinite, as do our perceptions of colour, heat, etc.

(G VII, 358; to Clarke, II.8 [1715].) I do not say the material world is a machine or watch that goes without God's interposition, and I have sufficiently insisted that the creation wants to be continually influenced by its creator. But I maintain it to be a watch that goes without wanting to be mended by him; otherwise we must say that God bethinks himself again. No, God has foreseen everything. He has provided a remedy for everything beforehand. There is in his works a harmony, a beauty, already pre-established.

(Couturat *Opuscules*, p. 525; Loemker, p. 269; Ariew & Garber, p. 33; "First Truths" [ca. 1685].) *If the diversity of soul and body be assumed, their union can be explained* from this without the common hypothesis of an *influx*, which is unintelligible, and without the hypothesis of occasional causes, which calls upon a God *ex machina*. For God has equipped both soul and body from the beginning with such great wisdom and workmanship that through the original constitution and essence of each, everything which happens in one corresponds perfectly to whatever happens in the other, just as if something had passed over from the one into the other. I call this the *hypothesis of concomitance*. This is true of all the substances in the whole universe but is not perceptible in all as it is in the soul and body.

COMMENTARY

In this pivotal section, Leibniz applies his theory of a pre-established harmony obtaining among all monadic operations (compare sec. 56) to the solution of the mind-body problem. The dominant mind-monad and the monads constituting its body agree in functioning—as Mark Twain asked, "When the body

is drunk, does the mind stay sober?" And they do so as part of the overall coordination of the behavior of all substances under the aegis of the universal
regulations of monadic comportment (i.e., natural laws).

The universal coördination of all monads that obtains by nature of their all
being variant representations of one selfsame universe thus harmonizes the
actions of souls (and spirits) on the one side and bodies on the other, and assures
the consonance of the "laws of mind" which govern our psychological doings
and the "laws of matter" which govern the physical operations of extra-mental
nature.

Leibniz regards his pre-established harmony as providing a *natural* explanation of mind-body coordination, in contrast to the view of the Occasionalists
like Malebranche who require the *deus ex machina* intervention of God, and
accordingly regard this coordination as the result of a perpetual miracle.

KEY WORDS:

principles/*principes*
to explain naturally/*expliquer naturellement*
pre-established harmony/*harmonie préétablie*
substance/*substance*
union of soul and body/*union de l'âme et du corps*
conformity/*conformité*
soul/*âme*
organic body/*corps organique*
laws/*lois*
representation/*représentation*
the universe/*l'univers*

SECTION 79

**79. Souls act according to the laws of final causes through appetition, ends,
and means. Bodies act according to the laws of efficient causes or of motions.
And the two realms, that of efficient causes and that of final causes, are harmonious with one another.**

*79. Les ames agissent selon les loix des causes finales par appetitions, fins
et moyens. Les corps agissent selon les loix des causes efficientes ou des
mouvemens. Et les deux regnes, celuy des causes efficientes et celuy des causes
finales, sont harmoniques entre eux.*

(PNG, sec. 3.) The perceptions in the monad arise from each other according
to the laws of the appetites or of the *final causes of good and of evil*, which
consist in observable perceptions, whether regulated or unregulated, in the
same way that bodily changes and external phenomena arise from each other
according to the laws of *efficient causality*, that is, of motions. Thus there is a
perfect *harmony* between the perceptions of the monad and the motions of the
body, pre-established from the beginning between the system of efficient causes
and that of final causes. It is in this that the accord and the physical union of

soul and body consist, without either one being able to change the laws of the other.

(PNG, sec. 11.) It is surprising that no reason can be given for the laws of motion which have been discovered in our own time, and part of which I myself have discovered, by a consideration of *efficient causes* or of matter alone. For I have found that we must have recourse to *final causes* and that these laws do not depend upon the *principle of necessity*, as to the truths of logic, arithmetic, and geometry, but upon the *principles of fitness*, that is to say, upon the choice of wisdom. This is one of the most effective and obvious proofs of the existence of God for those who can probe into these matters thoroughly.

(DM, sec. 13.) Whatever happens in conformity to these divine anticipations ⟨of God's universal foreknowledge⟩ is assured but not necessary and . . . if anyone were to do the contrary, he would not do anything impossible in itself, though it would be impossible ex hypothesi for it to happen. . . . For it will be found that the demonstration of the predicate of Caesar ⟨i.e., crossing the Rubicon etc.⟩ is not as absolute as that of numbers or of geometry but that it supposes the sequence of things which God has freely chosen and what is founded on the first decree of God and on the decree which God has made about human nature (following the primary one), which is that man shall do, though freely, that which appears to him to be best.

(DM, sec. 18.) It appears more and more clear that although all the particular phenomena of nature can be explained mathematically or mechanically by those who understand them, yet nevertheless, the general principles of corporeal nature and even of mechanics are metaphysical rather than geometric, and belong rather to certain indivisible forms or natures as the causes of the appearances, than to the corporeal mass or to extension. This reflection is able to reconcile the mechanical philosophy of the moderns with the circumspection of the intelligent and well-meaning persons who, with a certain justice, fear that we are becoming too far removed from immaterial beings and that we are thus prejudicing piety.

(G VII, 412; to Clarke, V.92 [1716].) It is true, that, according to me, the soul does not disturb the laws of the body, nor the body those of the soul; and that the soul and body do only agree together; the one acting freely, according to the rules of final causes; and the other acting mechanically, according to the laws of efficient causes. . . . For, every agent which acts according to final causes, is free, though it happens to agree with an agent acting only by efficient causes without knowledge, or mechanically; because God, foreseeing what the free cause would do, did from the beginning regulate the machine in such manner, that it cannot fail to agree with that free cause.

(G II, 57–58; Loemker, p. 338; to Arnauld [1686].) The hypothesis of occasional causes is not satisfactory, it seems to me, to a philosopher, because it introduces a sort of continuous miracle as though God at every moment was changing the laws of bodies on the occasions when minds had thoughts, or was changing the regular course of the thinking of the soul by exciting in it other thoughts on the occasion of a bodily movement; and in general as though God was interfering otherwise for the ordinary events of life than in preserving each substance in its course and in the laws established for it. Only the hypothesis of the concomitance or the agreement of substances among themselves therefore is able to explain these things in a manner wholly conceivable and worthy of God. And as this hypothesis alone is demonstrative and inevitable in my opinion, according to the proposition which we have just established, it seems also that it agrees better with the freedom of reasonable creatures than the hypothesis of impressions or of occasional causes. God created the soul from the very start in such a manner that for the ordinary events it has no need of these interventions, and whatever happens to the soul comes from its own being, without any necessity, on its part, of accommodation in the sequence of events to the body, any more than there is of the body's accommodating itself to the soul. Each one follows its laws, the one acts freely, the other without choice, and they accord with one another in the same phenomena. The soul is nevertheless the form of its body, because it expresses the phenomena of all other bodies according to their relation to its own.

(G IV, 391; "Animadversions Against Cartesian Principles" [1697].) I fully agree that all the particular phenomena of nature can be explained mechanically if we explore them enough and that we cannot understand the causes of material things on any other basis. But I hold nevertheless that we must also consider how these mechanical principles and general laws of nature themselves arise from higher principles . . . ; that there is something metaphysical in them, which is devoid of the concepts which the imagination offers, and which is to be referred to a subject void of extension. For, in addition to extension and its variations, there is in matter a force or power of action by which the transition is made from metaphysics to nature, and from material to immaterial things.

(G IV, 559; Loemker, p. 559; "Response to Bayle" [1702].) The body is made in such a way that the soul never makes any resolutions to which the movements of the body do not correspond; even the most abstract reasonings play their part in this by means of the characters which represent them to the imagination. In a word, so far as the details of phenomena are concerned, everything takes place in the body as if the evil doctrine of those who believe that the soul is material were true, or as if man himself were only a body or an automaton. And since this perception cannot be explained by figures and movements, it establishes the other half of my hypothesis and makes us recognize an indivisible substance in ourselves which must itself be the source of its phenomena. According to this second half of my hypothesis, therefore, everything occurs in the soul as if there were no body, just as everything occurs in the body as if there were no soul, according to the first half. And reason makes us conclude that other men have the same prerogative as we. Besides, I have frequently shown with regard to bodies themselves that although there are mechanical reasons for the details of phenomena, the final analysis of the laws of mechanics and the nature of substances compels us to resort to active indivisible principles. And the wonderful order which prevails here shows us that there is a universal principle whose intelligence is supreme as well as his power. . . . The pre-established harmony is a good interpreter of each to the other. This shows that our view combines what is good in the hypotheses of both Epicurus and Plato, of both the greatest materialists and the greatest idealists, and that there is nothing surprising here except only the supreme perfection of the ruling principle, which is now shown in its works to be far above all that we have believed until now. What wonder, then, that everything goes well and with precision, since all things work together and lead each other by the hand, if we first assume that the whole has been perfectly thought out. It would rather be the greatest of all wonders or better, the strangest of absurdities, if this vessel, designed to go so well, if this machine whose route has been plotted for all time, should fail in spite of the measures which God has taken. Our hypothesis with respect to corporeal mass should therefore not be compared to a vessel which brings itself to port but to the ferry boats which are attached to a cable across the river. It is like the theatrical machines and fireworks whose regularity we no longer find strange when we know how everything is done.

(G VI, 532; Loemker, p. 556; "On the Doctrine of a Single Universal Spirit" [1702].) I have carefully examined this matter and I have shown that there are really in the soul some materials of thoughts or objects of the understanding, which the external senses do not supply, namely the soul itself and its functions (*nihil est in intellectu quod non fuerit in sensu, nisi ipse intellectus*) ... but I find nevertheless, that there is never an abstract thought which is not accompanied by some material images or marks, and I have made out a perfect parallelism between what passes in the soul and what takes place in matter, having shown that the soul, with its functions, is something distinct from matter but yet is always accompanied by material organs, and also that the functions of the soul are always accompanied by functions of its organs, which must correspond to them, and that this is and always will be reciprocal.

(G VII, 321; Loemker, p. 365; "Distinguishing Real from Imaginary Phenomena" [ca. 1690].) And certainly there is nothing to prevent innumerable other minds from existing as well as ours, although not all possible minds exist. This I demonstrate from the fact that all existing things are interrelated (*inter se commercium habent*). However, minds of another nature than ours can be conceived which also are interrelated with ours here. That all existing things have this intercourse with each other can be proved, moreover, both from the fact that otherwise no one could say whether anything is taking place in existence now or not, so that there would be no truth or falsehood for such a proposition, which is absurd; but also because there are no extrinsic denominations, and no one becomes a widower in India by the death of his wife in Europe unless a real change occurs in him. For every predicate is in fact contained in the nature of a subject. Now, if some possible minds exist, the question is: Why not all? Furthermore, since all existents must be interrelated, there must be a cause of their interrelations; indeed, everything must necessarily express the same nature but in a different way. But the cause which leads all minds to have intercourse with each other or to express the same nature, and therefore to exist, is that cause which perfectly expresses the universe, namely God.

COMMENTARY

The two realms of the psychological and the physical harmonize because both root in exactly the same foundation: the all-pervasive pre-established harmony that prevails among all existing monads. It is this which aligns the perceptions and appetitions of a monad with the activities of its natural environment. Accordingly, the physical realm of mechanically operative efficient causes and the psychological realm of voluntaristically operative final causes accord with one another in complete coordination. Mind-body coordination simply constitutes no problem.

KEY WORDS:

souls/*âmes*
bodies/*corps*
appetition/*appétition*
ends and means/*fins et moyens*
laws/*lois*
motions/*mouvements*
realm/*règne*
final causes/*causes finales*
efficient causes/*causes efficientes*
to harmonize/*être harmonique*

SECTION 80

80. Descartes recognized that souls are wholly unable to impart force to bodies because there is always the same quantity of force in matter <i.e. the material world>. However, he believed that the soul could change the direction of <force in> bodies. But this was because people did not know in his time the law of nature which also maintains the conservation of the same total of directed force in matter. If he had recognized this, he would have hit upon my system of pre-established harmony. (See *Theodicy*, Preface; secs. 22, 59–61, 63, 66, 345–48, 354, 355).

80. *Des-Cartes a reconnu, que les Ames ne peuvent point donner de la force aux corps, parce qu'il y a toûjours la même quantité de la force dans la matière. Cependant il a crû que l'ame pouvoit changer la direction* des corps. Mais c'est parce qu'on n'a point sû de son temps la loy de la nature qui porte encor la conservation de la même direction totale dans la matière. S'il l'avoit remarquée, il seroit tombé dans mon Système de l'Harmonie préétablie.* (Theodicée, *Préface*, ****; *secs. 22, 59–61, 63, 66, 345 seqq., 354, 355.)*
    <*Note that *direction* is used here for *force directive = vis directiva*.>

(*Theodicy*, Preface; G VI 44.) In order to explain this marvel of the formation of animals, I made use of a Pre-established Harmony, that is to say, of the same means I had used to explain another marvel, namely the correspondence of soul with body. . . . <Bayle> was not yet disposed to believe that God, with all his power over Nature and with all the foreknowledge which he has of the contingencies that may arrive, could have so disposed things that by the laws of mechanics alone a vessel (for instance) should go to its port of destination without being steered during its passage by some intelligent guide. I was surprised to see that limits were placed on the power of God, without the adduction of any proof and without indication that there was any contradiction to be feared on the side of the object or any imperfection on God's side. Whereas I had shown before in my Rejoinder that even men often produce through automata something like the movements that come from reason, and that even a finite mind (but one far above ours) could accomplish what M. Bayle thinks impossible to the Divinity. Moreover, as God orders all things at once beforehand, the accuracy of the path of this vessel would be no more strange than that of a fuse passing along a cord in fireworks, since the whole disposition of things preserves a perfect harmony between them by means of their influence one upon the other. . . . I explain this opinion and throw more light upon the possibility of it through the system of preformation. Whereafter there will be no cause for surprise that God has so made the body that by virtue of its own laws it can carry out the intentions of the reasoning soul: for all that the reasoning soul can demand of the body is less difficult than the organization which God has demanded of the seeds. . . . But I admit the supernatural here only in the beginnings of things, in respect of the first formation of animals or in respect of the original constitution of pre-established harmony between the soul and the body. Once that has come to pass, I hold that the formation of animals and the relation between the soul and the body are something as natural now as the other most ordinary operations of Nature.

(*Theodicy*, sec. 22.) In mechanics compound movement results from all the tendencies that concur in one and the same moving body, and satisfies each one equally, in so far as it is possible to do all at one time. It is as if the moving body took equal account of these tendencies, as I once showed in an issue of the *Journal de Paris* (7 Sept. 1693), when giving the general law of the compositions of movement. In this sense also it may be said that the antecedent will is efficacious in a sense and even effective with success.

(*Theodicy*, sec. 59.) The Scholastic philosophers believed that there was a reciprocal physical influence between body and soul: but since it has been recognized that thought and dimensional mass have no mutual connexion, and that they are creatures differing *toto genere*, many moderns have acknowledged that there is no *physical communication* between soul and body, despite the *metaphysical communication* always subsisting, which causes soul and body to compose one and the same suppositum, or what is called a person. This physical communication, if there were such, would cause the soul to change the degree of speed and the directional line of some motions that are in the body, and *vice versa* the body to change the sequence of the thoughts that are in the soul. But this effect cannot be inferred from any notion conceived in the body and in the soul; though nothing be better known to us than the soul, since it is inmost to us, that is to say inmost to itself.

(*Theodicy*, sec. 60.) M. Descartes wished to compromise and to make a part of the body's action dependent upon the soul. He believed in the existence of a rule of Nature to the effect, according to him, that the same quantity of movement is conserved in bodies. He deemed it not possible that the influence of the soul should violate this law of bodies, but he believed that the soul notwithstanding might have power to change the direction of the movements that are made in the body; much as a rider, though giving no force to the horse he mounts, nevertheless controls it by guiding that force in any direction he pleases. But as that is done by means of the bridle, the bit, the spurs and other material aids, it is conceivable how that can be; there are, however, no instruments such as the soul may employ for this result, nothing indeed either in the soul or in the body, that is, either in thought or in the mass, which may serve to explain this change of the one by the other. In a word, that the soul should change the quantity of force and that it should change the line of direction, both these things are equally inexplicable.

(*Theodicy*, sec. 61.) Moreover, two important truths on this subject have been discovered since M. Descartes' day. The first is that the quantity of absolute force which is in fact conserved is different from the quantity of move-ment, as I have demonstrated elsewhere. The second discovery is that the same direction is still conserved in all bodies together that are assumed as interact-ing, in whatever way they come into collision. If this rule had been known to M. Descartes, he would have taken the direction of bodies to be as independent of the soul as their force; and I believe that that would have led direct to the Hypothesis of Pre-established Harmony, whither these same rules have led me. For apart from the fact that the physical influence of one of these substances on the other is inexplicable, I recognized that without a complete derangement of the laws of Nature the soul could not act physically upon the body. And I did not believe that one could here listen to philosophers, competent in other respects, who produce a God, as it were, *ex machina*, to bring about the final solution of the piece, maintaining that God exerts himself deliberately to move bodies as the soul pleases, and to give perceptions to the soul as the body re-quires. For this system, which is called that of *occasional causes* (because it teaches that God acts on the body at the instance of the soul, and *vice versa*) besides introducing perpetual miracles to establish communication between these two substances, does not obviate the derangement of the natural laws obtaining in each of these same substances, which, in the general opinion, their mutual influence would cause.

(*Theodicy*, sec. 63.) Far from its being prejudicial, nothing can be more fa-vourable to freedom than that system. And M. Jacquelot has demonstrated well in his book on the *Conformity of Faith with Reason* that it is just as if he who knows all that I shall order a servant to do the whole day long on the morrow made an automaton entirely resembling this servant, to carry out to-morrow at the right moment all that I should order; and yet that would not prevent me from ordering freely all that I should please, although the action of the autom-aton that would serve me would not be in the least free.

(*Theodicy*, sec. 66.) One may however give a true and philosophic sense to this mutual dependence which we suppose between the soul and the body. It is that the one of these two substances depends upon the other ideally, in so far as the reason of that which is done in the one can be furnished by that which is in the other. This had already happened when God ordered beforehand the harmony that there would be between them. Even so would that automaton, that should fulfil the servant's function, depend upon me ideally, in virtue of the knowledge of him, who foreseeing my future orders, would have rendered it capable of serving me at the right moment all though the morrow. The knowl-edge of my future intentions would have actuated this great craftsman, who would accordingly have fashioned the automaton: my influence would be ob-jective, and his physical. For in so far as the soul has perfection and distinct thoughts, God has accommodated the body to the soul, and has arranged be-forehand that the body is impelled to execute its orders. And in so far as the soul is imperfect and as its perceptions are confused, God has accommodated the soul to the body, in such sort that the soul is swayed by the passions arising out of corporeal representations. This produces the same effect and the same appearance as if the one depended immediately upon the other, and by the agency of a physical influence. Properly speaking, it is by its confused thoughts that the soul represents the bodies which encompass it. The same thing must apply to all that we understand by the actions of simple substances one upon another. For each one is assumed to act upon the other in proportion to its perfection, although this be only ideally, and in the reasons of things, as God in the beginning ordered one substance to accord with another in proportion to the perfection or imperfection that there is in each.

(*Theodicy*, sec. 345.) The reason for the belief held by many that the laws of motion are arbitrary comes from the fact that few people have properly examined them. It is known now that M. Descartes was much mistaken in his statement of them. I have proved conclusively that conservation of the same quantity of motion cannot occur, but I consider that the same quantity of force is conserved, whether absolute or directive and respective, whether total or partial. My principles, which carry this subject as far as it can go, have not yet been published in full; but I have communicated them to friends competent to judge of them, who have approved them, and have converted some other persons of acknowledged erudition and ability. I discovered at the same time that the laws of motion actually existing in Nature, and confirmed by experiments, are not in reality absolutely demonstrable, as a geometrical proposition would be; but neither is it necessary that they be so. They do not spring entirely from the principle of necessity, but rather from the principle of perfection and order; they are an effect of the choice and the wisdom of God. I can demonstrate these laws in diverse ways, but must always assume something that is not of an absolutely geometrical necessity. Thus these admirable laws are wonderful evidence of an intelligent and free being, as opposed to the system of absolute and brute necessity, advocated by Strato or Spinoza.

(*Theodicy*, sec. 346.) I have found that one may account for these laws by assuming that the effect is always equal in force to its cause, or, which amounts to the same thing, that the same force is conserved always: but this axiom of higher philosophy cannot be demonstrated geometrically. One may again apply other principles of like nature, for instance the principle that action is always equal to reaction, one which assumes in things a distaste for external change, and cannot be derived either from extension or impenetrability; and that other principle, that a simple movement has the same properties as those which might belong to a compound movement such as would produce the same phenomena of locomotion. These assumptions are very plausible, and are successful as an explanation of the laws of motion: nothing is so appropriate, all the more since they are in accord with each other. But there is to be found in them no absolute necessity, such as may compel us to admit them, in the way one is compelled to admit the rules of logic, of arithmetic and geometry.

(*Theodicy*, sec. 347.) It seems, when one considers the indifference of matter to motion and to rest, that the largest body at rest could be carried along without any resistance by the smallest body in motion, in which case there would be action without reaction and an effect greater than its cause. There is also no necessity to say of the motion of a ball which runs freely on an even, horizontal plane, with a certain degree of speed, say A, that this motion must have the properties of that motion which it would have if it were going with lesser speed in a boat, itself moving in the same direction with the residue of the speed, to ensure that the ball, seen from the bank, advance with the same degree A. For, although the same appearance of speed and of direction results through this medium of the boat, it is not because it is the same thing. Nevertheless it happens that the effects of the collision of the balls in the boat, the motion in each one separately combined with that of the boat giving the appearance of the effects that these same balls colliding would have outside the boat. All that is admirable, but one does not see its absolute necessity. A movement on the two sides of the right-angled triangle composes a movement on the hypotenuse; but it does not follow that a ball moving on the hypotenuse must produce the effect of two balls of its own size moving on the two sides: yet that is true. Nothing is so appropriate as this result, and God has chosen the laws that produce it: but one sees no geometrical necessity therein. Yet it is this very lack of necessity which enhances the beauty of the laws that God has chosen, wherein divers admirable axioms exist in conjunction, and it is impossible for one to say which of them is the primary.

(*Theodicy*, sec. 348.) I have also shown that therein is observed that excellent law of continuity, which I have perhaps been the first to state, and which is a kind of touchstone whose test the rules of M. Descartes, of Father Fabry, Father Pardies, Father de Malebranche and others cannot pass. In virtue of this law, one must be able to regard rest as a movement vanishing after having continually diminished, and likewise equality as an inequality that vanishes also, as would happen through the continual diminution of the greater of two unequal bodies, while the smaller retains its size. As a consequence of this consideration, the general rule for unequal bodies, or bodies in motion, must apply also to equal bodies or to bodies one of which is at rest, as to a particular case of the rule. This does result in the true laws of motion, and does not result in certain laws invented by M. Descartes and by some other men of talent, which already on that score alone prove so ill-concerted that one may predict <*a priori*> that experiment will not favour them.

(*Theodicy*, secs. 354–55.) M. Bayle . . . <maintains that>: "It is true that since the laws of motion were instituted in such forms as we see now in the world, it is an inevitable necessity that a hammer striking a nut should break it, and that a stone falling on a man's foot should cause some bruise or some derangement of its parts. . . . ⟨But⟩ it is by an arbitrary institution God has ordained that wounds in the body should cause pain in the soul which is united to this body. It therefore only rested with him to have chosen another system of union between soul and body: he was therefore able to choose one in accordance wherewith wounds only evoke the idea of the remedy and an intense but agreeable desire to apply it. He was able to arrange that all bodies which were on the point of breaking a man's head or piercing his heart should evoke a lively sense of danger, and that this sense should cause the body to remove itself promptly out of reach of the blow. All that would have come to pass without miracles, since there would have been general laws on this subject." . . . It is evident that M. Bayle believes that everything accomplished through general laws is accomplished without miracles. But I have shown sufficiently that if the law is not founded on reasons and does not serve to explain the event through the nature of things, it can only be put into execution by a miracle. If, for example God had ordained that bodies must have a circular motion, he would have needed perpetual miracles, or the ministry of angels, to put this order into execution: for that is contrary to the nature of motion, whereby the body naturally abandons the circular line to continue in the tangent straight line if nothing holds it back. Therefore it is not enough for God to ordain simply that a wound should excite an agreeable sensation: natural means must be found for that purpose. The real means whereby God causes the soul to be conscious of what happens in the body have their origin in the nature of the soul, which represents the bodies, and is so made beforehand that the representations which are to spring up one from another within it, by a natural sequence of thoughts, correspond to the changes in the body.

(PNG, sec. 11.) The supreme wisdom of God has made him choose especially those *laws of motion* which are best adjusted and most fitted to abstract or metaphysical reasons. There is conserved the same quantity of total and absolute force or of action, also the same quantity of relative force or of reaction, and finally, the same quantity of directive force. Furthermore, action is always equal to reaction, and the entire effect is always equal to its full cause. It is surprising that no reason can be given for the laws of motion which have been discovered in our own time, and part of which I myself have discovered, by a consideration of *efficient causes* or of matter alone. For I have found that we must have recourse to *final causes* and that these laws do not depend upon the *principle of necessity*, as do the truths of logic, arithmetic, and geometry, but upon the *principle of fitness*, that is to say, upon the choice of wisdom. This is one of the most effective and obvious proofs of the existence of God for those who can probe into these matters thoroughly.

(DM, sec. 17.) Our new philosophers are unanimous in employing that famous law that God always preserves the same amount of motion in the universe. In fact it is a very plausible law, and in times past I held it for indubitable. But since then I have learned in what its fault consists. Monsieur Descartes and many other clever mathematicians have thought that the quantity of motion, that is to say the velocity multiplied by the mass of the moving body, is exactly equivalent to the moving force, or to speak in mathematical terms that the force varies as the velocity multiplied by the mass. Now it is reasonable that the same force is always preserved in the universe. . . . But force ought to be estimated by the quantity of the effect which it is able to produce, for example, by the height to which a body of certain weight can be raised. This is a very different thing from the velocity which can be imparted to it, and in order to impart to it double the velocity we must have double the force. Monsieur Descartes has fallen into error here, only because he trusted too much to his thoughts even when they had not been ripened by reflection. But it astonishes me that his disciples have not noticed this error.

(G IV, 497–98; "Clarification of the New System" [1696].) You know that M. Descartes believed that the same quantity of motion is conserved in bodies. It has been demonstrated that he was mistaken in this; but I have shown that it is always true that the same motive force—instead of, as he thought, the same quantity of motion—is conserved. Even so, the changes which take place in the body as a consequence of the modifications of the soul caused him embarrassment, because they seemed to violate this law. He thought therefore that he had found a way out of this difficulty, which is certainly ingenious, by saying that we must distinguish motion and direction of motion; and that the soul cannot increase or diminish the motive force, but that it changes the direction or determination of the course of the animal spirits, and it is in this way that voluntary motions take place. It is true that he made no attempt to explain how the soul sets about changing the course of bodies—and in fact this seems as inconceivable as saying that it gives them motion, unless you have recourse, as I do, to pre-established harmony. But the truth is that there is *another law of nature*, which I have discovered and proved, and which M. Descartes did not know: namely, that *there is conserved* not only the same quantity of motive force, but also *the same quantity of direction from whatever side in the world it be taken*. That is to say: take any straight line you like, and take also any number of bodies, chosen as you please; you will find that, considering all these bodies together without leaving out any of those which act on any of those which you have taken, there will always be the same quantity of progression from the same side in all the lines parallel to the straight line you have chosen: provided care is taken that the sum total of progression is estimated by deducting that of the bodies which go in the opposite direction from that of those which go in the direction chosen. This law is as beautiful and as general as the other, and deserves as little to be violated: and this is so in my system, which conserves both force and direction, and in a word, all the natural laws of bodies, notwithstanding the changes which occur in them as a result of those in the soul.

(G VI, 540–41; Loemker, p. 587; "On the Principles of Life and on Plastic Natures" [1705].) Descartes ... thought it unnecessary to give the soul the power of increasing or diminishing the force of the body but only that of changing its direction by changing the course of the animal spirits. And those Cartesians who have given vogue to the doctrine of occasional causes hold that since the soul can have no influence whatever upon the body, it is necessary for God to change the course and direction of the animal spirits in accordance with the wishes of the soul. But if this new law of nature which I have demonstrated had been known in Descartes's day, according to which not only the same quantity of total force of bodies in interrelation is conserved but also their total direction, he would undoubtedly have been led to my system of pre-established harmony, for he would have recognized that it is just as reasonable to say that the soul does not change the quantity of the direction of the body as it is to deny to the soul the power of changing the quantity of its force, both being equally contrary to the order of things and the laws of nature, since both are equally inexplicable. Therefore souls or vital principles, according to my system, change nothing in the ordinary course of bodies and do not even give God the occasion for doing so. The souls follow their laws, which consist in a definite development of perceptions according to goods and evils, and the bodies follow theirs, which consist in the laws of motion; nevertheless, these two beings of entirely different kind meet together and correspond to each other like two clocks perfectly regulated to the same time. It is this that I call the theory of *pre-established harmony*, which excludes every concept of miracle from purely natural actions and makes things run their course regulated in an intelligible manner. Instead of this, the common system has recourse to absolutely inexplainable influences, while in the system of occasional causes God is compelled at every moment, by a kind of general law and as if by compact, to change the natural course of the thoughts of the soul to adapt them to the impressions of the body and to interfere with the natural course of bodily movements in accordance with the volitions of the soul. This can only be explained by a perpetual miracle, whereas I explain the whole intelligently by the nature which God has established in things.

COMMENTARY

Leibniz prided himself on having discovered the conservation of momentum (a physical quantity which he himself called "force") not just as an aggregate total, but in any given direction throughout all mechanical interactions. He regarded this physical principle as establishing a clear circumscription of the modificatory influence of mind on the physical processes of nature, and this impelled him toward the idea of the pre-established harmony between mind and body, which he judged to be the only feasible way to reconcile the facts of psychology with those of physics.

Descartes had thought that whereas the aggregate quantity of "force" in nature was constant, its direction could be modified through the intervention of human minds. Leibniz thus saw the discovery of the conservation of "force" *in any given direction* as having far-reaching philosophical consequences, requiring a principle of preestablished harmony for its accommodation.

KEY WORDS:

soul/*âme*
force/*force*
bodies/*corps*
matter/*matière*
law of nature/*loi de la nature*
conservation/*conservation*
quantity of force/*quantité de la force*
directed force/*force directive (direction)*
system of pre-established harmony/*système de l'harmonie préétablie*

PERSONS:

René Descartes

SECTION 81

81. This system <of pre-established harmony> has it that bodies act as though (to suppose the impossible) there were no souls at all, and souls act as though there were no bodies at all, and both act as though each influenced the other.

81. Ce Systeme fait que les corps agissent comme si (per impossibile) il n'y avoit point d'Ames, et que les Ames agissent comme s'il n'y avoit point de corps; et que tous deux agissent comme si l'un influoit sur l'autre.

(PNG, sec. 3.) The perceptions in the monad arise from each other according to the laws of the appetites or of the *final causes of good and of evil,* which consist in observable perceptions, whether regulated or unregulated, in the same way that bodily changes and external phenomena arise from each other according to the laws of *efficient causality,* that is, of motions. Thus there is a perfect *harmony* between the perceptions of the monad and the motions of the body, pre-established from the beginning between the system of efficient causes and that of final causes. It is in this that the accord and the physical union of soul and body consist, without either one being able to change the laws of the other.

(G IV, 559; Loemker, p. 577; "Response to Bayle" [1702].) All that ambition or any other passion brings to pass into the soul of Caesar is also represented in his body, and all the motions of these passions come from the impressions of objects combined with internal motions. And the body is so constituted that the soul never makes any resolution without the motions of the body agreeing with it. This applies even to the most abstract reasonings, because of the characters which represent them to the imagination. In a word, everything takes place in bodies, as regards the detail of their phenomena, as if the evil doctrine of those who, like Epicurus and Hobbes, believe that the soul is material, were true; or as if man himself were only a body or an automaton. . . . Those who show the Cartesians that their way of proving that the lower animals are only automata amounts to justifying him who should say that all men, except himself, are also mere automata, have said exactly what I need for that half of my hypothesis which concerns body. But, apart from the principles which make it certain that there are Monads, of which compound substances are only the results, the Epicurean doctrine is refuted by inner experience, by our consciousness of the Ego which consciously perceives the things which take place in the body; and as perception cannot be explained by figures and motions, the other half of my hypothesis is established, and we are obliged to recognize that there is in us an *indivisible substance* which must be itself the source of its phenomena. Consequently, according to this second half of my hypothesis, everything takes place in the soul as if there were no body; just as, according to the first half, everything takes place in the body as if there were no soul. . . . Whatever of good there is in the hypotheses of Epicurus and of Plato, of the greatest Materialists and the greatest Idealists, is combined here.

COMMENTARY

This section provides a compact and elegant statement of pre-established harmony: though bodies and souls/spirits consist in monadic substances that go along in their own internally pre-programmed ways, the creation-choice of God looks to the most comprehensive and ample coordination between their respective doings. In this, the real world, mind and matter accordingly follow their own internally complete and mutually concordant laws—together constituting a rationally harmonious whole.

KEY WORDS:

bodies/*corps*
souls/*âmes*
to act/*agir*
as if/*comme si*
to influence/*influencer*
system (of pre-established harmony)/*système (de l'harmonie préétablie)*

SECTION 82

82. As regards *spirits* or rational souls, while I find that at bottom the same situation prevails in all organisms and animals, as just said (namely that the animal and the soul begin only with the world and end only with the world), there is nevertheless this peculiarity in rational animals, that their minute spermatic animacules, as long as they are only this, have merely ordinary or sensitive souls. But as soon as those who are, so to speak, elect arrive through an actual conception at human nature, their sensitive souls are elevated to the rank of reason and to the prerogative of spirits. (See *Theodicy*, secs. 91, 397.)

82. Quant aux Esprits, *ou* Ames raisonnables, *quoique je trouve qu'il y a dans le fond la même chose dans tous les vivans et animaux, comme nous venons de dire; (sçavoir que l'Animal et l'Ame ne commencent qu'avec le monde, et ne finissent pas non plus que <avec> le monde), il y a pourtant cela de particulier dans les Animaux raisonnables, que leurs petits Animaux Spermatiques, tant qu'ils ne sont que cela, ont seulement des Ames ordinaires ou sensitives; mais dès que ceux, qui sont élûs, pour ainsi dire, parviennent par une actuelle conception à la nature humaine, leurs ames sensitives sont elevées au degré de la raison et à la prerogative des Esprits.* (Théodicée, *secs. 91, 397.)*

(*Theodicy*, sec. 91.) Considering that so admirable an order and rules so general are established in regard to animals, it does not appear reasonable that man should be completely excluded form that order, and that everything in relation to his soul should come about in him by miracle. Besides, I have pointed out repeatedly that it is of the essence of God's wisdom that all should be harmonious in his works, and that nature should be parallel with grace. It is thus my belief that those souls which one day shall be human souls, like those of other species, have been in the seed, and in the progenitors as far back as Adam, and have consequently existed since the beginning of things, always in a kind of organic body. . . . This doctrine is also sufficiently confirmed by the microscope observations of M. Leeuwenhoek and other good observers. But it also for divers reasons appears likely to me that they existed then as sentient or animal souls only, endowed with perception and feeling, and devoid of reason. Further I believe that they remained in this state up to the time of the generation of the man to whom they were to belong, but that then they received reason, whether there be a natural means of raising a sentient soul to the degree of a reasoning soul (a thing I find it difficult to imagine) or whether God may have given reason to this soul through some special operation, or (if you will) by a kind of *transcreation*. This latter is easier to admit, inasmuch as revelation teaches much about other forms of immediate operation by God upon our souls.

(*Theodicy*, sec. 397.) Souls cannot spring up naturally, or be derived from one another, and . . . it is necessary that ours either be created or be pre-existent. I have even pointed out a certain middle way between a creation an an entire pre-existence. I find it appropriate to say that the soul pre-existing in the seeds from the beginning of things was only sentient, but that it was elevated to the superior degree, which is that of reason, when the man to whom this soul should belong was conceived, and when the organic body, always accompanying this soul from the beginning, but under many changes, was determined for forming the human body. I considered also that one might attribute this elevation of the sentient soul (which makes it reach a more sublime degree of being, namely reason) to the extraordinary operation of God. Nevertheless it will be well to add that I would dispense with miracles in the generating of man, as in that of the other animals. It will be possible to explain that, if one imagines that in this great number of souls and of animals, or at least of living organic bodies which are in the seeds, those souls alone which are destined to attain one day to human nature contain the reason that shall appear therein one day, and the organic bodies of these souls alone are preformed and predisposed to assume one day the human shape, while the other small animals or seminal living beings, in which no such thing is pre-established, are essentially different from them and possessed only of an inferior nature. This production is a kind of *traduction* but more manageable than that kind which is commonly taught: it does not derive the soul from a soul, but only the animate from an animate, and it avoids the repeated miracles of a new creation, which would cause a new and pure soul to enter a body that must corrupt it.

(N.S., sec. 4.) I saw that these forms and these souls must be indivisible, just as is our mind; in fact, I remembered that this was the opinion of St. Thomas with regard to the souls of beasts. But this truth revived the great difficulties about the origin and duration of souls and forms. For since every substance which has a true unity can begin and end only by a miracle, it follows that souls can begin only by creation and end only by annihilation. So I was obliged to recognize that except for the souls which God still expressly wills to create, the forms which constitute substances have been created with the world and that they will subsist always. Moreover, certain Scholastics like Albert the Great and John Bacon had glimpsed a part of the truth about the origin of these forms. Nor should this opinion appear extraordinary, since we are merely ascribing to the forms the duration which the Gassendists grant to their atoms.

(G II, 75; to Arnauld [1686].) I agree, also, <with St. Thomas> that every substantial form, or, indeed, every substance is indestructible and also ingenerable, which latter was also the opinion of Albertus Magnus. . . . They can come into being therefore only by an act of creation. I am a good deal inclined to believe that all the births of unreasoning animals, which do not deserve a new act of creation, are only transformations of another animal already living, but at times invisible, as for example, with the changes which happen to a silkworm and other like creatures, where nature has disclosed its secrets in certain instances while it conceals them in others. Thus, brute souls would have all been created from the very beginning of the world, in accordance with that fertility of seeds mentioned in Genesis, but the reasoning soul is <as such> created only at the time of the formation of its body, being entirely different from the other souls which we know because it is capable of reflection and imitates on a small scale the divine nature.

COMMENTARY

The three grades of monads—simple monads, souls, and spirits—do not differ in kind but merely in mode of operation. However, whatever capacity they exhibit when operating at higher levels (as souls or as spirits) is always present in potential, and makes for a difference in degree of perceptual functioning that is tantamount to a difference in kind among the substances at issue. As Leibniz thus sees it, the rational souls or spirits occupy a very special status in the world's scheme of things, a status they acquire at the very moment of conception. On the "elect" souls see also section 75.

KEY WORDS:

spirits/*esprits*
souls/*âmes*
organisms/*vivants*
animal/*animal*
reason/*raison*
to begin/*commencer*
to finish/*finir*
ordinary souls/*âmes ordinaires*
sensitive souls/*âmes sensitives*
rational souls/*ames raisonnables*
rational animals/*animaux raisonnables*
spermatic animacules/*petits animaux spermatiques*
the world/*le monde*
elect/*élû*
human nature/*nature humaine*
conception/*conception*
prerogative of spirits/*prérogative des esprits*

SECTION 83

83. Among other differences between ordinary souls and spirits, a part of which I have already noted <in secs. 29–30>, there is also this, that souls in general are living mirrors or images of the universe of created beings. But the spirits are also images of divinity itself—of the very Author of nature. They are capable of knowing the system of the universe, and of imitating it to some extent through constructive samples, each spirit being like a minute divinity within its own sphere. (See *Theodicy*, sec. 147.)

83. Entre autres differences qu'il y a entre les Ames ordinaires et les Esprits, dont j'en ai deja marqué une partie, il y a encore celle-ci, que les Ames en general sont des miroirs vivans ou images de l'univers des creatures, mais que les Esprits sont encore des images de la Divinité même, ou de l'Auteur même de la Nature; capables de connoître le Systeme de l'univers et d'en imiter quelque chose par des echantillons architectoniques; chaque Esprit étant comme une petite divinité dans son departement. (Théodicée, sec. 147.)

(*Theodicy*, sec. 147.) God, in giving man intelligence, has presented him with an image of the Divinity. He leaves him to himself, in a sense, in his small department . . . It is there that free will plays its game: and God makes game (so to speak) of these little Gods that he has thought good to produce, as we make game of children who follow pursuits which we secretly encourage or hinder according as it pleases us. Thus man is there like a little god in his own world or *Microcosm*, which he governs after his own fashion. . . . But he also commits great errors, because he abandons himself to the passions, and because God abandons him to his own way. God punishes him also for such errors, now like a father or tutor, training or chastising children, now like a just judge, punishing when these intelligences or their small worlds come into collision. . . . Thus the apparent deformities of our little worlds combine to become beauties in the great world, and have nothing in them which is opposed to the oneness of an infinitely perfect universal principle: on the contrary, they increase our wonder at the wisdom of him who makes evil serve the greater good.

(PNG, sec. 14.) As for the reasonable soul or *spirit* there is something more in it than in monads or even in simple souls. It is not only a mirror of the universe of creatures but also an image of divinity. The spirit not only has a perception of the works of God but is even capable of producing something which resembles them, though in miniature. For not to mention the wonders of dreams in which we invent, without effort but also without will, things which we should have to think a long time to discover when awake, our soul is architectonic also in its voluntary actions and in discovering the sciences according to which God has regulated things (by weight, measure, number, etc.). In its own realm and in the small world in which it is allowed to act, the soul imitates what God performs in the great world.

(N.S., sec. 5.) I concluded, nevertheless, that we must not mix up indifferently, or confuse, minds or rational souls with other forms or souls, for they are of a superior order and have incomparably more perfection than have the forms which are sunk in matter, which I believe are found everywhere. For in comparison with these, minds or rational souls are as little gods made in the image of God and having in them some ray of the light of the Divinity. This is why God governs minds as a prince governs his subjects or indeed as a father cares for his children, while he deals with other substances, instead, as an engineer handles his machines. Minds thus have special laws which place them beyond the revolutions of matter, and one can say that all the rest is made only for them, these revolutions themselves being adapted to the happiness of the good and the punishment of the evil.

(DM, sec. 34.) Supposing that the bodies which constitute a *unum per se*, as human bodies, are substances, and have substantial forms, and supposing that animals have souls, we are obliged to grant that these souls and these substantial forms cannot entirely perish, any more than can the atoms or the ultimate elements of matter, according to the position of other philosophers; for no substance perishes, although it may become very different. Such substances also express the whole universe, although more imperfectly than do spirits. The principal difference, however, is that they do not know that they are, nor what they are. Consequently, not being able to reason, they are unable to discover necessary and universal truths. It is also because they do not reflect regarding themselves that they have no moral qualities, whence it follows that undergoing a thousand transformations, as we see a caterpillar change into a butterfly, the result from a moral or practical standpoint is the same as if we said that they perished in each case, and we can indeed say it from the physical standpoint in the same way that we say bodies perish in their dissolution. But the intelligent soul, knowing that it is and having the ability to say that word "I" so full of meaning, not only continues and exists, metaphysically far more certainly than do the others, but it remains the same from the moral standpoint, and constitutes the same personality, for it is its memory or knowledge of this ego which renders it open to punishment and reward. Also the immortality which is required in morals and in religion does not consist merely in this perpetual existence, which pertains to all substances, for if in addition there were no remembrance of what one had been, immortality would not be at all desirable. Suppose that some individual could suddenly become King of China on condition, however, of forgetting what he had been, as though being born again, would it not amount to the same practically, or as far as the effects could be perceived, as if the individual were annihilated, and a king of China were the same instant created in his place? The individual would have no reason to desire this.

(DM, sec. 35.) The difference between intelligent substances and those which are not so is as great as the difference between a mirror and one who looks into it.

(Loemker, p. 280; "On the Elements of Natural Science" [ca. 1682].) Every science is to be sought after, not for the sake of curiosity or ostentation, but for the sake of action. However, we act to attain happiness or a state of enduring joy, and joy is the sense of perfection. Every thing is to be held as more perfect to the degree that it is freer by nature; that is, to the degree that its power is greater over the things that surround it, and its suffering from external things is less. Hence, since the power proper to the mind is understanding, it follows that we will be the happier the clearer our comprehension of things and the more we act in accordance with our proper nature, namely, reason. Only to the extent that our reasonings are right are we free, and exempt from the passions which are impressed upon us by surrounding bodies. Yet it is impossible to evade these passions entirely, since the mind is affected in various ways by its body, while our body, which is but a small part of the universe, can be helped and harmed by the bodies which surround it. The knowledge of bodies is therefore most important on two grounds—first to perfect our mind through an understanding of the purposes and causes of things; second, to conserve and nurture our body, which is the organ of the soul, by furthering what is wholesome for it and reducing what is harmful.

COMMENTARY

Spirits are *architectonic* in that, like God, the supreme architect, they play an actively creative role in the world's scheme, mentally conceiving ideas that guide action.

Like God himself, spirits are free agents capable of planning, deciding, implementing. The essence of free will for Leibniz is freedom of choice—but clearly not freedom to choose *independently* of reasons, but rather freedom to choose *in the light* of reasons, in line with those reasons we deem best, those which, to the best of one's insight, stand forth as the strongest. Thus a determination of choice by reasons nowise inhibits or constrains the will—constraint is a matter of limitation through the operation of factors *external* to one's reasons. (In this regard, Leibniz's view of freedom of choice is much the same as Spinoza's.)

What is so special about spirits in Leibniz's view is exactly that they share certain preeminent capacities with God, in particular *reason* (the capacity to grasp necessary truths), *intelligence* (the capacity to apprehend laws of nature), and *creativity* (the capacity to act through free will in the pursuit of values). Thus each spirit is, or has the potential of being, "a minute divinity in its own sphere."

This state of affairs is, as Leibniz sees it, deeply satisfying to human reason. For it is of reason's very essence to search for intelligible order and this is to be found principally and optimally in the perfection of things. We thus take rational pleasure in understanding the lawful structure of this world (think of Archimedes' *Eureka!*) because this search for intelligible order is of the very essence of reason. Our rationality delights in discovering the rational order that God has actualized in the world's scheme of things.

Considering Leibniz's stress in the *Theodicy* on the fact that spirits are rational, creative, and diminutively God-like agents, it is striking that the terms *freedom, free agent, liberty of action,* or the like, never once occur in the *Monadology* or in the *Principles of Nature and of Grace*. It is odd that these final summaries of his philosophical system omit mention of this most central of its doctrines.

KEY WORDS:

ordinary souls/*âmes ordinaires*
spirits/*esprits*
created beings/*créatures*
living mirror/*miroir vivant*
image of the universe/*image de l'univers*
image of divinity/*image de la Divinité*
author of nature/*auteur de la nature*
system of the universe/*système de l'univers*
minute divinity/*petite divinité*
constructive samples/*échantillons architectoniques*
department/*département*

SECTION 84

84. This brings it about that spirits are capable of entering into a kind of community with God, and that he is in regard to them not only what an inventor is to his machine (as God is in relation to other created beings), but also what a prince is to his subjects, and even a father to his children.

84. C'est ce qui fait que les Esprits sont capables d'entrer dans une manière de Société avec Dieu, et qu'il est à leur égard non seulement ce qu'un inventeur est à sa Machine (comme Dieu l'est par rapport aux autres creatures) mais encore ce qu'un Prince est à ses sujets, et même un pere à ses enfans.

(PNG, sec. 14.) As for the reasonable soul or *spirit*, there is something more in it than in monads or even in simple souls. It is not only a mirror of the universe of creatures but also an image of divinity. The spirit not only has a perception of the works of God but is even capable of producing something which resembles them, though in miniature. . . . In its own realm and in the small world in which it is allowed to act, the soul imitates what God performs in the great world.

(PNG, sec. 15.) For this reason all spirits, whether of men or of higher beings (*génies*), enter by virtue of reason and the eternal truths into a kind of society with God and are members of the City of God, that is to say, the most perfect state, formed and governed by the action without a proportionate reward, and finally, as much virtue and happiness as is possible. And this takes place, not by a dislocation of nature, as if what God has planned for souls could disturb the laws of bodies, but by the very order of natural things itself, by virtue of the harmony pre-established from all time between the realms of nature and of grace, between God as architect and God as monarch, in such a way that nature leads to grace, and grace perfects nature by using it.

(PNG, sec. 16.) Though reason cannot teach us the details of the great future, these being reserved for revelation, we can be assured by this same reason that things are arranged in a way which surpasses our desires. God being also the most perfect, the happiest, and therefore the most lovable of substances, and *true pure love* consisting in the state which causes pleasure to be taken in the perfections and the felicity of the beloved, this love must give us the greatest pleasure of which one is capable, since God is its object.

(DM, sec. 36.) Spirits are of all substances the most capable of perfection. . . . Hence it follows that God who in all things has the greatest perfection will have the greatest care for spirits and will give not only to all of them in general, but even to each one in particular the highest perfection which the universal harmony will permit. We can even say that it is because he is a spirit that God is the originator of existences, for if he had lacked the power of will to choose what is best, there would have been no reason why one possible being should exist rather than any other. Therefore God's being a spirit himself dominates all the consideration which he may have toward created things. Spirits alone are made in his image, being as it were of his blood or as children in the family, since they alone are able to serve him of free will, and to act consciously imitating the divine nature. A single spirit is worth a whole world, because it not only expresses the whole world, but it also knows it and governs itself as does God. . . . This nature of spirits, so noble that it enables them to approach divinity as much as is possible for created things, has as a result that God derives infinitely more glory from them than from the other beings, or rather the other beings furnish to spirits the material for glorifying him. This moral quality of God which constitutes him Lord and Monarch of spirits influences him so to speak personally and in a unique way. It is through this that he humanizes himself, that he is willing to tolerate anthropomorphisms, and that he enters into social relations with us. And this consideration is so dear to him that the happy and prosperous condition of his empire which consists in the greatest possible felicity of its inhabitants, becomes supreme among his laws. Happiness is to persons what perfection is to beings. And if the dominant principle in the existence of the physical world is the decree to give it the greatest possible perfection, the primary purpose in the moral world or in the city of God which constitutes the noblest part of the universe ought to be to extend the greatest happiness possible. We must not therefore doubt that God has so ordained everything that spirits not only shall live forever, because this is un-avoidable, but that they shall also preserve forever their moral quality, so that his city may never lose a person, quite in the same way that the world never loses a substance. Consequently they will always be conscious of their being, otherwise they would be open to neither reward nor punishment, a condition which is the essence of a republic, and above all of the most perfect republic where nothing can be neglected. In fine, God being at the same time the most just and the most benevolent of monarchs, and requiring only a good will on the part of men, provided that it be sincere and intentional, his subjects cannot desire a better condition. To render them perfectly happy he desires only that they love him.

(G II, 124–25; Loemker, p. 346; to Arnauld [1687].) With regard to spirits, that is to say, substances which think and which are able to recognize God and to discover eternal truths, I hold that God governs them according to laws different from those with which he governs the rest of substances; for, while all the forms of substances express the whole universe, it can be said that animal substances express the world rather than God, while spirits express God rather than the world. God governs the animal substances according to the material laws of force and of the transfer of motion, but spirits, according to spiritual laws of justice, of which the others are incapable. It is for this reason that animal substances can be called material, because the economy which God observes with regard to them is that of a worker or of a machinist, but with regard to spirits God performs the functions of a prince or of a legislator, which is infinitely higher; with regard to material substances, God is only what he is with regard to everything, namely, the universal author of beings. He assumes, however, another aspect with regard to spirits who conceive of him as endowed with will and with moral qualities; because he is, himself, a spirit and, like one among us, to the point of entering with us into a social relation, where he is the head. It is this universal society or republic of spirits under this sovereign monarch which is the noblest part of the universe, composed of so many little gods under this one great God; for, it can be said that created spirits differ from God only in degree, only as the finite differs from the infinite, and it can be truly said that the whole universe has been made only to contribute to the beautifying and to the happiness of this city of God. This is why everything is so constructed that the laws of force or the purely material laws work together in the whole universe to carry out the laws of justice or of love, so that nothing will be able to injure the souls that are in the hands of God, and so that every-thing should result for the greatest good of those who love him; this is why, furthermore, it must be that spirits keep their personalities and their moral qualities so that the city of God shall lose no member and they must in particular preserve some sort of memory or consciousness or the power to know what they are, upon which depends all their morality.

(G VII, 307–08; Loemker, p. 490; "On the Radical Origination of Things" [1697].) As for the afflictions, especially of good men, however, we must take it as assured that these lead to their greater good and that this is true not only theologically but also naturally. . . . In general, one may say that, though af-flictions are temporary evils, they are good in effect, for they are shortcuts to greater perfection. . . . We may call this backing up the better to spring forward ("*qu'on recule pour mieux sauter*").

COMMENTARY

A kinship of sorts exists between the spirits and God by virtue of the fact that they too are rational agents capable of creative action and of knowing eternal truths. This circumstance establishes a special, virtually familial tie between him and them.

In invoking the analogy of a machine and its inventor, it is likely that Leibniz had in mind his own invention of an arithmetical calculating machine, which he always viewed as one of his prime achievements.

Regarding the analogy of prince and father, compare Aristotle:

> For the relationship of a father to his sons bears the form of monarchy, since the father cares for his children, and this is why Homer calls Zeus "father"; it is the ideal of monarchy to be a paternal rule. (*Nichomachean Ethics*, 1060b24.)

KEY WORDS:

spirits/*esprits*
God/*Dieu*
created beings/*créatures*
community with God/*société avec Dieu*
inventor/*inventeur*
machine/*machine*
prince/*prince*
subjects/*sujets*
father/*père*

SECTION 85

85. From this it is readily concluded that the assemblage of all spirits must compose the City of God, that is, the most perfect state possible, under the most perfect of monarchs. (See *Theodicy*, sec. 146; Abridgment, obj. 2.)

*85. D'où il est aisé de conclure, que l'assemblage de tous les Esprits doit composer la Cité de Dieu, c'est à dire le plus parfait état qui soit possible, sous le plus parfait des Monarques. (*Théodicée, sec. 146; Abrégé, obj. 2.)

(*Theodicy*, sec. 118.) I agree that the happiness of intelligent creatures is the principal part of God's designs, for they most resemble him; but I do not see how it can be proved that this is his sole aim. It is true that the kingdom of nature must be helpful to the kingdom of grace; but as everything is connected in God's great design, we must believe that the kingdom of grace is also in some way fitted to the kingdom of nature, in such a manner that this keeps the greatest order and beauty, so as to render the whole composed of both the most perfect possible.

(*Theodicy*, sec. 146.) Every time we see . . . (a finished) work of God, we find it so perfect that we must wonder at the contrivance and the beauty thereof: but when we do not see an entire work, when we only look upon scraps and fragments, it is no wonder if the good order is not evident there. Our planetary system composes such an isolated work, which is complete also when it is taken by itself; each plant, each animal, each man furnishes one such work, to a certain point of perfection: one recognizes therein the wonderful contrivance of the author. But the human kind, so far as it is known to us, is only a fragment, only a small portion of the City of God or of the republic of Spirits, which has an extent too great for us, and whereof we know too little, to be able to observe the wonderful order therein. . . . But the harmony existing in all the rest allows of a strong presumption that it would exist also in the government of men, and generally in that of Spirits, if the whole were known to us.

(*Theodicy*, Abridgment, obj. 2.) I cannot admit . . . that there is more evil than good in intelligent creatures. One need not even agree that there is more evil than good in the human kind. For it is possible, and even a very reasonable thing, that the glory and the perfection of the blessed may be incomparably greater than the misery and imperfection of the damned, and that here the excellence of the total good in the smaller number may exceed the total evil which is in the greater number. . . . Even should one admit that there is more evil than good in the human kind, one still has every reason for not admitting that there is more evil than good in all intelligent creatures. For there is an inconceivable number of Spirits, and perhaps of other rational creatures besides: and an opponent cannot prove that in the whole City of God, composed as much of Spirits as of rational animals without number and of endless different kinds, the evil exceeds the good. Although one need not, in order to answer an objection, prove that a thing is, when its mere possibility suffices, I have nevertheless shown in this present work that it is a result of the supreme perfection of the Sovereign of the Universe that the kingdom of God should be the most perfect of all states or governments possible, and that in consequence what little evil there is should be required to provide the full measure of the vast good existing there.

(PNG, sec. 15.) For this reason all spirits, whether of men or of higher beings (*génies*), enter by virtue of reason and the eternal truths into a kind of society with God and are members of the City of God, that is to say, the most perfected state, formed and governed by the greatest and best of monarchs. Here there is no crime without punishment, no good action without a proportionate reward, and finally, as much virtue and happiness as is possible. And this takes place, not by a dislocation of nature, as if what God has planned for souls could disturb the laws of bodies, but by the very order of natural things itself, by virtue of the harmony pre-established from all time between the realms of nature and of grace, between God as architect and God as monarch, in such a way that nature leads to grace, and grace perfects nature by using it.

(DM, sec. 36.) Spirits are of all substances the most capable of perfection and their perfections are different in this that they interfere with one another the least, or rather they aid one another the most, for only the most virtuous can be the most perfect friends. Hence it follows that God who in all things has the greatest perfection will have the greatest care for spirits and will give not only to all of them in general, but even to each one in particular the highest perfection which the universal harmony will permit. We can even say that it is because he is a spirit that God is the originator of existences, for if he had lacked the power of will to choose what is best, there would have been no reason why one possible being should exist rather than any other. Therefore God's being a spirit himself dominates all the consideration which he may have toward created things. Spirits alone are made in his image, being as it were of his blood or as children in the family, since they alone are able to serve him of free will, and to act consciously imitating the divine nature. A single spirit is worth a whole world, because it not only expresses the whole world, but it also knows it and governs itself as does God. In this way we may say that though every substance expresses the whole universe, yet the other substances express the world rather than God, while spirits express God rather than the world. This nature of spirits, so noble that it enables them to approach divinity as much as is possible for created things, has as a result that God derives infinitely more glory from them than from the other beings, or rather the other beings furnish to spirits the material for glorifying him. This moral quality of God which constitutes him Lord and Monarch of spirits influences him so to speak personally and in a unique way. It is through this that he humanizes himself, that he is willing to suffer anthropologies, and that he enters into social relations with us and this consideration is so dear to him that the happy and prosperous condition of his empire which consists in the greatest possible felicity of its inhabitants, becomes supreme among his laws. . . . In fine, God being at the same time the most just and the most benevolent of monarchs, and requiring only a good will on the part of men, provided that it be sincere and intentional, his subjects cannot desire a better condition. To render them perfectly happy he desires only that they love him.

(NS, sec. 5.) Spirits have special laws which put them above the revolutions of matter through the very order which God has placed there; and it may be said that everything else is made only for them, these revolutions themselves being arranged for the felicity of the good and the punishment of the wicked.

(NS, sec. 8.) Rational souls, however, follow much more elevated laws and are exempt from everything which might make them lose the quality of citizens of the society of minds, since God has provided so well that no changes in matter can make them lose the moral qualities of their personality.

(G IV, 391; "Against the Principles of the Cartesians" [1697].) Nature has, as it were, an empire within an empire, and so to speak a double kingdom, of reason and of necessity, or of forms and of particles of matter.

COMMENTARY

Leibniz maintains that the group of all of the monads of the highest level—the rational souls or spirits (esprits)—constitutes a special sector of reality. For these intelligent, rational, free agents constitute a separate category of select beings, who share in the salient features of God himself (knowledge, power, morality). Because of this kinship, God takes a special interest in and feels a special responsibility for the spirits. He is not merely their creator but their paternalistic monarch. Here we enter upon the guiding idea of Leibniz's political philosophy, which is predicated on the paternalistic ideal of a benevolent ruler promoting the best interests of his subjects under the guidance of wise and knowledgeable counselors.

Latta offers some helpful observations regarding Leibniz's idea of a City of God:

The reference is to the *civitas Dei* of St. Augustine; but the difference of meaning is very great. St. Augustine's *civitas Dei* is the Christian Church as opposed to the *civitas terrena* or earthly state. Leibniz's City of God, on the other hand, is not set in opposition to an earthly state, but is the moral order of the universe, as distinct from its natural order. The City of God according to Leibniz, includes not Christians alone, but all men. (Latta, p. 267n.)

KEY WORDS:

spirits/*esprits*
God/*Dieu*
assemblage of all spirits/*assemblage de tous les esprits*
city of God/*cité de Dieu*
the most perfect state/*le plus parfait état*
the possible/*le possible*
monarch/*monarque*
the most perfect of monarchs/*le plus parfait des monarques*

SECTION 86

86. This City of God, this truly universal monarchy, is a moral world within the natural world, and is the most exalted and the most divine of the works of God. And it is in it that the glory of God truly consists, for there would be none at all if his grandeur and goodness were not known and admired by the spirits. It is also in relation to this divine city that he particularly has goodness, whereas his wisdom and power are manifested everywhere.

86. Cette Cité de Dieu, cette Monarchie veritablement universelle, est un Monde Moral, dans le Monde Naturel, et ce qu'il y a de plus elevé et de plus divin dans les ouvrages de Dieu: et c'est en luy que consiste veritablement la gloire de Dieu, puisqu'il n'y en auroit point, si sa grandeur et sa bonté n'étoient pas connues et admirées par les esprits; c'est aussi par rapport à cette cité divine, qu'il a proprement de la Bonté, au lieu que sa Sagesse et sa Puissance se monstrent partout.

(NS, sec. 16.) In metaphysical strictness we are in a state of perfect independence as concerns the influence of all the other created beings. This throws a wonderful light on the immortality of our soul as well and on the always uniform conservation of our individual being, which is perfectly regulated by its own nature and fully sheltered from all accidents from without, whatever appearance there may be to the contrary. Never has a system so clearly exhibited our elevation. Since each mind is as a world apart and sufficient unto itself, independent of every other created being, enveloping the infinite and expressing the universe, it is as durable, as subsistent, as absolute as the universe of creatures itself. We must therefore conclude that it must always play such a part as is most fitting to contribute to the perfection of the society of all minds, which is their moral union in the City of God.

(DM, sec. 35.) God must be considered not only as the principle and the cause of all substances and of all existing things, but also as the chief of all persons or intelligent substances, as the absolute monarch of the most perfect city or republic, such as is constituted by all the spirits together in the universe, God being the most complete of all spirits at the same time that he is greatest of all beings. For assuredly the spirits are the most perfect of substances and best express the divinity. Since all the nature, purpose, virtue and function of substances is, as has been sufficiently explained, to express God and the universe, there is no room for doubting that those substances which give the expression, knowing what they are doing and which are able to understand the great truths about God and the universe, do express God and the universe incomparably better than do those natures which are either brutish and incapable of recognizing truths, or are wholly destitute of sensation and knowledge. The difference between intelligent substances and those which are not intelligent is quite as great as between a mirror and one who sees. As God is himself the greatest and wisest of spirits it is easy to understand that the spirits with which he can, so to speak, enter into conversation and even into social relations by communicating to them in particular ways his feelings and his will so that they are able to know and love their benefactor, must be much nearer to him than the rest of created things which may be regarded as the instruments of spirits. In the same way we see that all wise persons consider far more the condition of a man than of anything else however precious it may be; and it seems that the greatest satisfaction which a soul, satisfied in other respects, can have is to see itself loved by others. However, with respect to God there is this difference that his glory and our worship can add nothing to his satisfaction, the recognition of creatures being nothing but a consequence of his sovereign and perfect felicity and being far from contributing to it or from causing it even in part. Nevertheless, that which is reasonable in finite spirits is found eminently in him and as we praise a king who prefers to preserve the life of a man before that of the most precious and rare of his animals, we should not doubt that the most enlightened and most just of all monarchs has the same preference.

(DM, sec. 36.) Felicity is to persons what perfection is to beings. And if the first principle of the existence of the physical world is the decree giving it as much perfection as possible, the first design of the moral world or City of God, which is the noblest part of the universe, must be to distribute through it the greatest possible felicity.

(DM, sec. 37.) God, inasmuch as he cares for the sparrows, will not neglect reasoning beings, who are infinitely more dear to him; how all the hairs of our heads are numbered; how heaven and earth may pass away but the word of God and that which belongs to the means of our salvation will not pass away; how God has more regard for the least one among intelligent souls than for the whole machinery of the world; how we ought not to fear those who are able to destroy the body but are unable to destroy the soul, since God alone can render the soul happy or unhappy; and how the souls of the righteous are protected by his hand against all the upheavals of the universe, since God alone is able to act upon them; how none of our acts are forgotten; how everything is to be accounted for; even careless words and even a spoonful of water which is well used; in fact how everything must result in the greatest welfare of the good, for then shall the righteous become like suns and neither our sense nor our minds have ever tasted of anything approaching the joys which God has laid up for those that love him.

COMMENTARY

God's goodness and benevolence find a suitable sphere of operation only through his relationship to other intelligent moral agents, namely the spirits: only in this relationship is God's grandeur fully realized. A world without spirits—without intelligent moral agents—would be wholly beneath the dignity of a divine being, even as a king would be degraded by ruling over a tank of fish rather than fellow humans as subjects. Here Leibniz once again echoes Nicholas of Cusa, who wrote, "God wishes to be known and therefore, because of this, all things are" (*Excerptationes ex sermonibus*, vi, 104a).

KEY WORDS:

city of God/*cité de Dieu (cité divine)*
universal monarchy/*monarchie universelle*
moral world/*monde moral*
natural world/*monde naturel*
glory/*gloire*
grandeur/*grandeur*
divine/*divin*
works of God/*ouvrages de Dieu*
spirits/*esprits*
goodness/*bonté*
wisdom/*sagesse*
power/*puissance*

SECTION 87

87. As we have already established a perfect harmony between two natural realms <in secs. 78–79>, the one of efficient and the other of final causes, we must here also recognize a further harmony between the physical realm of nature and the moral realm of grace, that is, between God considered as architect of the mechanism of the universe, and God considered as monarch of the divine city of spirits. (See *Theodicy*, secs. 62, 74, 112, 118, 130, 247, 248.)

87. *Comme nous avons établi ci-dessus une Harmonie parfaite entre deux Regnes Naturels, l'un des causes Efficientes, l'autre des Finales, nous devons remarquer ici encore une autre harmonie entre le regne Physique de la Nature et le regne Moral de la Grace, c'est à dire entre Dieu consideré comme Architecte de la Machine de l'univers, et Dieu consideré comme Monarque de la Cité divine des Esprits. (Théodicée, secs. 62, 74, 112, 118, 130, 247, 248.)*

(*Theodicy*, sec. 62.) Being on other considerations already convinced of the principle of Harmony in general, I was in consequence convinced likewise of the preformation and the Pre-established Harmony of all things amongst themselves, of that between nature and grace, between the decrees of God and our actions foreseen, between all parts of matter, and even between the future and the past, the whole in conformity with the sovereign wisdom of God, whose works are the most harmonious it is possible to conceive. Thus I could not fail to arrive at the system which declares that God created the soul in the beginning in such a fashion that it must produce and represent to itself successively that which takes place within the body, and the body also in such a fashion that it must do of itself that which the soul ordains. Consequently the laws that connect the thoughts of the soul in the order of final causes and in accordance with the evolution of perceptions must produce pictures that meet and harmonize with the impressions of bodies on our organs; and likewise the laws of movements in the body, which follow one another in the order of efficient causes, meet and so harmonize with the thoughts of the soul that the body is induced to act at the time when the soul wills it.

(*Theodicy*, sec. 74.) The *principle of the fitness of things* has seen to it that affairs were so ordered that the evil action must bring upon itself a chastisement. There is good reason to believe, following the parallelism of the two realms, that of final causes and that of efficient causes, that God has established in the universe a connexion between punishment or reward and bad or good action, in accordance wherewith the first should always be attracted by the second, and virtue and vice obtain their reward and their punishment in consequence of the natural sequence of things, which contains still another kind of pre-established harmony than that which appears in the communication between the soul and the body. For, in a word, all that God does, as I have said already, is harmonious to perfection.

(*Theodicy*, sec. 112.) The contemplation of divine wisdom leads us to believe that the realm of nature serves that of grace; and that God as an Architect has done all in a manner befitting God considered as a Monarch. We do not sufficiently know the nature of the forbidden fruit, or that of the action, or its effects, to judge of the details of this matter: nevertheless we must do God justice so far as to believe that it comprised something other than what painters depict for us.

(*Theodicy*, sec. 118.) I grant that the happiness of intelligent creatures is the principal part of God's design, for they are most like him; but nevertheless I do not see how one can prove that to be his sole aim. It is true that the realm of nature must serve the realm of grace: but, since all is connected in God's great design, we must believe that the realm of grace is also in some way adapted to that of nature, so that nature preserves the utmost order and beauty, to render the combination of the two the most perfect that can be. And there is no reason to suppose that God, for the sake of some lessening of moral evil, would reverse the whole order of nature. Each perfection or imperfection in the creature has its value, but there is none that has an infinite value. Thus the moral or physical good and evil of rational creatures does not infinitely exceed the good and evil which is simply metaphysical, namely that which lies in the perfection of the other creatures; and yet one would be bound to say this if the present maxim were strictly true. . . . It is certain God sets greater store by a man than a lion; nevertheless it can hardly be said with certainty that God prefers a single man in all respects to the whole of lion-kind. Even should that be so, it would by no means follow that the interest of a certain number of men would prevail over the consideration of a general disorder diffused through an infinite number of creatures. This opinion would be a remnant of the old and somewhat discredited maxim, that all is made solely for man.

(*Theodicy*, sec. 130.) It is true that God makes of matter and of spirits whatever he wills; but he is like a good sculptor, who will make from his block of marble only that which he judges to be the best, and who judges well. God makes of matter the most excellent of all possible machines; he makes of spirits the most excellent of all governments conceivable; and over and above all that, he establishes for their union the most perfect of all harmonies, according to the system I have proposed. Now since physical evil and moral evil occur in this perfect world, one must conclude (contrary to M. Bayle's assurance here) that *otherwise a still greater evil would have been altogether inevitable.* This great evil would be that God would have chosen ill if he had chosen otherwise than he has chosen. It is true that God is infinitely powerful; but his power is indeterminate, goodness and wisdom combined determine him to produce the best.

(*Theodicy*, sec. 247.) The system of general harmony which I assume . . . holds that the realm of efficient causes and that of final causes are parallel to each other; that God has no less the quality of the best monarch than that of the greatest architect; that matter is so disposed that the laws of motion serve as the best guidance for spirits; and that consequently it will prove that he has attained the utmost good possible, provided one reckon the metaphysical, physical and moral goods together.

(*Theodicy*, sec. 248.) But (M. Bayle will say) God having power to avert innumerable evils by one small miracle, why did he not employ it? . . . I have sufficiently met objections of this sort with this general answer, that God ought not to make choice of another universe since he has chosen the best, and has only made use of the miracles necessary thereto. Thus I answered M. Bayle's charge that miracles change the natural order of the universe. . . . But they in fact are part of God's plan from the start. And one must bear in mind that once the best plan of things has been chosen nothing can be changed therein.

(PNG, sec. 15.) For this reason all spirits, whether of men or of higher beings (*génies*), enter by virtue of reason and the eternal truths into a kind of society with God and are members of the City of God, that is to say, the most perfect state, formed and governed by the greatest and best of monarchs. Here there is no crime without punishment, no good action without a proportionate reward, and finally, as much virtue and happiness as is possible. And this takes place, not by a dislocation of nature, as if what God has planned for souls could disturb the laws of bodies, but by the very order of natural things itself, by virtue of the harmony pre-established from all time between the realms of nature and of grace, between God as architect and God as monarch, in such a way that nature leads to grace, and grace perfects nature by using it.

(NS, sec. 5.) Minds or rational souls are as little gods made in the image of God and having in them some ray of the light of the Divinity. This is why God governs minds as a prince governs his subjects or indeed as a father cares for his children, while he deals with other substances, instead, as an engineer handles his machines. Minds thus have special laws which place them beyond the revolutions of matter, and one can say that all the rest is made only for them, these revolutions themselves being adapted to the happiness of the good and the punishment of the evil.

(NS, sec. 14.) The organized mass in which the point of view of the soul is found <i.e., the body> is itself expressed more immediately by the soul and is in turn ready to act by itself following the laws of the corporeal mechanism, at the moment at which the soul wills but without either disturbing the laws of the other, the animal spirits and the blood taking on, at exactly the right moment, the motions required to correspond to the passions and the perceptions of the soul.

COMMENTARY

As Leibniz sees it, *Homo sapiens* is an amphibian—a creature of two realms. As an embodied spirit, we occupy the highest place in the kingdom of nature— while in the kingdom of grace, we occupy the lowest place. As embodied beings, we are subject to the material order of efficient causation. But as created intelligences, we operate in the order of final causation as well.

The harmony of the two realms of final and efficient causes which provide for mind-body coordination at the human level stands coordinate with the harmony of the two realms of nature and of grace at the theological level. (This section makes clear why Leibniz gave the companion essay to the *Monadology* the title "Principles of Nature and of Grace.")

In Leibniz's thought there are various levels or layers of harmonization:

• the voluntaristic harmony of mind-body interaction (of will and action)
• the cognitive harmony, between perception and its focus (of thought and its object)
• the causal harmony between the order of efficient and final causation (of physical causality and of purpose)
• the moral harmony of desert and reward (of nature and of grace)

All are aspects of the grand universal pre-established harmony ordained through the optimizing realization choice of a benevolent creator.

KEY WORDS:

(perfect) harmony/*harmonie (parfaite)*
natural realm/*règne naturel*
efficient and final causes/*causes efficientes et causes finales*
God as architect/*Dieu comme architecte*
God as monarch/*Dieu comme monarque*
mechanism of the universe/*machine de l'univers*
the realm of nature and the realm of grace/*le règne physique de la nature et le règne moral de la grâce*
divine city of spirits/*cité divine des esprits*

SECTION 88

88. This harmony brings it about that all things lead to grace by the ways of nature themselves, so that this globe, for example, must be destroyed and renewed in natural ways at those moments that the government of the spirits requires for the punishment of some and the reward of others. (See *Theodicy*, secs. 18–20, 110, 244, 245, 340.)

*88. Cette Harmonie fait que les choses conduisent à la grace par les voyes mêmes de la nature, et que ce globe par exemple doit être détruit et reparé par les voyes naturelles dans les momens, que le demande le gouvernement des Esprits; pour le chatiment des uns et la recompense des autres. (*Théodicée, *secs. 18 seqq., 110, 244, 245, 340.)*

(*Theodicy*, sec. 18.) Jesus Christ came to save men. He is the eternal Son of God, even as he is his only Son; but (according to some ancient Christians, and according to the author of this hypothesis) having taken upon him at first, from the beginning of things, the most excellent nature among created beings, to bring them all to perfection, he set himself amongst them: and this is the second filiation, whereby he is the first-born of all creatures. . . . And when the time of judgement shall draw near, when the present face of our globe shall be about to perish, he will return to it in visible form, thence to withdraw the good, transplanting them, it may be, in the sun, and to punish here the wicked with the demons that have allured them; then the globe of the earth will begin to burn and will be perhaps a comet. This fire will last for aeons upon aeons. The tail of the comet is intended by the smoke which will rise incessantly, according to the Apocalypse, and this fire will be hell, or the second death whereof Holy Scripture speaks. But at last hell will render up its dead, death itself will be destroyed; reason and peace will begin to hold sway again in the spirits that had been perverted; they will be sensible of their error, they will adore their Creator, and will even begin to love him all the more for seeing the greatness of the abyss whence they emerge. Simultaneously (by virtue of the *harmonic parallelism* of the Realms of Nature and of Grace) this long and great conflagration will have purged the earth's globe of its stains. It will become again a sun; its Presiding Angel will resume his place with the angels of his train; humans that were damned shall be with them numbered amongst the good angels; this chief of our globe shall render homage to the Messiah, chief of created beings.

(*Theodicy*, sec. 19.) It seemed to the ancients that there was only one earth inhabited, and even of that men held the antipodes in dread: the remainder of the world was, according to them, a few shining globes and a few crystalline spheres. Today, whatever bounds are given or not given to the universe, it must be acknowledged that there is an infinite number of globes, as great as and greater than ours, which have as much right as it to hold rational inhabitants, though it follows not at all that they are human. It is only one planet, that is to say one of the six principal satellites of our sun; and as all fixed stars are suns also, we see how small a thing our earth is in relation to visible things, since it is only an appendix of one amongst them. It may be that all suns are peopled only by blessed creatures, and nothing constrains us to think that many are damned, for few instances or few samples suffice to show the advantage which good extracts from evil. Moreover, since there is no reason for the belief that there are stars everywhere, is it not possible that there may be a great space beyond the region of the stars? Whether it be the Empyrean Heaven, or not, this immense space encircling all this region may in any case be filled with happiness and glory. It can be imagined as like the Ocean, whither flow the rivers of all blessed creatures, when they shall have reached their perfection in the system of the stars. What will become of the consideration of our globe and its inhabitants? Will it not be something incomparably less than a physical point, since our earth is as a point in comparison with the distance of some fixed stars? Thus since the proportion of that part of the universe which we know is almost lost in nothingness compared with that which is unknown, and which we yet have cause to assume, and since all the evils may be raised in objection before us are in this near nothingness, haply it may be that all evils are almost nothingness in comparison with the good things which are in the universe.

(*Theodicy*, sec. 20.) But it is necessary also to meet the more speculative and metaphysical difficulties which have been mentioned, and which concern the cause of evil. The question is asked first of all, whence does evil come? *Si Deus est, unde malum? Si non est, unde bonum?* The ancients attributed the cause of evil to matter which they believed uncreate and independent of God: but we, who derive all being from God, where shall we find the source of evil? The answer is, that it must be sought in the ideal nature of the creature, in so far as this nature is contained in the eternal verities which are in the understanding of God, independently of his will. For we must consider that there is an *original imperfection in the creature before sin*, because the creature is limited in its essence; whence ensues that it cannot know all, and that it can deceive itself and commit other errors.

(*Theodicy*, sec. 110.) One must dwell a little on what is said here, that he chose the possible beings "whom it pleased him to choose." For it must be borne in mind that when I say, "that pleases me," it is as though I were saying, "I find it good." Thus it is the ideal goodness of the object which pleases, and which makes me choose it among many others which do not please or which please less, that is to say, which contain less of that goodness which moves me. Now it is only the genuinely good that is capable of pleasing God: and consequently that which pleases God most, and which meets his choice, is the best.

(*Theodicy*, sec. 242.) It should be no cause for astonishment that I endeavour to elucidate these things by comparisons taken from pure mathematics, where everything proceeds in order, and where it is possible to fathom them by a close contemplation which grants us an enjoyment, so to speak, of the vision of the ideas of God. One may propose a succession or series of numbers perfectly irregular to all appearance, where the numbers increase and diminish variably without the emergence of any order; and yet he who knows the key to the formula, and who understands the origin and the structure of this succession of numbers, will be able to give a rule which, being properly understood, will show that the series is perfectly regular, and that it even has excellent properties. One may make this still more evident in lines. A line may have twists and turns, ups and downs, points of reflexion and points of inflexion, interruptions and other variations, so that one sees neither rhyme nor reason therein, especially when taking into account only a portion of the line; and yet it may be that one can give its equation and construction, wherein a geometrician would find the reason and the fittingness of all these so-called irregularities. That is how we must look upon the irregularities constituted by monstrosities and other so-called defects in the universe.

(*Theodicy*, sec. 244.) When I mention monstrosities I include numerous other apparent defects besides. We are acquainted with hardly anything but the surface of our globe; we scarce penetrate into its interior beyond a few hundred fathoms. That which we find in this crust of the globe appears to be the effect of some great upheavals. It seems that this globe was once on fire, and that the rocks forming the base of this crust of the earth are scoria remaining from a great fusion. In their entrails are found metal and mineral products, which closely resemble those emanating from our furnaces. . . . For when the earth's surface cooled after the great conflagration the moisture that the fire had driven into the air fell back upon the earth, washed its surface and dissolved and absorbed the solid salt that was left in the cinders, finally filling up this great cavity in the surface of our globe, to form the ocean filled with salt water.

(*Theodicy*, sec. 245.) But, after the fire, one must conclude that earth and water made ravages no less. It may be that the crust formed by the cooling, having below it great cavities, fell in, so that we live only on ruins, as among others Thomas Burnet, Chaplain to the late King of Great Britain, aptly observed. Sundry deluges and inundations have left deposits, whereof traces and remains are found which show that the sea was in places that to-day are most remote from it. But these upheavals ceased at last, and the globe assumed the shape that we see. Moses hints at these changes in few words: the separation of light from darkness indicates the melting caused by the fire; and the separation of the moist from the dry marks the effects of inundations. But who does not see that these disorders have served to bring things to the point where they now are, that we owe to them our riches and our comforts, and that through their agency this globe became fit for cultivation by us. These disorders passed into order. The disorders, real or apparent, that we see from afar are sunspots and comets; but we do not know what uses they supply, nor the rules prevailing therein. Time was when the planets were held to be wandering stars: now their motion is found to be regular. Peradventure it is the same with the comets: posterity will know.

(*Theodicy*, sec. 340.) For nothing gives clearer indication of the imperfection of a philosophy than the necessity experienced by the philosopher to confess that something comes to pass, in accordance with his system, for which there is no reason. That applies to the idea of Epicurus on the deviation of atoms. Whether it be God or Nature that operates, the operation will always have its reasons. In the operations of Nature, these reasons will depend either upon necessary truths or upon the laws that God has found the most reasonable; and in the operations of God, they will depend upon the choice of the supreme reason which causes them to act.

COMMENTARY

As Leibniz sees it, the harmonic coordination of the realms of nature and of grace means that it was not (for example) by a "miracle" that the Red Sea parted for Moses, but that the whole course of world history, human and natural alike (as encoded in the complete individual concepts of the monads involved) has so functioned as to yield that particular phenomenon at that particular time.

KEY WORDS:

harmony/*harmonie*
grace/*grâce*
natural ways/*voies naturelles*

destroyed and renewed/*détruit et réparé*
spirits/*esprits*
government of spirits/*gouvernement des esprits*
reward and punishment/*récompense et châtiment*

SECTION 89

89. It can also be said that God as architect fully satisfies God as lawgiver. Thus sins must carry their penalty with them through the order of nature, and even in virtue of the mechanical make-up of things. And similarly, good deeds will obtain their rewards in ways that are mechanical as regards bodies, even though this cannot and need not always happen immediately.

89. On peut dire encore, que Dieu comme Architecte contente en tout Dieu comme Legislateur, et qu'ainsi les pechés doivent porter leur peine avec eux par l'ordre de la nature, et en vertu même de la structure mecanique des choses; et que de même les belles actions s'attireront leurs recompenses par des voyes machinales par rapport aux corps, quoique cela ne puisse et ne doive pas arriver toujours sur le champ.

(*Theodicy*, sec. 211.) Rules are the expression of general will: the more one observes rules, the more regularity there is; simplicity and productivity are the aim of rules. I shall be met with the objection that a uniform system will be free to be too uniform, that would offend against the rules of harmony. . . . I believe therefore that God can follow a simple, productive, regular plan; but I do not believe that the best and the most regular is always opportune for all creatures simultaneously; and I judge *a posteriori*, for the plan chosen by God is not so. I have however, also shown this *a priori* in examples taken from mathematics. . . .

(NE, p. 189.) I find that it is essential to the happiness of created beings that their happiness never consists in complete attainment, which would make them insensate and stupified, but in continual and uninterrupted progress towards greater goods. Such progress is inevitably accompanied by desire or at least by constant disquiet, but of the kind I have just explained: it does not amount to discomfort, but is restricted to the elements or rudiments of suffering, which we cannot be aware of in themselves but which suffice to act as spurs and to stimulate the will. That is what a healthy man's appetite does, unless it amounts to that discomfort which unsettles us and gives us a tormenting obsession with the idea of whatever it is that we are without.

(NS, sec. 5.) Minds or rational souls . . . are of a superior order and have incomparably more perfection than have the forms which are sunk in matter, which I believe are found everywhere. For in comparison with these, minds or rational souls are as little gods made in the image of God and having in them some ray of the light of the Divinity. This is why God governs minds as a prince governs his subjects or indeed as a father cares for his children, while he deals with other substances, instead, as an engineer handles his machines. Minds thus have special laws which place them beyond the revolutions of matter, and one can say that all the rest is made only for them, these revolutions themselves being adapted to the happiness of the good and the punishment of the evil.

(G VII, 308; Loemker, p. 490; "On the Radical Origination of Things" [1697].) As for the afflictions, especially of good men, however, we must take it as certain that these lead to their greater good and that this is true not only theologically but also naturally. So a seed sown in the earth suffers before it bears fruit. In general, one may say that though afflictions are temporary evils, they are good in effect, for they are short cuts to greater perfection. So in physics the liquids which ferment slowly also are slower to settle, while those in which there is a stronger disturbance settle more promptly, throwing off impurities with greater force. We may well call this drawing back the better to spring forward [*qu'on recule pour mieux sauter*]. These views must therefore be affirmed not merely as gratifying and comforting but also as most true. And in general, I hold that there is nothing truer than happiness and nothing happier and sweeter than truth.

(G VII, 358–59; to Clarke, II.12 [1715].) If God is obliged to mend the course of nature from time to time, it must be done either supernaturally or naturally. If it be done supernaturally, we must have recourse to miracles in order to explain natural things, which is reducing a hypothesis *ad absurdum*, for everything may easily be accounted for by miracles. But if it be done naturally, then God will not be *intelligentia supramundana*; he will be comprehended under the nature of things, that is, he will be the soul of the world (*intelligentia mundana*).

(Loemker, pp. 565–66; "On the Common Concept of Justice" [ca. 1702].) We may say that it is the same in the government of intelligent substances under the kingship of God, in which everything seems confused to our eyes. Nevertheless, it must be the most beautiful and most marvelous arrangement of the world, since it comes from an Author who is the source of all perfection. But it is too great and too beautiful for spirits with our present range to be able to perceive it so soon. To try to see it here is like wishing to take a novel by the tail and to claim to have deciphered the plot from the first book; the beauty of a novel, instead, is great in the degree that order emerges from very great apparent confusion. The composition would thus contain a fault if the reader could divine the entire issue at once. But what is only interest and beauty in novels, which imitate creation, so to speak, is also utility and wisdom in this great and true poem, this word-by-word creation, the universe. The beauty and justice of the divine government have been hidden in part from our eyes, not only because it could not be otherwise without changing the entire harmony of the world, but also because it is proper in order that there may be more exercise of free virtue, wisdom, and a love of God which is not mercenary, since the rewards and punishments are still outwardly invisible and appear only to the eyes of our reason or faith.

COMMENTARY

On bodies as mechanisms or automata see sections 64 and 77. As Leibniz sees it, the mechanical order of the world's physical processes is so arranged that the spirits, which always harmonize with bodies, will ultimately get their just deserts. Leibniz is persuaded that the course of world history is so arranged, overall and in the long run, that every creature (and every person) will ultimately automatically get its proper due—that the great story of universal history will have a happy ending with the good duly rewarded and the evil duly punished. It is this view of the course of history as a theater of divine justice where all will come right in due course in this "best of possible worlds" that marks Leibniz as an optimist.

KEY WORDS:

God as architect/*Dieu comme Architecte*
God as legislator/*Dieu comme Législateur*
rewards/*récompenses*
punishment/*châtiment*
good deeds and sins/*belles actions et péchés*
mechanical make-up of things/*structure mécanique des choses*
bodies/*corps*
mechanical means/*voies machinales*
the order of nature/*l'ordre de la nature*

SECTION 90

90. Finally, under this perfect government no good deed whatever will be unrewarded and no wicked one unpunished. And all must result for the benefit of the good, that is, of those who are nowise malcontents in this great state, who trust in providence after having done their duty, and who love and imitate, as is proper, the author of all good, taking pleasure in the consideration of his perfections according to the nature of a genuine *pure love*, which makes one take pleasure in the felicity of the beloved. It is this that makes wise and virtuous people work for everything that seems in conformity with the presumptive or antecedent divine will, and nevertheless content themselves with what God actually brings to pass by his secret, consequent or decisive will. They recognize that, if only we could sufficiently understand the order of the universe, we should find that it surpasses all the desires of the wisest, and that it is impossible to make it any better than it is, not only for the whole generally, but also for ourselves in particular, if we are properly attached to the author of all, not only as the architect and efficient cause of our being, but also as our master and as the final cause, who ought to be the whole aim of our will and who alone can bring us happiness. (See *Theodicy*, Preface; secs. 134 *ad fin.*, 278.)

90. *Enfin sous ce gouvernement parfait il n'y aura point de bonne Action sans recompense, point de mauvaise sans chatiment: et tout doit reussir au bien des bons, c'est à dire de ceux qui ne sont point des mécontents dans ce grand Etat, qui se fient à la providence, après avoir fait leur devoir et qui aiment et imitent, comme il faut, l'Auteur de tout bien, se plaisant dans la consideration de ses perfections suivant la nature du pur amour veritable, qui fait prendre plaisir à la felicité de ce qu'on aime. C'est ce qui fait travailler les personnes sages et vertueuses à tout ce qui paroit conforme à la volonté divine presomptive ou antecedente; et se contenter cependant de ce que Dieu fait arriver effectivement par sa volonté secrete, consequente ou decisive; en reconnaissant que, si nous pouvions entendre assez l'ordre de l'univers, nous trouverions qu'il surpasse tous les souhaits des plus sages, et qu'il est impos-*

sible de le rendre meilleur qu'il est, non seulement pour le tout en general,
mais encore pour nous mêmes en particulier, si nous sommes attachés comme
il faut à l'Auteur du tout, non seulement comme à l'Architecte et à la cause
efficiente de nôtre être, mais encore comme à notre Maître, et à la cause Finale
qui doit faire tout le but de nôtre volonté, et peut seul faire nôtre bonheur.
*(*Théodicée, *Préface,* *4a-b; secs. *134* ad fin., *278.)*

(*Theodicy*, Preface; G VI, 27–28.) Moreover, the fall of the first man having happened only with God's permission, and God having resolved to permit it only when once he had considered its consequences, which are the corruption of the mass of the human race and the choice of a small number of elect, with the abandonment of all the rest, it is useless to conceal the difficulty by limiting one's view to the mass already corrupt. One must, in spite of oneself, go back to the knowledge of the consequences of the first sin, preceding the decree whereby God permitted it, and whereby he permitted simultaneously that the damned should be involved in the mass of perdition and should not be delivered: for God and the sage make no resolve without considering its consequences. I hope to remove all these difficulties. . . . I will show that God himself, although he always chooses the best, does not act by an absolute necessity, and that the laws of nature laid down by God, founded upon the fitness of things, keep the mean between geometrical truths, absolutely necessary, and arbitrary decrees; which M. Bayle and other modern philosophers have not sufficiently understood. Further I will show that there is an indifference in freedom, because there is no absolute necessity for one course or the other; but yet that there is never an indifference of perfect equipoise. And I will demonstrate that there is in free actions a perfect spontaneity beyond all that has been conceived hitherto. Finally I will make it plain that the hypothetical and the moral necessity which subsist in free actions are open to no objection. . . . Likewise concerning the origin of evil in its relation to God, I offer a vindication of his perfections that shall extol not less his holiness, his justice and his goodness than his greatness, his power and his independence. I show how it is possible for everything to depend upon God, for him to co-operate in all the actions of creatures, even, if you will, to create these creatures continually, and nevertheless not to be the author of sin. Here also it is demonstrated how the private nature of evil should be understood. Much more than that, I explain how evil has a source other than the will of God, and that one is right therefore to say of moral evil that God wills it not, but simply permits it. Most important of all, however, I show that it has been possible for God to permit sin and misery, and even to co-operate therein and promote it, without detriment to his holiness and his supreme goodness: although, generally speaking, he could have avoided all these evils.

(*Theodicy*, sec. 23.) Thence it follows that God wills *antecedently* the good and *consequently* the best. And as for evil, God wills moral evil not at all, and physical evil or suffering he does not will absolutely. Thus it is that there is no absolute predestination to damnation; and one may say of physical evil, that God wills it often as a penalty owing to guilt, and often also as a means to an end, that is, to prevent greater evils or to obtain greater good.

(*Theodicy*, sec. 24.) Concerning sin or moral evil, although it happens very often that it may serve as a means of obtaining good or of preventing another evil, it is not this that renders it a sufficient object of the divine will or a legitimate object of a created will. It must only be admitted or *permitted* in so far as it is considered to be a certain consequence of an indispensable duty.

(*Theodicy*, sec. 25.) But in relation to God nothing is open to question, nothing can be opposed to *the rule of the best*, which suffers neither exception nor dispensation. It is in this sense that God permits sin: for he would fail in what he owes to himself, in what he owes to his wisdom, his goodness, his perfection, if he followed not the grand result of all his tendencies to good, and if he chose not that which is absolutely best, not withstanding the evil of guilt, which is involved therein by the supreme necessity of the eternal verities. Hence the conclusion that God wills all good *in himself antecedently*, that he wills the best *consequently* as an *end*, that he wills what is indifferent, and physical evil, sometimes as a *means*, but that he will only permit moral evil as the *sina qua non* or as a hypothetical necessity which connects it with the best. Therefore the *consequent will* of God, which has sin for its object, is only *permissive*.

(*Theodicy*, sec. 119.) It is not strictly true (though it appear plausible) that the benefits God imparts to the creatures who are capable of felicity tend solely to their happiness. All is connected in Nature; and if a skilled artisan, an engineer, an architect, a wise politician often makes one and the same thing serve several ends, if he makes a double hit with a single throw, when that can be done conveniently, one may say that God, whose wisdom and power are perfect, does so always. That is husbanding the ground, the time, the place, the material, which make up as it were his outlay. Thus God has more than one purpose in his projects. The felicity of all rational creatures is one of the aims he has in view; but it is not his whole aim, nor even his final aim. Therefore it happens that the unhappiness of some of these creatures may come about *by concomitance*, and as a result of other greater goods. . . . The goods as such, considered in themselves, are the object of the antecedent will of God. God will produce as much reason and knowledge in the universe as his plan can admit. One can conceive of a mean between an antecedent will altogether pure and primitive, and a consequent and final will. The *primitive antecedent will* has as its object each good and each evil in itself, detached from all combination, and tends to advance the good and prevent the evil. The *mediate will* relates to combinations, as when one attaches a good to an evil: then the will will have some tendency towards this combination when the good exceeds the evil therein. But the *final and decisive will* results from consideration of all the goods and all the evils that enter into our deliberation, it results from a total combination. This shows that a mediate will, although it may in a sense pass as consequent in relation to a pure and primitive will, must be considered antecedent in relation to the final and decretory will. God gives reason to the human race; misfortunes arise thence by concomitance. His pure antecedent will tends towards giving reason, as a great good, and preventing the evils in question. But when it is a question of the evils that accompany this gift which God has made to us of reason, the compound, made up of the combination of reason and of these evils, will be the object of a mediate will of God, which will tend towards producing or preventing this compound, according as the good or the evil prevails therein. But even though it should prove that reason did more harm than good to men (which, however, I do not admit), whereupon the mediate will of God would discard it with all its concomitants, it might still be the case that it was more in accordance with the perfection of the universe to give reason to men, notwithstanding all the evil consequences which it might have with reference to them. Consequently, the final will or the decree of God, resulting from all the considerations he can have, would be to give it to them. And, far from being subject to blame for this, he would be blameworthy if he did not so. Thus the evil, or the mixture of goods and evils wherein the evil prevails, happens only *by concomitance*, because it is connected with greater goods that are outside this mixture. This mixture, therefore, or this compound, is not to be conceived as a grace or as a gift from God to us; but the good that is found mingled therein will nevertheless be good. Such is God's gift of reason to those who make ill use thereof. It is always a good in itself; but the combination of this good with the evils that proceed from its abuse is not a good with regard to those who in consequence thereof become unhappy. Yet it comes to be by concomitance, because it serves a greater good in relation to the universe. And it is doubtless that which prompted God to give reason to those who have made it an instrument of their unhappiness. Or, to put it more precisely, in accordance with my system God, having found among the possible beings some rational creatures who misuse their reason, gave existence to those who are included in the best possible plan of the universe.

(*Theodicy*, sec. 134.) God wishes to save all men: that means that he would save them if men themselves did not prevent it, and did not refuse to receive his grace; and he is not bound or prompted by reason always to overcome their evil will. He does so sometimes nevertheless, when superior reasons allow of it, and when his consequent and decretory will, which results from all his reasons, makes him resolve upon the election of a certain number of men. He give aids to all for their conversion and for perseverance, and these aids suffice in those who have good will, but they do not always suffice to give good will. Men obtain this good will either through particular aids or through circumstances which cause the success of the general aids. God cannot refrain from offering other remedies which he knows men will reject, bringing upon themselves all the greater guilt: but shall one wish that God be unjust in order that man may be less criminal? Moreover, the grace that does not serve the one may serve the other, and indeed always serves the totality of God's plan, which is the best possible in conception. Shall God not give the rain, because there are low-lying places which will be thereby incommoded? . . . God's object has in it something infinite, his cares embrace the universe: what we know thereof is almost nothing, and we desire to gauge his wisdom and his goodness by our knowledge. What temerity, or rather what absurdity! . . . God does all the best possible, in accordance with the infinite wisdom which guides his actions. It is true that we have already before our eyes proofs and tests of this, when we see something entire, some whole complete in itself, and isolated, so to speak, among the works of God. Such a whole, shaped as it were by the hand of God, is a plant, an animal, a man. We cannot wonder enough at the beauty and the contrivance of its structure. But when we see some broken bone, some piece of animal's flesh, some sprig of a plant, there appears to be nothing but confusion, unless an excellent anatomist observe it: and even he would recognize nothing therein if he had not before seen like pieces attached to their whole. It is the same with the government of God: that which we have been able to see hitherto is not a large enough piece for recognition of the beauty and the order in the Divine City, which we see not yet here on earth, would be an object of our faith, of our hope, of our confidence in God. If there are any who think otherwise, so much the worse for them, they are malcontents in the State of the greatest and the best of all monarchs; and they are wrong not to take advantage of the examples he has given them of his wisdom and his infinite goodness, whereby he reveals himself as being not only wonderful, but also worthy of love beyond all things.

(*Theodicy*, sec. 278.) All *pleasure* is a feeling of some perfection; one *loves* an object in proportion as one feels its perfections; nothing surpasses the divine perfections. Whence it follows that charity and love of God give the greatest pleasure that can be conceived, in that proportion in which one is penetrated by these feelings, which are not common among men, busied and taken up as men are with the objects that are concerned with their passions.

(*Theodicy*, Abridgment, Obj. 4.) It may be that one can prevent the sin, but that one ought not to do so, because one could not do so without committing a sin oneself, or (when God is concerned) without acting unreasonably. I have given instances of that, and have applied them to God himself. It may be also that one contributes to the evil, and that one even opens the way to it sometimes, in doing things one is bound to do. And when one does one's duty, or (speaking of God) when, after full consideration, one does that which reason demands, one is not responsible for events, even when one foresees them. One does not will these evils; but one is willing to permit them for a greater good, which one cannot in reason help preferring to other considerations. This is a *consequent* will, resulting from acts of *antecedent* will, in which one wills the good. I know that some persons, in speaking of the antecedent and consequent will of God, have meant by the antecedent that which wills that all men be saved, and by the consequent that which wills, in consequence of persistent sin, that there be some damned, damnation being a result of sin. But these are only examples of a more general notion, and one may say with the same reason, that God wills by his antecedent will that men sin not, and that by his consequent or final and decretory will (which is always followed by its effect) he wills to permit that they sin, this permission being a result of superior reasons. One has indeed justification for saying, in general, that the antecedent will of God tends towards the production of good and the prevention of evil, each taken in itself, and as it were detached (*particulariter et secundum quid:* St. Thomas, *Summa Theol.*, I, qu. 19, art. 6) according to the measure of the degree of each good or of each evil. Likewise one may say that the consequent, or final and total, divine will tends towards the production of as many goods as can be put together, whose combination thereby becomes determined, and involves also the permission of some evils and the exclusion of some goods, as the best possible plan of the universe demands. Arminius . . . explained very well that the will of God can be called consequent not only in relation to the action of the creature considered beforehand in the divine understanding, but also in relation to other anterior acts of divine will. But it is enough to consider the passage cited from Thomas Aquinas, and that from Scotus (I, dist. 46, qu. 11), to see that they make this distinction as I have made it here.

(PNG, sec. 16.) Thus, though reason cannot teach us the details of the great future, these being reserved for revelation, we can be assured by this same reason that things are arranged in a way which surpasses our desires. God being also the most perfect, the happiest, and therefore the most lovable of substances, and *true pure love* consisting in the state which causes pleasure to be taken in the perfections and the felicity of the beloved, this love must give us the greatest pleasure of which one is capable, since God is its object.

(PNG, sec. 17.) And it is easy to love him as we ought if we know him as I have said. For though God is not visible to our external senses, he is nonetheless most love-worthy and gives very great pleasure. We see how much pleasure honors give to men, although they do not consist of qualities which appear to the external senses. Martyrs and fanatics, though the affection of the latter is not well ordered, show what power the pleasure of the spirit has. What is more, even the pleasures of sense are reducible to intellectual pleasures, known confusedly. Music charms us, although its beauty consists only in the agreement of numbers and in the counting, which we do not perceive but which the soul nevertheless continues to carry out, of the beats or vibrations of sounding bodies which coincide at certain intervals. The pleasures which the eye finds in proportions are of the same nature, and those caused by other senses amount to something similar, although we may not be able to explain them so distinctly.

(PNG, sec. 18.) It may even be said that the love of God already gives us, here and now, a foretaste of future felicity. And although it is disinterested, by itself it constitutes our greatest good and interest, even when we do not seek these in it and when we consider only the pleasure it gives and disregard the utility it produces. For it gives us a perfect confidence in the goodness of our Author and Master, and this produces a true tranquility of spirit, not such as the Stoics have who resolutely force themselves to be patient, but by a present contentment which itself assures us of future happiness. And apart from the present pleasure, nothing could be more useful for the future, for the love of God also fulfils our hopes and leads us in the way of supreme happiness, since, by virtue of the perfect order established in the universe, everything is done in the best possible way, as much for the general good as for the greatest particular good of those who are convinced of it and are satisfied by the divine government. This cannot fail to be true of those who know how to love the source of all good. It is true that the supreme happiness (with whatever *beatific vision* or knowledge of God it may be accompanied) cannot ever be full, because God, being infinite, cannot ever be known entirely. Thus our happiness will never consist, and ought never to consist, in complete happiness, which leaves nothing to be desired and which would stupefy our spirit, but in a perpetual progress to new pleasures and new perfections.

(DM, 35.) God must be considered not only as the principle and the cause of all substances and of all existing things, but also the chief of all persons or intelligent substances, as the absolute monarch of the most perfect city or republic, such as is constituted by all the spirits together in the universe, God being the most complete of all spirits at the same time that he is greatest of all beings. For assuredly the spirits are the most perfect of substances and best express the divinity. Since all the nature, purpose, virtue and function of substances is, as has been sufficiently explained, to express God and the universe, there is no room for doubting that those substances which give the expression, knowing what they are doing and which are able to understand the great truths about God and the universe, do express God and the universe incomparably better than do those natures which are either brutish and incapable of recognizing truths, or as wholly destitute of sensation and knowledge. The difference between intelligent substances and those which are not intelligent is quite as great as between a mirror and one who sees. As God himself is the greatest and wisest of spirits it is easy to understand that the spirits with which he can, so to speak, enter into conversation and even into social relations by communicating to them in particular ways his feelings and his will so that they are able to know and love their benefactor, must be much nearer to him than the rest of created things which may be regarded as the instruments of spirits.

(DM, 36.) God's being a spirit himself dominates all the consideration which he may have toward created things. Spirits alone are made in his image, being as it were of his blood or as children in the family, since they alone are able to serve him of free will, and to act consciously imitating the divine nature. A single spirit is worth a whole world, because it not only expresses the whole world, but it also knows it and governs itself as does God. In this way we may say that though every substance expresses the whole universe, yet the other substances express the world rather than God, while spirits express God rather than the world. This nature of spirits, so noble that it enables them to approach divinity as much as is possible for created things, has as a result that God derives infinitely more glory from them than from the other beings, or rather the other beings furnish to spirits the material for glorifying him. This moral quality of God which constitutes him Lord and Monarch of spirits influences him so to speak personally and in a unique way. It is through this that he humanizes himself, that he is willing to tolerate anthropomorphisms, and that he enters into social relations with us and this consideration is so dear to him that the happy and prosperous condition of his empire which consists in the greatest possible felicity of its inhabitants, becomes supreme among his laws. . . . In fine, God being at the same time the most just and the most benevolent of monarchs, and requiring only a good will on the part of men, provided that it be sincere and intentional, his subjects cannot desire a better condition. To render them perfectly happy he desires only that they love him.

(G III, 387; *Codex iuris diplomaticus* [1693].) Thus the contemplation of beautiful things is itself pleasant, and a painting of Raphael affects him who understands it, even if it offers no material gains, so that he keeps it in his sight and takes delight in it, in a kind of image of love. But when the beautiful object is at the same time itself capable of happiness, this affection passes over into true love. The *divine love* moreover, excels over those loves because God can be loved with the happiest result, since nothing is happier than God, and at the same time nothing can be conceived more beautiful and more worthy of happiness. And since he possesses supreme power and supreme wisdom, his happiness is not only built into ours (if we are wise; that is, if we love him), but it also constitutes ours.

(G VII, 88; "Notes for a *Scientia Generalis*" [ca. 1680].) Nothing serves our happiness better than the illumination of our understanding and the exercise of our will to act according to our understanding, and this illumination is to be sought especially in the knowledge of such things as can bring our understanding ever further into a higher light. For there springs from such knowledge an enduring progress in wisdom and virtue, and therefore also in perfection and joy, the advantage of which remains with the soul even after this life.

(Loemker, pp. 219–20; "Dialogue Between Polidore and Théophide" [ca. 1678].) Since you have acknowledged this great point, let us draw its practical consequences. *First*, it follows that the world is governed in such a way that a wise person who is well informed will have nothing to find fault with and can find nothing more to desire. *Second*, every wise man ought to be content, not only out of necessity as if he were compelled to be patient, but with pleasure and a kind of extreme satisfaction, knowing that everything happens in such a way that the interests of each individual person who is persuaded of this truth will be achieved with every possible advantage. For when God admits us a little further into his secrets than he has until now, then among other surprises, there will be that of seeing the wonderful inventions which he has used to make us happy beyond our possible conception. *Third*, we ought to love God above all things, since we find everything with greater perfection in him than in things themselves, and since his goodness provides us with our whole power. For it is by this goodness that we obtain everything with greater perfection in him than in things themselves, and since his goodness provides us with our power. *Fourth*, with these opinions we can be happy in advance here below, before enjoying everything which God has prepared for us; those who are discontent, on the other hand, expose themselves to losing voluntarily everything that God has tried to give them. It can be said that this resignation of our will to that of God, whom we have every reason to trust, follows from the truly divine love, whereas our dissatisfaction and even our disappointment in mundane matters contain something of hatred toward God, which is the ultimate of misery. *Fifth*, we ought to give witness of the supreme love which we bear toward God through the charity we owe to our neighbor. And we ought to make every effort imaginable to contribute something to the public good. For it is God who is the Lord; it is to him that the public good pertains as his own. And all that we do unto the least of these, his subjects, whom he has the goodness to treat as brothers, we have done unto him; all the more will he receive as brother whoever contributes to the general good. *Sixth*, we must try to perfect ourselves as much as we can, and especially the mind, which is properly what we call ourself. And since perfection of mind consists in the knowledge of truth and the exercise of virtue, we should be persuaded that those who in this life have had the best entrance into eternal truths and the most transparent and clearest knowledge of God's perfection, and as a result have loved him more and witnessed with more ardor for the general good, will be susceptible of greater happiness in the life to come. For *finally*, nothing is neglected in nature; nothing is lost with God; all our hairs are numbered, and not a glass of water will be forgotten; . . . no good action goes without reward, no each one without some punishment; no perfection without a series of others unto infinity.

(Riley, p. 59; "The Common Concept of Justice" [ca. 1703].) What Cicero said allegorically of ideal justice is really true in relation to this substantial justice (i.e., what "coincides with the good pleasure of God"): that if we could see this justice, we would be inflamed by its beauty. One can compare the divine monarchy to a kingdom whose sovereign would be a queen more spiritual and more wise than Queen Elizabeth; more judicious, more happy and, in a word, greater than Queen Anne; more clever, more wise, and more beautiful than the Queen of Prussia: in short, as accomplished as it is possible to be. Let us imagine that the perfections of this queen make such an impression on the minds of her subjects that they take the greatest pleasure in obeying and pleasing her: in this case everyone would be virtuous and just by inclination. It is this which happens literally, and beyond everything one can describe, with respect to God and those who know him. It is in him that wisdom, virtue, justice, and greatness are accompanied by sovereign beauty. One cannot know God as one ought without loving him above all things, and one cannot love him thus without willing what he wills. His perfections are infinite and cannot end, and this is why the pleasure which consists in the feeling of his perfections is the greatest and most durable which can exist. That is, the greatest happiness, which causes one to love him, causes one to be happy and virtuous at the same time.

COMMENTARY

The idea that "all should result for the benefit of the good" is evidently an allusion to Romans 8:28 ("all things work together for the benefit of those who love God"). For Leibniz, as for the Stoics and many Christian thinkers as well, contentment with the order established by a benevolent deity is a cardinal virtue.

Leibniz holds that there is indeed such a thing as moral evil, which arises when spirits comport themselves as malcontent malingerers within the City of God. But the reason for this lies in their own nature and not in the world's being somehow a thing of evil or imperfection. At the cosmic level, evil is nothing positive but is the product of a lack or privation inherent in the nature of things, akin to the cold that is an absence of warmth on the earth's shady side: "Evil needs no explanation through a particular principle, *per principium maleficium*, any more than do cold and darkness need a *principium frigidum* or a principle of darkness. Evil itself comes only from privation; the positive enters therein only by concomitance" (*Theodicy*, sec. 153). Note that Leibniz does not say that evil *is* mere privation but rather that it *comes from* mere privation.

The distinction between the antecedent and the consequent will of God derives from St. Thomas Aquinas, who wrote: "This distinction is not founded upon the Divine will itself, for in it there is neither before nor after; but it is founded upon the objects of His will. . . . A thing may be considered either in itself, absolutely, or with some particular circumstance, which forms a subsequent consideration. For instance it is good in itself that man should live and bad that he should be killed, considering the matter absolutely; but if we add, with regard to some particular man, that he is a murderer or that his living is a source of danger to a large number of people, in this case it will be good that the man should be killed, and bad that he should live. Accordingly it may be said that a judge wills with an antecedent will that every man should continue to live, but wills with a consequent will that a murderer should be hanged." (*Summa Theologica*, I, qu. 19, art., 6; compare *De Veritate*, qu. 23, art., 30, and see Leibniz, G VI, 442.)

God's antecedent (presumptive) unconditional will is that we should all be good—this is what he would like us to do—absolutely and ideally. But his consequent and circumstance-conditioned will, as embodied in the world created through his ultimate, all-inclusive decisions (hence here called "decisive") is that we should do what we choose to do as free agents. And so, even though we choose to do evil (even in the best possible world), as the best available prospect this world nevertheless still remains the one he (consequently) chooses.

For Leibniz, animals can have well-being (*bien être*) but only rational agents have the self-awareness (*apperception*) required for the realization of *happiness* (*bonheur*). Note, however, that for Leibniz the happiness of finite agents does not consist in the attainment of a stable state, but in a progress, a striving, a teleological nisus toward an improved condition of things. He sees the highest duty of the intelligent spirits to reside in an imitation of God's creative activity, an *imitatio dei* of sorts (secs. 83, 90), which, in the case of limited beings, lies in an effort to achieve a condition of greater perfection.

As L. E. Loemker informatively indicates, Leibniz's discussion reflects

> the bitter debate on the issue of disinterested love, which broke out between Fénelon and Bossuet after the appearance of the former's *Explication des maximes des saints sur la vie intérieure* in 1697. Fénelon asserted that pure love must "exclude every interested motive" and that "the soul must make the absolute sacrifice of its self-interest for eternity." The theological conflict which followed led to Fénelon's banishment from the court in August, 1697, and the pope's condemnation of the *Explication* in March, 1699 (see A. Cherel, *Fénelon ou la réligion du pur amour* [Paris, 1934]). (Loemker, p. 430n.)

Leibniz's closing strikes a powerfully optimistic note, setting out in strong terms his personal vision of what a genuine love of God demands—confident faith in a divinely ordained order of justice and benevolence. Leibniz does not, however, hold that this present state (or indeed any other particular state) of the world could not be better. On the contrary, he inclines toward a conception of progress that sees the world as always (or generally) getting better in the future than it was earlier on. What cannot be improved upon, as he sees it, is not the present conditional things, but the world's course taken all in all, in its historical totality. Any way of improving this-here-now would exact a sacrifice in the goodness embodied in the world's good overall.

KEY WORDS:

good deed/*bonne action*
perfect government/*gouvernement parfait*
reward/*récompense*
punishment/*châtiment*
the good/*les bons*
the bad/*les mauvaises*
malcontents/*mécontents*
best possible world/*le meilleur univers*
antecedent and consequent will/*volonté antécédente* (or *présomptive*) *et conséquente* (or *décisive*)
pure love/*pur amour (de Dieu)*
true happiness/*bonheur véritable* (*félicité*)
God/*Dieu*
God as architect/*Dieu comme architecte*
the author of all/*l'auteur du tout*
efficient cause/*cause efficiente*

final cause/*cause finale*
order of the universe/*ordre de l'univers*
divine will/*volonté divine*
the best/*le meilleur*
perfection/*perfection*
the wise/*les sages*
the virtuous/*les vertueuses*
will/*volonté*

APPENDIX

THE MYTH OF SEXTUS

(From the final sections [414–17] of the *Theodicy*)

Theodorus journeyed to Athens where he was bidden to lie down to sleep in the temple of the Goddess. Dreaming, he found himself transported into an unknown country. There stood a palace of unimaginable splendor and prodigious size. The Goddess Pallas appeared at the gate, surrounded by rays of dazzling majesty. . . . She touched the face of Theodorus with an olive-branch, which she was holding in her hand. And lo! he had become able to confront the divine radiancy of the daughter of Jupiter, and of all that she should show him. Jupiter who loves you (she said to him) has commended you to me to be instructed. You see here the palace of the fates, where I keep watch and ward. Here are representations not only of that which happens but also of all that which is possible. Jupiter, having surveyed them before the beginning of the existing world, classified the possibilities into worlds, and chose the best of all. He comes sometimes to visit these places, to enjoy the pleasure of recapitulating things and of renewing his own choice, which cannot fail to please him. I have only to speak, and we shall see a whole world that my father might have produced, wherein will be represented anything that can be asked of him; and in this way one may know also what would happen if any particular possibilities should attain unto existence. And whenever the conditions are not determinate enough, there will be as many such worlds differing from one another as one shall wish, which will answer differently the same question, in as many ways as possible. You learnt geometry in your youth, like all well-instructed Greeks. You know therefore that when the conditions of a required point do not sufficiently determine it, and there is an infinite number of them, they all fall into what geometricians call a locus, and this locus at least (which is often a line) will be determinate. Thus you can picture to yourself an ordered succession of worlds, which shall contain each and every one the case that is in question, and shall vary its circumstances and its consequences. But if you put a case that differs from the actual world only in one single definite thing and in its results, a certain one of those determinate worlds will answer you. These worlds are all here, that is, in ideas. I will show you some, wherein shall be found, not absolutely the same Sextus as you have seen (that is not possible, he carries with him always that which he shall be) but several Sextuses resembling him, possessing all that you know already of the true Sextus, but not all that is already in him imperceptibly, nor in consequence all that shall yet happen to him. You will find in one world a very happy and noble Sextus, in another a Sextus content with a mediocre state, a Sextus, indeed of every kind and endless diversity of forms. Thereupon the Goddess led Theodorus into one of the halls of the palace: when he was within, it was no longer a hall, it was a world. . . . At the command of Pallas there came within view Dodona with the temple of Jupiter, and Sextus issuing thence; he could be heard saying that he would obey the God. And lo! he goes to a city lying between two seas, resembling Corinth. He buys there a small garden; cultivating it, he finds a treasure; he becomes a rich man, enjoying affection and esteem; he dies at a great age, beloved of the whole city. Theodorus saw the whole life of Sextus as at one glance, and as in a stage presentation. There was a great volume of writings in this hall: Theodorus could not refrain from asking what that meant. It is the history of this world which we are now visiting, the Goddess told him; it is the book of its fates. You have seen a number on the forehead of Sextus. Look in this book for the place which it indicates. Theodorus looked for it, and found there the history of Sextus in a form more ample than the outline he had seen. Put your finger on any line you please, Pallas said to him, and you will see represented actually in all its detail that which the line broadly indicates. He obeyed, and he saw coming into view all the characteristics of a portion of the life of that Sextus. They passed into another hall, and lo! another world, another Sextus, who, issuing from the temple, and having resolved to obey Jupiter, goes to Thrace. There he marries the daughter of the king, who had no other children; he succeeds him, and he is adored by his subjects. They went into other rooms, and always they saw new scenes. The halls rose in a pyramid, becoming even more beautiful as one mounted towards the apex, and representing more beautiful worlds. Finally they reached the highest one which was the most beautiful one of all: for the pyramid had a beginning, but one could not see its end; it had an apex, but no base; it went on increasing to infinity. That is (as the Goddess explained) because amongst an endless number of possible worlds there is the best of all, else would God not have determined to create any; but there is not any one which has not also less perfect worlds below it: that is why the pyramid goes on descending to infinity. Theodorus, entering this highest hall, became entranced in ecstasy; he had to receive succour from the Goddess, a drop of a divine liquid placed on his tongue restored him; he was beside himself for joy. We are in the real true world (said the Goddess) and you are at the source of happiness. Behold what Jupiter makes ready for you, if you continue to serve him faithfully. Here is Sextus as he is, and as he will be in reality. He issues from the temple in a rage, he scorns the counsel of the Gods. You see him going to Rome, bringing confusion everywhere, violating the wife of his friend. There he is driven out with his father, beaten, unhappy. If Jupiter had placed here a Sextus happy at Corinth or King in Thrace, it would be no longer this world. And nevertheless he could not have failed to choose this world, which surpasses in perfection all the others, and which forms the apex of the pyramid. Else would Jupiter have renounced his wisdom, he would have banished me, me his daughter. You see that my father did not make Sextus wicked; he was so from all eternity, he was so always and freely. My father only granted him the existence which his wisdom could not refuse to the world where he is included: he made him pass from the region of the possible to that of the actual beings. The crime of Sextus serves for great things: it renders Rome free; thence will arise a great empire, which will show noble examples to mankind. But that is nothing in comparison with the worth of this whole world, at whose beauty you will marvel, when, after a happy passage from this mortal state to another and better one, the Gods shall have fitted you to know it. At this moment Theodorus wakes up, he gives thanks to the Goddess, he owns the justice of Jupiter. His spirit pervaded by what he has seen and heard, he carries on the office of High Priest, with all the zeal of a true servant of God, and with all the joy whereof a mortal is capable.

COMMENTARY

There are three materially different approaches to optimism:

1. *Absolutistic optimism.* Everything is literally for the best. All negativity is only *seemingly* such. Anything bad is, even at worst, only a lack of imperfection—a shortfall of the good. Negativity (badness, evil) is nothing substantial as such; everything there is is good, though doubtless in varying degrees.

2. *Instrumentalistic optimism.* There is actual negativity (badness, evil), but whenever present, it serves as a causal means to a greater good. There is always a chain of causes and effects through which any evil is ultimately productive of a predominating good. All those clouds have silver linings; any item of negativity is in fact a causally productive means operating toward augmenting the good. The bads of the world are causally necessary conditions for the realization of greater goods.

3. *Compensatory optimism.* There indeed is evil and negativity. And it is not always causally productive of a predominating good—not in every case simply a means causally conducive to a greater good in just exactly that same causal locality. But at the overall, collective level, the good outweighs the bad. The world is a systemic whole of interlocking elements, and matters are so arranged that a preponderant good always *compensates* for the presence of evil. The good and the bad stand in a relationship of *systemic interconnection*: evil is an integral and irremovable part of a holistic world order that embodies a greater good.

Quite different things are at issue here. With (1) we have a "blind" optimism that refuses to see negativity as something real. With (2) we have a theory of *causal facilitation* that acknowledges the reality of negativity but sees it as a means to greater good. With (3) we have a theory of *compensation* that sees negativity outweighed by a coordinated positivity in the world's overall systemic arrangements.

It would seem that (1) is not squarely held by any (Western) philosopher since the neo-Platonism of classical antiquity—apart from mystics and spiritualists. (Mary Baker Eddy wrote that "evil is but an illusion, and it has no real basis. Evil is a false belief." *Science and Health,* authorized ed. [Boston: Christian Science Press, 1934], p. 480, secs. 23–24.) This position is clearly at odds with the usual Christian view of the Fall of Man, and so to find its more common expression, we must turn to the Oriental religions, which see the phenomenal world with all its evils as *maya* or illusion. Voltaire's Dr. Pangloss, who sometimes talks in the manner of (1), comes closer to holding (2). But Leibniz, who sometimes talks in the instrumentalistic manner of (2), actually holds the compensatory version at issue in (3). The world's evil is simply part of a "package deal," accepted by God because only thus is it possible to realize the greatest attainable balance of good over evil. Accordingly, Voltaire's parody of the instrumentalistic bad-will-lead-to-good idea in *Candide* did not really hit its target, Leibniz.

Leibniz was not one of those rosy-visioned theologians who argue that all of the world's evils and imperfections are mere illusions—that if only we saw things more fully and deeply, we would come to realize our mistake and reclassify all those negativities as goods. As they see it, all imperfection is only *seeming* imperfection—evils are simply shadows needed to secure the painting's overall effectiveness, and any complaint about the badness of things reflects a misunderstanding arising from an *incomplete* understanding. (This was essentially the doctrine of Plotinus, for whom evil is not something positive and real as such, but only something negative, a mere lack or deficiency of good. See especially *Enneads*, III, ii, 3–18; IV, iii, 13–18; IV, iv, 45; and passim.) But this (problematic) neo-Platonic line of absolutistic optimism just is not Leibniz's. Leibniz was quite prepared to recognize that much is wrong in the world. But all the other possibilities are worse. (Even a half-full barrel can be fuller than all the others.) Leibniz recognized evil as real. But he saw it as a systemically necessary price to be paid for realizing the best available net balance of good or evil. The myth of Sextus illustrates this: "The crime of Sextus serves for great things: It renders Rome free, thence will arise a great empire, which will show noble examples to mankind." (*Theodicy*, sec. 416.) The world's arrangements are systemically interconnected. If we improved something here, even more would come unstruck over there—an "improvement" at one point of the system always has damaging repercussions at another. (As with the harmony of a painting, however, the connections are matters of harmonization and systemic interlinkage, not of causal interaction.)

A further aspect of Leibnizian optimism is a meliorism with respect to the conditions of life for organic creatures in general and rational beings in particular. Of course, this is not to say that they are superbly good or (given the inherent imperfections of finite creatures) that they can ever become so. But things will improve on balance in the long run.

The salient feature of Leibniz's position remains in its commitment to a compensatory optimism that sees the world as good on the whole. For Leibniz this is simply an aspect of the fact that the world is the creation of a benevolent deity. But this Leibnizian optimism is certainly not one of the facile ostrich-head-in-the-ground sort, which maintains that everything is just fine and sees no evil simply because it refuses, in a Pollyannaish fashion, to look evil in the face.

❧ Index of Key Terms and Ideas

Note: References to the *Monadology* are by section number. LL references are by page number to the substantially informative entries in Reinhard Finster, et. al., eds., *Leibniz Lexicon* (Hildesheim: Georg Olms, 1988).

❧ Index of French Terms and Expressions

❧ Index of References